CLYMER®

KAWASAKI

700-750cc VULCAN • 1985-2001

The world's finest publisher of mechanical how-to manuals

INTERTEC PUBLISHING
P.O. Box 12901, Overland Park, Kansas 66282-2901

Copyright ©2001 Intertec Publishing

FIRST EDITION
First Printing May, 1995
Second Printing September, 1999
SECOND EDITION
First Printing August, 2001

Printed in U.S.A.

CLYMER and colophon are registered trademarks of Intertec Publishing.

ISBN: 0-89287-794-4

Library of Congress: 2001093615

MEMBER

 MOTORCYCLE INDUSTRY COUNCIL, INC.

Technical photography by Ed Scott.

Technical and photographic assistance by Curt Jordan, Jordan Engineering, Santa Ana, California.

Technical illustrations by Mitzi McCarthy and Robert Caldwell.

COVER: Photographed by Mark Clifford, Mark Clifford Photography, Los Angeles, California.

PRODUCTION: Dylan Goodwin.

CONTENTS

QUICK REFERENCE DATA

TIRE SIZE AND INFLATION PRESSURE (COLD)*

Tire size	
Front	100/90-19H tubeless
Rear	150/90-15 74H, 150/90 B15 M/C 74H or
	150/90-15 M/C 74H tubeless

	Tire Pressure			
	Front		Rear	
Load	psi	kPa	psi	kPa
Up to 215 lbs (97.5 kg)	28	200	28	200
U.S., Canada, Australia, South Africa models				
215 to 406 lbs (97 to 184 kg)	28	200	32	225
All other models				
215 to 397 lbs (97 to 180 kg)	28	200	32	225

* Tire inflation pressure for factory equipped tires. Aftermarket tires may require different inflation pressure; refer to manufacturer's specifications.

RECOMMENDED LUBRICANTS AND FLUIDS

Fuel
  U.S. and Canada _____ Regular unleaded 87 [(R + M)/2 method] or 91 octane or higher
  U.K. and all others — 85-95 octane
Engine oil
  Grade — API SE or SF
  Viscosity _____ SAE 10W/40, 10W/50, 20W/40 or 20W/50
  Capacity
    Oil change only _____ 3.6 L (3.8 U.S. qt. [3.16 Imp. qt.])
    Change and filter _____ 4.0 L (4.2 U.S. qt. [3.52 Imp. qt.])
  Coolant — Ethylene glycol
    Capacity at change — 1.5 L (1.58 U.S. qt. [1.32 Imp. qt.])
Final drive oil
  Grade _____ GL-5 under API classification
  Viscosity
    When above 5°C (41°F) — SAE 90 hypoid gear oil with
    When below 5°C (41°F) — SAE 80 hypoid gear oil with
    Capacity at change _____ 150 ml (5.07 U.S. oz. [4.2 Imp. oz.])
Brake fluid _____ DOT 3
Battery refilling _____ Distilled water
Fork oil
  Viscosity _____ SAE 10W/20
  Capacity per leg
    Oil change only — 310-320 ml (10.48-10.82 U.S. oz. [8.73-9.0 Imp. oz.])
    After disassembly
      U.S. and Canadian models — 359-364 ml (12.04-12.31 U.S. oz. [10.11-10.25 Imp. oz.])
      All other models — 370-375 ml (12.51-12.68 U.S. oz. [10.42-10.56 Imp. oz.])

(continued)

RECOMMENDED LUBRICANTS AND FLUIDS (continued)

Fork oil (continued)
  Oil level each leg
    U.S. and Canadian models   220-240 mm (8.66-9.45 in.)
    All other models   205-225 mm (8.07-8.86 in.)
  Air pressure
    Standard   Atmospheric pressure
    Usable range   0-49 kPa (0-7.1 psi)
  Cables   Cable lube or SAE 10W/30 motor oil
  Pivot points   SAE 10W/30 motor oil
  Air filter oil   SAE 30

MAINTENANCE AND TUNE UP TIGHTENING TORQUES

Item	N•m	ft.-lb.
Oil drain plug	18	13
Oil filter	18	13
Fork drain bolt	7.8	69 in.-lb.
Final drive unit drain bolt	20	14.5
Front brake caliper mounting bolts	32	24
Engine coolant drain plugs	8.8	78 in.-lb.
Radiator drain plug	2.9	26 in.-lb.
Thermostat housing bleed valve	7.8	69 in.-lb.

TUNE-UP SPECIFICATIONS

Spark plug type
  Standard heat range
    U.S., Canadian, Australia, Italy, So. Africa models   NGK DP7EA-9, ND X22EP-U9
    All other models   NGK DPR7EA-9, ND X22EPR-U9
  Optional heat range
    U.S., Canadian, Australia, Italy, So. Africa models   NGK DP8EA-9, ND X24EP-U9
    All other models   NGK DPR8EA-9, ND X24EPR-U9
  Spark plug gap   0.8-0.9 mm (0.03-0.04 in.)
  Idle speed
    Switzerland (1988-1989)   1,300 ±50 rpm
    All other models   1,100 ±50 rpm
  Cylinder compression   890-1,370 kPa (129-199 psi)

REPLACEMENT BULBS

Item	U.S. and Canadian Models Voltage/wattage
Headlight (high/low beam)	12V 60/55W
Taillight/brake light	12V 8/27W
Directional signal	
Front (plus running position)	12V 23/8W
Rear	12V 23W
License plate light	12V 8W
Indicator lights	12V 3.4W
Instrument illumination lights	12V 3W

(continued)

REPLACEMENT BULBS (continued)

Item	Other than U.S. and Canadian Models Voltage/wattage
Headlight (high/low beam)	12V 60/55W
City light	12V 4W
Taillight/brake light	
South Africa	12V 8/27W
All other models	12V 5/21W
Directional signal (front and rear)	
Australia and South Africa	12V 23W
All other models	12V 21W
License plate light	
Australia and South Africa	12V 8W
All other models	12V 5W
Indicator lights	12V 3.4W
Instrument illumination lights	12V 3W

CLYMER®

KAWASAKI

700-750cc VULCAN • 1985-2001

INTRODUCTION

This detailed, comprehensive manual covers the U.S. and U.K. models of the Kawasaki Vulcan 700-750 cc V-twins from 1985-2001.

The expert text gives complete information on maintenance, tune-up, repair and overhaul. Hundreds of photos and drawings guide you through every step. The book includes all you will need to know to keep your Kawasaki running right. Throughout this book where differences occur among the models, they are clearly identified.

A shop manual is a reference. You want to be able to find information fast. As in all Clymer books, this one is designed with you in mind. All chapters are thumb tabbed. Important items are extensively indexed at the rear of the book. All procedures, tables, photos, etc., in this manual are for the reader who may be working on the bike for the first time or using this manual for the first time. All the most frequently used specifications and capacities are summarized in the *Quick Reference Data* pages at the front of the book.

Keep the book handy in your tool box. It will help you better understand how your bike runs, lower repair costs and generally improve your satisfaction with the bike.

CHAPTER ONE

GENERAL INFORMATION

This detailed, comprehensive manual covers the U.S. and the U.K. models of the Kawasaki Vulcan 700-750 cc V-twins from 1985-2001.

Troubleshooting, tune-up, maintenance and repair are not difficult, if you know what tools and equipment to use and what to do. Step-by-step instructions guide you through jobs ranging from simple maintenance to complete engine and suspension overhaul.

This manual can be used by anyone from a first time do-it-yourselfer to a professional mechanic. Detailed drawings and clear photographs give you all the information you need to do the work right.

Some procedures will require the use of special tools. The resourceful mechanic can, in many cases, think of acceptable substitutes for special tools, there is always another way. This can be as simple as using a few pieces of threaded rod, washers and nuts to remove or install a bearing or fabricating a tool from scrap material. However, using a substitute for a special tool is not recommended as it can be danger-

ous to and may damage the part. If you find that a tool can be designed and safely made, but will require some type of machine work, you may want to search out a local community college or high school that has a machine shop curriculum. Some shop teachers welcome outside work that can be used as practical shop applications for advanced students.

Table 1 lists the engine and chassis numbers (VIN) for models covered in this manual. Metric and U.S. standards are used throughout this manual and U.S. to metric conversion is given in **Table 2**.

Tables 1-5 are found at the end of the chapter.

MANUAL ORGANIZATION

This chapter provides general information and discusses equipment and tools useful both for preventive maintenance and troubleshooting.

Chapter Two provides methods and suggestions for quick and accurate diagnosis and repair of problems. Troubleshooting procedures discuss typical symptoms and logical methods to pinpoint the trouble.

Chapter Three explains all periodic lubrication and routine maintenance necessary to keep your Kawasaki in top operating condition. Chapter Three also includes recommended tune-up procedures, eliminating the need to consult other chapters on the various assemblies.

Subsequent chapters describe specific systems such as the engine top end, engine bottom end, clutch, transmission, fuel, exhaust, electrical, cooling, suspension, drive train, steering and brakes. Each chapter provides disassembly, repair and assembly procedures in simple step-by-step form. If a repair is impractical for a home mechanic, it is so indicated. It is usually faster and less expensive to take such repairs to a Kawasaki dealer or competent repair shop. Specifications concerning a particular system are included at the end of the appropriate chapter.

NOTES, CAUTIONS AND WARNINGS

The terms NOTE, CAUTION and WARNING have specific meanings in this manual. A NOTE provides additional information to make a step or procedure easier or clearer. Disregarding a NOTE could cause inconvenience, but would not cause damage or personal injury.

A CAUTION emphasizes an area where equipment damage could occur. Disregarding a CAUTION could cause permanent mechanical damage; however, personal injury is unlikely.

A WARNING emphasizes an area where personal injury or even death could result from negligence. Mechanical damage may also occur. WARNINGS *are to be taken seriously.* In some cases, serious injury and death has resulted from disregarding similar warnings.

SAFETY FIRST

Professional mechanics can work for years and never sustain a serious injury. If you observe a few rules of common sense and safety, you can enjoy many safe hours servicing your own machine. If you

ignore these rules you can hurt yourself or damage the equipment.

1. *Never* use gasoline as a cleaning solvent.

2. *Never* smoke or use a torch in the vicinity of flammable liquids, such as cleaning solvent, in open containers.

3. If welding or brazing is required on the machine, remove the fuel tank and rear shock to a safe distance, at least 50 feet away.

4. Use the proper sized wrenches to avoid damage to fasteners and injury to yourself.

5. When loosening a tight or stuck nut, be guided by what would happen if the wrench should slip. Be careful; protect yourself accordingly.

6. When replacing a fastener, make sure to use one with the same measurements and strength as the old one. Incorrect or mismatched fasteners can result in damage to the bike and possible personal injury. Beware of fastener kits that are filled with cheap and poorly made nuts, bolts, washers and cotter pins.

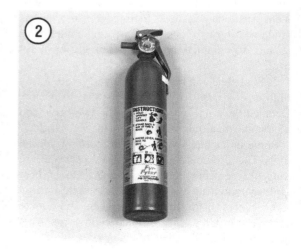

Refer to *Fasteners* in this chapter for additional information.

7. Keep all hand and power tools in good condition. Wipe greasy and oily tools after using them. They are difficult to hold and can cause injury. Replace or repair worn or damaged tools.

8. Keep your work area clean and uncluttered.

9. Wear safety goggles (**Figure 1**) during all operations involving drilling, grinding, the use of a cold chisel or anytime you feel unsure about the safety of your eyes. Safety goggles should also be worn anytime solvent and compressed air is used to clean a part.

10. Keep an approved fire extinguisher nearby (**Figure 2**). Be sure it is rated for gasoline (Class B) and electrical (Class C) fires.

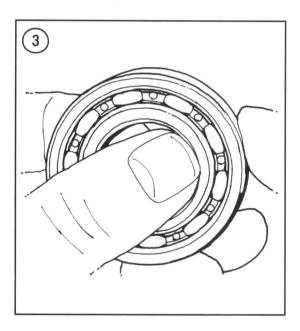

11. When drying bearings or other rotating parts with compressed air, never allow the air jet to rotate the bearing or part. The air jet is capable of rotating them at speeds far in excess of those for which they were designed. The bearing or rotating part is very likely to disintegrate and cause serious injury and damage. To prevent bearing damage when using compressed air, hold the inner bearing race by hand (**Figure 3**).

SERVICE HINTS

Most of the service procedures covered are straightforward and can be performed by anyone reasonably handy with tools. It is suggested, however, that you consider your own capabilities carefully before attempting any operation involving major disassembly of the engine or transmission.

Take your time and do the job right. Do not forget that a newly rebuilt engine must be broken-in the same way as a new one. Keep the rpm within the limits given in your owner's manual when you get back on the road or out in the dirt.

1. "Front," as used in this manual, refers to the front of the bike; the front of any component is the end closest to the front of the bike. The "left-" and "right-hand" sides refer to the position of the parts as viewed by a rider sitting on the seat facing forward. For example, the throttle control is on the right-hand side. These rules are simple, but confusion can cause a major inconvenience during service.

2. Whenever servicing the engine or clutch, or when removing a suspension component, the bike should be secured in a safe manner.

> *WARNING*
> *Never disconnect the positive (+) battery cable unless the negative (–) cable has first been disconnected. Disconnecting the positive cable while the negative cable is still connected may cause a spark. This could ignite hydrogen gas given off by the battery, causing an explosion.*

3. Disconnect the negative battery cable (**Figure 4**) when working on or near the electrical, clutch, or starter systems and before disconnecting any electrical wires. On most batteries, the negative terminal

will be marked with a minus (–) sign and the positive terminal with a plus (+) sign.

4. Tag all similar internal parts for location and mark all mating parts for position (A, **Figure 5**). Record number and thickness of any shims as they are removed. Small parts such as bolts can be identified by placing them in plastic sandwich bags (B, **Figure 5**). Seal and label them with masking tape.

5. Place parts from a specific area of the engine (e.g. cylinder head, cylinder, clutch, shift mechanism, etc.) into plastic boxes (C, **Figure 5**) to keep them separated.

6. When disassembling transmission shaft assemblies, use an egg flat (the type that restaurants get their eggs in) (D, **Figure 5**) and set the parts from the shaft in one of the depressions in the same order as removed.

NOTE
Some of the procedures or service specifications listed in this manual may not be applicable if your Kawasaki has been modified or if it has been equipped with non-stock equipment. When modifying or installing non-stock equipment, file all printed instruction or technical information regarding the new equipment in a folder or notebook for future reference. If your Kawasaki was purchased second hand, the previous owner may have installed non-stock parts. If necessary, consult with your dealer or the accessory manufacturer on components that may affect tuning or repair procedures.

7. Wiring should be tagged with masking tape and marked as each wire is removed. Again, do not rely on memory alone.

8. Finished surfaces should be protected from physical damage or corrosion. Keep gasoline and brake fluid off painted surfaces.

9. Use penetrating oil on frozen or tight bolts, then strike the bolt head a few times with a hammer and punch (use a screwdriver on screws). Avoid the use of heat where possible, as it can warp, melt or affect the temper of parts. Heat also ruins finishes, especially paint and plastics.

10. No parts removed or installed (other than bushings and bearings) in the procedures given in this manual should require unusual force during disas-

sembly or assembly. If a part is difficult to remove or install, find out why before proceeding.

11. Cover all openings after removing parts or components to prevent dirt, small tools, etc. from falling in.

12. Read each procedure *completely* while looking at the actual parts before starting a job. Make sure you *thoroughly* understand what is to be done and then carefully follow the procedure, step by step.

13. Recommendations are occasionally made to refer service or maintenance to a Kawasaki dealer or a specialist in a particular field. In these cases, the work will be done more quickly and economically than if you performed the job yourself.

14. In procedural steps, the term "replace" means to discard a defective part and replace it with a new or exchange unit. "Overhaul" means to remove, disassemble, inspect, measure, repair or replace defective parts, reassemble and install major systems or parts.

15. Some operations require the use of a hydraulic press. Unless you have a press, it would be wiser to have these operations performed by a shop equipped for such work, rather than to try to do the job yourself with makeshift equipment that may damage your machine.

16. Repairs go much faster and easier if your machine is clean before you begin work. There are many special cleaners on the market, like Simple Green or Bel-Ray Degreaser, for washing the engine and related parts. Follow the manufacturer's directions on the container for the best results. Clean all oily or greasy parts with cleaning solvent as you remove them.

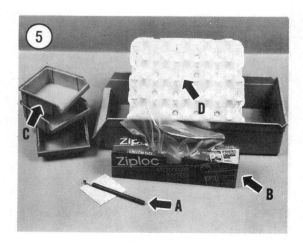

WARNING
Never *use gasoline as a cleaning agent. It presents an extreme fire hazard. Be sure to work in a well-ventilated area when using cleaning solvent. Keep a fire extinguisher, rated for gasoline fires, handy in any case.*

CAUTION
If you use a car wash to clean your bike, don't direct the high pressure water hose at steering bearings, carburetor hoses, suspension linkage components, wheel bearings and electrical components. The water will flush grease out of the bearings or damage the seals.

17. Much of the labor charges for repairs made by dealers are for the time involved during the removal, disassembly, assembly, and reinstallation of other parts in order to reach the defective part. It is frequently possible to perform the preliminary operations yourself and then take the defective unit to the dealer for repair at considerable savings.

18. If special tools are required, make arrangements to get them before you start. It is frustrating and time-consuming to get partly into a job and then be unable to complete it.

19. Make diagrams (or take a picture) wherever similar-appearing parts are found. For instance, crankcase bolts are often not the same length. You may think you can remember where everything came from—but mistakes are costly. There is also the possibility that you may be sidetracked and not return to work for days or even weeks—during which time the carefully laid out parts may have become disturbed.

20. When assembling parts, be sure all shims and washers are replaced exactly as they came out.

21. Whenever a rotating part butts against a stationary part, look for a shim or washer. Use new gaskets if there is any doubt about the condition of the old ones. A thin coat of oil on non-pressure type gaskets may help them seal more effectively.

22. High spots may be sanded off a piston with sandpaper, but fine emery cloth and oil will do a much more professional job.

23. Carbon can be removed from the head, the piston crowns and the exhaust ports with a dull screwdriver. Do *not* scratch machined surfaces. Wipe off the surface with a clean cloth when finished.

24. A baby bottle makes a good measuring device for adding oil to the front forks. Get one that is graduated in fluid ounces and milliliters(ml). After it has been used for this purpose, do *not* let a small child drink out of it as there will always be an oil residue in it.

25. If it is necessary to make a clutch cover or ignition cover gasket and you do not have a suitable old gasket to use as a guide, you can use the outline of the cover and gasket material to make a new gasket. Apply engine oil to the cover gasket surface. Then place the cover on the new gasket material and apply pressure with your hands. The oil will leave a very accurate outline on the gasket material that can be cut around.

CAUTION
When purchasing gasket material to make a gasket, measure the thickness of the old gasket and purchase gasket material with the same approximate thickness.

26. Heavy grease can be used to hold small parts in place if they tend to fall out during assembly. However, keep grease and oil away from electrical and brake components.

27. The carburetor is best cleaned by disassembling it and soaking the parts in a commercial cleaning solvent. Never soak gaskets and rubber parts in these cleaners. Never use wire to clean out jets and air passages. They are easily damaged. Use compressed air to blow out the carburetor only if the float has been removed first.

28. There are many items available that can be used on your hands before and after working on your bike. A little preparation prior to getting "all greased up" will help when cleaning up later. Before starting out, work Vaseline, soap or a product such as Invisible Glove onto your forearms, into your hands and under your fingernails and cuticles. This will make cleanup a lot easier. For cleanup, use a waterless hand soap such as Sta-Lube and then finish up with powdered Boraxo and a fingernail brush.

PARTS REPLACEMENT

When you order parts from the dealer or other parts distributor, always order by frame and engine serial numbers. Refer to **Table 1**. Compare new parts to old before purchasing them. If they are not alike, have the parts manager explain the difference to you.

TORQUE SPECIFICATIONS

Torque specifications throughout this manual are given in Newton-meters (N•m) and foot-pounds (ft.-lb.).

Existing torque wrenches calibrated in meter kilograms can be used by performing a simple conversion. All you have to do is move the decimal point one place to the right; for example, 3.5 mkg = 35 N•m. This conversion is accurate enough for mechanical work even though the exact mathematical conversion is 3.5 mkg = 34.3 N•m.

Refer to **Table 3** for general torque specifications for various size screws, bolts and nuts that may not be listed in the respective chapters. To use the table, first determine the size of the bolt or nut. Use a vernier caliper and measure the inside dimension of the threads of the nut (**Figure 6**) and across the threads for a bolt (**Figure 7**).

FASTENERS

The materials and designs of the various fasteners used on your Kawasaki are not arrived at by chance or accident. Fastener design determines the type of tool required to work the fastener. Fastener material is carefully selected to decrease the possibility of physical failure.

Nuts, bolts and screws are manufactured in a wide range of thread patterns. To join a nut and bolt, the diameter of the bolt and the diameter of the hole in

the nut must be the same. It is just as important that the threads on both be properly matched.

The best way to tell if the threads on 2 fasteners are matched is to turn the nut on the bolt (or the bolt into the threaded hole in a piece of equipment) with fingers only. Be sure both pieces are clean. If much force is required, check the thread condition on each fastener. If the thread condition is good but the fasteners jam, the threads are not compatible. A thread pitch gauge (**Figure 8**) can also be used to determine pitch. Kawasaki motorcycles are manufactured with ISO (International Organization for Standardization) metric fasteners. The threads are cut differently than those of American fasteners (**Figure 9**).

Most threads are cut so that the fastener must be turned clockwise to tighten it. These are called right-hand threads. Some fasteners have left-hand threads; they must be turned counterclockwise to be tightened. Left-hand threads are used in locations where

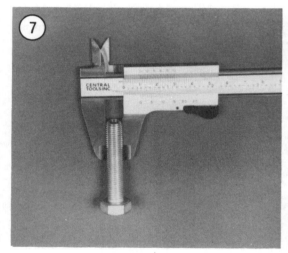

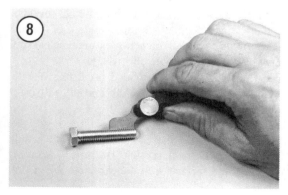

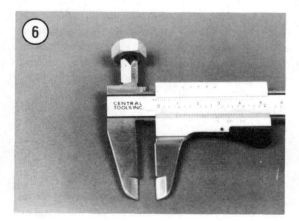

normal rotation of the equipment would tend to loosen a right-hand threaded fastener.

ISO Metric Screw Threads

ISO (International Organization for Standardization) metric threads come in 3 standard thread sizes: coarse, fine and constant pitch. The ISO coarse pitch is used for most all common fastener applications. The fine pitch thread is used on certain precision tools and instruments. The constant pitch thread is used mainly on machine parts and not for fasteners. The constant pitch thread, however, is used on all metric thread spark plugs.

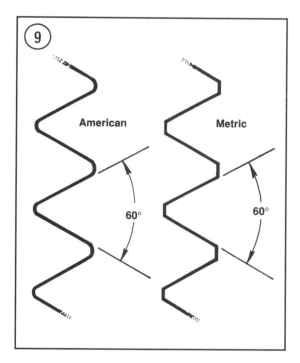

ISO metric threads are specified by the capital letter M followed by the diameter in millimeters and the pitch (or the distance between each thread) in millimeters separated by the sign ×. For example, a M8 × 1.25 bolt is one that has a diameter of 8 millimeters with a distance of 1.25 millimeters between each thread. The measurement across 2 flats on the head of the bolt (**Figure 10**) indicates the proper wrench size to be used. **Figure 7** shows how to determine bolt diameter.

> *NOTE*
> *When purchasing a bolt from a dealer or parts store, it is important to know how to specify bolt length. The correct way to measure bolt length is by measuring the length starting from underneath the bolt head to the end of the bolt (Figure 11). Always measure bolt length in this manner to avoid purchasing bolts that are too long.*

Machine Screws

There are many different types of machine screws. **Figure 12** shows a number of screw heads requiring different types of turning tools. Heads are also designed to protrude above the metal (round) or to be slightly recessed in the metal (flat). See **Figure 13**.

Bolts

Commonly called bolts, the technical name for these fasteners is cap screws. Metric bolts are described by the diameter and pitch (or the distance between each thread). For example a M8 × 1.25 bolt is one that has a diameter of 8 millimeters and a distance of 1.25 millimeters between each thread.

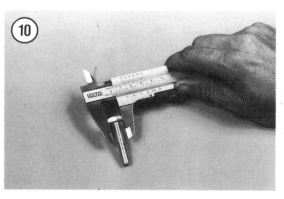

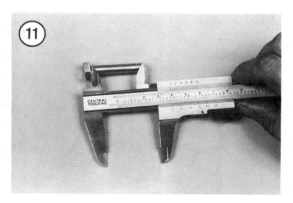

The measurement across 2 flats on the head of the bolt (**Figure 10**) indicates the proper wrench size to be used. Use a vernier caliper and measure across the threads (**Figure 7**) to determine the bolt diameter and to measure the length (**Figure 11**).

Nuts

Nuts are manufactured in a variety of types and sizes. Most are hexagonal (6-sided) and fit on bolts, screws and studs with the same diameter and pitch.

Figure 14 shows several types of nuts. The common nut is generally used with a lockwasher. Self-locking nuts have a nylon insert which prevents the nut from loosening; no lockwasher is required. Wing nuts are designed for fast removal by hand. Wing nuts are used for convenience in non-critical locations.

To indicate the size of a metric nut, manufacturers specify the diameter of the opening and the thread pitch. This is similar to bolt specifications, but without the length dimension. The measurement across

2 flats on the nut indicates the proper wrench size to be used (**Figure 15**).

Self-locking Fasteners

Several types of bolts, screws and nuts incorporate a system that develops an interference between the bolt, screw, nut or tapped hole threads. Interference is achieved in various ways: by distorting threads, coating threads with dry adhesive or nylon, distorting the top of an all-metal nut, using a nylon insert in the center or at the top of a nut, etc.

Prevailing torque fasteners offer greater holding strength and better vibration resistance. Some prevailing torque fasteners can be reused if in good condition. Others, like the nylon insert nut, form an initial locking condition when the nut is first installed; the nylon forms closely to the bolt thread pattern, thus reducing any tendency for the nut to loosen. When the nut is removed, the locking efficiency is greatly reduced. For greatest safety, it is

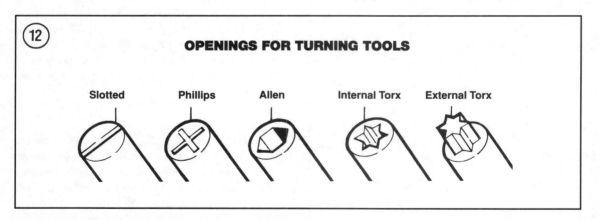

OPENINGS FOR TURNING TOOLS

Slotted   Phillips   Allen   Internal Torx   External Torx

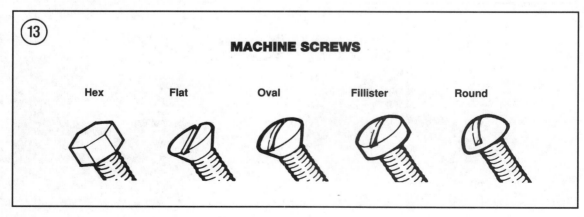

MACHINE SCREWS

Hex   Flat   Oval   Fillister   Round

recommended that you install new self-locking fasteners whenever they are removed.

Washers

There are 2 basic types of washers: flat washers and lockwashers. Flat washers are simple discs with a hole to fit a screw or bolt. Lockwashers are designed to prevent a fastener from working loose due to vibration, expansion and contraction. **Figure 16** shows several types of washers. Washers are also used in the following functions:

   a. As spacers.

   b. To prevent galling or damage of the equipment by the fastener.

   c. To help distribute fastener load during torquing.

   d. As seals.

Note that flat washers are often used between a lockwasher and a fastener to provide a smooth bearing surface. This allows the fastener to be turned easily with a tool.

Cotter Pins

Cotter pins (**Figure 17**) are used to secure fasteners in a special location. The threaded stud, bolt or

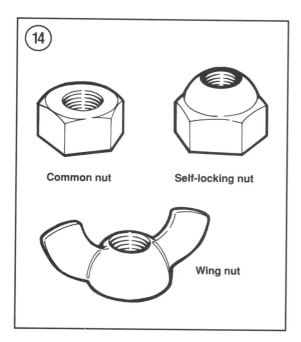

Common nut   Self-locking nut

Wing nut

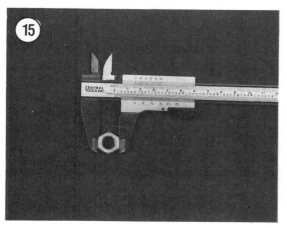

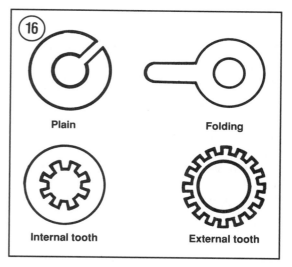

Plain   Folding

Internal tooth   External tooth

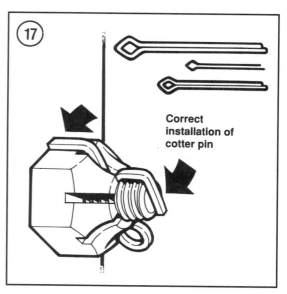

Correct
installation of
cotter pin

axle must have a hole in it. Its nut or nut lock piece has castellations around its upper edge into which the cotter pin fits to keep it from loosening. When properly installed, a cotter pin is a positive locking device.

The first step in properly installing a cotter pin is to purchase one that will fit snugly when inserted through the nut and the mating thread part. This should not be a problem when purchasing cotter pins through a Kawasaki dealer; you can order them by their respective part numbers. However, when you purchase them at a hardware or automotive store, keep this in mind. The cotter pin should not be so tight that you have to drive it in and out, but you do not want it so loose that it can move or float after it is installed.

Before installing a cotter pin, tighten the nut to the recommended torque specification. If the castellations in the nut do not line up with the hole in the bolt or axle, tighten the nut until alignment is achieved. Do not loosen the nut to make alignment. Insert a new cotter pin through the nut and hole, then tap the head lightly to seat it. Bend one arm over the flat on the nut and the other against the top of the axle or bolt. Cut the arms to a suitable length to prevent them from snagging on clothing, or worse, your hands, arms or legs; the exposed arms will cut flesh easily. When the cotter pin is bent and its arms cut to length, it should be tight. If you can wiggle the cotter pin, it is improperly installed.

Cotter pins should not be reused as their ends may break and allow the cotter pin to fall out and perhaps the fastener to unscrew itself.

Circlips

Circlips can be internal or external design. They are used to retain items on shafts (external type) or within bores (internal type). In some applications, circlips of varying thicknesses are used to control the end play of parts assemblies. These are often called selective circlips. Circlips should be replaced during installation, as removal weakens and deforms them.

Two basic styles of circlips are available: machined and stamped circlips. Machined circlips (**Figure 18**) can be installed in either direction (shaft or housing) because both faces are machined, thus creating two sharp edges. Stamped circlips (**Figure 19**) are manufactured with one sharp edge and one rounded edge. When installing stamped circlips in a

thrust situation (transmission shafts, fork tubes, etc.), the sharp edge must face away from the part producing the thrust. When installing circlips, observe the following:

    a. Compress or expand circlips only enough to install them.

    b. After the circlip is installed, make sure it is completely seated in its groove.

Transmission circlips become worn with use and increase side play. For this reason, always use new circlips whenever a transmission is to be reassembled.

LUBRICANTS

Periodic lubrication assures long life for any type of equipment. The *type* of lubricant used is just as important as the lubrication service itself, although in an emergency the wrong type of lubricant is better than none at all. The following paragraphs describe the types of lubricants most often used on motorcy-

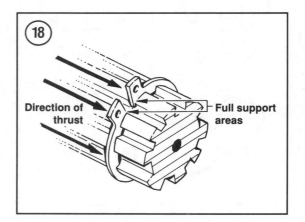

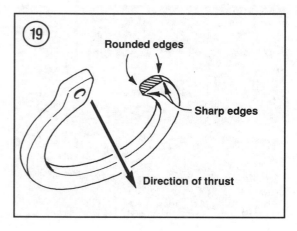

cle equipment. Be sure to follow the manufacturer's recommendations for lubricant types.

Generally, all liquid lubricants are called "oil." They may be mineral-based (including petroleum bases), natural-based (vegetable and animal bases), synthetic-based or emulsions (mixtures). "Grease" is an oil to which a thickening base has been added so that the end product is semi-solid. Grease is often classified by the type of thickener added; lithium soap is commonly used.

Engine Oil

Four-cycle oil for motorcycle and automotive engines is graded by the American Petroleum Institute (API) and the Society of Automotive Engineers (SAE) in several categories. Oil containers display these ratings on the top or label (**Figure 20**).

API oil grade is indicated by letters; oils for gasoline engines are identified by an "S." Kawasaki models described in this manual require SE or SF graded oil.

Viscosity is an indication of the oil's thickness. The SAE uses numbers to indicate viscosity; thin oils have low numbers while thick oils have high numbers. A "W" after the number indicates that the viscosity testing was done at low temperature to simulate cold-weather operation. Engine oils fall into the 5-50 range.

Multi-grade oils (for example 10W-40) are less viscous (thinner) at low temperatures and more viscous (thicker) at high temperatures. This allows the oil to perform efficiently across a wide range of engine operating conditions. The lower the number, the better the engine will start in cold climates. Higher numbers are usually recommended for engine running in hot weather conditions.

Grease

Greases are graded by the National Lubricating Grease Institute (NLGI). Greases are graded by number according to the consistency of the grease; these range from No. 000 to No. 6, with No. 6 being the most solid. A typical multipurpose grease is NLGI No. 2. For specific applications, equipment manufacturers may require grease with an additive such as molybdenum disulfide (MOS2).

Also recommended for some applications is an anti-seize lubricant (**Figure 21**). This is necessary to prevent pivot points from corroding and locking up.

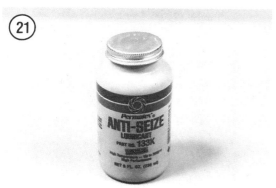

RTV GASKET SEALANT

Room temperature vulcanizing (RTV) sealant is used on some pre-formed gaskets and to seal some components. RTV is a silicone gel supplied in tubes and can be purchased in a number of different colors.

Moisture in the air causes RTV to cure. Always place the cap on the tube as soon as possible when using RTV. RTV has a shelf life of one year and will not cure properly when the shelf life has expired. Check the expiration date on RTV tubes before using and keep partially used tubes tightly sealed.

Applying RTV Sealant

Clean all gasket residue from mating surfaces. Surfaces should be clean and free of oil and dirt. Remove all RTV gasket material from blind attaching holes, as it can cause a "hydraulic" effect and affect bolt torque.

Apply RTV sealant in a continuous bead. Circle all mounting holes unless otherwise specified. Torque mating parts within 10 minutes after application.

THREADLOCK

A chemical locking compound should be used on all bolts and nuts, even if they are secured with lockwashers. A locking compound will lock fasteners against vibration loosening and seal against leaks. Loctite 242 (blue) and 271 (red) are recommended for many threadlock requirements described in this manual (**Figure 22**).

Loctite 242 (blue) is a medium strength threadlock and component disassembly can be performed with normal hand tools. Loctite 271 (red) is a high strength threadlock and heat or special tools, such as a press or puller, may be required for component disassembly.

Applying Threadlock

Surfaces should be clean and free of oil, grease, dirt and other residue; clean threads with an aerosol electrical contact cleaner before applying the Loctite. When applying Loctite, use a small amount. If too much is used, it can work its way down the threads and stick parts together not meant to be stuck.

GASKET REMOVER

Stubborn gaskets can present a problem during engine service as they can take a long time to remove. Consequently, there is the added problem of secondary damage occurring to the gasket mating surfaces from the incorrect use of gasket scraping tools. To quickly and safely remove stubborn gaskets, use a spray gasket remover. Spray gasket remover can be purchased through automotive parts houses. Follow the manufacturer's directions for use.

EXPENDABLE SUPPLIES

Certain expendable supplies are required during maintenance and repair work. These include grease, oil, gasket cement, wiping rags and cleaning solvent. Ask your dealer for the special locking compounds, silicone lubricants and other products which make bike maintenance simpler and easier. Cleaning solvent or kerosene is available at some service stations, paint or hardware stores.

WARNING
Having a stack of clean shop rags on hand is important when performing engine and suspension service work. However, to prevent the possibility of fire damage from spontaneous combustion from a pile of solvent soaked rags, store them in a lid sealed metal container until they can be washed or discarded.

NOTE
To avoid absorbing solvent and other chemicals into your skin while cleaning parts, wear a pair of petroleum-resis-

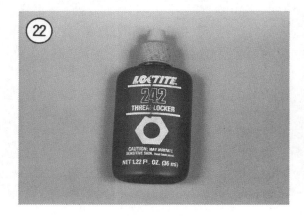

tant rubber gloves. These can be purchased through industrial supply houses or well-equipped hardware stores.

PARTS REPLACEMENT

Kawasaki makes frequent changes during a model year, some minor, some relatively major. When you order parts from the dealer or other parts distributor, always order by frame and engine numbers. The

frame number serial number is stamped on the left-hand side of the steering head (**Figure 23**). The vehicle identification number (VIN) plate is attached to the right-hand side of the frame down tube (**Figure 24**). The engine number is stamped on a raised pad on the right-hand side of the crankcase upper surface (**Figure 25**). The carburetor number (**Figure 26**) is on the side of the carburetor above the float bowl.

Write the numbers down and carry them with you. Compare new parts to old before purchasing them. If they are not alike, have the parts manager explain the difference to you. **Table 1** lists engine and frame serial numbers for the models covered in this manual.

NOTE
*If your Kawasaki was purchased second-hand and you are not sure of its model year, use the bike's VIN and frame serial numbers and the information listed in **Table 1**. Read your bike's serial number. Then compare the numbers listed in **Table 1**. If your bike's serial number is listed in **Table 1**, cross-reference the number with the adjacent model number and year.*

BASIC HAND TOOLS

Many of the procedures in this manual can be carried out with simple hand tools and test equipment familiar to the average home mechanic. Keep your tools clean and in a tool box. Keep them organized with the sockets and related drives together, the open-end combination wrenches together, etc. After using a tool, wipe off dirt and grease with a clean cloth and return the tool to its correct place.

Top-quality tools are essential; they are also more economical in the long run. If you are now starting to build your tool collection, stay away from the "advertised specials" featured at some parts houses, discount stores and chain drug stores. These are usually a poor grade tool that can be sold cheaply and that is exactly what they are—*cheap*. They are usually made of inferior material, and are thick, heavy and clumsy. Their rough finish makes them difficult to clean and they usually don't last very long. If it is ever your misfortune to use such tools, you will probably find out that the wrenches do not fit the heads of bolts and nuts correctly and will damage the fastener.

Quality tools are made of alloy steel and are heat treated for greater strength. They are lighter and better balanced than cheap ones. Their surface is smooth, making them a pleasure to work with and easy to clean. The initial cost of good-quality tools may be more but they are cheaper in the long run. Don't try to buy everything in all sizes in the beginning; buy a few at a time until you have the necessary tools.

The following tools are required to perform virtually any repair job on a bike. Each tool is described and the recommended size given for starting a tool collection. **Table 4** includes the tools that should be on hand for simple home repairs and/or major overhaul. Additional tools and some duplicates may be added as you become more familiar with the bike. Almost all motorcycles and vehicles (with the exception of the U.S. built Harley Davidson and some English motorcycles) use metric size bolts and nuts. If you are starting your collection now, buy metric sizes.

Screwdrivers

The screwdriver is a very basic tool, but if used improperly it will do more damage than good. The slot on a screw has a definite dimension and shape. A screwdriver must be selected to conform with that shape. Use a small screwdriver for small screws and a large one for large screws or the screw head will be damaged.

Two basic types of screwdriver are required: common (flat- or slot-blade) screwdrivers (**Figure 27**) and Phillips screwdrivers (**Figure 28**).

Note the following when selecting and using screwdrivers:

a. The screwdriver must always fit the screw head. If the screwdriver blade is too small for the screw slot, damage may occur to the screw slot and screwdriver. If the blade is too large, it cannot engage the slot properly and will result in damage to the screw head.

b. Standard screwdrivers are identified by the length of their blade. A 6-inch screwdriver has a blade six inches long. The width of the screwdriver blade will vary, so make sure that the blade engages the screw slot the complete width of the screw.

c. Phillips screwdrivers are sized according to their point size. They are numbered one, two, three and four. The degree of taper determines the point size; the No. 1 Phillips screwdriver will be the most pointed. The points become more blunt as their number increases.

NOTE
You should also be aware of another screwdriver similar to the Phillips, and that is the Reed and Prince tip. Like the Phillips, the Reed and Prince screwdriver tip forms an "X" but with one major exception, the Reed and Prince tip has a much more pointed tip. The Reed and Prince screwdriver should never be used on Phillips screws and vise versa. Intermixing these screwdrivers will cause damage to the screw and screwdriver. If you have both types in your tool box and they are similar in appearance, you may want to identify

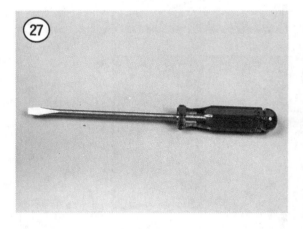

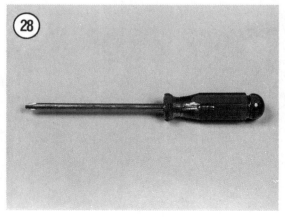

them by painting the screwdriver shank underneath the handle.

d. When selecting screwdrivers, note that you can apply more power with less effort with a longer screwdriver than with a short one. Of course, there will be situations where only a short handle screwdriver can be used. Keep this in mind though, when having to remove tight screws.

e. Because the working end of a screwdriver receives quite a bit of abuse, you should purchase screwdrivers with hardened-tips. The extra money will be well spent.

Screwdrivers are available in sets which often include an assortment of common and Phillips blades. If you buy them individually, buy at least the following:

a. Common screwdriver—5/16 × 6 in. blade.

b. Common screwdriver—3/8 × 12 in. blade.

c. Phillips screwdriver—size 2 tip, 6 in. blade.

d. Phillips screwdriver—size 3 tip, 6 and 8 in. blade.

Use screwdrivers only for driving screws. Never use a screwdriver for prying or chiseling metal. Do not try to remove a Phillips, Torx or Allen head screw with a standard screwdriver (unless the screw has a combination head that will accept either type); you can damage the head so that the proper tool will be unable to remove it.

Keep screwdrivers in the proper condition and they will last longer and perform better. Always keep the tip of a standard screwdriver in good condition. **Figure 29** shows how to grind the tip to the proper shape if it becomes damaged. Note the symmetrical sides of the tip.

Pliers

Pliers come in a wide range of types and sizes. Pliers are useful for cutting, bending and crimping.

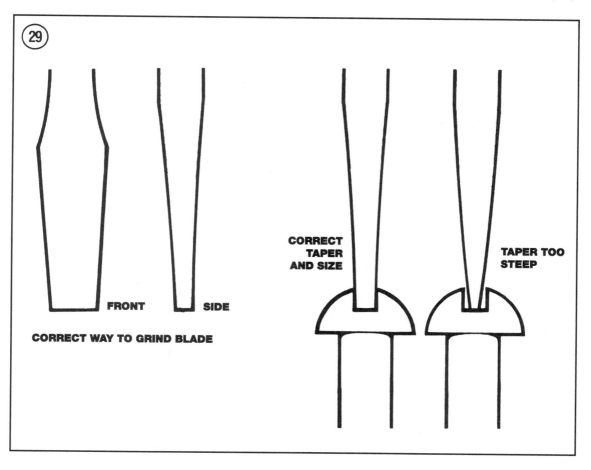

(29)

FRONT   SIDE

CORRECT WAY TO GRIND BLADE

CORRECT TAPER AND SIZE

TAPER TOO STEEP

They should never be used to cut hardened objects or to turn bolts or nuts. **Figure 30** shows several pliers useful in repairing your Kawasaki.

Each type of pliers has a specialized function. Slip-joint pliers are general purpose pliers and are used mainly for holding things and for bending. Needlenose pliers are used to hold or bend small objects. Water pump pliers can be adjusted to hold various sizes of objects; the jaws remain parallel to grip around objects such as pipe or tubing. There are many more types of pliers.

> *CAUTION*
> *Pliers should not be used for loosening or tightening nuts or bolts. The pliers' sharp teeth will grind off the nut or bolt corners and damage it.*

> *CAUTION*
> *If slip-joint or water pump pliers are going to be used to hold an object with a finished surface, wrap the object with tape or cardboard for protection.*

Vise-grip Pliers

Vise-grip pliers (**Figure 31**) are used to hold objects very tightly while another task is performed on the object. While vise-grip pliers work well, caution should be followed with their use. Because vise-grip pliers exert more force than regular pliers, their sharp jaws can permanently scar the object. In addition, when vise-grip pliers are locked into position, they can crush or deform thin wall material.

Vise-grip pliers are available in many types for more specific tasks.

Circlip Pliers

Circlip pliers (**Figure 32**) are special in that they are only used to remove circlips from shafts or within engine or suspension housings. When purchasing circlip pliers, there are two distinguishing kinds. External pliers (spreading) are used to remove circlips that fit on the outside of a shaft. Internal pliers (squeezing) are used to remove circlips which fit inside a gear or housing.

> *WARNING*
> *Because circlips can sometimes slip and "fly off" during removal and installation, always wear safety glasses.*

Box-end, Open-end and Combination Wrenches

Box-end, open-end and combination wrenches are available in sets or separately in a variety of sizes. On open- and box-end wrenches, the number stamped near the end refers to the distance between 2 parallel flats on the hex head bolt or nut. On combination wrenches, the number is stamped near the center.

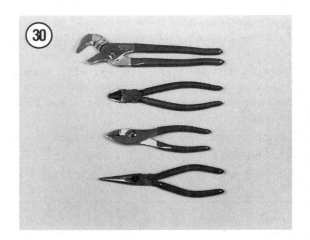

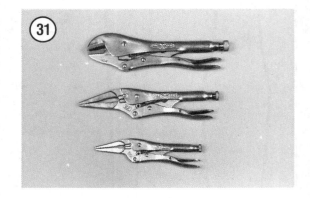

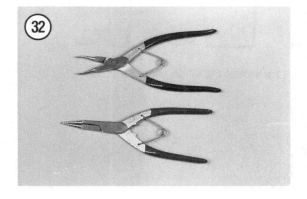

Box-end wrenches require clear overhead access to the fastener but can work well in situations where the fastener head is close to another part. They grip on all six edges of a fastener for a very secure grip. They are available in either 6-point or 12-point. The 6-point gives superior holding power and durability but requires a greater swinging radius. The 12-point works better in situations where the swinging radius is limited.

Open-end wrenches are speedy and work best in areas with limited overhead access. Their wide, flat jaws make them unstable for situations where the bolt or nut is sunken in a well or close to the edge of a casting. These wrenches grip only two flats of a fastener so if either the fastener head or the wrench jaws are worn, the wrench may slip off.

Combination wrenches (**Figure 33**) have open-end on one side and box-end on the other with both

ends being the same size. These wrenches are favored by professionals because of their versatility.

Adjustable (Crescent) Wrenches

An adjustable wrench (sometimes called crescent wrench) can be adjusted to fit nearly any nut or bolt head which has clear access around its entire perimeter. Adjustable wrenches (**Figure 34**) are best used as a backup wrench to keep a large nut or bolt from turning while the other end is being loosened or tightened with a proper wrench.

Adjustable wrenches have only two gripping surfaces, which make them more subject to slipping off the fastener, damaging the part and possibly injuring your hand. The fact that one jaw is adjustable only aggravates this shortcoming.

These wrenches are directional; the solid jaw must be the one transmitting the force. If you use the adjustable jaw to transmit the force, it will loosen and possibly slip off.

Adjustable wrenches come in all sizes but something in the 6 to 8 in. range is recommended as an all-purpose wrench.

Socket Wrenches

This type is undoubtedly the fastest, safest and most convenient to use. Sockets which attach to a ratchet handle (**Figure 35**) are available with 6-point or 12-point openings and 1/4, 3/8, 1/2 and 3/4 in. drives. The drive size indicates the size of the square hole which mates with the ratchet handle.

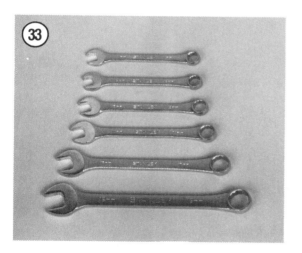

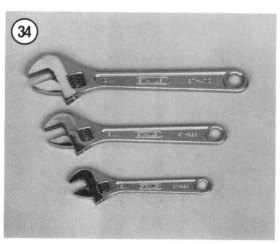

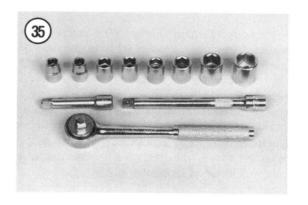

Allen Wrenches

Allen wrenches are available in sets or separately in a variety of sizes. These sets come in SAE and metric size, so be sure to buy a metric set. Allen bolts are sometimes called socket bolts. Sometimes the bolts are difficult to reach and it is suggested that a variety of Allen wrenches be purchased (e.g. socket driven, T-handle and extension type) as shown in **Figure 36**.

Torque Wrench

A torque wrench is used with a socket to measure how tightly a nut or bolt is installed. They come in a wide price range and with either 3/8 or 1/2 in. square drive (**Figure 37**). The drive size indicates the size of the square drive which mates with the socket. Purchase one that measures 0-280 N•m (0-200 ft.-lb.).

Impact Driver

This tool might have been designed with the bike in mind. This tool makes removal of fasteners easy and minimizes damage to bolts and screw slots. Impact drivers and interchangeable bits (**Figure 38**) are available at most large hardware, motorcycle or auto parts stores. Don't purchase a cheap one as it will not work as well and require more force (the "use a larger hammer" syndrome) than a moderately priced one. Sockets and Allen wrenches can also be used with a hand impact driver; however, make sure that the socket, or Allen wrench, is designed for use with an impact driver or air tool. Do not use regular hand sockets, as they may shatter during use.

Hammers

The correct hammer (**Figure 39**) is necessary for repairs. A hammer with a face (or head) of rubber or plastic or the soft-faced type that is filled with buckshot are sometimes necessary in engine tear downs. Never use a metal-faced hammer on engine or suspension parts, as severe damage will result in most cases. Ball-peen or machinist's hammers will be required when striking another tool, such as a punch or impact driver. When striking a hammer against a punch, cold chisel or similar tool, the face of the hammer should be at least 1/2 in. larger than the head

of the tool. When it is necessary to strike hard against a steel part without damaging it, a brass hammer should be used. A brass hammer can be used because brass will give when striking a harder object.

Note the following:

a. Always wear safety glasses when using a hammer.

b. Inspect hammers for damaged or broken parts. Repair or replace the hammer as required. Do not use a hammer with a taped handle.

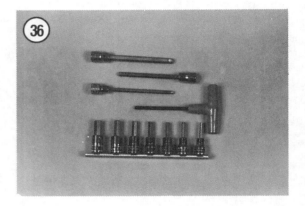

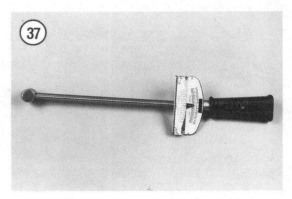

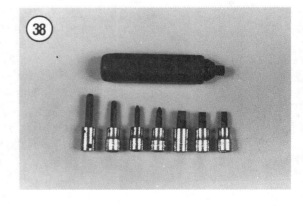

c. Always wipe oil or grease from the hammer before using it.

d. The head of the hammer should always strike the object squarely. Do not use the side of the hammer or the handle to strike an object.

e. Always use the correct hammer for the job.

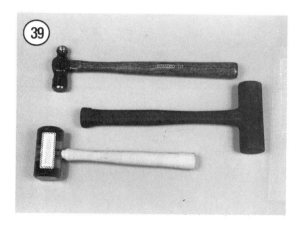

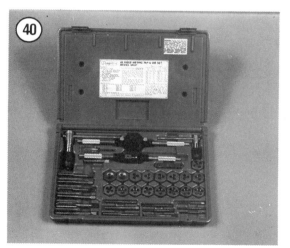

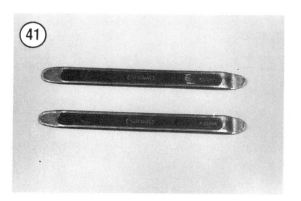

Tap and Die Set

A complete tap and die set (**Figure 40**) is a relatively expensive tool. But when you need a tap or die to clean up a damaged thread, there is really no substitute. Be sure to purchase one for metric threads when working on your Kawasaki.

Tire Levers

When changing tires, use a good set of tire levers (**Figure 41**). Never use a screwdriver in place of a tire lever; refer to Chapter Twelve for tire changing procedures using these tools. Before using the tire levers, check the working ends of the tool and remove any burrs. Don't use a tire lever for prying anything but tires. For better leverage when changing tires on your Kawasaki, you may want to invest in a set of 16 in. long tire irons. These can be ordered through your dealer.

Drivers and Pullers

These tools are used to remove and install oil seals, bushings, bearings and gears. These will be called out during service procedures in later chapters as required.

TEST EQUIPMENT

Multimeter or VOM

This instrument (**Figure 42**) is invaluable for electrical system troubleshooting. See *Electrical Troubleshooting* in Chapter Eight for its use.

Compression Gauge

An engine with low compression cannot be properly tuned and will not develop full power. A compression gauge (**Figure 43**) measures engine compression. Open the throttle all the way when checking engine compression. See Chapter Three.

Cylinder Leak Down Tester

By positioning a cylinder on its compression stroke so that both valves are closed and then pres-

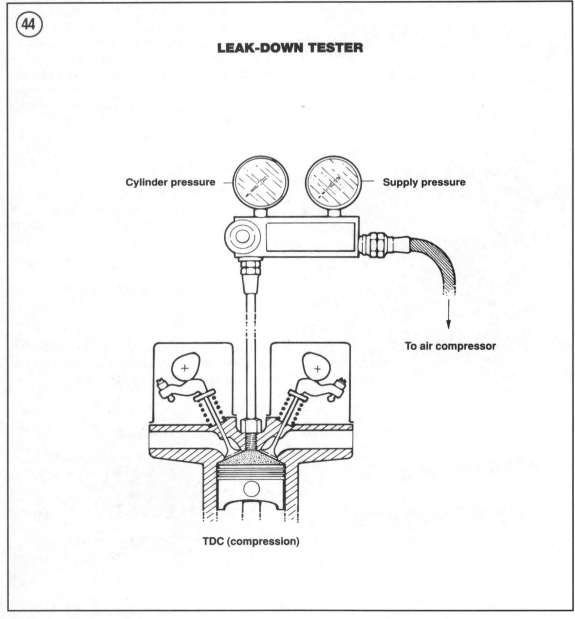

LEAK-DOWN TESTER

Cylinder pressure

Supply pressure

To air compressor

TDC (compression)

surizing the cylinder, you can isolate engine problem areas (e.g. leaking valve, damaged head gasket, broken, worn or stuck piston rings) by listening for escaping air through the carburetors, exhaust pipe, cylinder head mating surface, etc. To perform this procedure, a leak down tester (**Figure 44**) and an air compressor are required. This procedure is de-

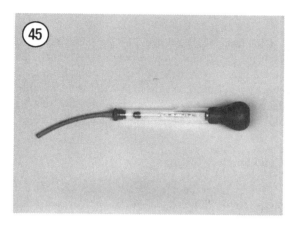

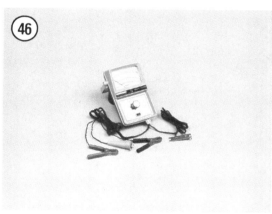

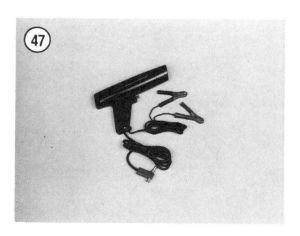

scribed in Chapter Three. Cylinder leak down testers can be purchased through Kawasaki dealers, accessory tool manufacturers and automotive tool suppliers.

Battery Hydrometer

A hydrometer (**Figure 45**) is the best way to check a battery's state of charge. A hydrometer measures the weight or density of the sulfuric acid in the battery's electrolyte in specific gravity.

Portable Tachometer

A portable tachometer (**Figure 46**) is necessary for tuning. Ignition timing and carburetor adjustments must be performed at specified engine speeds. The best instrument for this purpose is one with a low range of 0-1,000 or 0-2,000 rpm and a high range of 0-4,000 rpm. Extended range (0-6,000 or 0-8,000 rpm) instruments lack accuracy at lower speeds. This instrument should be capable of detecting 25 rpm on the low range.

Strobe Timing Light

This instrument is useful for checking ignition timing. By flashing a light at the precise instant the spark plug fires, the position of the timing mark can be seen. The flashing light makes a moving mark appear to stand still opposite a stationary mark.

Suitable lights range from inexpensive neon bulb types to powerful xenon strobe lights (**Figure 47**). A light with an inductive pickup is recommended to eliminate any possible damage to ignition wiring. Use according to manufacturer's instructions.

PRECISION MEASURING TOOLS

Measurement is an important part of motorcycle service. When performing many of the service procedures in this manual, you will be required to make a number of measurements. These include basic checks such as valve clearance, engine compression and spark plug gap. As you get deeper into engine disassembly and service, measurements will be required to determine the size and condition of the piston and cylinder bore, valve and guide wear, camshaft wear, crankshaft runout and so on. When making these measurements, the degree of accuracy will dictate which tool is required. Precision measuring tools are expensive. If this is your first experience at engine or suspension service, it may be more worthwhile to have the checks made at a Kawasaki dealer or machine shop. However, as your skills and enthusiasm increase for doing your own service work, you may want to purchase some of these specialized tools. The following is a description of the measuring tools required during engine and suspension overhaul.

Feeler Gauge

Feeler gauges come in assorted sets and types (**Figure 48**). The feeler gauge is made of either a piece of a flat or round hardened steel of a specified thickness. Wire gauges are frequently recommended to measure spark plug gap. Flat gauges are used for most other measurements. Feeler gauges may also be designed for specialized uses, such as for measuring valve clearances. The end of these gauges is usually small and angled to make checking valve clearances easier.

Vernier Caliper

This tool (**Figure 49**) is invaluable when reading inside, outside and depth measurements with close precision. It can be used to measure clutch spring length and the thickness of clutch plates, shims and thrust washers.

Outside Micrometers

One of the most reliable tools used for precision measurement is the outside micrometer (**Figure 50**).

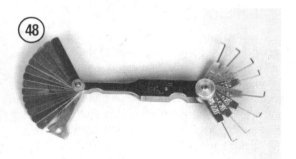

Outside micrometers will be required to measure valve shim thickness, piston diameter and valve stem diameter. Outside micrometers are also used with other tools to measure the cylinder bore and the valve guide inside diameters. Micrometers can be purchased individually or as a set.

Dial Indicator

Dial indicators (**Figure 51**) are precision tools used to check dimension variations on machined parts such as transmission shafts and axles and to check crankshaft and axle shaft end play. Dial indicators are available with various dial types; select a dial indicator with a continuous dial (**Figure 52**).

Cylinder Bore Gauge

The cylinder bore gauge is a very specialized precision tool. The gauge set shown in **Figure 53** is

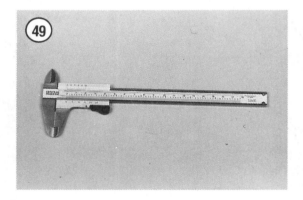

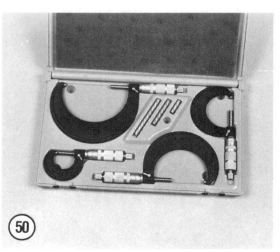

comprised of a dial indicator, handle and a number of length adapters to adapt the gauge to different bore sizes. The bore gauge can be used to make cylinder bore measurements such as bore size, taper and out-of-round. Depending on the bore gauge, it can sometimes be used to measure brake caliper and master cylinder bore sizes. An outside micrometer must be used together with the bore gauge to determine bore dimensions.

Small Hole Gauges

A set of small hole gauges (**Figure 54**) allows you to measure a hole, groove or slot ranging in size up to 13 mm (0.500 in.). A small hole gauge will be required to measure valve guide and brake master cylinder bore diameters. An outside micrometer must be used together with the small hole gauge to determine bore dimensions.

Telescoping Gauges

Telescoping gauges (**Figure 55**) can be used to measure hole diameters from approximately 5/16-6 in. (8-150 mm). Like the small hole gauge, the telescoping gauge does not have a scale gauge for direct readings. Thus, an outside micrometer is required to determine bore dimensions.

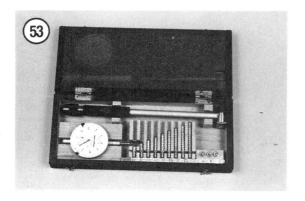

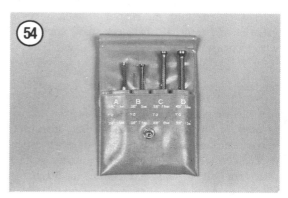

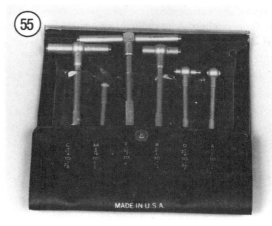

Screw Pitch Gauge

A screw pitch gauge (**Figure 56**) determines the thread pitch of bolts, screws, studs, etc. The gauge is made up of a number of thin plates. Each plate has a thread shape cut on one edge to match one thread pitch. When using a screw pitch gauge to determine a thread pitch size, try to fit different blade sizes onto the bolt thread until both threads match.

Magnetic Stand

A magnetic stand (**Figure 57**) is used to hold a dial indicator securely when checking the runout of a round object or when checking the end play of a shaft.

V-Blocks

V-blocks (**Figure 58**) are precision ground blocks used to hold a round object when checking its runout or condition. In motorcycle repair, V-blocks can be used when checking the runout of such items as valve stems, camshaft, balancer shaft, crankshaft, wheel axles and fork tubes.

Surface Plate

A surface plate can be used to check the flatness of parts or to provide a perfectly flat surface for minor resurfacing of cylinder head or other critical gasket surfaces. While industrial quality surface plates are quite expensive, the home mechanic can improvise. A thick metal plate can be put to use as a surface plate. The metal surface plate shown in **Figure 59** has a piece of sandpaper or dry wall surface sanding sheets glued to its surface that can be used for cleaning and smoothing cylinder head and crankcase mating surfaces.

> *NOTE*
> *Check with a local machine shop on the availability and cost of having a metal plate resurfaced for use as a surface plate.*

SPECIAL TOOLS

A few special tools may be required for major service. These are described in the appropriate chap-

ters and are available either from a Kawasaki dealer or other manufacturers as indicated.

This section describes special tools unique to this type of bike's service and repair.

The Grabbit (Clutch Holding Tool)

The Grabbit (**Figure 60**), or clutch holding tool (Kawasaki part No. 57001-305), is a special tool used to hold the clutch boss when removing and tightening the clutch nut.

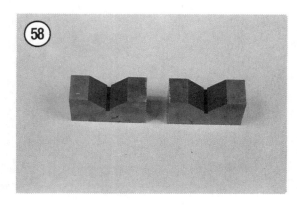

Other Special Tools

A few other special tools may be required for major service. These are described in the appropriate chapters and are available from Kawasaki dealers or other manufacturers as indicated.

CLEANING SOLVENT

With the environmental concern that is prevalent today concerning the disposal of hazardous solvents, the home mechanic should select a water soluble, biodegradable solvent. These solvents can be purchased through dealers, automotive parts houses and large hardware stores.

Selecting a solvent is only one of the problems facing the home mechanic when it comes to cleaning parts. You need some type of tank to clean parts as well as to store the solvent. There are a number of manufacturers offering different types and sizes of parts cleaning tanks. While a tank may seem a luxury to the home mechanic, you will find that it will

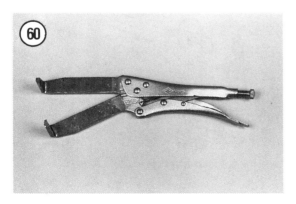

quickly pay for itself through its efficiency and convenience. When selecting a parts washer, look for one that can recycle and store the solvent, as well as separate the sludge and contamination from the clean solvent. Most important, check the warranty, if any, as it pertains to the tank's pump. Like most tools, when purchasing a parts washer, you get what you pay for.

WARNING
Having a stack of clean shop rags on hand is important when performing engine work. However, to prevent the possibility of fire damage from spontaneous combustion from a pile of solvent-soaked rags, store them in a lid-sealed metal container until they can be washed or discarded.

NOTE
To avoid absorbing solvent and other chemicals into your skin while cleaning parts, wear a pair of petroleum-resistant rubber gloves. These can be purchased through industrial supply houses or well-equipped hardware stores.

MECHANIC'S TIPS

Removing Frozen Nuts and Screws

When a fastener rusts and cannot be removed, several methods may be used to loosen it. First, apply penetrating oil such as Liquid Wrench or WD-40 (available at hardware or auto supply stores). Apply it liberally and let it penetrate for 10-15 minutes. Rap the fastener several times with a small hammer; do not hit it hard enough to cause damage. Reapply the penetrating oil if necessary.

For frozen screws, apply penetrating oil as described, then insert a screwdriver in the slot and rap the top of the screwdriver with a hammer. This loosens the rust so the screw can be removed in the normal way. If the screw head is too chewed up to use this method, grip the head with vise-grip pliers and twist the screw out.

Avoid applying heat unless specifically instructed, as it may melt, warp or remove the temper from parts.

Removing Broken Screws or Bolts

When the head breaks off a screw or bolt, several methods are available for removing the remaining portion.

If a large portion of the remainder projects out, try gripping it with vise-grip pliers. If the projecting portion is too small, file it to fit a wrench or cut a slot in it to fit a screwdriver. See **Figure 61**.

If the head breaks off flush, use a screw extractor. To do this, center punch the exact center of the remaining portion of the screw or bolt. Drill a small hole in the screw and tap the extractor into the hole.

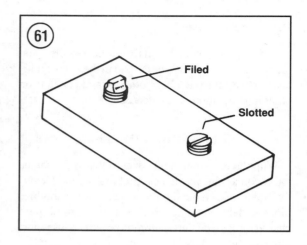

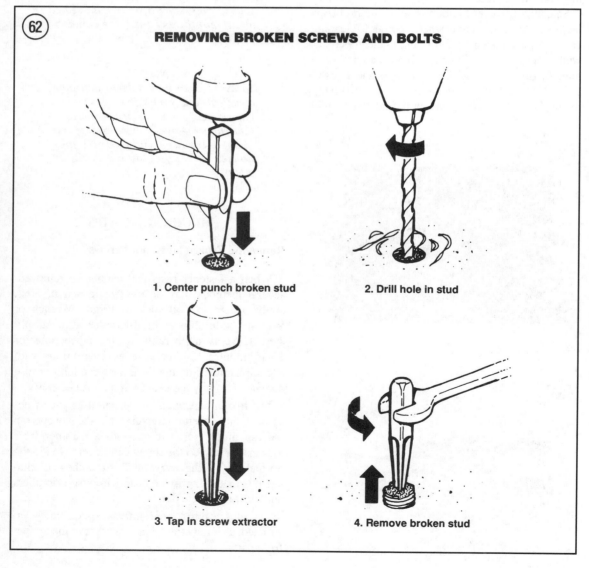

REMOVING BROKEN SCREWS AND BOLTS

1. Center punch broken stud

2. Drill hole in stud

3. Tap in screw extractor

4. Remove broken stud

Back the screw out with a wrench on the extractor. See **Figure 62**.

Remedying Stripped Threads

Occasionally, threads are stripped through carelessness or impact damage. Often the threads can be cleaned up by running a tap (for internal threads on nuts) or die (for external threads on bolts) through the threads. See **Figure 63**. To clean or repair spark plug threads, a spark plug tap can be used (**Figure 64**).

> *NOTE*
> *Tap and dies can be purchased individually or in a set as shown in* ***Figure 40***.

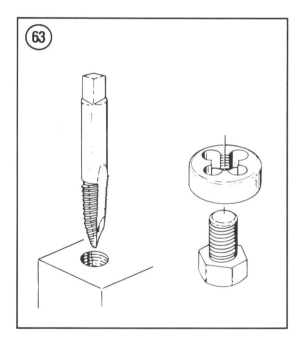

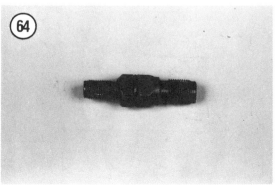

If an internal thread is damaged, it may be necessary to install a Helicoil (**Figure 65**) or some other type of thread insert. Follow the manufacturer's instructions when installing their insert.

Removing Broken or Damaged Studs

If a stud is broken or the threads severely damaged, perform the following. A tube of red Loctite (No. 271), 2 nuts, 2 wrenches and a new stud will be required during this procedure (**Figure 66**). Studs that are stripped or damaged will require the use of a stud remover.

1. Thread two nuts onto the damaged stud. Then tighten the 2 nuts against each other so that they are locked.

> *NOTE*
> *If the threads on the damaged stud do not allow installation of the 2 nuts, you will have to remove the stud with a stud remover.*

2. Turn the bottom nut counterclockwise and unscrew the stud.

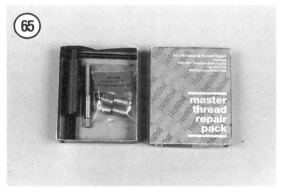

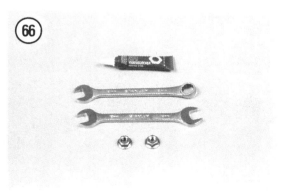

3. Threaded holes with a bottom surface should be blown out with compressed air as dirt buildup in the bottom of the hole may prevent the stud from being torqued properly. If necessary, use a bottoming tap to true up the threads and to remove any deposits.

4. Install 2 nuts on the top half of the new stud as in Step 1. Make sure they are locked securely.

5. Coat the bottom half of a new stud with red Loctite (No. 271).

6. Turn the top nut clockwise and thread the new stud securely.

7. Remove the nuts and repeat for each stud as required.

8. Follow Loctite's directions on cure time before assembling the component.

BALL BEARING REPLACEMENT

Ball bearings (**Figure 67**) are used throughout your Kawasaki's engine and chassis to reduce power loss, heat and noise resulting from friction. Because ball bearings are precision made parts, they must be maintained by proper lubrication and maintenance. When a bearing is found to be damaged, it should be replaced immediately. However, when installing a new bearing, care should be taken to prevent damage to the new bearing. While bearing replacement is described in the individual chapters where applicable, the following can be used as a guideline.

> *NOTE*
> *Unless otherwise specified, install bearings with the manufacturer's mark or number on the bearing facing outward.*

Bearing Removal

While bearings are normally removed only when damaged, there may be times when it is necessary to remove a bearing that is in good condition. Depending on the situation, you may be able to remove the bearing without damaging it. However, bearing removal in some situations, no matter how careful you are, will cause bearing damage. Care should always be given to bearings during their removal to prevent

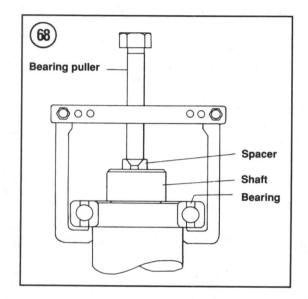

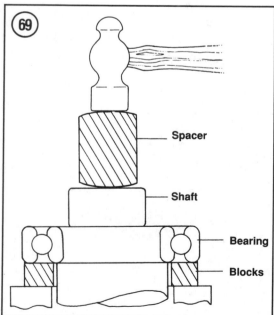

secondary damage to the shaft or housing. Note the following when removing bearings.

1. When using a puller to remove a bearing from a shaft, take care that the shaft is not damaged. Always place a piece of metal between the end of the shaft

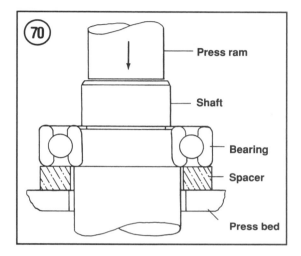

2. When using a hammer to remove a bearing from a shaft, do not strike the hammer directly against the shaft. Instead, use a brass or aluminum spacer between the hammer and shaft (**Figure 69**) and make sure to support both bearing races with wood blocks as shown.

3. The most ideal method of bearing removal is with a hydraulic press. However, certain procedures must be followed or damage may occur to the bearing, shaft or case half. Note the following when using a press:

    a. Always support the inner and outer bearing races with a suitable size wood or aluminum spacer ring (**Figure 70**). If only the outer race is supported, the balls and/or the inner race will be damaged.

    b. Always make sure the press ram (**Figure 70**) aligns with the center of the shaft. If the ram is not centered, it may damage the bearing and/or shaft.

    c. The moment the shaft is free of the bearing, it will drop to the floor. Secure or hold the shaft to prevent it from falling.

Bearing Installation

1. When installing a bearing in a housing, pressure must be applied to the outer bearing race (**Figure 71**). When installing a bearing on a shaft, pressure must be applied to the *inner* bearing race (**Figure 72**).

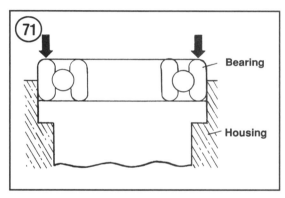

2. When installing a bearing as described in Step 1, some type of driver will be required. Never strike the bearing directly with a hammer or the bearing will be damaged. When installing a bearing, a piece of pipe or a socket with an outer diameter that matches the bearing race will be required. **Figure 73** shows the correct way to use a socket and hammer when installing a bearing over a shaft.

3. Step 1 describes how to install a bearing in a case half and over a shaft. However, when installing a bearing over a shaft and into a housing at the same time, a snug fit will be required for both outer and inner bearing races. In this situation, a spacer must be installed underneath the driver tool so that pressure is applied evenly across *both* races. See **Figure 74**. If the outer race is not supported as shown in

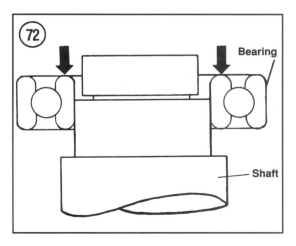

Figure 74, the balls will push against the outer bearing track and damage it.

Shrink Fit

1. *Installing a bearing over a shaft:* When a tight fit is required, the bearing inside diameter will be smaller than the shaft. In this case, driving the bearing on the shaft using normal methods may cause bearing damage. Instead, the bearing should be heated before installation. Note the following:
   a. Secure the shaft so that it is ready for bearing installation.
   b. Clean all residue from the bearing surface of the shaft. Remove burrs with a file or sandpaper.
   c. Fill a suitable pot or beaker with clean mineral oil. Place a thermometer (rated higher than 248° F [120° C]) in the oil. Support the thermometer so that it does not rest on the bottom or side of the pot.
   d. Remove the bearing from its wrapper and secure it with a piece of heavy wire bent to hold it in the pot. Hang the bearing in the pot so that it does not touch the bottom or sides of the pot.
   e. Turn the heat on and monitor the thermometer. When the oil temperature rises to approximately 248° F (120° C), remove the bearing from the pot and quickly install it. If necessary, place a socket on the inner bearing race and tap the bearing into place. As the bearing chills, it will tighten on the shaft so you must work quickly when installing it. Make sure the bearing is installed all the way.

2. *Installing a bearing in a housing:* Bearings are generally installed in a housing with a slight interference fit. Driving the bearing into the housing using normal methods may damage the housing or cause bearing damage. Instead, the housing should be heated before the bearing is installed. Note the following:

CAUTION
Before heating the crankcases in this procedure to remove the bearings, wash the cases thoroughly with detergent and water. Rinse and rewash the cases as required to remove all traces of oil and other chemical deposits.

   a. The housing must be heated to a temperature of about 212° F (100° C) in an oven or on a hot

plate. An easy way to check to see that it is at the proper temperature is to drop tiny drops of water on the case as it heats up; if they sizzle and evaporate immediately, the temperature is correct. Heat only one housing at a time.

CAUTION
Do not heat the housing with a torch (propane or acetylene) never bring a flame into contact with the bearing or housing. The direct heat will destroy the case hardening of the bearing and will likely warp the housing.

   b. Remove the housing from the oven or hot plate and hold onto the housing with a kitchen pot holder, heavy gloves or heavy shop cloths—it is hot.

NOTE
A suitable size socket and extension works well for removing and installing bearings.

   c. Hold the housing with the bearing side down and tap the bearing out. Repeat for all bearings in the housing.
   d. While heating up the housing halves, place the new bearings in a freezer if possible. Chilling them will slightly reduce their overall diameter

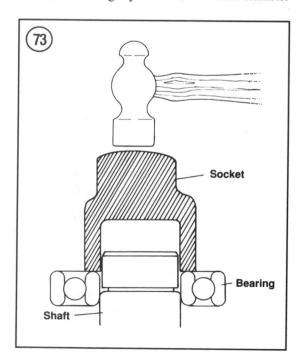

73

Socket

Bearing

Shaft

while the hot housing assembly is slightly larger due to heat expansion. This will make installation much easier.

NOTE
Always install bearings with the manufacturer's mark or number facing outward.

e. While the housing is still hot, install the new bearing(s) into the housing. Install the bearings

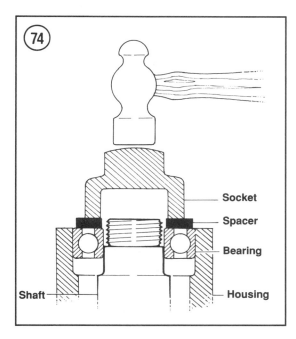

74

Socket

Spacer

Bearing

Shaft

Housing

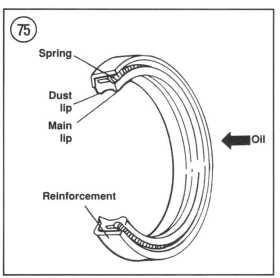

75

Spring

Dust lip

Main lip

Oil

Reinforcement

by hand, if possible. If necessary, lightly tap the bearing(s) into the housing with a socket placed on the outer bearing race. Do not install new bearings by driving on the inner bearing race. Install the bearing(s) until it seats completely.

OIL SEALS

Oil seals (**Figure 75**) are used to prevent leakage of oil, water, grease or combustion gasses from between a housing and a shaft. Improper removal of a seal can damage the housing or shaft. Improper installation of the seal can damage the seal. Note the following:

a. Prying is generally the easiest and most effective method of removing a seal from a housing. However, always place a rag underneath the pry tool to prevent damage to the housing.

b. Grease should be packed in the seal lips before the seal is installed.

c. Oil seals should be installed so that the manufacturer's numbers or marks face out.

d. Oil seals should be installed with a socket placed on the outside of the seal as shown in **Figure 76**. Make sure the seal is driven squarely into the housing. Never install a seal by hitting against the top of the seal with a hammer.

RIDING SAFETY

General Tips

1. Read your owner's manual and know your machine.

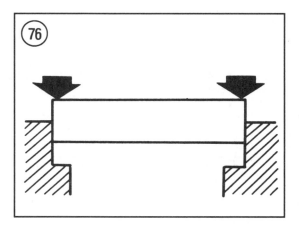

76

2. Check the throttle and brake controls before starting the engine.

3. Know how to make an emergency stop.

4. Never add fuel while anyone is smoking in the area or when the engine is running.

5. Never wear loose scarves, belts or boot laces that could catch on moving parts.

6. Always wear eye protection, head protection and protective clothing to protect your *entire* body. Today's riding apparel is very stylish and you will be ready for action as well as being well protected.

7. Riding in the winter months requires a good set of clothes to keep your body dry and warm, otherwise your entire trip may be miserable. If you dress properly, moisture will evaporate from your body. If you become too hot and if your clothes trap the moisture, you will become cold. Even mild temperatures can be very uncomfortable and dangerous when combined with a strong wind or traveling at high speed. See **Table 5** for wind chill factors. Always dress according to what the wind chill factor is, not the ambient temperature.

8. Never allow anyone to operate the bike without proper instruction. This is for their bodily protection and to keep your bike from damage or destruction.

9. Never attempt to repair your bike with the engine running except when necessary for certain tune-up procedures.

10. Check all of the machine components and hardware frequently, especially the wheels and the steering.

Table 1 FRAME SERIAL NUMBERS

U.S. and Canadian Models		
Year/model	Frame number	Engine number
1985		
VN700A1		
U.S.	JKAVN6A1 FA000001-006733	VN700AE000001-006762
Canada	JKAVNDA1 FA000001-on	VN700AE000001-006762
1986 VN750A2		
U.S. mfgr*	JKAVNDA1 GA002501-005500	VN750AE002501-012500
Japan mfgr*	JKAVNDA1 GB500001-508300	VN750AE002501-012500
1987 VN750A3		
U.S. mfgr*	JKAVNDA1 HB508301-509500	VN750AE012501-015000
Japan mfgr*	JKAVNDA1 HA005501-006700	VN750AE012501-015000
1988 VN750A4		
U.S. mfgr*	JKAVNDA1 JB509501-510700	VN750AE015001-on
Japan mfgr*	JKAVNDA1 JA006701-007900	VN750AE015001-on
1989 VN750A5		
U.S. mfgr*	JKAVNDA1 KB510701-on	VN750AE015001-on
Japan mfgr*	JKAVNDA1 KA007901-on	VN750AE015001-on
1990 VN750A6		
U.S. mfgr*	JKAVNDA1 LB512901-on	VN750AE017201-on
Japan mfgr*	JKAVNDA1 LA009001-on	VN750AE017201-on
1991 VN750A7	JKAVNDA1 MB515101-on	VN750AE017201-on
1992 VN750A8	JKAVNDA1 NB517301-on	VN750AE017201-on
1993 VN750A9	JKAVNDA1 PB520601-on	VN750AE017201-on
1994 VN750A10	JKAVNDA1 RB524801-on	VN750AE017201-on
1995 VN750A10	JKAVNDA1 SB529701-on	VN750AE017201-on
U.K. Models		
Year/model	Frame number	Engine number
1986 VN750A2	VN750A-002501-on	VN750AE002501-012500
1987 VN750A3	VN750A-005501-on	VN750AE012501-015000
1988 VN750A4	VN750A-006701-on	VN750AE015001-017200
1989 VN750A5	VN750A-007901-on	VN750AE017201-on
	(continued)	

Table 1 FRAME SERIAL NUMBERS (continued)

U.K. Models (continued)		
Year/model	Frame number	Engine number
1993 VN750A9	VN750A-600001-on	VN750AE017201-on
1994 VN750A10	JKAVNDA1 RB524807-529700	VN750AE017201-on
1995 VN750A11	JKAVNDA1 SB529701-534899	VN750AE017201-on
1996 VN750A12	JKAVNDA1TB534900-536700	VN750AE017201-on
1997 VN750A13	JKAVNDA1 VB536701-538600	VN750AE017201-on
1998 VN750A14	JKAVNDA1 WB538501-on	VN750AE017201-on
1999 VN750A15	JKAVNDA1 XB539901-541600	VN750AE017201-on
2000 VN750A16	JKAVNDA1 YB541601-on	VN750AE017201-on
2001 VN750A17	JKAZGCA1 1A059001-on*	VN750AE017201-on
	JKAZGCA1 1B514901-on	VN750AE017201-on

* U.S. mfgr = models manufactured in Lincoln, Nebraska U.S.A.
Japan mfgr = models manufactured in Japan.

Table 2 DECIMAL AND METRIC EQUIVALENTS

Fractions	Decimal in.	Metric mm	Fractions	Decimal in.	Metric mm
1/64	0.015625	0.39688	33/64	0.515625	13.09687
1/32	0.03125	0.79375	17/32	0.53125	13.49375
3/64	0.046875	1.19062	35/64	0.546875	13.89062
1/16	0.0625	1.58750	9/16	0.5625	14.28750
5/64	0.078125	1.98437	37/64	0.578125	14.68437
3/32	0.09375	2.38125	19/32	0.59375	15.08125
7/64	0.109375	2.77812	39/64	0.609375	15.47812
1/8	0.125	3.1750	5/8	0.625	15.87500
9/64	0.140625	3.57187	41/64	0.640625	16.27187
5/32	0.15625	3.96875	21/32	0.65625	16.66875
11/64	0.171875	4.36562	43/64	0.671875	17.06562
3/16	0.1875	4.76250	11/16	0.6875	17.46250
13/64	0.203125	5.15937	45/64	0.703125	17.85937
7/32	0.21875	5.55625	23/32	0.71875	18.25625
15/64	0.234375	5.95312	47/64	0.734375	18.65312
1/4	0.250	6.35000	3/4	0.750	19.05000
17/64	0.265625	6.74687	49/64	0.765625	19.44687
9/32	0.28125	7.14375	25/32	0.78125	19.84375
19/64	0.296875	7.54062	51/64	0.796875	20.24062
5/16	0.3125	7.93750	13/16	0.8125	20.63750
21/64	0.328125	8.33437	53/64	0.828125	21.03437
11/32	0.34375	8.73125	27/32	0.84375	21.43125
23/64	0.359375	9.12812	55/64	0.859375	22.82812
3/8	0.375	9.52500	7/8	0.875	22.22500
25/64	0.390625	9.92187	57/64	0.890625	22.62187
13/32	0.40625	10.31875	29/32	0.90625	23.01875
27/64	0.421875	10.71562	59/64	0.921875	23.41562
7/16	0.4375	11.11250	15/16	0.9375	23.81250
29/64	0.453125	11.50937	61/64	0.953125	24.20937
15/32	0.46875	11.90625	31/32	0.96875	24.60625
31/64	0.484375	12.30312	63/64	0.984375	25.00312
1/2	0.500	12.70000	1	1.00	25.40000

Table 3 STANDARD TIGHTENING TORQUES

Thread size	N•m	ft.-lb.
Bolt		
6 mm	6	4.5
8 mm	15	11
10 mm	30	22
12 mm	55	40
14 mm	85	61
16 mm	130	94
Nut		
10 mm	6	4.5
12 mm	15	11
14 mm	30	22
17 mm	55	40
19 mm	85	61
22 mm	130	94

* Use these torque figures for all fasteners not individually listed.

Table 4 WORKSHOP TOOLS

Tool	Size or specificaton
Screwdriver	
Common	1/8 x 4 in. blade
Common	5/16 x 8 in. blade
Common	3/8 x 12 in. blade
Phillips	Size 2 tip, 6 in. overall
Pliers	
Slip joint	6 in. overall
Vise-grip	10 in. overall
Needlenose	6 in. overall
Channel lock	12 in. overall
Snap ring	Assorted
Wrenches	
Box-end set	Assorted
Open-end set	Assorted
Crescent	6 in. and 12 in. overall
Socket set	1/2 in. drive ratchet with assorted metric sockets
Socket drive extensions	1/2 in. drive, 2 in., 4 in. and 6 in.
Socket universal joint	1/2 in. drive
Allen	Socket driven (long and short), T-handle driven and 90°
Hammers	
Soft faced	–
Plastic faced	–
Metal faced	–
Other special tools	
Impact driver	1/2 in. drive with assorted bits
Torque wrench	1/2 in. driver (ft.-lb.)
Flat feeler gauge	Metric set

Table 5 WINDCHILL FACTOR

Estimated wind speed in mph	Actual thermometer reading (°F)											
	50	40	30	20	10	0	−10	−20	−30	−40	−50	−60
	Equivalent temperature (°F)											
Calm	50	40	30	20	10	0	−10	−20	−30	−40	−50	−60
5	48	37	27	16	6	−5	−15	−26	−36	−47	−57	−68
10	40	28	16	4	−9	−21	−33	−46	−58	−70	−83	−95
15	36	22	9	−5	−18	−36	−45	−58	−72	−85	−99	−112
20	32	18	4	−10	−25	−39	−53	−67	−82	−96	−110	−124
25	30	16	0	−15	−29	−44	−59	−74	−88	−104	−118	−133
30	28	13	−2	−18	−33	−48	−63	−79	−94	−109	−125	−140
35	27	11	−4	−20	−35	−49	−67	−82	−98	−113	−129	−145
40 *	26	10	−6	−21	−37	−53	−69	−85	−100	−116	−132	−148

Little danger (for properly clothed person)

Increasing danger | Great danger

• Danger from freezing of exposed flesh •

*Wind speeds greater than 40 mph have little additional effect.

CHAPTER TWO

TROUBLESHOOTING

Every motorcycle engine requires an uninterrupted supply of fuel and air, proper ignition and adequate compression. If any of these is lacking, the engine will not run.

Diagnosing mechanical problems is relatively simple if you use orderly procedures and keep a few basic principles in mind.

The troubleshooting procedures in this chapter analyze typical symptoms and show logical methods of isolating causes. These are not the only methods. There may be several ways to solve a problem, but only a systematic approach can guarantee success.

Never assume anything. Do not overlook the obvious. If you are riding along and the bike suddenly quits, check the easiest, most accessible problem spots first.

If nothing obvious turns up in a quick check, look a little further. Learning to recognize and describe symptoms will make repairs easier for you or a mechanic at the shop. Describe problems accurately and fully. Saying that it won't run isn't the same thing as saying it quit at high speed and won't start, or that "it sat in my garage for 3 months and then wouldn't start."

Gather as many symptoms as possible to aid in diagnosis. Note whether the engine lost power gradually or all at once. Remember that the more complicated a machine is, the easier it is to troubleshoot because symptoms point to specific problems.

After the symptoms are defined, areas which could cause problems are tested and analyzed.

Guessing at the cause of a problem may provide the solution, but it can easily lead to frustration, wasted time and a series of expensive, unnecessary parts replacements.

You do not need fancy equipment or complicated test gear to determine whether repairs can be attempted at home. A few simple checks could save a large repair bill and lost time while the bike sits in a dealer's service department. On the other hand, be realistic and don't attempt repairs beyond your abilities. Service departments tend to charge heavily for

putting together a disassembled engine that may have been abused. Some won't even take on such a job, so use common sense and don't get in over your head.

OPERATING REQUIREMENTS

An engine needs 3 basics to run properly: correct fuel/air mixture, compression and a spark at the correct time (**Figure 1**). If one or more are missing, the engine will not run. Four-stroke engine operating principles are described under *Engine Principles* in Chapter Four.

If the machine has been sitting for any length of time and refuses to start, check and clean the spark plugs and then look to the gasoline delivery system. This includes the fuel tank, fuel shutoff valve and fuel line to the carburetor. Gasoline deposits may have formed and gummed up the carburetor jets and air passages. Gasoline tends to lose its potency after standing for long periods. Condensation may contaminate the fuel with water. Drain the old fuel (fuel tank, fuel lines and carburetors) and try starting with a fresh tankful.

TROUBLESHOOTING INSTRUMENTS

Refer to Chapter One for a list of the instruments needed.

STARTING THE ENGINE

When experiencing engine starting troubles, it is easy to work out of sequence and forget basic engine starting procedures. The following sections list factory recommended starting procedures for the Vulcan VN700 and VN750 engine at the following ambient temperatures and engine conditions:

   a. Cold engine with normal air temperature.
   b. Cold engine with low air temperature.
   c. Warm engine and/or high air temperature.
   d. Flooded engine.

Starting Notes

1. A sidestand ignition cut-off system is used on all models. The position of the sidestand will affect engine starting. Note the following:

a. The engine cannot start when the sidestand is down and the transmission is in gear.

b. The engine can start when the sidestand is down and the transmission is in NEUTRAL. The engine will stop if the transmission is put in gear with the sidestand down.

c. The engine can be started when the sidestand is up and the transmission is in NEUTRAL or in gear with the clutch lever pulled in.

2. Before starting the engine, shift the transmission into NEUTRAL and confirm that the engine stop switch is at RUN.

3. Turn the ignition switch to ON and confirm the following:

a. The neutral indicator light is ON (when transmission is in NEUTRAL).

b. The engine oil pressure warning light is ON.

4. The engine is now ready to start. Refer to the starting procedure in this section that best meets the air temperature and engine condition.

5. If the engine is idled at a fast speed for more than 5 minutes and/or the throttle is snapped on and off repeatedly at normal air temperatures, the exhaust pipes may discolor.

6. Excessive choke use can cause an excessively rich fuel mixture. This condition can wash oil off of the piston and cylinder walls, causing piston and cylinder scuffing.

CAUTION
Once the engine starts, the red oil pressure warning light should go off in a few seconds. If the light stays on longer than a few seconds, stop the engine immediately. Check the engine oil level as described in Chapter Three. If the oil level is okay, the oil pressure may be too low or the oil pressure switch may be shorted. Check the oiling system and correct the problem before starting the engine. If the oil pressure switch is okay, the system is warning you that some type of stoppage has occurred in the lubrication system and that oil is not being delivered to engine components. Severe engine damage will occur if the engine is run with low oil pressure. Refer to **Engine Lubrication** *in this chapter.*

NOTE
Do not operate the starter motor for more than 5 seconds at a time. Wait

approximately 10 seconds between starting attempts.

Starting Procedure

Cold engine with normal air temperature

Normal air temperature is considered to be between 50-95° F (10-35° C).

1. Perform the procedures under *Starting Notes*.

2. Install the ignition key and turn the ignition switch to ON.

3. Pull the choke lever (**Figure 2**) to the fully ON position.

4. Make sure the engine stop switch is in the RUN position (A, **Figure 3**).

5. Depress the starter button (B, **Figure 3**) and start the engine. Do not open the throttle when pressing the starter button.

NOTE
When a cold engine is started with the throttle open and the choke ON, a lean mixture will result and cause hard starting.

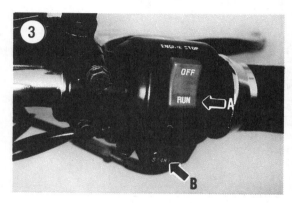

6. With the engine running, operate the choke lever as required to keep the engine idling at 1,500-2,500 rpm.

7. After approximately 30 seconds, push the choke lever to the fully OFF position (**Figure 4**). If the idling is rough, open the throttle lightly until the engine warms up.

Cold engine with low air temperature

Low air temperature is considered to be 50° F (10° C) or lower.

1. Perform the procedures under *Starting Notes*.

2. Install the ignition key and turn the ignition switch to ON.

3. Pull the choke lever (**Figure 2**) to the fully ON position.

4. Make sure the engine stop switch is in the RUN position (A, **Figure 3**).

5. Depress the starter button (B, **Figure 3**) and start the engine. Do not open the throttle when pressing the starter button.

6. Once the engine is running, open the throttle slightly to help warm the engine. Continue warming

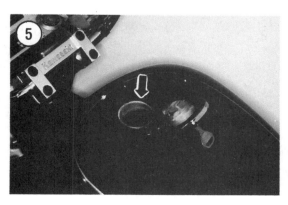

the engine until the choke can be turned to the fully OFF position and the engine responds to the throttle cleanly.

Warm engine and/or high air temperature

High air temperature is considered to be 95° F (35° C) or higher.

1. Perform the procedures under *Starting Notes*.

2. Install the ignition key and turn the ignition switch to ON.

3. Open the throttle slightly and depress the starter button (B, **Figure 3**). Do not use the choke.

Flooded engine

If the engine will not start after a few attempts it may be flooded. If you smell gasoline after attempting to start the engine, and the engine did not start, the engine is probably flooded. To start a flooded engine:

1. Turn the engine stop switch off.

2. Push the choke lever (**Figure 4**) to the OFF position.

3. Open the throttle completely and depress the starter button (B, **Figure 3**) for 5 seconds. Then release the start button and close the throttle.

4. Wait 10 seconds, then continue with Step 5.

5. Turn the engine stop switch on.

6. Turn the ignition switch on.

7. Open the throttle slightly and depress the starter button to start the engine. Do not use the choke.

EMERGENCY TROUBLESHOOTING

When the bike is difficult to start, or won't start at all, it doesn't help to wear down the battery by using the electric starter. Check for obvious problems even before getting out your tools. Go down the following list step by step. Do each one; you may be embarrassed to find the engine stop switch off, but that is better than wearing down the battery. If the bike still will not start, refer to the appropriate troubleshooting procedure in this chapter.

1. Is there fuel in the tank? Open the filler cap (**Figure 5**) and rock the bike. Listen for fuel sloshing around.

WARNING
Do not use an open flame to check in the tank. A serious explosion is certain to result.

2. Is the fuel supply valve in the ON position? Turn the valve to the ON position (**Figure 6**) (or the RES position) (**Figure 7**). This will ensure you get the last remaining gas.
3. Is the engine stop switch in the correct position? The engine should start and operate when the switch is in the RUN position (A, **Figure 3**). This switch is used primarily as an emergency or safety switch. Check that the switch is in the RUN position when starting the engine. Test the switch as described under *Switches* in Chapter Eight.
4. Are all 4 spark plug caps on tight? Push the spark plug caps (**Figure 8**) on each side of both cylinders and slightly rotate them to clean the electrical connection between the plug and the connector.
5. Is the choke lever in the right position? The choke lever should be OFF (**Figure 4**) for a warm engine and ON (**Figure 2**) for a cold engine.

ENGINE STARTING TROUBLESHOOTING

An engine that refuses to start or is difficult to start is very frustrating. More often than not, the problem is very minor and can be found with a simple and logical troubleshooting approach.

First, review the steps under *Engine Starting Procedures* in this chapter. You may be working out of sequence and may have flooded the engine. If the engine will not start by following the engine starting steps, continue with this section.

The following are beginning points from which to isolate engine starting problems.

NOTE
Do not operate the starter motor for more than 5 seconds at a time. Wait approximately 10 seconds between starting attempts.

Engine Fails to Start (Spark Test)

Perform the following spark test to determine if the ignition system is operating properly.

1. Remove both spark plugs from each cylinder head as described in Chapter Three.

NOTE
*If the spark plugs are wet after attempting to start the engine or if they appear fouled, refer to **Fuel System** in this chapter.*

2. Connect each spark plug wire and connector to a spark plug and touch each spark plug base to a good

ground like the engine cylinder head. Position the spark plugs so you can see the electrode.

WARNING
During the next step, do not hold the spark plugs or connectors with your fingers or a serious electrical shock may result. If necessary, use a pair of insulated pliers to hold the spark plugs or wires. The high voltage generated by the ignition system could produce serious or fatal shocks.

3. Crank the engine over with the starter. A fat blue spark should be evident across each spark plug electrode. If the spark is good, continue with Step 4. If the spark is weak or if there is no spark, perform Step 6.

NOTE
*If the starter does not operate or if the starter motor rotates but the engine does not turn over, refer to **Engine Will Not Crank** in this section.*

4. Check engine compression as described in Chapter Three. If the compression is good, perform Steps 5-7. If the compression is low, check for one or more of the following:
   a. Leaking cylinder head gasket(s).
   b. Cracked or warped cylinder head(s).
   c. Worn piston rings, pistons and cylinders.
   d. Valve stuck open.
   e. Seized valve(s).
   f. Worn or damaged valve seat(s).
   g. Incorrect valve timing.
5. Turn the fuel valve to the OFF position (**Figure 9**).
6. Disconnect the fuel tube from the carburetors (**Figure 10**) and insert the open end into a clear, glass container.
7. Turn the fuel valve to ON, RES and OFF. A steady flow of fuel should be noticed with the fuel valve in the ON and RES positions. The fuel flow should stop with the fuel valve in the OFF position. If the fuel flow is okay, perform Step 8. If there is no fuel flow or if the flow is slow and intermittent, check for one or more of the following conditions:
   a. Empty fuel tank.
   b. Plugged fuel tank cap vent hole (**Figure 11**).
   c. Clogged fuel filter or fuel line.
   d. Stuck or clogged carburetor fuel valve.
8. If the spark was weak or if there was no spark at one or more plugs, note the following:
   a. If there is no spark at all of the plugs, there may be a problem in the input side of the ignition system IC ignitor, pickup coil(s), sidestand switch or neutral switch. Test these parts as described in Chapter Eight.
   b. If there is no spark at one of the spark plugs, the spark plug is probably faulty or there is a problem with the spark plug wire or plug cap. Replace the spark plug and retest. If there is still no spark at that one plug, test the spark plug

wire and plug cap as described in Chapter Eight. If those test good, the problem may be in the primary side of the ignition system (ignition coil or IC ignitor). Test these parts as described in Chapter Eight.

Engine is Difficult to Start

Check for one or more of the following possible malfunctions:
a. Fouled spark plug(s).
b. Improperly adjusted choke.
c. Intake manifold air leak.
d. Contaminated fuel system.
e. Improperly adjusted carburetors.
f. Ignition system malfunction.
g. Weak ignition coil(s).
h. Poor compression.
i. Engine and transmission oil too heavy.

Engine Will Not Crank

Check for one or more of the following possible malfunctions:
a. Blown fuse.
b. Discharged battery.
c. Defective starter motor, starter relay or start switch.
d. Seized piston(s).
e. Seized crankshaft bearings.
f. Broken connecting rod(s).
g. Locked-up transmission or clutch assembly.
h. Defective starter clutch.

ENGINE PERFORMANCE

In the following check list, it is assumed that the engine runs, but is not operating at peak performance. This will serve as a starting point from which to isolate a performance malfunction. Where ignition timing is mentioned as a problem, remember that there is no method of adjusting the ignition timing. If you check the ignition timing with a timing light as described in Chapter Three and it is incorrect, there is a faulty part within the ignition system. The individual parts must be checked and the faulty part(s) replaced.

Engine Will Not Start or Is Hard to Start

a. Fuel tank empty.
b. Obstructed fuel line, fuel shutoff valve or fuel filter.
c. Sticking float valve in carburetor(s).
d. Carburetors incorrectly adjusted.
e. Improper starter valve (choke) operation.
f. Improper throttle operation.
g. Fouled or improperly gapped spark plug(s).
h. Ignition timing incorrect.
i. Broken or shorted ignition coil(s).
j. Weak or faulty IC ignitor or pickup coils.
k. Improper valve timing.
l. Clogged air filter element.
m. Contaminated fuel.
n. Engine flooded with fuel.

Engine Starts but Then Stops

a. Incorrect choke adjustment.
b. Incorrect pilot air screw setting (closed).
c. Incorrect ignition timing.
d. Contaminated fuel.
e. Intake manifold air leak.

Engine Will Not Idle

a. Carburetors incorrectly adjusted (too lean or too rich).
b. Fouled or improperly gapped spark plug(s).
c. Leaking head gasket(s) or vacuum leak.
d. Ignition timing incorrect.
e. Improper valve timing.
f. Obstructed fuel line or fuel shutoff valve.
g. Low engine compression.
h. Starter valve (choke) stuck in the open position.
i. Incorrect pilot screw adjustment.
j. Clogged slow jet(s) in the carburetor(s).
k. Clogged air filter element.
l. Valve(s) and valve seat(s) require service.

Poor High Speed Performance

1. Check ignition timing as described in Chapter Three. If ignition timing is correct, perform Step 2. If the timing is incorrect, test the following ignition system components as described in Chapter Eight:
a. IC ignitor.
b. Pickup coil(s).

c. Ignition coils.

2. Turn the fuel valve in the OFF position (**Figure 9**).

3. Disconnect the fuel tube from the carburetors (**Figure 10**) and insert the open end into a clear, glass container.

4. Turn the fuel valve to ON, RES and OFF. A steady flow of fuel should be noticed with the fuel valve in the ON and RES positions. The fuel flow should stop with the fuel valve in the OFF position. If the fuel flow is okay, perform Step 5. If there is no fuel flow or if the flow is slow and intermittent, check for one or more of the following conditions:

    a. Empty fuel tank.

    b. Plugged fuel tank cap vent hole (**Figure 11**).

    c. Clogged fuel filter or fuel line.

    d. Stuck or clogged carburetor fuel valve.

5. Remove the carburetors as described in Chapter Seven. Then remove the float bowls and check for contamination and plugged jets. If any contamination is found, disassemble and clean each carburetor. You should also pour out and discard the remaining fuel in the fuel tank and flush the fuel tank thoroughly. If no contamination was found and the jets were not plugged, perform Step 6.

6. Incorrect valve timing and worn or damaged valve springs can cause poor high speed performance. If the valve timing was set just prior to the bike experiencing this type of problem, the valve timing may be incorrect. If the valve timing was not set or changed, and you performed all of the other inspection procedures in this section without locating the problem area, the cylinder head covers should be removed and the valve train assembly inspected.

Low or Poor Engine Power

1. Support the bike with the rear wheel off the ground, then spin the rear wheel by hand. If the wheel spins freely, perform Step 2. If the wheel does not spin freely, check for the following conditions:

    a. Dragging rear brake.

    b. Excessive rear axle tightening torque (1986-1989).

    c. Worn or damaged rear wheel bearings.

2. Check the clutch adjustment and operation. If the clutch slips, refer to *Clutch* in this chapter.

3. If Steps 1 and 2 did not locate the problem, test ride the bike and accelerate lightly. If the engine speed increased according to throttle position, per-

form Step 4. If the engine speed did not increase, check for one or more of the following problems:

    a. Clogged or damaged air filter.

    b. Restricted fuel flow.

    c. Clogged fuel tank cap vent.

    d. Incorrect choke adjustment or operation.

    e. Clogged or damaged muffler.

4. Check for one or more of the following problems:

    a. Low engine compression.

    b. Fouled spark plug(s).

    c. Clogged carburetor jet(s).

    d. Incorrect ignition timing.

    e. Incorrect oil level (too high or too low).

    f. Contaminated oil.

    g. Worn or damaged valve train assembly.

    h. Engine overheating.

Engine Overheating

    a. Incorrect coolant level.

    b. Incorrect carburetor adjustment or jet selection.

    c. Improper spark plug heat range.

    d. Cooling system malfunction.

    e. Clogged radiator and/or cooling fins.

    f. Oil level low.

    g. Oil not circulating properly.

    h. Valves leaking.

    i. Heavy engine carbon deposits.

    j. Dragging brake(s).

    k. Clutch slipping.

Engine Overheating (Cooling System Malfunction)

Note the above, then proceed with the following items:

    a. Clogged radiator.

    b. Thermostat stuck closed.

    c. Worn or damaged radiator cap.

    d. Water pump worn or damaged.

    e. Fan relay malfunction.

    f. Thermostatic fan switch malfunction.

    g. Damaged fan blade(s).

    h. Clogged or blocked coolant passages in radiator, hoses or engine.

2

Excessive Exhaust Smoke and Engine Runs Roughly

a. Clogged air filter element.
b. Carburetor adjustment incorrect; mixture too rich.
c. Choke not operating correctly.
d. Water or other contaminants in fuel.
e. Clogged fuel line.
f. Spark plugs fouled.
g. Ignition coil defective.
h. Loose or defective ignition circuit wire.
i. Short circuit from damaged wire insulation.
j. Loose battery cable connection(s).
k. Valve timing incorrect.

Engine Lacks Acceleration

a. Carburetor mixture too lean.
b. Clogged fuel line.
c. Improper ignition timing.
d. Dragging brake(s).
e. Slipping clutch.

Engine Backfires

a. Improper ignition timing.
b. Carburetors improperly adjusted.
c. Lean fuel mixture.

Engine Misfires During Acceleration

a. Improper ignition timing.
b. Lean fuel mixture.

ENGINE NOISES

Often the first evidence of an internal engine problem is a strange noise. That knocking, clicking or tapping sound which you never heard before may be warning you of impending trouble.

While engine noises can indicate problems, they are difficult to interpret correctly; inexperienced mechanics can be seriously misled by them.

Professional mechanics often use a special stethoscope (which looks like a doctor's stethoscope) for isolating engine noises. You can do nearly as well with a "sounding stick" which can be an ordinary piece of doweling, or a section of small hose. By placing one end in contact with the area to which you want to listen and the other end to the front of your ear (not directly on your ear), you can hear sounds emanating from that area. The first time you do this, you may be confused at the strange sounds coming from even a normal engine. If you can, have an experienced friend or mechanic help you sort out the noises.

Consider the following when troubleshooting engine noises:

1. *Knocking or pinging during acceleration*—Caused by using a lower octane fuel than recommended. May also be caused by poor fuel. Pinging can also be caused by a spark plug of the wrong heat range or carbon build-up in the combustion chamber. Refer to *Correct Spark Plug Heat Range and Compression Test* in Chapter Three.

2. *Slapping or rattling noises at low speed or during acceleration*—May be caused by piston slap, i.e., excessive piston-cylinder wall clearance.

NOTE
Piston slap is easier to detect when the engine is cold and before the pistons have expanded. Once the engine has warmed up, piston expansion reduces piston-to-cylinder clearance.

3. *Knocking or rapping while decelerating*—Usually caused by excessive rod bearing clearance.

4. *Persistent knocking and vibration occurring every crankshaft rotation*—Usually caused by worn rod or main bearing(s). Can also be caused by broken piston rings or damaged piston pins.

5. *Rapid on-off squeal*—Compression leak around cylinder head gasket(s) or spark plug(s).

6. *Valve train noise*—Check for the following:
a. Valve hydraulic lash adjuster(s) defective.
b. Valve sticking in guide.
c. Low oil pressure.
d. Damaged camshaft cap or loose mounting bolts.

ENGINE LUBRICATION

An improperly operating engine lubrication system will quickly lead to engine seizure. The engine oil level should be checked weekly and topped up, as described in Chapter Three. Oil pump service is described in Chapter Four.

Oil Consumption High or Engine Smokes Excessively

a. Worn valve guides.
b. Worn or damaged piston rings.

Excessive Engine Oil Leaks

a. Clogged air filter breather hose.
b. Loose engine parts.
c. Damaged gasket sealing surfaces.

Black Smoke

a. Clogged air filter.
b. Incorrect carburetor fuel level (too high).
c. Choke stuck open.
d. Incorrect main jet (too large).

White Smoke

a. Worn valve guide.
b. Worn valve oil seal.
c. Worn piston ring oil ring.
d. Excessive cylinder and/or piston wear.
e. Coolant leaking into cylinders.

Oil Pressure Too High

a. Clogged oil filter.
b. Clogged oil gallery or metering orifices.
c. Pressure relief valve stuck closed.

Low Oil Pressure

a. Low oil level.
b. Damaged oil pump.
c. Clogged oil screen.
d. Clogged oil filter.
e. Internal oil leakage.
f. Pressure relief valve stuck open.

No Oil Pressure

a. Damaged oil pump.
b. Excessively low oil level.
c. No oil in crankcase.
d. Internal oil leakage.
e. Damaged oil pump drive chain.

f. Damaged oil pump drive shaft.

Oil Pressure Warning Light Stays On

a. Low oil pressure.
b. No oil pressure.
c. Damaged oil pressure switch.
d. Short circuit in warning light circuit.

Oil Level Too Low

a. Oil level not maintained at correct level.
b. Worn piston rings.
c. Worn cylinder(s).
d. Worn valve guides.
e. Worn valve stem seals.
f. Piston rings incorrectly installed during engine overhaul.
g. External oil leakage.
h. Oil leaking into the cooling system.

Oil Contamination

a. Blown cylinder head gasket(s) allowing coolant leakage.
b. Water contamination.
c. Oil and filter not changed at specified intervals or when abnormal operating conditions demand more frequent changes.

CLUTCH

The basic clutch troubles and causes are listed in this section.

Excessive Clutch Lever Operation

If the clutch lever is too hard to pull in, check the following:
a. Clutch cable not properly adjusted.
b. Clutch cable requires lubrication.
c. Clutch cable improperly routed or bent.
d. Damaged clutch lifter bearing.
e. Push rod bent.

Rough Clutch Operation

This condition can be caused by excessively worn, grooved or damaged clutch housing slots.

Clutch Slippage

If the engine sounds like it is winding out without accelerating, the clutch is probably slipping. Some of the main causes of clutch slipping are:
a. Worn clutch plates.
b. Weak clutch springs.
c. No clutch lever free play.
d. Loose clutch lifter bolts.
e. Damaged clutch lifter.
f. Engine oil additive being used (clutch plates contaminated).

Clutch Drag

If the clutch will not disengage or if the bike creeps with the transmission in gear and the clutch disengaged, the clutch is dragging. Some of the main causes of clutch drag are:
a. Excessive clutch lever free play.
b. Warped clutch plates.
c. Damaged clutch lifter.
d. Loose clutch housing locknut.
e. Clutch lifter rod improperly installed.
f. Engine oil level too high.
g. Incorrect oil viscosity.
h. Engine oil additive being used.

GEARSHIFT LINKAGE

The gearshift linkage assembly connects the gearshift pedal (external shift mechanism) to the shift drum (internal shift mechanism).

The external shift mechanism can be examined after removing the external shift mechanism cover on the left-hand side of the crankcase. The internal shift mechanism can only be examined once the engine has been removed from the frame and the crankcase disassembled. Common gearshift linkage troubles and checks to make are listed below.

Transmission Jumps out of Gear

a. Loose stopper arm bolt.
b. Damaged stopper arm.
c. Weak or damaged stopper arm spring.
d. Loose or damaged shifter cam.
e. Bent shift fork shaft(s).
f. Bent or damaged shift fork.
g. Worn gear dogs or slots.

h. Damaged shift drum grooves.

Difficult Shifting

a. Damaged clutch system.
b. Incorrect oil viscosity.
c. Bent shift fork shaft(s).
d. Bent or damaged shift fork(s).
e. Worn gear dogs or slots.
f. Damaged shift drum grooves.

TRANSMISSION

Transmission symptoms are sometimes hard to distinguish from clutch symptoms. Common transmission troubles and checks to make are listed below. Refer to Chapter Six for transmission service procedures. Prior to working on the transmission, make sure the clutch and gearshift linkage assembly are not causing the trouble.

Difficult Shifting

a. Damaged clutch system.
b. Incorrect oil viscosity.
c. Bent shift fork shaft(s).
d. Bent or damaged shift fork(s).
e. Worn gear dogs or slots.
f. Damaged shift drum grooves.

Jumps out of Gear

a. Loose or damaged shift drum stopper arm.
b. Bent or damaged shift fork(s).
c. Bent shift fork shaft(s).
d. Damaged shift drum grooves.
e. Worn gear dogs or slots.
f. Broken shift linkage return spring.

Incorrect Shift Lever Operation

a. Bent shift lever.
b. Stripped shift lever splines.
c. Damaged shift lever linkage.

Excessive Gear Noise

a. Worn bearings.
b. Worn or damaged gears.

c. Excessive gear backlash.

ELECTRICAL TROUBLESHOOTING

This section describes the basics of electrical troubleshooting, how to use test equipment and the basic test procedures with the various pieces of test equipment.

Electrical troubleshooting can be very time-consuming and frustrating without proper knowledge and a suitable plan. Refer to the wiring diagrams at the end of the book and at the individual system diagrams included with the Charging System, Ignition System and Starting System sections in this chapter. Wiring diagrams will help you determine how the circuit should work by tracing the current

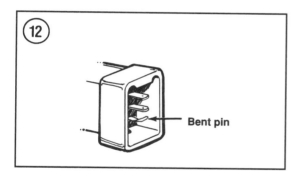

Bent pin

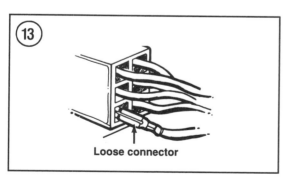

Loose connector

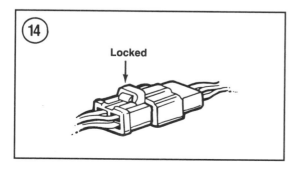

Locked

paths from the power source through the circuit components to ground. Also check any circuits that share the same fuse, ground or switch, etc. If the other circuits work properly, the shared wiring is okay and the cause must be in the wiring used only by the suspect circuit. If all related circuits are faulty at the same time the probable cause is a poor ground connection or a blown fuse(s).

As with all troubleshooting procedures, analyze typical symptoms in a systematic procedure. Never assume anything and don't overlook the obvious like a blown fuse or an electrical connector that has separated. Test the simplest and most obvious cause first and try to make tests at easily accessible points on the bike.

Preliminary Checks and Precautions

Prior to starting any electrical troubleshooting procedure perform the following:

a. Check the main fuse; make sure it is not blown. Replace if necessary.

b. Check the individual fuse(s) for each circuit; make sure it is not blown. Replace if necessary.

c. Inspect the battery. Make sure it is fully charged, the electrolyte level is correct and that the battery leads are clean and securely attached to the battery terminals. Refer to *Battery* in Chapter Eight.

d. Disconnect each electrical connector in the suspect circuit and check that there are no bent metal pins on the male side of the electrical connector (**Figure 12**). A bent pin will not connect to its mating receptacle in the female end of the connector, causing an open circuit.

e. Check each female end of the connector. Make sure that the metal connector on the end of each wire (**Figure 13**) is pushed all the way into the plastic connector. If not, carefully push them in with a narrow blade screwdriver.

f. Check all electrical wires where they enter the individual metal connector in both the male and female plastic connector.

g. Make sure all electrical connectors within the connector are clean and free of corrosion. Clean, if necessary, and pack the connectors with a dielectric grease.

h. After all is checked out, push the connectors together and make sure they are fully engaged and locked together (**Figure 14**).

i. Never pull on the electrical wires when disconnecting an electrical connector-pull only on the connector plastic housing.

j. Never use a self-powered test light on circuits that contain solid-state devices. The solid-state devices may be damaged.

TEST EQUIPMENT

Test Light or Voltmeter

A test light can be constructed of a 12-volt light bulb with a pair of test leads carefully soldered to the bulb. To check for battery voltage (12 volts) in a circuit, attach one lead to ground and the other lead to various points along the circuit. Where battery voltage is present the light bulb will light.

A voltmeter is used in the same manner as the test light to find out if battery voltage is present in any given circuit. The voltmeter, unlike the test light, will also indicate how much voltage is present at each test point. When using a voltmeter, attach the red lead (+) to the component or wire to be checked and the negative (–) lead to a good ground.

Self-powered Test Light and Ohmmeter

A self-powered test light can be constructed of a 12-volt light bulb, a pair of test leads and a 12-volt battery. When the test leads are touched together the light bulb will go on.

Use a self-powered test light as follows:

a. Touch the test leads together to make sure the light bulb goes on. If not, correct the problem prior to using it in a test procedure.

b. Disconnect the bike's battery or remove the fuse(s) that protects the circuit to be tested.

c. Select 2 points within the circuit where there should be continuity.

d. Attach one lead of the self-powered test light to each point.

e. If there is continuity, the self-powered test light bulb will come on.

f. If there is no continuity, the self-powered test light bulb will not come on indicating an open circuit.

An ohmmeter can be used in place of the self-powered test light. The ohmmeter, unlike the test light, will also indicate how much resistance is present between each test point. Low resistance means good

continuity in a complete circuit. Before using an ohmmeter, it must first be calibrated. This is done by touching the leads together and turning the ohms calibration knob until the meter reads zero.

> *CAUTION*
> *An ohmmeter must never be connected to any circuit which has power applied to it. Always disconnect the battery negative lead before using the ohmmeter.*

Jumper Wire

When using a jumper wire always install an inline fuse/fuse holder (available at most auto supply stores or electronic supply stores) to the jumper wire. Never use a jumper wire across any load (a component that is connected and turned on). This would result in a direct short and will blow the fuse(s) and/or damage components and wiring in that circuit.

BASIC TEST PROCEDURES

Voltage Testing

Unless otherwise specified, all voltage tests are made with the electrical connector still connected. Insert the test leads into the backside of the connector and make sure the test lead touches the electrical wire or metal connector within the connector. If the test lead only touches the wire insulation you will get a false reading.

Always check both sides of the connector as one side may be loose or corroded thus preventing electrical flow through the connector. This type of test can be performed with a test light or a voltmeter. A voltmeter will give the best results.

> *NOTE*
> *If using a test light, it doesn't make any difference which test lead is attached to ground.*

1. Attach the negative test lead (if using a voltmeter) to a good ground (bare metal). If necessary, scrape away paint from the frame or engine (retouch later with paint). Make sure the part used for ground is *not* insulated with a rubber gasket or rubber grommet.

2. Attach the positive test lead (if using a voltmeter) to the point (electrical connector, etc.) you want to check.

3. Turn the ignition switch on. If using a test light, the test light will come on if voltage is present. If using a voltmeter, note the voltage reading. The reading should be within 1 volt of battery voltage (12 volts). If the voltage is 11 volts or less there is a problem in the circuit.

Voltage Drop Test

A voltage drop of 1 volt means there is a problem in the circuit. All components within the circuit are designed for low resistance in order to conduct electricity within a minimum loss of voltage.

1. Connect the voltmeter positive test lead to the end of the wire or switch closest to the battery.

2. Connect the voltmeter negative test lead to the other end of the wire or switch.

3. Turn the components on in the circuit.

4. The voltmeter should indicate 12 volts. If there is a drop of 1 volt or more, there is a problem within the circuit.

5. Check the circuit for loose or dirty connections within an electrical connector(s).

Continuity Test

A continuity test is made to determine if the circuit is complete with no opens in either the electrical wires or components within that circuit.

Unless otherwise specified, all continuity tests are made with the electrical connector still connected. Insert the test leads into the backside of the connector and make sure the test lead touches the electrical wire or metal connector within the connector. If the test lead only touches the wire insulation you will get a false reading.

Always check both sides of the connectors as one side may be loose or corroded thus preventing electrical flow through the connector. This type of test can be performed with a self-powered test light or an ohmmeter. An ohmmeter will give the best results.

If using an ohmmeter, calibrate the meter by touching the leads together and turning the ohms calibration knob until the meter reads zero. This is necessary in order to get accurate results.

1. Disconnect the battery negative lead as described under *Battery* in Chapter Three.

2. Attach one test lead (test light or ohmmeter) to one end of the part of the circuit to be tested.

3. Attach the other test lead to the other end of the part of the circuit to be tested.

4. The self-powered test light will come on if there is continuity. The ohmmeter will indicate either a low or no resistance (means good continuity in a complete circuit) or infinite resistance (means an open circuit).

Testing for a Short with a Self-powered Test Light or Ohmmeter

This test can be performed with either a self-powered test light or an ohmmeter.

1. Disconnect the battery negative lead as described under *Battery* in Chapter Three.

2. Remove the blown fuse from the fuse panel.

3. Connect one test lead of the test light or ohmmeter to the load side (battery side) of the fuse terminal in the fuse panel.

4. Connect the other test lead to a good ground (bare metal). If necessary, scrape away paint from the frame or engine (retouch later with paint). Make sure the part used for a ground is not insulated with a rubber gasket or rubber grommet.

5. With the self-powered test light or ohmmeter attached to the fuse terminal and ground, wiggle the wiring harness relating to the suspect circuit at 6 in. (15.2 cm) intervals. Start next to the fuse panel and work your way away from the fuse panel. Watch the self-powered test light or ohmmeter as you progress along the harness.

6. If the test light blinks or the needle on the ohmmeter moves, there is a short-to-ground at that point in the harness.

Testing For a Short with a Test Light or Voltmeter

This test can be performed with either a test light or voltmeter.

1. Remove the blown fuse from the fuse panel.

2. Connect the test light or voltmeter across the fuse terminals in the fuse panel. Turn the ignition switch on and check for battery voltage (12 volts).

3. With the test light or voltmeter attached to the fuse terminals, wiggle the wiring harness relating to

the suspect circuit at 6 in. (15.2 cm) intervals. Start next to the fuse panel and work your way away from the fuse panel. Watch the test light or voltmeter as you progress along the harness.

4. If the test light blinks or the needle on the voltmeter moves, there is a short-to-ground at that point in the harness.

ELECTRICAL PROBLEMS

If light bulbs burn out frequently, the cause may be excessive vibration, a loose connection that permits sudden current surges or the installation of the wrong type of bulb.

Most light and ignition problems are caused by loose or corroded ground connections. Check these prior to replacing a light bulb or electrical component.

CHARGING SYSTEM TROUBLESHOOTING

The charging system (**Figure 15**) consists of the battery, alternator and a voltage regulator/rectifier. A 30 amp main fuse protects the circuit.

Alternating current generated by the alternator is rectified to direct current. The voltage regulator maintains the voltage to the battery and additional

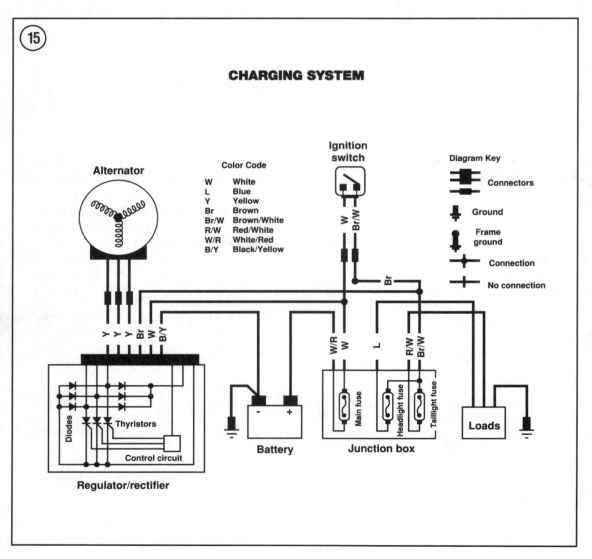

electrical loads (lights, ignition, etc.) at a constant voltage regardless of variations in engine speed and load.

The basic charging system complaints are:
a. Battery discharging.
b. Battery overcharging.

Battery Discharging

1. Check all of the connections. Make sure they are tight and free of corrosion.

2. Perform the *Charging System Leakage Test* as described in Chapter Eight. Note the following:
   a. Current leakage under 1.2 mA, perform Step 3.
   b. Current leakage 1.2 mA or higher, perform Step 4.

3. Perform the *Regulator/Rectifier Unit Resistance Test* as described in Chapter Eight. Note the following:
   a. If the resistance readings are correct, perform the *Wiring Harness Test* as described in Chapter Eight. If the wiring harness tests are correct, the ignition switch is probably faulty; test the ignition switch as described in Chapter Eight.
   b. If the resistance readings are incorrect, replace the regulator/rectifier unit and retest.

4. Perform the *Charging Voltage Test* in Chapter Eight. Note the following:
   a. If the test readings are correct, perform Step 5.
   b. If the test readings are incorrect, perform Step 6.

5. Test the battery with a battery tester and note the following:

NOTE
If you do not have access to the battery tester, remove the battery from the bike

and take it to a Kawasaki dealer for testing.

   a. If the test readings are correct, the battery is faulty or the charging system is being overloaded, probably from accessory electrical items.
   b. If the test readings are incorrect, check for an open circuit in the wiring harness and for dirty or loose-fitting terminals; clean and repair as required.

6. Perform the battery charging line and ground line tests as described under *Wiring Harness Test* in Chapter Eight. Note the following:
   a. If the test readings are correct, perform Step 7.
   b. If the test readings are incorrect, check for an open circuit in the wiring harness and for dirty or loose-fitting terminals; clean and repair as required.

7. Perform the charging coil line tests as described under *Wiring Harness Test* in Chapter Eight. Note the following:
   a. If the test readings are incorrect, perform Step 8.
   b. If the test readings are correct, perform Step 9.

8. Perform the *Charging Coil Resistance Test* as described in Chapter Eight. Note the following:
   a. If the test readings are correct, check for a dirty or loose-fitting alternator electrical connector; clean and repair as required.
   b. If the test readings are incorrect, replace the alternator assembly as described in Chapter Eight.

9. Perform the *Regulator/Rectifier Unit Resistance Test* as described in Chapter Eight. Note the following:
   a. If the resistance readings are correct, the battery is faulty. Replace the battery and retest.
   b. If the resistance readings are incorrect, replace the regulator/rectifier unit and retest.

Battery Overcharging

If the battery is overcharging, the regulator/rectifier unit (**Figure 16**) is faulty. Replace the regulator/rectifier unit as described in Chapter Eight.

⑰

IGNITION SYSTEM

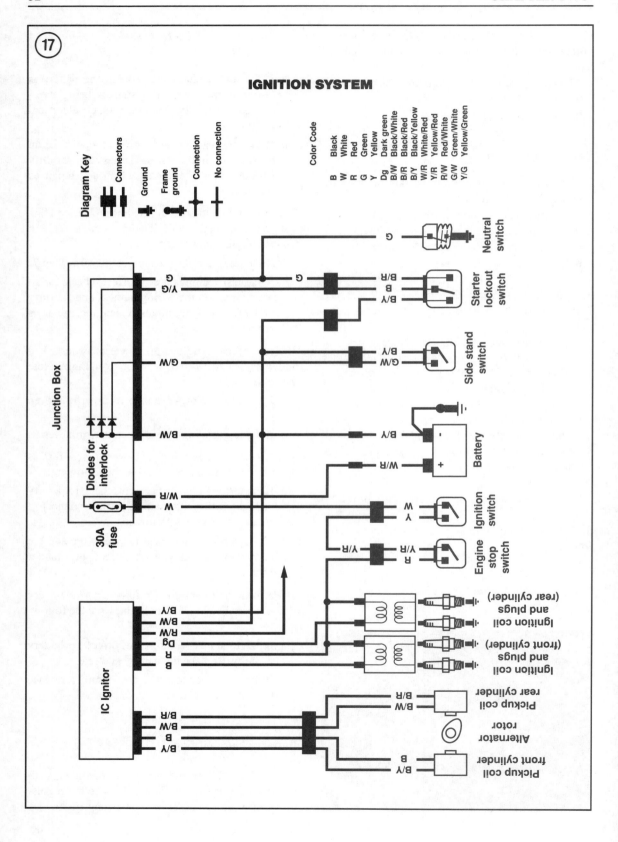

IGNITION SYSTEM TROUBLESHOOTING

The ignition system (**Figure 17**) consists of an IC ignitor, 2 ignition coils, a pickup coil assembly and 4 spark plugs (2 per cylinder). The basic ignition system complaints are:

a. No spark at all 4 spark plugs.

b. No spark at one spark plug.

c. Engine starts and runs but sidestand switch does not operate.

Prior to troubleshooting the ignition system, perform the following:

1. Check the battery to make sure it is fully charged and in good condition. A weak battery will result in a slower engine cranking speed.

2. Perform the spark test as described under *Engine Fails to Start (Spark Test)* in this chapter. Then refer to the appropriate ignition system complaint.

3. Because a loose or dirty electrical connector can prevent the ignition system from operating properly, check for dirty or loose-fitting connector terminals. The ignition system electrical diagram and the wiring diagrams at the end of this book can be used to locate the appropriate electrical connectors. Also, refer to *Preliminary Checks and Precautions* under *Electrical Troubleshooting* in this chapter for additional information.

No Spark at All Four Spark Plugs

1. Check for dirty or loose-fitting connector terminals as previously described. Clean and repair as required.

> *NOTE*
> *If the ignition system does not operate properly after inspecting and cleaning*

the connector terminals, proceed with Step 2.

2. Measure the IC Ignitor resistance as described under *IC Ignitor Resistance Test* in Chapter Eight. Note the following:

a. If the resistance reading is incorrect, the IC Ignitor is faulty and should be replaced.

b. If the resistance reading is correct, check for an open circuit between the IC Ignitor and the pickup coil assembly.

> *NOTE*
> *The IC Ignitor is located just behind the battery (A, **Figure 18**).*

> *NOTE*
> *When switching between ohmmeter scales, always cross the test leads and zero the meter to assure a correct reading.*

3. Measure the pickup coil resistance as described under *Pickup Coil Resistance Test* in Chapter Eight. Note the following:

a. If the resistance reading is incorrect, the pulse generator is faulty and should be replaced.

b. If the resistance reading is correct, check for an open circuit between the ignition control module and the pulse generator.

> *NOTE*
> *The pickup coil connector is the upper 4-pin electrical connector (B, **Figure 18**) on the IC ignitor.*

4. Test the neutral switch as described in Chapter Eight. Note the following:

a. If the neutral switch is faulty, replace it and retest.

b. If the neutral switch is okay, check for an open circuit between the neutral switch and the ignition control module.

5. Test the sidestand switch as described in Chapter Eight. Note the following:

a. If the sidestand switch is faulty, replace it and retest.

b. If the sidestand switch is okay, check for an open circuit between the sidestand switch and the ignition control module.

6. When finished, install all previously removed parts.

No Spark at One Spark Plug

If there is no spark at one spark plug, replace the plug and repeat the spark test. If the new plug will not fire, perform the following.

1. Measure the coil's secondary resistance as described under *Ignition Coil Resistance Test* in Chapter Eight. Note the following:

   a. If the test results are incorrect, perform Step 2.

   b. If the test results are correct, repeat the spark test by switching the ignition coils. If you now

have a spark, the original coil is faulty and should be replaced.

2. Remove the spark plug wire from the ignition coil and repeat the test made in Step 1. Note the following:

   a. If the test results are still incorrect, the ignition coil is faulty and should be replaced.

   b. If the test results are now correct, check for poor contact between the spark plug wire and coil. If this is okay, the spark plug wire is faulty and should be replaced.

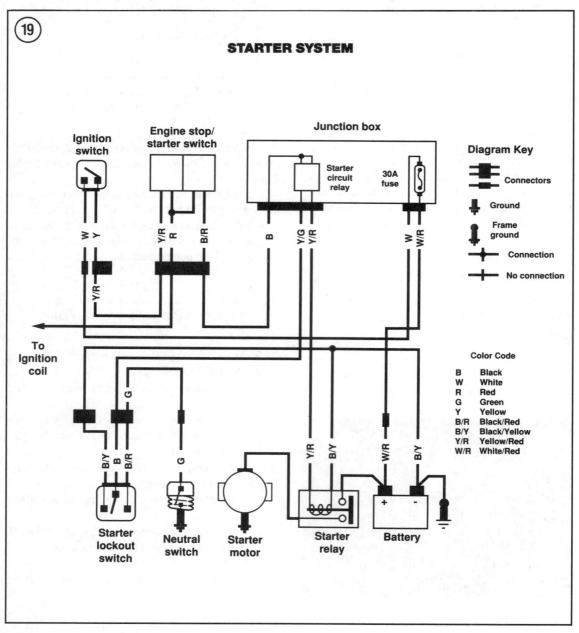

(19) **STARTER SYSTEM**

Engine Starts and Runs but Sidestand Switch Does Not Operate

When the engine is running and the transmission is in NEUTRAL, it should continue to run when the sidestand is moved down.

When the engine is running and the transmission is in gear, the engine should stop when the sidestand is moved down.

Check the sidestand switch continuity as described in Chapter Eight. Note the following:

a. If there is no continuity, the sidestand switch is faulty; replace the switch and retest.

b. If there is continuity, check for an open circuit in the non-grounded wire (brown wire on U.S. and Canadian models, black/yellow wire, on all other models) or for dirty or loose-fitting sidestand switch connector terminals.

STARTER SYSTEM TROUBLESHOOTING

The starting system (**Figure 19**) consists of the starter motor, starter gears, starter relay, starter button, ignition switch, clutch switch (starter lockout), neutral switch, main and auxiliary fuses and battery.

When the starter button is pressed, it allows current flow through the solenoid coil. The coil contacts close, allowing electricity to flow from the battery to the starter motor.

> *CAUTION*
> *Do not operate the starter for more than 5 seconds at a time. Let it rest approximately 10 seconds, then use it again.*

The starter should turn when the starter button is depressed when the transmission is in neutral and the clutch disengaged. If the starter does not operate properly, perform the following test procedures. Starter troubleshooting is grouped under the following:

a. Starter motor does not turn.

b. Starter motor turns slowly.

c. Starter motor turns but the engine does not.

d. Starter motor and engine turn but the engine does not start.

1. Check the battery to make sure it is fully charged and in good condition. Refer to Chapter Three for battery service.

2. Check the starter electrical cables for loose or damaged connections.

3. Check the battery electrical cables for loose or damaged connections. Then check the battery state of charge as described under *Battery Testing* in Chapter Eight.

4. If the starter does not operate correctly after making these checks and adjustments, perform the test procedure that best describes the starting trouble.

Starter Motor Does Not Turn

1. Remove the frame right side cover as described in Chapter Thirteen to expose the starter relay switch (**Figure 20**).

2. Check the starter relay connector for dirty or loose-fitting terminals. Clean and repair as required.

3. Check the starter relay switch. Turn the ignition switch on and depress the starter switch button. When the starter button is depressed, the starter relay switch should click once. Note the following:

a. If there was a click, perform Step 4.

b. If there was no click, perform Step 5.

> *CAUTION*
> *Because of the large amount of current that will flow from the battery to the starter in Step 4, a large cable should be used to make the connection.*

4. Remove the starter from the motorcycle as described in Chapter Eight. Using an auxiliary battery, apply battery voltage directly to the starter. The starter should turn when battery voltage is directly applied. Note the following:

a. If the starter motor runs, disassemble and inspect the starter motor as described in Chapter

Eight. Test the starter components and replace worn or damaged parts as required.

b. If the starter motor turns, check for loose or damaged starter cables. If the cables are okay, check the starter relay switch as described in Chapter Eight. Replace the starter relay switch if necessary.

5. Remove the starter relay switch (**Figure 20**). Note the following:

a. Connect the positive (+) lead of a fully charged 12-volt battery to the starter relay switch yellow/red wire terminal and the battery negative wire to the black/yellow wire terminal.

b. Connect an ohmmeter between the battery lead terminal and the starter motor lead terminal.

c. There should be continuity when the battery leads are connected to the starter relay switch and no continuity when they are disconnected.

6. If continuity was shown in each test, perform Step 7. If there is no continuity in one or more tests, check for dirty or loose-fitting terminals; clean and repair as required and retest. Then check for a short circuit in the wiring. If the connectors and wiring are okay, test the following components as described in Chapter Eight:

a. Clutch switch.

b. Clutch switch diode.

c. Neutral switch.

d. Sidestand switch.

7. Pull the rubber cover away from the starter relay switch electrical connector to expose the wire terminals in the connector (**Figure 21**). Then connect a voltmeter between the starter relay switch connector yellow/red terminal (+) and ground (−). Turn the ignition switch to ON and the engine stop switch to RUN. Press the starter button and read the voltage indicated on the voltmeter. It should be 12 volts. Turn the ignition switch off and note the following:

a. If battery voltage is shown, perform Step 8.

b. If no battery voltage is shown, check for a blown main or sub-fuse; see *Fuses* in Chapter Eight. If the fuses are okay, check for an open circuit in the wiring harness or for dirty or loose-fitting terminals. If the wiring and connectors are okay, check for a faulty ignition and/or starter switch as described in Chapter Eight.

8. Test the starter relay switch as described in Chapter Eight. Note the following:

a. If the starter relay switch is normal, check for dirty or loose-fitting terminals in its connector block.

b. If the starter relay switch is faulty, replace it and retest.

Starter Motor Turns Slowly

If the starter motor turns slowly and all engine components and systems are normal, perform the following:

1. Test the battery as described in Chapter Three.

2. Check for the following:

a. Loose or corroded battery terminals.

b. Loose or corroded battery ground cable.

c. Loose starter motor cable.

3. Remove, disassemble and bench test the starter as described under *Starter* in Chapter Eight.

4. Check the starter for binding during operation. Disassemble the starter and check the armature shafts for bending or damaged. Also check the starter clutch as described in Chapter Four.

Starter Motor Turns but the Engine Does Not

If the starter motor turns but the engine does not, perform the following:

1. If the starter motor is running backwards and the starter was just reassembled or if the starter motor cables were disconnected and then reconnected to the starter:

a. The starter motor was reassembled incorrectly.

b. The starter motor cables were incorrectly installed.

2. Check for a damaged starter clutch (Chapter Four).

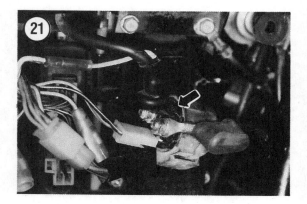

3. Check for a damaged or faulty starter pinion gear (Chapter Four).

4. Check for damaged starter clutch and reduction gears (Chapter Four).

Starter Relay Switch Clicks but Engine Does Not Turn Over

1. Excessive reduction gear friction.
2. Crankshaft cannot turn over because of mechanical failure.

Starter Motor Works with the Transmission in Neutral but Does Not Turn with the Transmission in Gear with the Clutch Lever Pulled in and the Sidestand Up

1. Test the clutch switch as described in Chapter Eight. Note the following:
   a. Clutch switch okay, perform Step 2.
   b. Clutch switch faulty, replace switch and retest.
2. Test the sidestand switch as described in Chapter Eight. Note the following:
   a. Sidestand switch okay, perform Step 3.
   b. Sidestand switch faulty, replace switch and re-test.
3. Check for an open circuit in the wiring harness. Check for loose or damaged electrical connector.

CARBURETOR TROUBLESHOOTING

The following lists isolate basic carburetor problems under specific complaints.

Engine Will Not Start

If the engine will not start and you have determined that the electrical and mechanical systems are working correctly, check the following:
1. If there is no fuel going to the carburetors, note the following:
   a. Clogged fuel tank breather cap hole.
   b. Clogged fuel tank-to-carburetor tube.
   c. Clogged fuel valve screen.
   d. Incorrect float adjustment.
   e. Stuck or clogged fuel valve in carburetor.
2. If the engine is flooded (too much fuel), note the following:

a. Flooded carburetors. Fuel valve in carburetor stuck open.
   b. Clogged air filter element(s).
3. A faulty emission control system (if equipped) can cause fuel problems. Note the following:
   a. Faulty purge control valve (PCV).
   b. Faulty air injection control valve (AICV).
   c. Loose, disconnected or plugged emission control system hoses.
4. If you have not located the problem in Steps 1-3, check for the following:
   a. Contaminated or deteriorated fuel.
   b. Intake manifold air leak.
   c. Clogged pilot or choke circuit.

Engine Starts but Idles and Runs Poorly or Stalls Frequently

An engine that idles roughly or stalls may have one or more of the following problems:
   a. Clogged air cleaner.
   b. Contaminated fuel.
   c. Incorrect pilot screw adjustment.
   d. Incorrect carburetor synchronization.
   e. Incorrect idle speed.
   f. Bystarter or slow circuit clogged.
   g. Loose, disconnected or damaged fuel and emission control vacuum hoses.
   h. Intake air leak.
   i. Lean fuel mixture.
   j. Rich fuel mixture.

Incorrect Fast Idle Speed

A fast idle speed can be due to one of the following problems:
   a. Faulty bystarter valve.
   b. Incorrect choke cable free play.
   c. Incorrect carburetor synchronization.

Poor Gas Mileage and Engine Performance

Poor gas mileage and engine performance can be caused by infrequent engine tune-ups. Check your records to see when your bike was last tuned up and compare against the recommended tune-up service intervals in Chapter Three. If the last tune-up was within the specified service intervals, check for one or more of the following problems:

a. Clogged air filter.

b. Clogged fuel system.

c. Loose, disconnected or damaged fuel and emission control vacuum hoses.

Rich Fuel Mixture

A rich carburetor fuel mixture can be caused by one or more of the following conditions:

a. Clogged or dirty air filter.

b. Worn or damaged fuel valve and seat.

c. Clogged air jets.

d. Incorrect float level (too high).

e. Bystarter valve damaged or stuck ON.

f. Flooded carburetors.

Lean Fuel Mixture

A lean carburetor fuel mixture can be caused by one or more of the following conditions:

a. Clogged carburetor air vent hole.

b. Clogged fuel filter.

c. Restricted fuel line.

d. Intake air leak.

e. Incorrect float level (too low).

f. Worn or damaged fuel valve.

g. Faulty throttle valve.

h. Faulty vacuum piston.

Engine Backfires

a. Lean fuel mixture.

b. Incorrect carburetor adjustment.

Engine Misses During Acceleration

When there is a pause before the engine responds to the throttle, the engine is missing. An engine miss can occur when starting from a dead stop or at any speed. An engine miss may be due to one of the following:

a. Lean fuel mixture.

b. Faulty ignition coil secondary wires; check for cracking, hardening or bad connections.

c. Faulty vacuum hoses; check for kinks, splits or bad connections.

d. Vacuum leaks at the carburetor and/or intake manifold(s).

e. Fouled spark plug(s).

f. Low engine compression, especially at one cylinder only. Check engine compression as described in Chapter Three. Low compression can be caused by worn engine components.

EXCESSIVE VIBRATION

Usually this is caused by loose engine mounting hardware.

If mounting hardware is okay, vibration can be difficult to find without disassembling the engine.

FRONT SUSPENSION AND STEERING

Poor handling may be caused by improper tire pressure, a damaged or bent frame or front steering components, a worn front fork assembly, worn wheel bearings or dragging brakes.

Bike Steers to One Side

a. Bent axle.

b. Bent frame.

c. Worn or damaged front wheel bearings.

d. Worn or damaged swing arm pivot bearings.

e. Damaged steering head bearings.

f. Uneven front fork adjustment.

g. Incorrectly installed wheels.

Suspension Noise

a. Loose mounting fasteners.

b. Damaged fork(s) or rear shock absorber.

c. Incorrect front fork oil.

Wobble/Vibration

a. Loose front or rear axle.

b. Loose or damaged wheel bearing(s).

c. Damaged wheel rim(s).

d. Damaged tire(s).

e. Loose swing arm pivot bolt.

f. Unbalanced tire and wheel.

Hard Suspension
(Front Forks)

a. Insufficient tire pressure.

b. Damaged steering head bearings.

c. Incorrect steering head bearing adjustment.

d. Bent fork tubes.

e. Binding slider.

f. Incorrect fork oil.

g. Plugged fork oil hydraulic passage.

Hard Suspension
(Rear Shock Absorbers)

a. Excessive tire pressure.

b. Bent damper rod.

c. Incorrect shock adjustment.

d. Damaged shock absorber bushing(s).

e. Damaged shock absorber bearing.

f. Damaged swing arm pivot bearing.

Soft Suspension
(Front Forks)

a. Insufficient tire pressure.

b. Insufficient fork oil level or fluid capacity.

c. Incorrect oil viscosity.

d. Weak or damaged fork springs.

Soft Suspension
(Rear Shock Absorbers)

a. Insufficient tire pressure.

b. Weak or damaged shock absorber spring.

c. Damaged shock absorber.

d. Incorrect shock absorber adjustment.

e. Leaking damper unit.

BRAKE PROBLEMS

Sticking disc brakes may be caused by a stuck piston(s) in a caliper assembly or warped pad shim(s) or improper rear brake adjustment.

Brake Drag

a. Clogged brake hydraulic system.

b. Sticking caliper pistons.

c. Sticking master cylinder piston.

d. Incorrectly installed brake caliper.

e. Warped brake disc.

f. Sticking caliper side slide pin.

g. Incorrect wheel alignment.

h. Worn or weak drum return springs.

i. Brake lining dry pivot and cam bushings.

Brakes Grab

a. Contaminated brake pads or linings.

b. Incorrect wheel alignment.

c. Warped brake disc or out-of-round brake drum.

d. Glazed pads or linings.

Brake Squeal or Chatter

a. Contaminated brake pads or linings.

b. Incorrectly installed brake caliper.

c. Warped brake disc.

d. Incorrect wheel alignment.

e. Anti-rattle spring missing in caliper.

Soft or Spongy Front Brake Lever

a. Low brake fluid level.

b. Air in brake hydraulic system.

c. Leaking brake hydraulic system.

Hard Front Brake Lever Operation

a. Clogged brake hydraulic system.

b. Sticking caliper pistons.

c. Sticking master cylinder piston.

d. Glazed or worn brake pads.

2

CHAPTER THREE

LUBRICATION, MAINTENANCE AND TUNE-UP

A motorcycle, even in normal use, is subjected to tremendous heat, stress and vibration. When neglected, any bike becomes unreliable and actually dangerous to ride.

To gain the utmost in safety, performance and useful life from the Kawasaki Vulcan, it is necessary to make periodic inspections and adjustments. Frequently minor problems are found during these inspections that are simple and inexpensive to correct at the time. If they are not found and corrected at this time, they could lead to major and more expensive problems later on.

Start out by doing simple tune-up, lubrication and maintenance, then tackle more involved jobs as you become more acquainted with the bike.

Table 1 is a suggested factory maintenance schedule. **Tables 1-6** are located at the end of this chapter.

NOTE
Where differences occur relating to the United Kingdom (U.K.) models they are identified. If there is no (U.K.) designation relating to a procedure, photo or illustration it is identical to the United States (U.S.) models.

ROUTINE CHECKS

The following simple checks should be performed at each stop at a service station for gas.

Engine Oil Level

Refer to *Engine Oil Level Check* under *Periodic Lubrication* in this chapter.

Fuel

All Vulcan engines are designed to use gasoline that has an antiknock index number (RON+MON)/2 of 87 or higher or a gasoline with a research octane number (RON) of 91 or higher. The pump octane number is normally displayed at service station gas pumps. Using a gasoline with a lower octane number can cause pinging or spark knock, either condition can lead to engine damage. Unleaded fuel is recommended because it reduces engine and spark plug deposits.

When choosing gasoline and filling the fuel tank, note the following:

NOTE
On California models, never fill the fuel tank so the fuel level rises into the filler neck. If the fuel tank is overfilled, heat may cause the fuel to expand and the fuel will overflow into the Evaporative Emission Control system resulting in hard starting and engine hesitation.

a. When filling the tank, do not overfill it. Fuel expands in the tank due to engine heat or heating by the sun. Stop adding fuel when the fuel level reaches the bottom of the filler tube inside the fuel tank.

b. To help meet clean air standards in some areas of the United States and Canada, oxygenated fuels are being used. Oxygenated fuels are conventional gasolines that are blended with an alcohol or ether compound to increase the gasoline's octane. When using an oxygenated fuel, make sure that it meets the minimum octane rating as previously specified.

c. Because oxygenated fuels can damage plastic and paint, make sure not to spill fuel onto the fuel tank during fuel stops.

d. An ethanol (ethyl or grain alcohol) gasoline that contains more than 10 percent ethanol by volume may cause engine starting and performance related problems.

e. A methanol (methyl or wood alcohol) gasoline that contains more than 5 percent methanol by volume may cause engine starting and performance related problems. Gasoline that contains methanol must have corrosion inhibitors to protect the metal, plastic and rubber parts in the fuel system from damage.

f. If your bike is experiencing fuel system damage or performance related problems from the use of oxygenated fuels, consult with a knowledgeable mechanic in an area where this type of fuel is widely sold and used.

Coolant Level

Check the coolant level in the reservoir tank only when the engine is **COOL** (at room or ambient temperature), preferably prior to the first ride of the day.

WARNING
*Do not remove the radiator cap when the engine is **HOT**. The coolant is under pressure and scalding and severe burns could result.*

1. Set the bike on the centerstand on a level surface.

2. The coolant level should be between the FULL and LOW marks (**Figure 1**) on the side of the tank. If necessary, add coolant to the reservoir tank.

NOTE
*If the coolant level is very low, there may be a leak in the cooling system. If this condition exists, refer to **Cooling System Inspection** in this chapter.*

NOTE
Never add just water to the system as this will dilute the coolant-to-water mixture to an unsafe level.

3. Unscrew the cap (**Figure 2**) from the reservoir tank and insert a small funnel into the radiator filler neck. Add a 50:50 mixture of distilled water and antifreeze to bring the level to the FULL mark on the tank.

4. Remove the funnel and install the cap. Tighten the cap securely.

General Inspection

1. Quickly inspect the engine for signs of oil, fuel or coolant leakage.
2. Check the tires for embedded stones. Pry them out with a suitable tool.
3. Make sure all lights work.

> *NOTE*
> *At least check the brake light. It can burn out at any time. Motorists cannot stop as quickly as you and need all the warning you can give.*

Tire Pressure

Tire pressure must be checked with the tires cold. Correct tire pressure varies with the load you are carrying or if you have a passenger. See **Table 2**.

Brake Operation

Check that the brakes operate with full hydraulic (front) or mechanical (rear) advantage. Check the front brake fluid level as described under *Disc Brake Fluid Level Inspection* in this chapter. Check that there is no brake fluid leakage from the front master cylinder, front calipers or brake lines.

Battery

The electrolyte level must be between the upper and lower level marks on the case. For complete details see *Battery Removal, Installation and Electrolyte Level Check* in this chapter.

Check the level frequently in hot weather, because the electrolyte will evaporate rapidly as ambient heat increases.

Throttle

Sit on the bike, with the brake ON, the transmission in NEUTRAL and the engine idling, move the handlebars from side to side. The engine idle speed should not increase or decrease as the handlebars are moved. Check that the throttle moves smoothly in all steering positions. Shut off the engine.

Engine Stop Switch

The engine stop switch (**Figure 3**) is designed primarily as an emergency switch. It is part of the right-hand switch assembly next to the throttle housing and it has 2 operating positions: OFF and RUN. When the switch is in the OFF position, the engine will not start or run. In the RUN position, the engine should start and run with the ignition switch on, the clutch lever pulled in, while pressing the starter button. With the engine idling, move the switch to OFF. The engine should turn off.

Sidestand Check Switch System Inspection

1. Place the bike on the centerstand, on level ground, with the rear wheel off the ground.
2. Check the sidestand spring (A, **Figure 4**). Make sure the spring is in good condition and has not lost tension.
3. Swing the sidestand (B, **Figure 4**) down and up a few times. The sidestand should swing smoothly

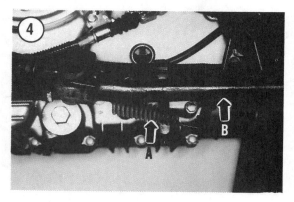

and the spring should provide proper tension in the raised position.

4. While sitting on the motorcycle, shift the transmission into NEUTRAL and move the sidestand up.

5. Start the engine and allow it to warm up. Then pull in the clutch lever and shift the transmission into gear.

6. Lower the sidestand with your foot. The engine should stop as the sidestand is lowered.

7. If the sidestand check switch did not operate as described, inspect the sidestand check switch as described in Chapter Eight.

Crankcase Breather Hose

Inspect the hose for cracks and deterioration and make sure that the hose clamps are tight.

**Evaporative Emission
Control System
(California Models)**

Inspect the hoses to make sure they are not kinked or bent and that they are securely connected to their respective parts.

Lights and Horn

With the engine running, check the following.

1. Pull the front brake lever on and check that the brake light comes on.

2. Push the rear brake pedal down and check that the brake light comes on soon after you have begun depressing the pedal.

3. With the engine running, check to see that the headlight and taillight are on.

4. Move the dimmer switch up and down between the HI and LO positions and check to see that the headlight elements are working in the headlight(s).

5. On U.K. models, move turn the switch on and off and check to see that the headlight elements are working in the headlight.

6. Push the turn signal switch to the left and right positions and check that all 4 turn signals are working.

7. Push the horn button and make sure that the horn blows loudly.

8. If during the test, the rear brake pedal traveled too far before the brake light came on, adjust the rear brake light switch as described in Chapter Eight.

9. If the horn or any of the lights failed to operate properly, refer to Chapter Eight.

PRE-CHECKS

The following checks should be performed prior to the first ride of the day.

1. Inspect all fuel lines and fittings for wetness.

2. Make sure the fuel tank is full of fresh gasoline.

3. Make sure the engine oil level is correct. Add oil if necessary.

4. Make sure the final drive unit oil level is correct. Add oil if necessary.

5. Check the operation of the front brake. Add hydraulic fluid to the front brake master cylinder if necessary.

6. Check the operation of the rear brake. Adjust the rear brake pedal free play as described in this chapter if necessary.

7. Check the operation of the clutch. Adjust clutch free play as described in Chapter Five if necessary.

8. Check the throttle and the rear brake pedal. Make sure they operate properly with no binding.

9. Inspect the front and rear suspension; make sure they have a good solid feel with no looseness.

10. Check tire pressure. Refer to **Table 2**.

11. Check the exhaust system for damage.

12. Check the tightness of all fasteners, especially engine mounting hardware.

SERVICE INTERVALS

The services and intervals shown in **Table 1** are recommended by the factory. Strict adherence to these recommendations will ensure long service from the Kawasaki. If the bike is run in an area of high humidity, the lubrication services must be done more frequently to prevent possible rust damage.

For convenience when maintaining your motorcycle, most of the services shown in these tables are described in this chapter. However, some procedures which require more than minor disassembly or adjustment are covered elsewhere in the appropriate chapter. The *Table of Contents* and *Index* can help you locate a particular service procedure.

TIRES AND WHEELS

Tire Pressure

Tire pressure should be checked and adjusted to maintain the tire profile, good traction and handling and to get the maximum life out of the tire. A simple, accurate gauge (**Figure 5**) can be purchased for a few dollars and should be carried in your motorcycle tool kit. Tire pressure should be checked when the tires are cold. The appropriate tire pressures are shown in **Table 2**.

> *NOTE*
> *After checking and adjusting the air pressure, make sure to install the air valve cap (**Figure 6**). The cap prevents small pebbles and dirt from collecting in the valve stem; this could allow air leakage or result in incorrect tire pressure readings.*

> *NOTE*
> *A loss of air pressure may be due to a loose or damaged valve core. Put a few drops of water on the top of the valve core. If the water bubbles, tighten the valve core and recheck. If air is still leaking from the valve after tightening it, replace the valve stem assembly.*

Tire Inspection

The tires take a lot of punishment so inspect them periodically for excessive wear. Inspect the tires for the following:

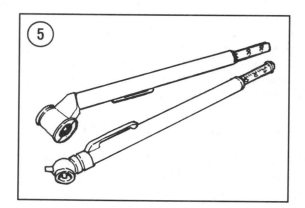

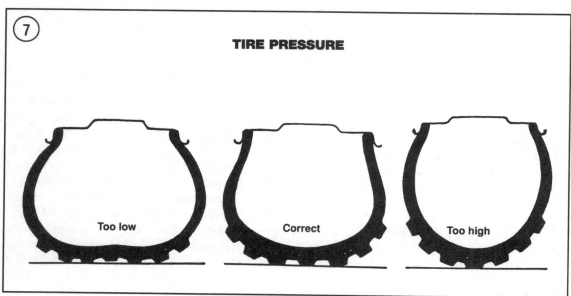

a. Deep cuts and imbedded objects (i.e., stones, nails, etc.). If you find a nail or other object in a tire, mark its location with a light crayon prior to removing it. This will help to locate the hole for repair. Refer to Chapter Ten for tire changing and repair information.

b. Flat spots.

c. Cracks.

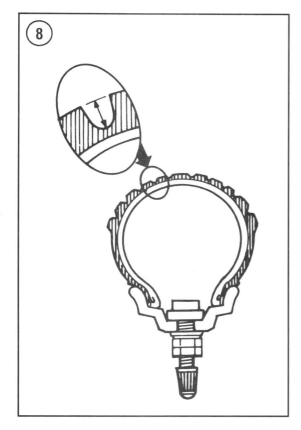

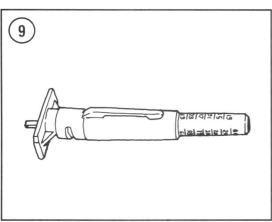

d. Separating plies.

e. Sidewall damage.

Tire Wear Analysis

Abnormal tire wear should be analyzed to determine its causes. The most common causes are the following:

a. Incorrect tire pressure: Check tire pressure as described in this chapter.

b. Overloading.

c. Incorrect wheel balance: The tire/wheel assembly should be balanced when installing a new tire and or tube and then re-balanced each time the tire is removed and reinstalled.

d. Worn or damaged wheel bearings.

Incorrect tire pressure is the biggest cause of abnormal tire wear **Figure 7**. Under-inflated tires will result in higher tire temperatures, hard or imprecise steering and abnormal tire wear. Overinflated tires will result in a hard ride and abnormal tire wear. Examine the tire tread, comparing wear in the center of the contact patch with tire wear at the edge of the contact patch. Note the following:

a. If a tire shows excessive wear at the edge of the contact patch, but the wear at the center of the contact patch is okay, the tire has been under-inflated.

b. If a tire shows excessive wear in the center of the contact patch, but the wear at the edge of the contact patch is okay, the tire has been overinflated.

Tread Depth

Check local traffic regulations concerning minimum tread depth. Measure the tread depth at the center of tire and to the center of the tire tread (**Figure 8**) using a tread depth gauge (**Figure 9**) or a small ruler. Kawasaki recommends that *original equipment tires* be replaced when the front tire tread depth is 1 mm (1/16 in.) or less, when the rear tread depth is 2.0 mm (3/32 in.) or less or when tread wear indicators appear at the designated area on the tire indicating the minimum tread depth.

Rim Inspection

Frequently inspect the wheel rims (**Figure 10**). If a rim has been damaged, it might have been enough to knock it out of alignment. Improper wheel alignment can cause severe vibration and result in an unsafe riding condition. If the rim portion of an alloy wheel is damaged, the wheel must be replaced as it cannot be serviced or repaired.

BATTERY

The battery is an important component in the electrical system. It is also the one most frequently neglected. In addition to checking and correcting the battery electrolyte level on a weekly basis, the battery should be cleaned and inspected at periodic intervals listed in **Table 1**.

The battery should be checked periodically for electrolyte level, state of charge and corrosion. During hot weather periods, frequent checks are recommended. If the electrolyte level is below the fill line, add distilled water as required. To assure proper mixing of the water and acid, operate the engine immediately after adding water. *Never* add battery acid instead of water; this will shorten the battery's life.

> *CAUTION*
> *If it becomes necessary to remove the battery breather tube when performing any of the following procedures, make sure to route the tube correctly during installation to prevent electrolyte or gas from spewing onto the battery case or any other component. Incorrect breather tube routing can cause structural and/or cosmetic damage.*

Removal, Installation and Electrolyte Level Check

1. Place the bike on the centerstand on level ground.
2. Remove the seat as described in Chapter Thirteen.

3. Disconnect the battery negative (–) cable (A, **Figure 11**).

4. Disconnect the battery positive (+) cable (B, **Figure 11**).

5. Remove the bolt (C, **Figure 11**) securing the battery hold down bracket (D, **Figure 11**). Unhook the front of the bracket and remove the bracket and protective pad.

6. Carefully pull the battery straight up and out of the battery box and remove it from the frame.

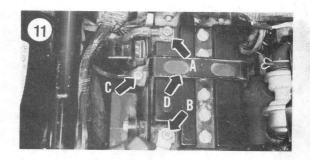

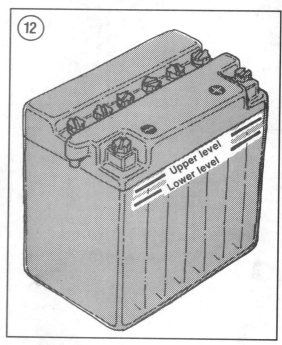

7. Set the battery on some newspapers or shop cloths to protect the workbench surface from any spilled acid residue.

8. The electrolyte level should be maintained between the 2 marks on the battery case (**Figure 12**).

WARNING
Protect your eyes, skin and clothing. If electrolyte gets into your eyes, flush your eyes thoroughly with clean water and get prompt medical attention.

CAUTION
Be careful not to spill battery electrolyte on plastic, painted or plated surfaces. The liquid is highly corrosive and will damage the finish. If it is spilled, wash it off immediately with soapy water and thoroughly rinse with clean water.

9. Rinse the battery off with clean water and wipe dry.

10. If the electrolyte level is low, remove the caps from the battery cells and add distilled water to correct the level. Never add electrolyte (acid) to correct the level.

NOTE
After distilled water has been added, reinstall the battery caps and gently shake the battery for several minutes to mix the existing electrolyte with the new water.

11. After the fluid level has been corrected and the battery allowed to stand for a few minutes, remove the battery caps and check the specific gravity (**Figure 13**) of the electrolyte with a hydrometer. See *Battery Testing* in this chapter.

CAUTION
*If distilled water has been added to a battery in freezing or near freezing weather, add it to the battery, dress warmly and then ride the bike for a **minimum of 30 minutes**. This will help mix the water thoroughly into the electrolyte in the battery. Distilled water is lighter than electrolyte and will float on top of the electrolyte if it is not mixed in properly. If the water stays on the top, it may freeze and fracture the battery case, ruining the battery.*

12. After the battery has been refilled, recharged or replaced, install it as follows:

   a. Clean the battery terminals of all corrosion and/or oxidation. After a thorough cleaning, coat the terminals with a thin layer of dielectric grease to retard corrosion and decomposition of the terminals.

   b. Visually inspect the battery cable connectors for corrosion and/or damage. If necessary, clean the cable connectors prior to attaching them to the battery.

   c. Position the battery on the ground with the negative (–) terminal (A, **Figure 11**) toward the *left-hand* side of the bike. The positive (+) terminal and the breather outlet are on the right-hand side (B, **Figure 11**).

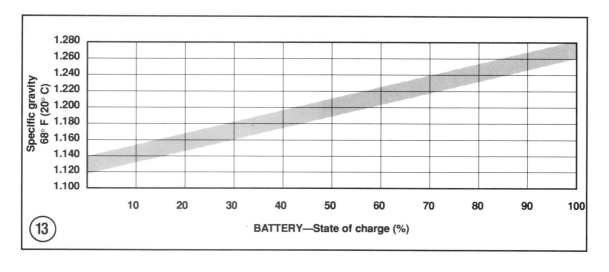

13 BATTERY—State of charge (%)

d. Make sure the breather tube is in place on the battery prior to installing the battery.

e. Carefully lower the battery into the battery case.

f. Install the bracket and protective pad and attach with the bolt at the rear. Tighten the bolt securely.

g. Attach the red positive (+) cable and bolt first then the black negative (–) cable. Tighten the bolts securely.

h. Install the seat.

Testing

Hydrometer testing is the best way to check battery condition. Use a hydrometer with numbered graduations from 1.100 to 1.300 rather than one with color-coded bands. To use the hydrometer, squeeze the rubber ball, insert the tip into the cell and release the pressure on the ball. Draw enough electrolyte to float the weighted float inside the hydrometer. Note the number in line with the surface of the electrolyte; this is the specific gravity for this cell. Squeeze the rubber ball again and return the electrolyte to the cell from which it came.

The specific gravity of the electrolyte in each battery cell is an excellent indication of that cell's condition. A fully charged cell will read from 1.265-1.280, while a cell in good condition reads from 1.225-1.265 and anything below 1.225 is practically dead.

> *NOTE*
> *Specific gravity varies with temperature. For each 10° the electrolyte temperature above 27° C (80° F), add 0.004 to readings indicated on the hydrometer. Subtract 0.004 for each 10° below 27° C (80° F).*

If the cells test in the poor range, the battery requires recharging. The hydrometer is useful for checking the progress of the charging operation. **Table 3** shows approximate state of charge.

Charging

> *WARNING*
> *During the charging process, highly explosive hydrogen gas is released from the battery. The battery should be charged only in a well-ventilated area away from any open flames (including pilot lights on home gas appliances). Do not allow any smoking in the area. Never check the charge by arcing (connecting pliers or other metal objects) across the terminals; the resulting spark can ignite the hydrogen gas.*

> *CAUTION*
> *Do **NOT** use an automotive-type battery charger as you will run the risk of overheating the battery and causing internal plate damage. Use only a small trickle charger designed specifically for use on motorcycle batteries.*

> *CAUTION*
> *Always remove the battery from the bike's frame before connecting the battery charger. Never recharge a battery in the bike's frame; the corrosive mist that is emitted during the charging process will corrode all surrounding surfaces.*

1. Connect the positive (+) charger lead to the positive (+) battery terminal and the negative (–) charger lead to the negative (–) battery terminal.

2. Remove all vent caps from the battery, set the charger to 12 volts and switch the charger ON. If the output of the charger is variable, it is best to select a low setting—1 1/2 to 2 amps. Normally, a battery should be charged at a slow charge rate of 1/10 its given capacity.

> *CAUTION*
> *The electrolyte level must be maintained at the upper level during the charging cycle; check and refill as necessary.*

3. The charging time depends on the discharged condition of the battery. The chart in **Figure 14** can be used to determine approximate charging times at different specific gravity readings. For example, if the specific gravity of your battery is 1.180, the approximate charging time would be 6 hours.

4. After the battery has been charged for about 6 hours, turn the charger OFF, disconnect the leads and check the specific gravity of each cell. It should be within the limits specified in **Table 3**. If it is, and remains stable for 1 hour, the battery is considered charged.

5. To ensure good electrical contact, cables must be clean and tight on the battery's terminals. If the

cables terminals are badly corroded, even after performing the above cleaning procedures, the cables should be disconnected, removed from the bike and cleaned separately with a wire brush and a baking soda solution. After cleaning, apply a very thin coating of dielectric grease, petroleum jelly (Vaseline) or silicone spray to the battery terminals before reattaching the cables.

NEW BATTERY INSTALLATION

When replacing the old battery with a new one, be sure to charge it completely (specific gravity 1.260-1.280) before installing it in the bike. Failure to do so or using the battery with a low electrolyte level will permanently damage the new battery.

NOTE
Recycle your old battery. *When you re-place the old battery, be sure to turn in the old battery at that time. The lead plates and the plastic case can be recycled. Most motorcycle dealers will accept your old battery in trade when you purchase a new one, but if they will not, many automotive supply stores certainly will.* ***Never*** *place an old battery in your household trash since it is illegal, in most states, to place any acid or lead (heavy metal) contents in landfills. There is also the danger of the battery being crushed in the trash truck and spraying acid on the truck operator.*

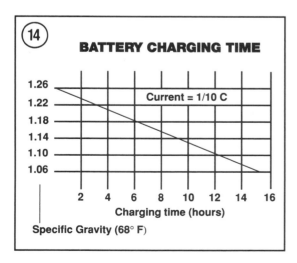

BATTERY ELECTRICAL CABLE CONNECTORS

To ensure good electrical contact between the battery and the electrical cables, the cables must be clean and free of corrosion.

1. If the electrical cable terminals are badly corroded, disconnect them from the bike's electrical system.

2. Thoroughly clean each connector with a wire brush and then with a baking soda solution. Rinse thoroughly with clean water and wipe dry with a clean cloth.

3. After cleaning, apply a thin layer of dielectric grease to the battery terminals before reattaching the cables.

4. If disconnected, attach the electrical cables to the bike's electrical system.

5. After connecting the electrical cables, apply a light coating of dielectric grease to the electrical terminals of the battery to retard corrosion and decomposition of the terminals.

PERIODIC LUBRICATION

Oil

Oil is graded according to its viscosity, which is an indication of how thick it is. The Society of Automotive Engineers (SAE) system distinguishes oil viscosity by numbers. Thick oils have higher viscosity numbers than thin oils. For example, an SAE 5 oil is a thin oil while an SAE 90 oil is relatively thick. If the oil has been tested in cold weather it is denoted with a "W" after the number as "SAE 10W."

Grease

A good-quality grease (preferably waterproof) should be used. Water does not wash grease from parts as easily as it washes oil off. In addition, grease maintains its lubricating qualities better than oil on long and strenuous rides. In a pinch, though, the wrong lubricant is better than none at all. Correct the situation as soon as possible.

Engine Oil Level Check and Adding Oil

Engine oil level is checked with the oil level inspection window, located at the right-hand side of the engine on the clutch cover.

1. Place the bike on the centerstand on level ground.

2. Start the engine and let it idle for 1-2 minutes.

3. Shut off the engine and let the oil settle for 1-2 minutes.

4. Make sure the bike is in the true vertical position. A false reading will be given if the bike is tipped to either side.

5. Look at the oil level inspection window. The oil level should be between the 2 lines (**Figure 15**). If the level is below the lower "H" line, add the recommended weight engine oil to correct the level.

6. Remove the oil filler cap (**Figure 16**).

7. Insert a funnel into the oil fill hole and fill the engine with the correct viscosity and quantity of oil. Refer to **Table 4**.

8. Remove the funnel, then install the oil filler cap and tighten securely.

9. Repeat Steps 2-5 and recheck the oil level.

Engine Oil and Oil Filter Change

Change the engine oil and the oil filter at the same time as the factory-recommended oil change interval indicated in **Table 1**. This assumes that the motorcycle is operated in moderate climates. In extreme climates, oil should be changed every 30 days. The time interval is more important than the mileage interval because acids formed by combustion blowby will contaminate the oil even if the motorcycle is not run for several months. If the motorcycle is operated under dusty conditions, the oil will get dirty more quickly and should be changed more frequently.

Use only a high-quality detergent motor oil with an API rating of SE or SF. The API rating is stamped on top of the can or printed on the label on the plastic bottle (**Figure 17**). Try to use the same brand of oil at each change. Use of oil additives is not recommended. Kawasaki recommends the use of SAE 10W-40 oil viscosity under normal conditions. Refer to **Figure 18** for correct oil viscosity to use under anticipated ambient temperatures (not engine oil temperature).

To change the engine oil and filter you will need the following:

  a. Drain pan.

  b. Funnel.

  c. Open-end wrench (drain plug).

  d. Kawasaki oil filter wrench or equivalent.

  e. Oil (refer to **Table 4** for quantity).

  f. New oil filter element.

There are a number of ways to discard the old oil safely. Some service stations and oil retailers will

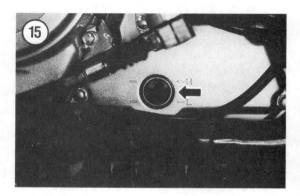

accept your used oil for recycling; some may even give you money for it. Never drain the oil onto the ground nor place it in your household trash.

> NOTE
> If you are going to recycle the oil, do not add any other type of chemical (fork oil, brake fluid, etc) to the oil as the oil recycler will probably not accept the oil. Final drive gear oil is acceptable.

1. Start the engine and let it reach operating temperature; 15-20 minutes of stop-and-go riding is usually sufficient.

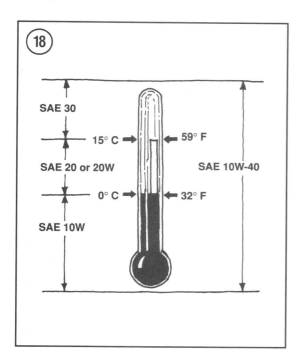

2. Turn the engine off and place the bike on level ground on the sidestand.

> NOTE
> Behind the drain plug is a spring, washer and oil screen. When the drain plug is removed, the spring and washer may come off with it. If they fall off or come out while the oil is draining, be sure to remove them from the oil pan after the draining is complete.

> WARNING
> Do **not** try to catch the spring and washer as the HOT oil is draining from the crankcase as this may result in burned fingers. Wait until later and remove them from the drain pan.

3. Place a drain pan under the left-hand rear portion of the crankcase below the drain plug (**Figure 19**). Remove the oil filler cap (**Figure 16**) this will speed up the flow of oil.

> NOTE
> Steps 4-8 are shown with the engine removed from the frame for clarity. It is not necessary to remove the engine for this procedure.

4. Unscrew and remove the oil drain plug (**Figure 20**).

5. Remove the spring, washer and oil screen from the crankcase.

6. Thoroughly clean the oil screen in a cleaning solvent. During the cleaning process, check for any small metal particles that may indicate internal engine damage. Dry with compressed air and inspect

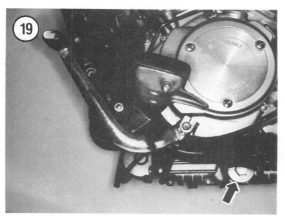

the oil screen (**Figure 21**) for any damage, broken areas or holes. Replace the oil screen as necessary.

7. Inspect the O-ring seal (**Figure 22**) on the crankcase drain plug. Replace if its condition is in doubt.

8. Install the oil screen (**Figure 23**), washer (**Figure 24**) and spring (**Figure 25**).

9. Install the drain plug and O-ring (**Figure 20**) and tighten to the torque specification listed in **Table 5**.

NOTE
Before removing the oil filter, clean off all road dirt and any oil residue around it.

10. Move the drain pan under the oil filter at the front of the engine.

NOTE
*The easiest way to remove the oil filter is to use a Kawasaki "cap type" oil filter wrench (**Figure 26**). For 1985-1993 models, use part No. 57001-1212, on 1994 and later models, use part No. 57001-1249.*

11. Use the special tool and socket wrench and unscrew the oil filter (**Figure 27**) from the engine. Place the old filter in a reclosable plastic bag and close it to prevent residual oil from draining out. Discard the used oil filter properly.

12. Clean off the oil filter mating surface on the crankcase with a shop rag and cleaning solvent. Remove any sludge or road dirt. Wipe it dry with a clean, lint-free cloth.

13. Apply a light coat of clean engine oil to the O-ring seal (**Figure 28**) on the new oil filter.

14. Screw on the new oil filter by hand until the O-ring seal contacts the crankcase mating surface,

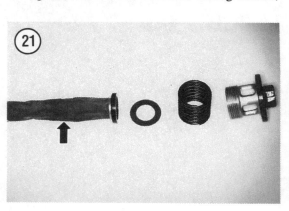

then tighten to the torque specification listed in **Table 5**.

15. Insert a funnel into the oil fill hole and fill the engine with the correct quantity of oil. Refer to **Table 4**.

16. Install the oil filler cap (**Figure 16**) and tighten securely.

17. Start the engine, let it run at idle speed and check for leaks.

18. Turn the engine off and check for correct oil level as described in this chapter; adjust as necessary.

Final Drive Oil Level Check

The final drive case should be cool. If the bike has been run, allow it to cool down (minimum of 10 minutes), then check the oil level. When checking or changing the final drive oil, do not allow any dirt or foreign matter to enter the case opening.

1. Place the bike on the centerstand on a level surface.

2. Wipe the area around the oil filler cap clean and unscrew the oil filler cap (**Figure 29**).

3. The oil level is correct if the oil is up to the lower edge of the filler cap hole. If the oil level is low, add hypoid gear oil until the oil level is correct. Refer to **Table 4** for correct oil viscosity and type to use under anticipated ambient temperatures.

4. Inspect the O-ring seal on the oil filler cap. If it is deteriorated or starting to harden it must be replaced.

5. Install the oil filler cap and tighten securely.

Final Drive Oil Change

The factory-recommended oil change interval is listed in **Table 1**.

To drain the oil you will need the following:
a. Drain pan.
b. Funnel.
c. The quantity of hypoid gear oil listed in **Table 4**.

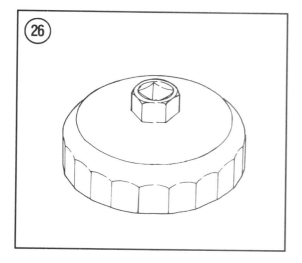

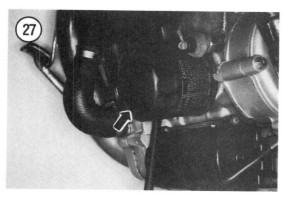

d. New aluminum gasket for the drain bolt.

Discard old oil as outlined under *Engine Oil and Filter Change* in this chapter.

1. Ride the bike until normal operating temperature is obtained. Usually 15-20 minutes of stop-and-go riding is sufficient.

2. Place the bike on the centerstand and shift the transmission in to neutral.

3. Place a drain pan under the drain plug.

> *WARNING*
> *Cover the wheel and rim to protect it from any oil that may accidentally spill onto it. Clean off all oil residue from the tire tread with a high-flash point solvent and thoroughly dry. If the tire is not thoroughly cleaned of all oil, the tire will have a slippery spot that may lead to an accident.*

4. Remove the oil filler cap (**Figure 29**) and the drain plug (**Figure 30**).

5. Let the oil drain for at least 15-20 minutes to ensure that the majority of the oil has drained out.

6. With the transmission in neutral and the rear wheel off the ground, slowly spin the rear wheel to expel any residual oil from the final drive unit.

7. Install a new aluminum sealing washer on the drain plug.

8. Install the drain plug and tighten it to the torque specification listed in **Table 5**.

9. Insert a funnel into the oil filler cap hole.

10. Add hypoid gear oil until the oil level is correct. Refer to **Table 4** for correct oil viscosity and type to use under anticipated ambient temperatures.

> *NOTE*
> *In order to measure the correct amount of fluid, use a plastic baby bottle. These have measurements in milliliters (ml) and fluid ounces (oz.) on the side.*

11. Make sure the O-ring seal is in place. Install the oil filler cap (**Figure 29**) and tighten securely.

12. Test ride the bike and check for oil leaks. After the test ride recheck the oil level as described in this chapter and readjust if necessary.

Front Fork Oil Change

It is a good practice to change the fork oil at the interval listed in **Table 1** or once a year. If it becomes

contaminated with dirt or water, change it immediately.

1. Place the bike on the centerstand on a level surface.

2. Remove the cap (**Figure 31**) from the top of both fork tubes.

> *WARNING*
> *Always bleed off all air pressure; failure to do so may cause personal injury when partially disassembling the fork for changing the oil.*

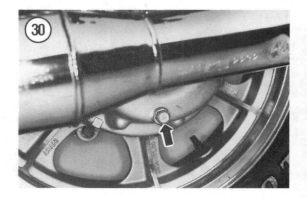

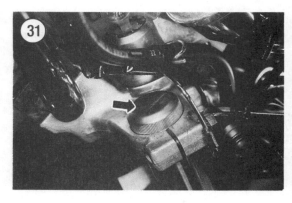

NOTE
Release air pressure gradually. If released too fast, fork oil will spurt out with the air. Protect your eyes and clothing accordingly.

3. On models so equipped, depress the valve stem and bleed off *all* air pressure. Repeat for the other fork assembly.

4. Use a suitable size socket and T-handle extension (**Figure 32**); depress the top cap and remove the retaining ring (**Figure 33**). Discard the old retaining ring as a new one must be installed every time the ring is removed.

5. Remove the top cap and spring spacer.

6. Place a clean shop cloth around the upper fork bridge to catch any fork oil during fork spring removal.

7. Carefully withdraw the fork spring and spring seat from the fork tube.

8. Place a drain pan under the fork leg.

WARNING
Cover the wheel and rim to protect it from any fork oil that may accidentally

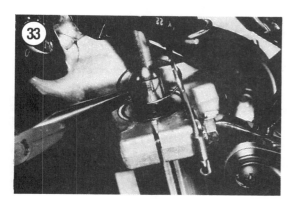

spill onto it. Clean off all oil residue from the tire tread with a high-flash point solvent and thoroughly dry. If the tire is not thoroughly cleaned of all fork oil, the tire will have a slippery spot that may lead to an accident.

9. A locking agent was applied to the drain bolt during assembly and may be difficult to loosen. If necessary, use an impact driver to loosen the bolt.

10. Unscrew the drain bolt (**Figure 34**) from the fork slider and drain the oil.

11. Place a jack under the engine with a piece of wood between the jack and the crankcase. Apply jack pressure to hold the bike in this position. Do not raise the front wheel off the ground at this time.

12. Repeat Steps 4-10 for the other fork assembly.

13. Apply jack pressure until the front wheel clears the ground. Remove the front wheel and front fender as described in Chapter Ten and Thirteen.

14. Place a shop cloth over the drain opening in the fork slider to catch any remaining oil that may spurt out in the following step.

15. Pump the fork several times by hand to expel most of the remaining oil. Repeat for the other fork assembly.

16. Dispose of the fork oil properly.

NOTE
*If you recycle your engine oil, do **not** add the fork oil to the oil as the oil recycler will probably not accept the oil.*

17. Clean the drain bolt threads of all old locking agent and dry with compressed air.

18. Apply blue Loctite (No. 242) to the drain bolt threads prior to installation and install the bolt (**Figure 34**). Tighten the bolt to the torque specification listed in **Table 5**. Install both drain bolts.

NOTE
Kawasaki recommends that the fork oil level be measured, if possible, to ensure a more accurate filling.

NOTE
To measure the correct amount of fluid, use a plastic baby bottle or a mixing container. These bottles or containers have measurements in milliliters (ml) on the side.

19. Add the recommended amount of fork oil to the fork assembly (**Figure 35**). Refer to **Table 4** for the recommended viscosity and quantity.

20. Compress the fork assembly completely and measure the fork oil level.

21. Use an accurate ruler or oil level gauge (**Figure 36**), to achieve the correct oil level listed in **Table 4**.

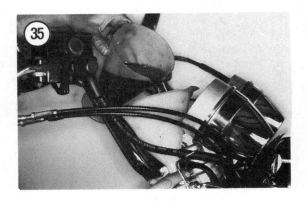

NOTE
*An oil level measuring device can be made as shown in **Figure 37**. Position the lower edge of the hose clamp the specified oil level distance up from the small diameter hole. Fill the fork with a few ml's more than the required amount of oil. Position the hose clamp on the top edge of the fork tube and draw out the excess oil. Oil is sucked out until the level reaches the small diameter hole. A precise oil level can be achieved with this simple device.*

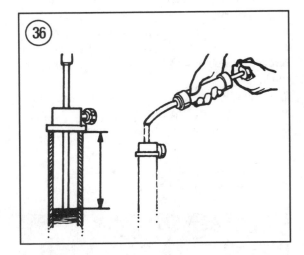

22. Allow the oil to settle completely and recheck the oil level measurement. Adjust the oil level if necessary.

23. Extend the fork slider.

24. Repeat Steps 19-22 for the other fork assembly.

25. Install the front fender and the front wheel. Maintain jack pressure under the engine.

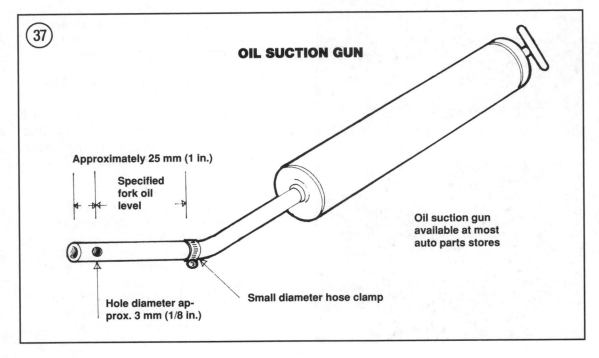

OIL SUCTION GUN

Approximately 25 mm (1 in.)

Specified fork oil level

Oil suction gun available at most auto parts stores

Small diameter hose clamp

Hole diameter approx. 3 mm (1/8 in.)

26. Install the fork spring with the smaller diameter coils going in first.

27. Install the spring seat, spacer and top cap (**Figure 38**).

> *WARNING*
> *Make sure the retaining ring is seated correctly in the fork tube groove. If the ring works loose while riding, the fork assembly will compress and could result in an accident.*

28. Use a suitable size socket and extension; depress the top cap and spring. Install a *new* retaining ring (**Figure 33**). Make sure the retaining ring is seated correctly in the fork tube groove (**Figure 39**).

29. Repeat Steps 26-28 for the other fork assembly.

30. Remove the jack from under the engine.

31. On models so equipped, add air pressure to the fork assemblies if so desired. Refer to **Table 4** for recommended air pressure.

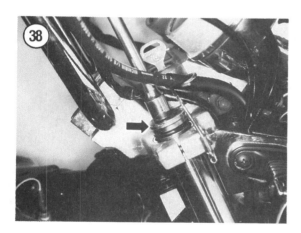

32. Install the cap (**Figure 31**) onto the top of both fork tubes.

Control Cables

The control cables should be lubricated at the cable inspection intervals specified in **Table 1** or when they become stiff or sluggish. At this time, it should also be inspected for fraying, and the cable sheath should be checked for chafing. The cables are relatively inexpensive and should be replaced when found to be faulty.

The cable should be lubricated with a cable lubricant and a cable lubricator.

> *CAUTION*
> *If the stock cable has been replaced with nylon-lined cables, do **not** oil them as described in the following procedure. Oil and most cable lubricants will cause the liner to expand, pinching the liner against the cable. Nylon lined cables are normally used dry. When servicing nylon-lined cables, follow the cable manufacturer's instructions.*

> *NOTE*
> *The main cause of cable breakage or cable stiffness is improper lubrication. Maintaining the cables as described in this section will assure long service life.*

1. Disconnect the clutch cable as follows:
   a. At the cable center adjuster, loosen the cable adjuster locknut (A, **Figure 40**) and turn the adjuster (B, **Figure 40**) all the way in to allow maximum slack in the cable.

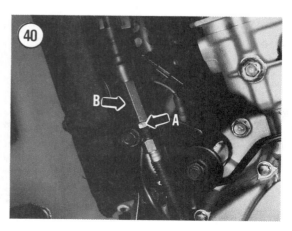

   b. At the hand lever on the handlebar, loosen the cable adjuster locknut (A, **Figure 41**) and turn the adjuster (B, **Figure 41**) all the way in to allow maximum slack in the cable.

   c. Align the slot in the cable adjuster locknut and the cable with the cable and release the cable from the adjuster and the hand lever.

2. Disconnect the throttle cables as follows:

   a. At the throttle control on the handlebar, loosen both cable adjuster locknuts (A, **Figure 42**) and turn both adjusters (B, **Figure 42**) all the way in to allow maximum slack in both cables.

   b. Remove the screws securing the right-hand switch assembly (C, **Figure 42**) together to gain access to the throttle cable ends. Separate the switch assembly.

   c. Disconnect the throttle cables from the grip assembly and the upper portion of the switch assembly.

   d. Remove the fuel tank as described under *Fuel Tank Removal/Installation* in Chapter Seven.

3. Disconnect the choke cable as follows:

   a. At the choke control lever on the handlebar, loosen the cable adjuster locknut (A, **Figure 43**) and turn the adjuster (B, **Figure 43**) all the way in to allow maximum slack in the cable.

   b. Remove the screws securing the left-hand switch assembly (**Figure 44**) together to gain access to the choke cable end. Separate the switch assembly.

   c. Disconnect the choke cable from the choke lever assembly.

   d. If not already removed, remove the fuel tank as described under *Fuel Tank Removal/Installation* in Chapter Seven.

4. Disconnect the rear brake cable as follows:

   a. At the rear brake panel, completely unscrew the adjust nut (A, **Figure 45**).

   b. Depress the brake pedal and disconnect the brake rod (B, **Figure 45**) from the pivot joint in the brake panel cam lever. Remove the pivot joint and reinstall the joint and the adjust nut onto the rod to avoid misplacing them.

   c. Remove the frame right-hand side cover.

   d. Remove the circlip securing the brake cable to the frame mounting tab (**Figure 46**).

   e. Slide the cable dust cover out of place.

   f. Pull the brake outer cable forward and slip the inner cable out of the slot in the mounting tab.

5. Attach a lubricator following the manufacturer's instructions (**Figure 47**).

6. Place a clean shop cloth at the other end of the cable to catch the excess lubricant as it exits the cable end.

7. Insert the nozzle of the lubricant can in the lubricator, press the button on the can and hold down until the lubricant begins to flow out of the other end of the cable.

8. Remove the lubricator, reconnect the cable(s) and adjust the cable(s) as described in this chapter:

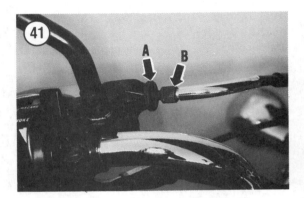

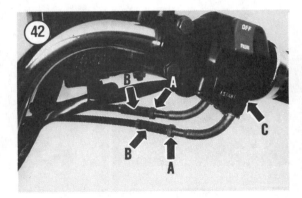

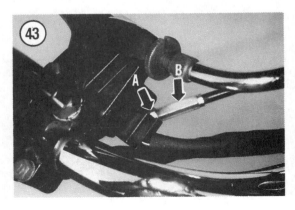

a. *Throttle Cable Adjustment.*
b. *Choke Cable Adjustment.*
c. *Clutch Cable Adjustment.*
d. *Rear Brake Adjustment.*

Brake System

The following brake components should be lubricated with silicone grease (specified for brake use) whenever the components are removed for service:
  a. Master cylinder rubber boots (inside).

b. Brake caliper boots (inside).
c. Brake caliper pin bolt sliding surface.

Brake Pedal
Pivot Shaft Lubrication

The brake pedal should be removed periodically, as described in Chapter Twelve, and the pivot shaft lubricated with waterproof grease.

Speedometer Cable Lubrication

The inner speedometer cable should be lubricated periodically or whenever needle operation is erratic. At the same time, check the outer cable for damage.

1. Unscrew the knurled speedometer cable ring (**Figure 48**) from the meter case.

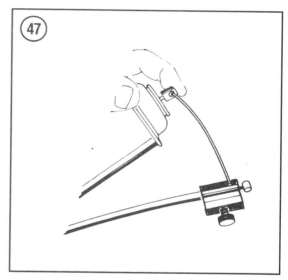

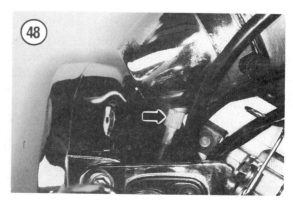

2. At the front wheel, remove the speedometer cable (**Figure 49**) from the speedometer gear housing.

3. Pull the cable from the sheath.

4. Clean the cable with a rag soaked in solvent and thoroughly dry with a lint-free cloth.

5. Examine the cable ends for damage. Check the cable for bending or broken strands. Replace the cable if necessary.

6. Thoroughly coat the cable with a good grade of multi-purpose grease and insert the cable back into the sheath. Push the cable back and forth through the sheath making sure there is no binding or roughness. The cable should move smoothly.

7. Reconnect the upper end of the speedometer cable to the speedometer housing.

8. Install the speedometer cable into the speedometer gear housing at the front wheel. If necessary, slowly rotate the front wheel until cable alignment is achieved.

Steering Stem Lubrication

The retainer-type ball bearings used in the steering system should be removed, cleaned and lubricated with bearing grease as described in Chapter Ten.

Miscellaneous Lubrication Points

Lubricate the clutch lever, front brake lever, sidestand pivot point, centerstand pivot points and the footpeg pivot points. Use SAE 10W-40 engine oil.

PERIODIC MAINTENANCE

Disc Brake Fluid Level Check and Adding Brake Fluid

The fluid level should be up between the upper and lower mark within the reservoir. If the brake fluid level reaches the lower level mark (**Figure 50**) on the side of the master cylinder reservoir, the fluid level must be corrected by adding fresh brake fluid.

1. Place the bike on the centerstand on level ground.

2. Position the handlebars so the front master cylinder reservoir is in its normal riding position.

3. Clean the top of the master cylinder of all dirt and foreign matter.

NOTE
*There are 2 different types of master cylinders used among the different models. The master cylinder shown in **Figure 51** is for 1985-1990 models. Service procedure for 1991 and later models is identical except that the top cover is round instead of rectangular.*

4. Remove the screws securing the cover (**Figure 51**). Remove the cover and the diaphragm (**Figure 52**).

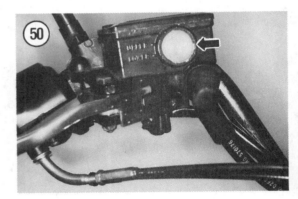

5. Add brake fluid until the level is to the upper level line within the master cylinder reservoir (**Figure 53**). Use fresh brake fluid from a sealed brake fluid container.

WARNING
Use brake fluid from a sealed container clearly marked DOT 3 only (specified for disc brakes). Others may vaporize

and cause brake failure. Do not inter-mix different brands or types of brake fluid as they may not be compatible. Do not intermix a silicone based (DOT 5) brake fluid as it can cause brake com-ponent damage leading to brake system failure.

CAUTION
Be careful when handling brake fluid. Do not spill it on painted or plated surfaces or plastic parts as it will de-stroy the surface. Wash the area imme-diately with soapy water and thoroughly rinse it off.

6. Reinstall the diaphragm (**Figure 52**) and the top cover (**Figure 51**). Tighten the screws securely.

Front Disc Brake Line

Check hydraulic brake lines between the front master cylinder (**Figure 54**) and the front brake calipers (**Figure 55**). If there is any leakage, tighten the connections and bleed the brakes as described under *Bleeding the System* in Chapter Twelve. If this does not stop the leak or if a brake line(s) is obvi-ously damaged, cracked or chafed, replace the brake line and bleed the system.

Disc Brake Pad Wear

Inspect the brake pads for excessive or uneven wear, scoring and oil or grease on the friction sur-face.

1. Place the bike on the centerstand on level ground.

2. Remove the bolts (**Figure 56**) securing the caliper assembly to the fork slider.

3. Carefully pull the caliper off the disc and check the wear lines on the brake pads (**Figure 57**).

4. Replace both pads if the wear line (**Figure 58**) on the pads reaches the brake disc.

5. Repeat for the other caliper.

6. If this condition exists, replace the pads as described in Chapter Twelve.

7. Reinstall the caliper assembly onto the brake disc being careful not to damage the leading edge of the pads during installation.

8. Tighten the mounting bolts to the torque specification listed in **Table 5**.

Disc Brake Fluid Change

Every time the reservoir cap is removed, a small amount of dirt and moisture enters the brake fluid. The same thing happens if a leak occurs or any part of the hydraulic system is loosened or disconnected. Dirt can clog the system and cause unnecessary wear. Water in the brake fluid vaporizes at a high temperature, impairing the hydraulic action and reducing the brake's stopping ability.

To maintain peak performance, change the brake fluid as indicated in **Table 1**. To change brake fluid, follow the *Bleeding the System* procedure in Chapter Twelve. Continue adding new fluid to the master cylinder and bleeding out at the caliper until the fluid leaving the caliper is clean and free of contaminants.

WARNING
Use brake fluid from a sealed container clearly marked DOT 3 only (specified for disc brakes). Others may vaporize and cause brake failure. Do not intermix different brands or types of brake fluid as they may not be compatible. Do not intermix a silicone based (DOT 5) brake fluid as it can cause brake component damage leading to brake system failure.

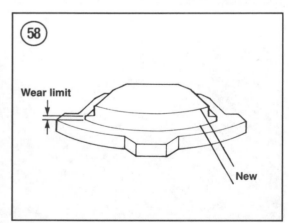

Wear limit

New

Rear Drum Brake Lining Wear Indicator

The rear drum brake is equipped with a brake lining wear indicator. This enables you to check the brake lining condition without removing the rear wheel and brake assembly for inspection purposes.

1. Apply the rear brake fully.

2. Observe where the wear indicator (A, **Figure 59**) falls within the embossed "usable range" (B, **Figure 59**) on the brake panel.

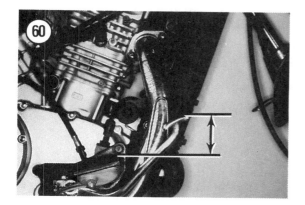

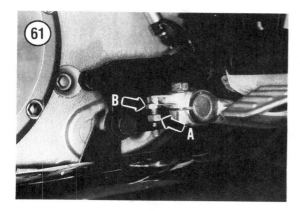

3. If the indicator falls within this range the brake lining thickness is within specification and does not require any service.

4. If the lines fall outside of this "usable range," the brake linings are worn to the point that they require replacement.

5. If necessary, replace the rear brake linings as described under *Rear Drum Brake* in Chapter Twelve.

Rear Brake Pedal Height Adjustment

The rear brake pedal height should be adjusted at the interval listed in **Table 1**. The pedal height will change with brake lining wear from use. The top of the brake pedal should be positioned above the top surface of the footpeg (**Figure 60**) 50-60 mm (2-1/2 in.).

1. Make sure the brake pedal is in the at-rest position.

2. To change height position, loosen the locknut (A, **Figure 61**) and turn the adjust bolt (B, **Figure 61**) until the correct height is achieved. Tighten the locknut (A) securely.

Rear Brake Pedal Freeplay Adjustment

The pedal freeplay should be 20-30 mm (0.8-1.2 mm).

1. Make sure the brake pedal is in the at-rest position.

2. Depress the brake pedal lightly by hand until the brake shoes make contact with the drum. This is the free play.

3. To change the freeplay adjustment, turn the adjust nut (**Figure 62**) at the end of the brake rod. Turn the adjust nut in either direction until the correct amount of freeplay is achieved.

Rear Brake Cam Lever Angle Adjustment

The rear brake cam lever should be at 80-90° angle, or less, to the rear brake rod when the rear brake is fully applied. If the lever is positioned at greater than 90°, rear braking effectiveness is greatly reduced.

1. Have an assistant apply the rear brake and observe the rear brake cam lever. Note the angle of the lever (A, **Figure 63**) in relation to the brake rod (B, **Figure 63**). If the lever is not within the specified 80-90° range, it must be repositioned (to less than 80-90°) on the camshaft to maintain full braking ability.

2. At the rear brake panel, completely unscrew the adjust nut (**Figure 62**).

3. Depress the brake pedal and disconnect the brake rod from the pivot joint in the brake panel cam lever. Remove the pivot joint and reinstall the joint and the adjust nut onto the rod to avoid misplacing them.

4. Use a fine-line permanent marking pen and mark the existing location of the cam lever split in relation to the end of the camshaft.

5. Remove the bolt (A, **Figure 64**) securing the brake cam lever and remove the lever (B, **Figure 64**) from the camshaft.

6. Reposition the cam lever on the camshaft to achieve the recommended 80-90°, or less, relationship to the brake rod.

7. Install the bolt and tighten securely.

8. Reinstall the brake rod, pivot joint and adjust nut.

9. Adjust the rear brake free play as described in this chapter.

10. Repeat Step 1; readjust if necessary.

Throttle Cable Adjustment

The pull throttle cable should be adjusted so the throttle linkage lever stops against the idle adjusting screw with the throttle grip in the closed position. If adjustment is necessary, perform the following.

1. At the throttle assembly end of the throttle cable, loosen the locknuts (A, **Figure 65**) on both the pull and push throttle cables.

2. Turn the adjusters (B, **Figure 65**) to allow maximum slack in both cables.

3. Rotate the throttle grip until it is *completely* closed.

4. Rotate the push cable adjuster until the cable becomes tight. Tighten the push cable locknut securely.

NOTE
__Figure 66__ is shown with the carburetor assembly removed for clarity.

5. Rotate the pull cable adjuster until the throttle linkage lever stops against the idle adjusting screw

(**Figure 66**). Make sure the throttle grip is still in the closed position.

6. Tighten the pull cable locknut securely.

NOTE
If the throttle cables cannot be properly adjusted using the cable upper adjusters at the throttle grip, continue with the cable lower adjusters at the carburetor assembly.

7. Disconnect the pull cable from the throttle wheel at the carburetor assembly.

8. Loosen the locknut on the push cable. Rotate the push cable adjuster until the cable becomes tight. Tighten the push cable locknut securely.

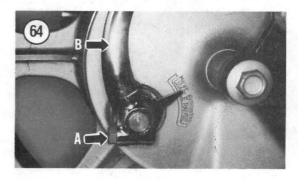

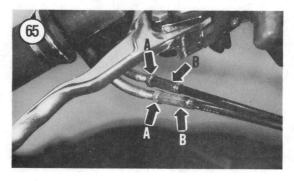

9. Reinstall the pull cable on to the throttle wheel.

10. Rotate the pull cable adjuster until the throttle linkage lever stops against the idle adjusting screw (**Figure 66**). Make sure the throttle grip is still in the closed position.

11. Tighten the pull cable locknut securely.

12. If the proper amount of adjustment cannot be achieved using this procedure, the cables have stretched to the point where they need replacing. Refer to *Throttle Cable Replacement* in Chapter Seven.

13. Check the throttle cables from the throttle grip to the throttle cable joint on the carburetor assembly. Make sure they are not kinked or chafed. Replace as necessary.

14. Make sure the throttle grip rotates freely from a fully closed to fully open position. Check with the handlebar at center, at full right and at full left. If necessary, remove the throttle grip and apply a lithium base grease to the rotating surfaces.

> *WARNING*
> *With the engine idling, move the handlebar from side to side.*

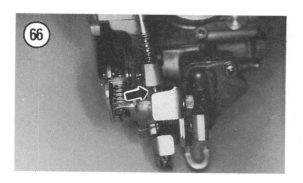

If idle speed increases during this movement, the throttle cable may need adjusting or may be incorrectly routed through the frame. Correct this problem immediately. Do **not** ride the bike in this unsafe condition.

Camshaft Chain Tensioner Adjustment

There is *no* provision for manual adjustment of the camshaft chain tension on this engine. Camshaft chain tension is maintained automatically.

Exhaust System

Check for leakage at all fittings. Tighten all bolts and nuts; replace any gaskets as necessary. Refer to *Exhaust System* in Chapter Seven.

Air Filter Elements

Both air filter elements should be removed and cleaned at the interval listed in **Table 1**. Always replace both air filter elements at the same time and they should be replaced sooner if soiled, severely clogged or broken in any area.

The air filter elements remove dust and abrasive particles from the air before the air enters each carburetor and the engine. Without the air filters, very fine particles could enter into the engine and cause rapid wear of the piston rings, cylinders and bearings and might clog small passages in the carburetors. Never run the bike without both air filter elements installed.

Proper air filter servicing can do more to ensure long service from your engine than almost any other single item.

Air Filter
Removal/Installation

There are two separate air filter assemblies on the Vulcan. Removal, cleaning, inspection and installation are the same for both assemblies.

The air filter elements should be replaced after 5 cleanings or when either is found to be damaged.

1. Remove the screws (A, **Figure 67**) securing the air filter cover and remove the cover (B, **Figure 67**).

2. Remove the 2 bolts and washers (A, **Figure 68**) securing the air filter element assembly (B, **Figure 68**) to the air filter housing and remove the element assembly from the housing.

3. Clean and inspect the elements as described in this chapter.

4. Position the element with the white sponge felt side (**Figure 69**) of the element facing in toward the air box and install the element assembly. Make sure it is correctly seated onto the air box so there is no air leak, then install the bolts and washers. Tighten the bolts securely.

5. Make sure the perimeter gasket (**Figure 70**) is in place in the air filter housing.

6. Install the air filter cover and screws. Tighten the screws securely.

7. Repeat for the other air filter assembly.

Element Cleaning and Inspection

1. Carefully remove the air filter element from the element holder (**Figure 71**).

> *CAUTION*
> *Do **not** clean the air filter element with gasoline, as it represents an extreme fire hazard.*

2. Fill a clean pan of appropriate size with a non-flammable solvent.

3. Submerge the air filter element into the cleaning solution and gently work the cleaning solution into the element pores.

4. Rinse the filter element under warm water and remove all solvent residue.

5. After cleaning the filter element (**Figure 72**), inspect it. If it is torn or damaged in any area, it should be replaced. Also, clean the air filter housing as described in Step 14. Do not run the engine with a damaged filter as it may allow dirt to enter the engine and cause severe engine wear.

6. Set the filter element aside and allow it to dry. thoroughly or apply *gentle* air pressure to the element.

7. Properly oiling an air filter element is a messy job. You may want to wear a pair of disposable latex gloves when performing the following steps of this procedure.

8. Purchase a box of gallon size clear reclosable storage bags. These bags can be used when cleaning

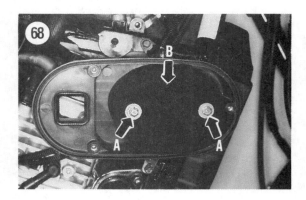

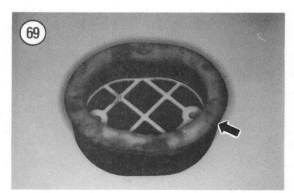

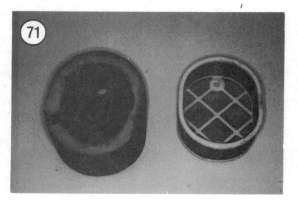

the filter as well as for storing engine and carburetor parts during disassembly.

9. Place the cleaned filter element into a plastic storage bag.

10. Pour SAE 30 motor oil onto the filter to soak it.

11. Place the filter element and plastic bag on a flat surface and work the oil into the element's pores.

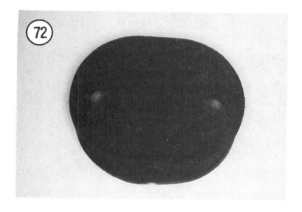

Continue until all of the filter's pores are discolored evenly with the oil.

12. Remove the filter element from the bag and check the pores for uneven oiling. This is indicated by light or dark areas. If necessary re-soak the filter element.

13. When the filter oiling is even, place the filter element on a shop cloth on a flat surface. Place another cloth on top of the element and press out the residual oil from the filter. Continue until the element is as dry as possible. Be careful not to damage the white sponge portion of the element as this is the sealing surface of the element.

14. If the filter element was torn or damaged, clean out the inside of the air filter housing with a shop rag and cleaning solvent. Remove any foreign matter that may have passed through a broken cleaner element.

15. Inspect the element holder (**Figure 73**) for damage; replace if necessary.

16. Carefully install the air filter element onto the element holder (**Figure 69**).

Fuel Line Inspection

Inspect the fuel line (**Figure 74**) from the fuel shutoff valve to the carburetor assembly. If it is cracked or starting to deteriorate, it must be replaced. Make sure the hose clamps are in place and holding securely.

> *WARNING*
> *A damaged or deteriorated fuel line presents a very dangerous fire hazard to both the rider and the vehicle if fuel should spill onto a hot engine or exhaust pipe.*

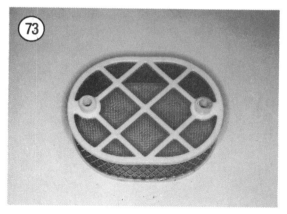

Vacuum Line Inspection

Inspect the condition of all vacuum lines for cracks or deterioration; and replace if necessary. Make sure the hose clamps are in place and holding securely.

Cooling System Inspection

At the interval indicated in **Table 1**, the following items should be checked. If you do not have the test equipment, the tests can be done by a Kawasaki

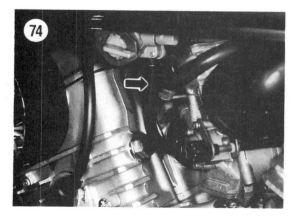

dealer, automobile dealer, radiator shop or service station.

1. Remove the steering head right-hand cover and remove the radiator cap (**Figure 75**).

2. Test the radiator cap pressure (**Figure 76**). The specified radiator cap relief pressure is 93-123 kPa (14-18 psi). The cap must be able to sustain this pressure for a minimum of 10 seconds. Replace the radiator cap if it does not hold pressure or if the relief pressure is too high or too low.

3. Leave the radiator cap off and install the tester to the radiator cap fitting (**Figure 77**).

4. Pressure test the entire cooling system (**Figure 78**). The entire cooling system should be pressurized up to, but not exceeding, 123 kPa (18 psi). The system must be able to sustain this pressure for a minimum of 6 seconds. Replace or repair any components that fail this test.

5. Test the specific gravity of the coolant with an antifreeze tester to ensure adequate temperature and corrosion protection. The system must have at least a 50:50 mixture of antifreeze and distilled water. Never let the mixture become less than 40% antifreeze or corrosion protection will be impaired.

6. Install the radiator cap and the steering head right-hand cover.

7. Check all cooling system hoses for damage or deterioration. Refer to **Figure 79**, **Figure 80** and **Figure 81**. Replace any hose that is questionable. Make sure all hose clamps are tight.

8. Remove the radiator cover (**Figure 82**).

9. Carefully clean any road dirt, bugs, mud, etc. from the front surface of the radiator core (**Figure**

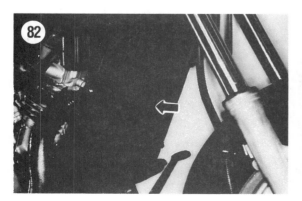

83). Use a whisk broom, compressed air or low-pressure water. If the radiator has been hit by a small rock or other item, *carefully* straighten out the fins with a screwdriver.

> **NOTE**
> *If the radiator has been damaged across approximately 20% or more of the frontal area, the radiator should be re-cored or replaced as described under **Radiator Removal/Installation** in Chapter Nine.*

10. Install the radiator cover (**Figure 82**).

Coolant Change

The cooling system should be completely drained and refilled at the interval indicated in **Table 1**.

It is sometimes necessary to remove the radiator or drain the coolant from the system in order to perform a service procedure on some parts of the bike. If the coolant is still in good condition (not time to replace the coolant), the coolant can be reused if it is kept clean. Drain the coolant into a *clean* drain pan and pour it into a *clean* sealable container like a plastic milk or bleach bottle. This coolant can then be reused if it is still clean.

> **CAUTION**
> *Antifreeze is poisonous and may attract animals. Do not leave the drained coolant where it is accessible to children or animals.*

> **CAUTION**
> *Use only a high-quality ethylene glycol antifreeze specifically labeled for use with aluminum engines. Do not use an alcohol-based antifreeze.*

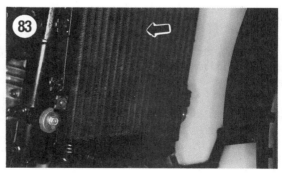

In areas where freezing temperatures occur, add a higher percentage of antifreeze to protect the system to temperatures far below those likely to occur.

The following procedure must be performed when the engine is cool.

> *WARNING*
> *Do **not** change the coolant while the engine is still hot or even warm. Do **not** remove the radiator fill cap (**Figure 75**) when the engine is HOT. The coolant is very hot and is under pressure. Severe scalding could result if the escaping coolant comes in contact with your skin. Allow the cooling system to cool down prior to loosening the cap and then loosen the cap slowly to the first detent to allow any built-up pressure to escape safely.*

> *CAUTION*
> *Be careful not to spill antifreeze on painted surfaces as it will destroy the surface. Wash immediately with soapy water and rinse thoroughly with clean water. Coolant is also slippery. Be sure to clean up any spilled coolant that may get on the ground or on the tire threads.*

1. Place the bike on the centerstand.
2. Remove the steering head right-hand cover.

> *NOTE*
> *A clean drain pan should be used to collect the spent coolant as the coolant will be inspected for possible internal engine problems after draining is completed.*

3. Place a clean drain pan under the right-hand crankcase.

> *NOTE*
> *Remove the crankcase drain bolt first as this will relieve the internal pressure prior to removing the radiator cap.*

4. Remove the main drain bolt (**Figure 84**) and gasket on the right-hand crankcase.
5. Remove the radiator drain bolt (**Figure 85**) and gasket.
6. Turn the radiator cap (**Figure 75**) counterclockwise to the first stop. Push down and turn the cap further counterclockwise and remove the cap. This will speed up the draining process.

7. Place a clean drain pan under the front cylinder on the right-hand side and remove the drain bolt (**Figure 86**) and gasket.

8. Place a clean drain pan under the rear cylinder on the left-hand side and remove the drain bolt (**Figure 87**) and gasket.

9. Remove the reservoir cap (A, **Figure 88**).

10. Remove the bolt securing the reservoir tank cover (B, **Figure 88**) and remove the cover.

11. Carefully pull the reservoir, with the hoses still attached, up out of the frame. Turn the reservoir

upside down and drain out all coolant. Reinstall the reservoir making sure the hoses are still attached and are not kinked.

12. Do not install the drain bolts yet.

13. Take the bike off the centerstand and tip the bike from side to side to drain any residual coolant from the cooling system. Place the bike back onto the centerstand.

14. Visually inspect the condition of the coolant as follows:

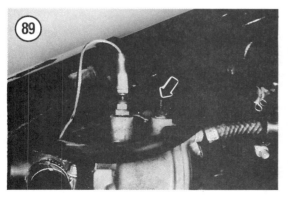

a. White "cotton-like" sediments in coolant indicate that aluminum parts in cooling system are corroded.

b. Brownish color to coolant indicates that iron parts in the cooling system are rusting.

c. An abnormal smell of the coolant may be indicate an exhaust or combustion leak into the cooling system.

15. If the drained coolant was contaminated or very dirty; flush the cooling system with freshwater. Allow the water to run through the cooling system for approximately 5 minutes. Shut off the water and allow the water to drain out.

16. Take the bike off the centerstand and tip the bike from side to side to drain all residual water from the cooling system. Place the bike back onto the centerstand.

17. Inspect the gaskets on the drain plugs; replace if necessary. Install all drain plugs and gaskets. Refer to **Figures 84-87**. Tighten the plugs to the torque specification listed in **Table 5**.

18. Refill the cooling system as follows:

    a. Insert a small funnel into the radiator filler neck.

> *CAUTION*
> *Do not use a higher percentage of coolant-to-water than 50:50. A higher concentration of antifreeze (60% or greater) will actually **decrease** the performance of the cooling system.*

    b. *Slowly* add a 50:50 mixture of distilled water and antifreeze into the radiator to bring the level to the cap inlet fitting on the filler neck. Adding the coolant slowly will help rid the system of trapped air.

    c. Add the same mixture of coolant to the reserve tank. Fill the tank to the full mark. Install the cap.

    d. Lean the bike from side to side to bleed out as much air from the system as possible.

    e. Remove the fuel tank as described under *Fuel Tank Removal/Installation* in Chapter Seven.

    f. Loosen the air bleeder bolt (**Figure 89**) on the thermostat housing.

    g. Place a shop cloth under the thermostat housing to catch the coolant as it comes out in the next step.

    h. Add additional coolant to the radiator fill cap and observe the bleed valve. Add coolant until the coolant flowing out of the bleed valve is free of bubbles. Tighten the bleed valve to the torque specification listed in **Table 5**.

i. Install the fuel tank as described in Chapter Seven.

j. Install the radiator cap (**Figure 75**) and turn it *clockwise* until it stops turning.

19. Start the engine and let it run at idle speed until the engine reaches normal operating temperature. Shut off the engine.

20. Check coolant level in the reservoir tank. Add coolant as necessary to bring the coolant level to the upper line (**Figure 90**).

21. Check for coolant leaks at all drain plugs. Tighten if necessary.

22. Test ride the bike and readjust the coolant level if necessary after the cooling system has cooled down.

23. Install the steering head right-hand cover.

Evaporative Emission Control System (California Models Only)

Fuel vapor from the fuel tank is routed into a charcoal canister when the engine is stopped. When the engine is started these vapors are drawn through the separator and into the carburetors and into the engine to be burned. Make sure all vacuum hoses are correctly routed and attached. Inspect the hoses and replace any if necessary.

Refer to Chapter Seven for detailed information on the *Evaporative Emission Control System* and for vacuum hose routing.

Wheel Bearings

There is no factory-recommended mileage interval for cleaning and repacking the wheel bearings. They should be inspected and serviced, if necessary, every time the wheel is removed or whenever there

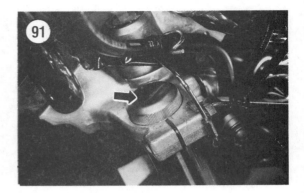

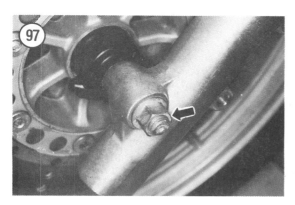

is a likelihood of water contamination. The correct service procedures are covered in Chapter Ten and Chapter Eleven.

Front Suspension Check

1. Apply the front brake and pump the forks up and down as vigorously as possible. Check for smooth operation and check for any fork oil leaks around the oil seal area on each fork leg.

2. Remove the cap (**Figure 91**) from the top of both fork tubes.

3. Make sure the retaining ring is seated correctly in the fork tube groove (**Figure 92**).

4. Make sure the upper and lower fork bridge bolts (**Figure 93**) are tight on both fork assemblies.

5. Remove the trim caps (**Figure 94**) and make sure the bolts (**Figure 95**) securing the handlebar holders to the upper fork bridge are tight.

6. Make sure the front axle pinch bolt and nut (**Figure 96**) and front axle nut (**Figure 97**) are tight.

> *CAUTION*
> *If any of the previously mentioned bolts and nuts are loose, refer to Chapter Ten for correct procedures and torque specifications.*

Rear Suspension Check

1. Place a wood block(s) under the engine to support the bike securely with the rear wheel off the ground.

2. Push hard on the rear wheel (sideways) to check for side play in the rear swing arm bearings. Remove the wood block(s).

3. Check the tightness of the shock absorber's upper (**Figure 98**) and lower (**Figure 99**) mounting cap nuts.

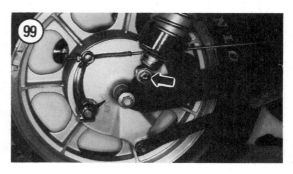

4. Remove the trim cap (**Figure 100**) on each side covering the swing arm pivot bolt nut.

5. Make sure the swing arm adjust bolt retainer bolts (A, **Figure 101**) are tight. Also make sure the adjust bolt locknut (B, **Figure 101**) is tight.

6. Make sure the nut (**Figure 102**) on the rear axle bolt is tight and that the cotter pin is in place.

7. Make sure the 4 nuts (**Figure 103**) securing the final drive unit to the swing arm are tight. Only 3 of the nuts are visible, be sure to check all 4 nuts for tightness.

8. Remove the retaining clips and check the tightness of the rear brake torque arm (**Figure 104**) nuts. Reinstall the retaining clips.

> *CAUTION*
> *If any of the previously mentioned bolts and nuts are loose, refer to Chapter Ten for correct procedures and torque specifications.*

Nuts, Bolts and Other Fasteners

Constant vibration can loosen many of the fasteners on the motorcycle. Check the tightness of all fasteners, especially those on:

 a. Engine mounting hardware.
 b. Engine crankcase covers.
 c. Handlebar and front forks.
 d. Gearshift lever.
 e. Brake pedal and lever.
 f. Final drive unit nuts.
 g. Exhaust system.
 h. Lighting equipment.

Steering Head Adjustment Check

Check the steering head bearings for looseness at the interval listed in **Table 1**.

1. Place a wood block(s) under the engine to support the bike securely with the front wheel off the ground.

2. Hold onto the front fork tube and gently rock the fork assembly back and forth. If you feel looseness, refer to Chapter Ten.

TUNE-UP

Perform a complete tune-up at the interval listed in **Table 1** of normal riding. More frequent tune-ups may be required if the bike is ridden in stop-and-go traffic. The purpose of the tune-up is to restore the performance lost due to normal wear and deterioration of parts.

Kawasaki does not recommend any specific time or mileage interval for replacing the spark plugs. If engine performance is reduced or if the spark plug electrodes show signs of erosion; replace all 4 spark plugs as a set. In addition, this is a good time to clean

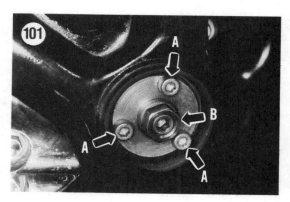

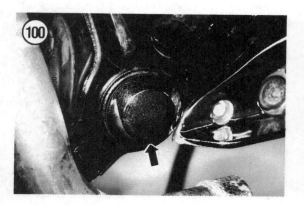

both air filter elements. Have all known new parts on hand before you begin.

Because the different systems in an engine interact, the procedures should be done in the following order:

  a. Run a compression test.
  b. Change spark plugs.
  c. Check ignition timing.
  d. Set the idle speed.
  e. Synchronize the carburetors.

Table 6 summarizes tune-up specifications.

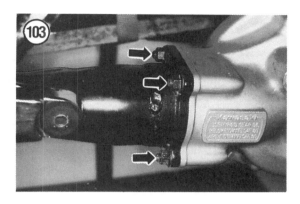

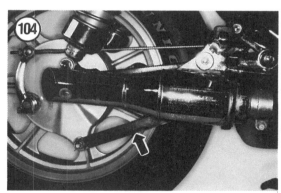

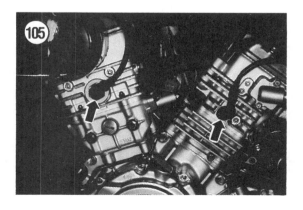

To perform a tune-up on your Kawasaki, you will need the following tools and equipment:

  a. 18 mm (5/8 in.) spark plug wrench.
  b. Socket wrench and assorted sockets.
  c. Compression gauge.
  d. Spark plug wire feeler gauge and gapper tool.
  e. Portable tachometer.
  f. Carburetor synchronization tool—to measure manifold vacuum.

Valve Clearance Measurement and Adjustment

The engine is equipped with a hydraulic valve train adjuster system and requires no periodic valve adjustment. The only time any type of adjustment is necessary is after a cylinder head has been overhauled: see Chapter Four.

Compression Test

Check the cylinder compression at the interval indicated in **Table 1**. Record the results and compare them to the results at the next interval. A running record will show trends in deterioration so that corrective action can be taken before complete failure.

The results when properly interpreted, can indicate general cylinder, piston ring and valve condition.

1. Warm the engine to normal operating temperature, then shut it off. Make sure the choke valves are completely open.
2. Remove one spark plug (**Figure 105**) from each cylinder as described in this chapter. Leave the other spark plug in place in order to seal off the cylinder.
3. Connect the compression tester to one cylinder following the manufacturer's instructions.
4. Crank the engine over until there is no further rise in pressure.
5. Remove the tester and record the reading. Repeat for the other cylinder.
6. When interpreting the results, actual readings are not as important as the difference between the readings. The usable cylinder compression pressure is listed in **Table 6**. Greater differences than those listed in **Table 6** indicate broken rings, leaky or sticking valves, a blown head gasket or a combination of all.

If the compression readings between the cylinders differ less than 10 psi, the rings and valves are in good condition.

If a low reading (10% or more) is obtained, it indicates valve or ring trouble. To determine which, pour about a teaspoon of engine oil through the spark plug hole onto the top of the piston. Turn the engine over once to clear the oil, then take another compression test and record the reading. If the compression returns to normal, the valves are good but the rings are defective. If the compression does not increase, the valves require servicing. A valve(s) could be hanging open but not burned or a piece of carbon could be on a valve seat.

Spark Plug Selection

Select plugs in a heat range designed for the loads and temperature conditions under which the engine will operate. Using incorrect heat ranges can cause piston seizure, scored cylinder walls or damaged piston crowns.

In general, use a hotter plug for low speeds, low loads and low temperatures. Use a colder plug for high speeds, high engine loads and high temperatures.

NOTE
In areas where seasonal temperature variations are great, the factory recommends a "two-plug system"—a cold plug for hard summer riding and a hot plug for slower winter operation— which may prevent spark plug and engine problems. The plug should operate hot enough to burn off unwanted deposits, but not so hot that it is damaged or causes preignition.

A spark plug of the correct heat range will show a light tan color on the portion of the insulator within the cylinder after the plug has been in service.

The reach (length) of a plug is also important (**Figure 106**). A longer than normal plug could interfere with the valves and pistons, causing permanent and severe damage. The recommended spark plugs are listed in **Table 6**.

Spark Plug Removal/Cleaning

1. Grasp each spark plug lead (**Figure 105**) and carefully pull it off the plug. If the boot is stuck to the plug, twist it slightly to break it loose.

CAUTION
If any dirt falls into the cylinder when the plugs are removed, it could cause serious engine damage.

2. Use compressed air and blow away any dirt that may have passed by the rubber boot on the spark plug lead and accumulated in the spark plug well.

3. Remove all 4 spark plugs with an 18 mm spark plug wrench. Keep the spark plugs in sets, 2 from the front cylinder and 2 from the rear cylinder, in the order that they were removed. If anything turns up during the inspection step, you will then know which cylinder it came from.

NOTE
If plugs are difficult to remove, apply penetrating oil around base of plugs and let it soak in about 10-20 minutes.

4. Inspect the spark plug carefully. Look for a plug with broken center porcelain, excessively eroded electrodes and excessive carbon or oil fouling. Replace such a plug. If deposits are light, the plug may be cleaned in solvent with a wire brush. Regap the plug as explained in this chapter.

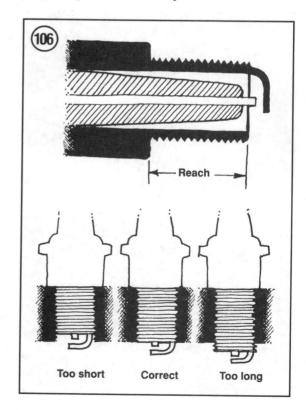

Reach

Too short　　　Correct　　　Too long

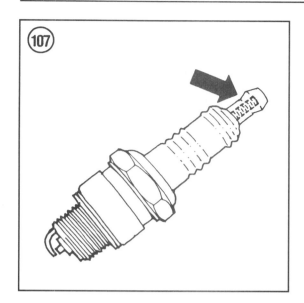

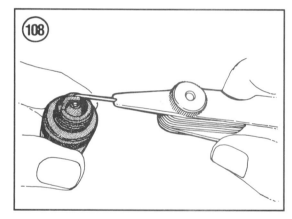

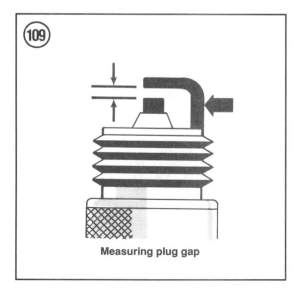

Measuring plug gap

NOTE
Spark plug cleaning with the use of a sand-blast type device is not recommended. While this type of cleaning is thorough, the plug must be perfectly free of all abrasive cleaning material when done. If not, it is possible for the cleaning material to fall into the engine during operation and cause damage.

Spark Plug Gapping and Installation

A new plug should be carefully gapped to ensure a reliable, consistent spark. You must use a special spark plug gapping tool with a wire feeler gauge.

1. Remove the new plug from the box. Do *not* screw on the small piece (**Figure 107**) that is sometimes loose in the box, they are not to be used.

2. Insert a wire feeler gauge between the center and each side electrode of each plug (**Figure 108**). The correct gap (**Figure 109**) is listed in **Table 6**. If the gap is correct, you will feel a slight drag as you pull the feeler gauge through. If there is no drag or the gauge won't pass through, bend the side electrode(s) with the gapping tool (**Figure 110**) to set the proper gap.

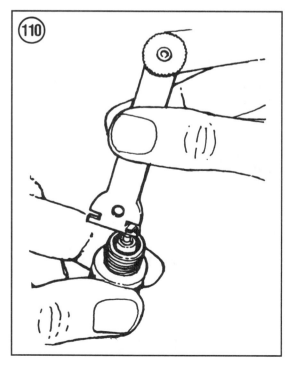

3. Put a *small* drop of oil or aluminum anti-seize compound on the threads of the spark plug.

4. Screw each spark plug in by hand until it seats. Very little effort is required. If force is necessary, you have the plug cross-threaded; unscrew it and try again.

NOTE
If a spark plug is difficult to install, the cylinder head threads may be dirty or slightly damaged. To clean the threads, apply grease to the threads of a spark plug tap and screw it carefully into the cylinder head. Turn the tap slowly until it is completely installed. If the tap cannot be installed, the threads are severely damaged and must be repaired.

5. Tighten the spark plugs an additional 1/2 turn after the gasket has made contact with the head. If you are reinstalling old, regapped plugs and are reusing the old gasket, only tighten an additional 1/4 turn.

CAUTION
Do not over tighten. Besides making the plug difficult to remove, the excessive torque will squash the gasket and destroy its sealing ability.

6. Install the spark plug leads; make sure the leads are on tight.

Reading Spark Plugs

Much information about engine and spark plug performance can be determined by careful examination of the spark plugs. This information is only valid after performing the following steps.

1. Ride the bike a short distance at full throttle in any gear.

2. Move the engine stop switch (**Figure 111**) to the OFF position before closing the throttle and simultaneously pull in the clutch or shift to NEUTRAL; coast and brake to a stop.

3. Remove one spark plug at a time and examine it. Compare it to **Figure 112**. If the insulator is white or burned, the plug is too hot and should be replaced with a colder one.

NOTE
A too-cold plug will have sooty or oily deposits ranging in color from dark

brown to black. Replace with a hotter plug and check for too-rich carburetion or evidence of oil blowby at the piston rings. If the plug has a light tan or gray colored deposit and no abnormal gap wear or electrode erosion is evident, the plug and the engine are running properly. If the plug exhibits a black insulator tip, a damp and oily film over the firing end and a carbon layer over the entire nose, it is oil fouled. An oil fouled plug can be cleaned, but it is better to replace it.

4. Repeat for the other spark plugs. If any one spark plug is found unsatisfactory, replace all 4 as a set.

Ignition Timing

All models are equipped with a solid state ignition system. This system uses no breaker points, is non-adjustable and requires no maintenance. The timing should be checked to make sure all ignition components are operating correctly.

Incorrect ignition timing can cause a drastic loss of engine performance and efficiency. It may also cause overheating.

Before starting on this procedure, check all electrical connections related to the ignition system. Make sure all connections are tight and free of corrosion and that all ground connections are tight.

1. Start the engine and let it reach normal operating temperature. Shut off the engine.

2. Place the bike on the centerstand.

3. Remove the screws securing the pickup coil cover (**Figure 113**) and remove the cover and O-ring gasket. Don't lose the O-ring on each bolt.

4. Connect a portable tachometer following the manufacturer's instructions. The bike's tachometer

3

SPARK PLUG CONDITION

NORMAL
- Identified by light tan or gray deposits on the firing tip.
- Can be cleaned.

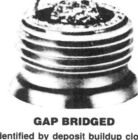

GAP BRIDGED
- Identified by deposit buildup closing gap between electrodes.
- Caused by oil or carbon fouling. If deposits are not excessive, the plug can be cleaned.

OIL FOULED
- Identified by wet black deposits on the insulator shell bore and electrodes.
- Caused by excessive oil entering combustion chamber through worn rings and pistons, excessive clearance between valve guides and stems or worn or loose bearings. Can be cleaned. If engine is not repaired, use a hotter plug.

CARBON FOULED
- Identified by black, dry fluffy carbon deposits on insulator tips, exposed shell surfaces and electrodes.
- Caused by too cold a plug, weak ignition, dirty air cleaner, too rich a fuel mixture or excessive idling. Can be cleaned.

LEAD FOULED
- Identified by dark gray, black, yellow or tan deposits or a fused glazed coating on the insulator tip.
- Caused by highly leaded gasoline. Can be cleaned.

WORN
- Identified by severely eroded or worn electrodes.
- Caused by normal wear. Should be replaced.

FUSED SPOT DEPOSIT
- Identified by melted or spotty deposits resembling bubbles or blisters.
- Caused by sudden acceleration. Can be cleaned.

OVERHEATING
- Identified by a white or light gray insulator with small black or gray brown spots and with bluish-burnt appearance of electrodes.
- Caused by engine overheating, wrong type of fuel, loose spark plugs, too hot a plug or incorrect ignition timing. Replace the plug.

PREIGNITION
- Identified by melted electrodes and possibly blistered insulator. Metallic deposits on insulator indicate engine damage.
- Caused by wrong type of fuel, incorrect ignition timing or advance, too hot a plug, burned valves or engine overheating. Replace the plug.

is not accurate enough in the low rpm range for this adjustment.

5. To check the timing on the *front* cylinder, perform the following:

    a. Connect a timing light according the manufacturer's instructions to one of the front spark plug leads.

    b. Start the engine and let it run at the idle speed listed in **Table 6**; aim the timing light at the alternator rotor (**Figure 114**) and pull the trigger.

    c. If the front cylinder's timing mark aligns with the index mark on the crankcase left-hand cover (**Figure 115**), the timing is correct.

    d. Shut off the engine and disconnect the timing light.

6. To check the timing on the *rear* cylinder, perform the following:

    a. Connect a timing light according the manufacturer's instructions to one of the rear spark plug leads.

    b. Start the engine and let it idle at the idle speed listed in **Table 6**; aim the timing light at the alternator rotor (**Figure 116**) and pull the trigger.

    c. If the rear cylinder's timing mark aligns with the index mark on the crankcase left-hand cover (**Figure 117**) the timing is correct.

    d. Shut off the engine and disconnect the timing light.

7. If either cylinder's timing is incorrect, refer to Chapter Eight and check the ignition components.

8. Disconnect the portable tachometer.

9. Inspect the O-ring perimeter seal (**Figure 118**) on the cover. Replace the gasket if it is damaged or starting to deteriorate.

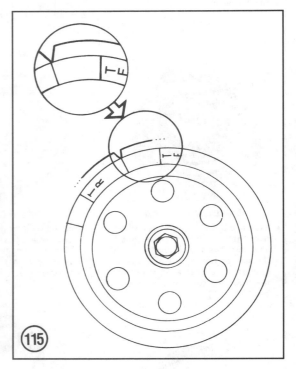

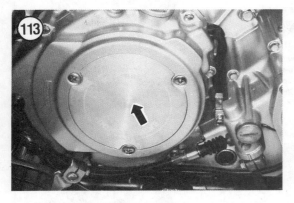

10. Make sure the O-rings (**Figure 119**) are in place on the screws. Install the pickup coil cover and screws. Tighten the screws securely.

Carburetor Idle Speed Adjustment

Prior to making this adjustment, the air filter elements must be clean and the engine must have adequate compression. See *Compression Test* in this chapter. Otherwise this procedure cannot be done properly.

1. Start and run the engine until it reaches normal operating temperature. Make sure the choke lever is in the open position, pushed in all the way forward toward the front of the bike (**Figure 120**).

2. Connect a portable tachometer following the manufacturer's instructions.

3. On the left-hand side of the bike, turn the idle adjust knob (**Figure 121**) in or out to adjust idle speed.

4. The correct idle speed is listed in **Table 6**.

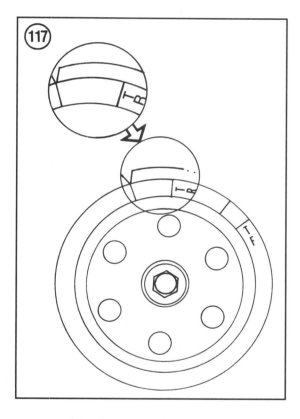

NOTE
The throttle linkage must stop against the idle adjust screw with the throttle in the completely closed position.

5. Open and close the throttle a couple of times; check for variations in idle speed. Readjust if necessary.

WARNING
*With the engine running at idle speed, move the handlebar from side to side. If the idle speed increases during this movement, the throttle cable may need adjusting or it may be incorrectly routed through the frame. Correct this problem immediately. Do **not** ride the bike in this unsafe condition.*

Carburetor Idle Mixture

The idle mixture (pilot screw) is preset at the factory and *is not to be reset*. Do not adjust the pilot screw unless the carburetors have been overhauled. If so, refer to Chapter Seven for service procedures.

Carburetor Synchronization

NOTE
Prior to synchronizing the carburetors, the air filters must be clean.

1. Warm the engine to normal operating temperature.
2. Check and if necessary, adjust the idle speed as described in this chapter. Shut off the engine.
3. Disconnect the vacuum lines from the carburetors.
4. Connect the vacuum lines from the carb-synch tool to the carburetor vacuum fittings, following the manufacturer's instructions. Be sure to route the vacuum lines to the correct cylinder. Balance the carb-synch tool at 1,000 rpm prior to starting this test following the manufacturer's instructions.
5. Start the engine and set the idle speed as specified in **Table 6**.

6. Check the gauge readings. If the difference in gauge readings is 12.7 kPa (2 cm Hg) or less between the 2 cylinders, the carburetors are considered synchronized.
7. If the carburetors are not synchronized, proceed as follows:

NOTE
To gain the utmost in performance and efficiency from the engine, adjust the carburetors so that the gauge readings are as close to each other as possible.

a. Continue to run the engine at idle speed.

NOTE
***Figure 122** is shown with the carburetor assembly removed for clarity. Do not remove the carburetor assembly for this procedure.*

b. Use a 7 mm wrench and turn the carburetor butterfly adjuster bolt (**Figure 122**).
c. Turning the bolt *in* will increase vacuum in the rear cylinder's carburetor.
d. Backing the bolt *out* will decrease vacuum in the rear cylinder's carburetor.
e. Reset the idle speed as listed in **Table 6** and shut off the engine.

8. Disconnect the carb-synch tool vacuum lines from the carburetors and reconnect the existing vacuum lines to the carburetors.
9. Install the vacuum port covers.

Table 1 MAINTENANCE SCHEDULE*

Prior to each ride	Inspect tires and rims and check inflation pressure
	Check steering for smooth operation
	with no excessive play or restrictions
	Check brake operation and for fluid leakage
	Check fuel supply. Make sure there is enough fuel
	for the intended ride
	Check for fuel leakage
	Check for coolant leakage
	Check all lights for proper operation
	Check engine oil level
	Check final drive oil level
	Check for smooth throttle operation
	Check gearshift pedal operation
	Check clutch operationand for fluid leakage
Initial 500 miles (800 km)	Replace engine oil and filter
	Clean oil screen
	Replace final drive oil
	Clean air filter elements
	Check engine idle speed; adjust if necessary
	Check carburetor synchronization; adjust if necessary
	Check evaporative emission control system**
	Check throttle grip free play; adjust if necessary
	Check clutch lever free play; adjust if necessary
	Check rear brake pedal free play; adjust if necessary
	Check fluid level in front brake master cylinder;
	add fluid if necessary
	Check rear brake light switch operation;
	adjust if necessary
	Check battery electrolyte level (more frequent
	in hot weather); add distilled water if necessary
	Inspect entire brake system
	Check all hoses--fuel, vacuum, emission,
	brake and coolant
	Check tightness of all fasteners
	Inspect steering for smooth operation;
	adjust if necessary
Every 3,100 miles (5,000 km)	Clean and inspect spark plugs; regap if necessary
	Check engine idle speed; adjust if necessary
	Check carburetor synchronization;
	adjust if necessary
	Check air suction valve***
	Check evaporative emission control system**
	Check clutch lever free play; adjust if necessary
	Inspect the brake pads and shoes for wear
	Check rear brake pedal free play;
	adjust if necessary
	Check fluid level in front brake master cylinder;
	add fluid if necessary
	Check rear brake light switch operation;
	adjust if necessary
	Inspect steering for smooth operation;
	adjust if necessary
	Check battery electrolyte level (more frequent in
	hot weather); add distilled water if necessary
	Check tire wear
	Lubricate all pivot points
	Lubricate control cables (throttle, choke,
	clutch, rear brake)

(continued)

Table 1 MAINTENANCE SCHEDULE* (continued)

Every 6,200 miles (10,000 km)	Clean and inspect spark plugs; regap if necessary
	Check engine idle speed; adjust if necessary
	Check carburetor synchronization; adjust if necessary
	Check air suction valve***
	Replace engine oil and filter
	Clean oil screen
	Check level of final drive oil; add oil if necessary
	Clean air filter elements
	Check engine idle speed; adjust if necessary
	Check carburetor synchronization; adjust if necessary
	Check fuel system for dirt or debris
	Check evaporative emission control system**
	Check throttle grip free play; adjust if necessary
	Check clutch lever free play; adjust if necessary
	Check rear brake pedal free play; adjust if necessary
	Check fluid level in front brake master cylinder; add fluid if necessary
	Check rear brake light switch operation; adjust if necessary
	Check battery electrolyte level (more frequent in hot weather); add distilled water if necessary
	Lubricate drive shaft
	Lubricate swing arm pivots
	Lubricate all pivot points
	Check tire wear
	Inspect entire brake system
	Check all hoses-- fuel, vacuum, emission, brake and coolant
	Check tightness of all fasteners
	Inspect steering for smooth operation; adjust if necessary
Every 12,400 miles (20,000 km) or every 2 years	Replace air filter elements (or after 5 cleanings)
	Drain and replace hydraulic brake fluid
	Drain and replace coolant
	Lubricate rear brake camshaft
	Lubricate steering stem bearings
	Replace rear brake cable
Every 30,000 miles (48,300 km) or every 2 years	Change the front fork oil
Every 4 years	Replace the brake hose
	Replace all coolant hoses
	Replace fuel lines

* This Kawasaki factory maintenance schedule should be considered as a guide to general maintenance and lubrication intervals. Harder than normal use and exposure to mud, water, sand, high humidity, etc. will naturally dictate more frequent attention to most maintenance items.
** California models only.
*** California and Switzerland models only.

Table 2 TIRE SIZE AND INFLATION PRESSURE (COLD)*

Tire	Size
Front	100/90-19H tubeless
Rear	150/90-15 74H, 150/90 B15 M/C 74H or 150/90-15 M/C 74H tubeless

(continued)

Table 2 TIRE SIZE AND INFLATION PRESSURE (COLD)* (continued)

| | Front | | Rear | |
Load	psi	kPa	psi	kPa
Up to 215 lbs (97.5 kg) U.S., Canada, Australia, South Africa models	28	200	28	200
215 to 406 lbs (97 to 184 kg) All other models	28	200	32	225
215 to 397 lbs (97 to 180 kg)	28	200	32	225

Tire Pressure

* Tire inflation pressure for factory equipped tires. Aftermarket tires may require different inflation pressure; refer to manufacturer's specifications.

Table 3 BATTERY STATE OF CHARGE

Specific gravity	State of charge
1.110-1.130	Discharged
1.140-1.160	Almost charged
1.170-1.190	One-quarter charged
1.200-1.220	One-half charged
1.230-1.250	Three-quarters charged
1.260-1.280	Fully charged

Table 4 RECOMMENDED LUBRICANTS AND FLUIDS

Fuel	
U.S. and Canada	Regular unleaded 87 [(R + M)/2 method] or 91 octane or higher
U.K. and all others	85-95 octane
Engine oil	
Grade	API SE or SF
Viscosity	SAE 10W/40, 10W/50, 20W/40 or 20W/50
Capacity	
Oil change only	3.6 L (3.8 U.S. qt. [3.16 Imp. qt.])
Change and filter	4.0 L (4.2 U.S. qt. [3.52 Imp. qt.])
Coolant	Ethylene glycol
Capacity at change	1.5 L (1.58 U.S. qt. [1.32 Imp. qt.])
Final drive oil	
Grade	GL-5 under API classification
Viscosity	
When above 5°C (41°F)	SAE 90 hypoid gear oil with
When below 5°C (41°F)	SAE 80 hypoid gear oil with
Capacity at change	150 ml (5.07 U.S. oz. [4.2 Imp. oz.])
Brake fluid	DOT 3
Battery refilling	Distilled water
Fork oil	
Viscosity	SAE 10W/20
Capacity per leg	
Oil change only	310-320 ml (10.48-10.82 U.S. oz. [8.73-9.0 Imp. oz.])
After disassembly	
U.S and Canadian models	359-364 ml (12.04-12.31 U.S. oz. [10.11-10.25 Imp. oz.])
All other models	370-375 ml (12.51-12.68 U.S. oz. [10.42-10.56 Imp. oz.])
Oil level each leg	
U.S. and Canadian models	220-240 mm (8.66-9.45 in.)
All other models	205-225 mm (8.07-8.86 in.)

(continued)

Table 4 RECOMMENDED LUBRICANTS AND FLUIDS (continued)

Fork oil (continued)	
Air pressure	
Standard	Atmospheric pressure
Usable range	0-49 kPa (0-7.1 psi)
Cables	Cable lube or SAE 10W/30 motor oil
Pivot points	SAE 10W/30 motor oil
Air filter oil	SAE 30

Table 5 MAINTENANCE AND TUNE UP TIGHTENING TORQUES

Item	N•m	ft.-lb.
Oil drain plug	18	13
Oil filter	18	13
Fork drain bolt	7.8	69 in.-lb.
Final drive unit drain bolt	20	14.5
Front brake caliper mounting bolts	32	24
Engine coolant drain plugs	8.8	78 in.-lb.
Radiator drain plug	2.9	26 in.-lb.
Thermostat housing bleed valve	7.8	69 in.-lb.

Table 6 TUNE-UP SPECIFICATIONS

Spark plug type	
Standard heat range	
U.S., Canadian, Australia, Italy, So. Africa models	NGK DP7EA-9, ND X22EP-U9
All other models	NGK DPR7EA-9, ND X22EPR-U9
Optional heat range	
U.S., Canadian, Australia, Italy, So. Africa models	NGK DP8EA-9, ND X24EP-U9
All other models	NGK DPR8EA-9, ND X24EPR-U9
Spark plug gap	0.8-0.9 mm (0.03-0.04 in.)
Idle speed	
Switzerland (1988-1989)	1,300 ±50 rpm
All other models	1,100 ±50 rpm
Cylinder compression	890-1,370 kPa (129-199 psi)

ENGINE

4

The engine is a V-twin liquid-cooled, 4-stroke design. The cylinders are offset and set at a 45° angle; the cylinders fire on alternate crankshaft rotations. Each cylinder is equipped with dual camshafts and 4 valves. The crankshaft is supported by 2 main bearings in a vertically split crankcase.

Both engine and transmission share a common case and the same wet sump oil supply. The clutch is a wet-type located on the right-hand side of the engine. Refer to Chapter Five for clutch and Chapter Six for transmission service procedures.

This chapter provides complete procedures and information for removal, inspection, service and reassembly of the engine.

> *NOTE*
> *Many of the upper end components on this engine are **almost** identical but slight variations do exist. These slight variations mean the component **must be installed** in the correct location—either on the front cylinder assembly or on the rear cylinder assembly. Where these similarities exist they are noted in the text and where it is necessary, mark the part with a "F" (front cylinder) or "R" (rear cylinder) to avoid confusion during assembly.*

Table 1 provides complete specifications for the engine and **Table 2** lists all of the engine torque specifications. **Tables 1-3** are located at the end of this chapter.

Before beginning work, re-read Chapter One in the front section of this book. You will do a better job with this information fresh in your mind.

ENGINE PRINCIPLES

Figure 1 explains how the engine works. This will be helpful when troubleshooting or repairing the engine.

SERVICING ENGINE IN FRAME

The following components can be serviced while the engine is mounted in the frame (the bike's frame is a great holding fixture for breaking loose stubborn bolts and nuts):

    a. Clutch (except for clutch outer housing).
    b. Carburetors.
    c. Starter motor.
    d. Alternator and electrical systems.

ENGINE

Removal/Installation

1. Place the bike on the centerstand on level ground.
2. Drain the engine oil and cooling system as described in Chapter Three.

① **4-STROKE ENGINE PRINCIPLES**

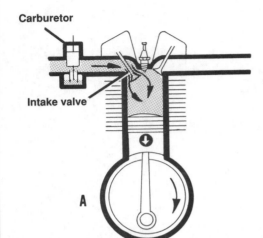

As the piston travels downward, the exhaust valve is closed and the intake valve opens, allowing the new air-fuel mixture from the carburetor to be drawn into the cylinder. When the piston reaches the bottom of its travel (BDC), the intake valve closes and remains closed for the next 1 1/2 revolutions of the crankshaft.

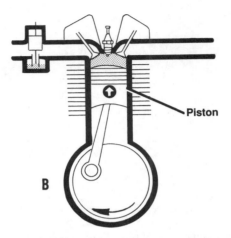

While the crankshaft continues to rotate, the piston moves upward, compressing the air-fuel mixture.

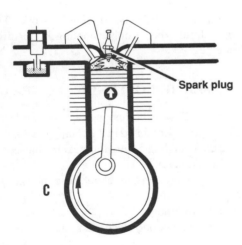

As the piston almost reaches the top of its travel, the spark plug fires, igniting the compressed air-fuel mixture. The piston continues to top dead center (TDC) and is pushed downward by the expanding gases.

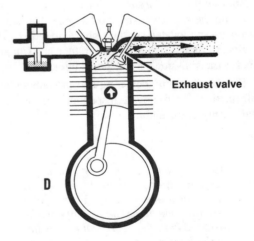

When the piston almost reaches BDC, the exhaust valve opens and remains open until the piston is near TDC. The upward travel of the piston forces the exhaust gases out of the cylinder. After the piston has reached TDC, the exhaust valve closes and the cycle starts all over again.

3. Remove the seat, both frame side covers and both frame head side covers as described in Chapter Thirteen.

4. Remove the fuel tank as described in Chapter Seven.

5. Remove the air filter assemblies and carburetor assembly as described in Chapter Seven. Move the throttle and choke cables out of the way.

6. Remove the radiator and fan assembly as described in Chapter Nine.

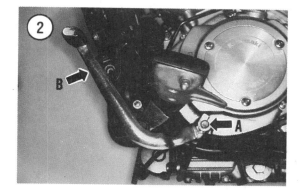

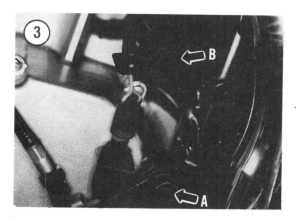

7. Remove the exhaust system as described in Chapter Seven.

8. On U.S. and Switzerland models, remove the left-hand air suction valve assembly and hose as described in Chapter Seven.

9. Disconnect the clutch cable from the release arm as described in Chapter Five. Move the cable out of the way.

10. Remove the front bevel gear case as described in this chapter.

11. Disconnect the spark plug leads from all 4 spark plugs. Move all 4 leads out of the way.

NOTE
After disconnecting the following electrical wires, move the loose ends out of the way and secure them to the frame. This will help to eliminate them catching on the engine assembly during removal from the frame.

12. Disconnect the following electrical wires from the engine:
   a. Starter motor.
   b. Alternator stator.
   c. Ignition pickup coils and ignition coils.
   d. Neutral switch.
   e. Oil pressure switch.
   f. Sidestand check switch.
   g. Engine ground.

13. Remove the bolt (A, **Figure 2**) securing the gearshift lever and remove the lever (B, **Figure 2**). Reinstall the bolt in the lever to avoid misplacing it.

14. Remove the rear brake pedal assembly (A, **Figure 3**) as described under *Rear Brake Pedal Removal/Installation* in Chapter Twelve.

15. Place wood block(s) and a small hydraulic jack under the engine to support it securely.

16. Take a final look all over the engine to make sure everything has been disconnected.

17. Make sure the hydraulic jack is still in place and supporting the engine securely.

CAUTION
The following steps require the aid of a helper to remove safely the engine assembly from the frame.

18. Loosen, but do not remove, all sub-frame and engine mounting bolts.

19. Remove the lower rear bolts (A, **Figure 4**) securing the frame sub-frame to the frame.

20. Remove the upper front bolts (**Figure 5**) securing the frame sub-frame to the frame.

21. Remove the frame sub-frame (B, **Figure 4**) from the frame.

22. Remove the front through bolt and nut (B, **Figure 3**).

23. On the right-hand side, perform the following:
   a. Remove the upper rear through bolt (A, **Figure 6**) and nut.
   b. Loosen the bolts (B, **Figure 6**) securing the engine upper rear bracket to the frame.
   c. Remove the engine bracket (C, **Figure 6**).

24. On the left-hand side, perform the following:
   a. Remove the nut (A, **Figure 7**) from the front through bolt.
   b. Remove the bolts (B, **Figure 7**) securing the engine bracket to the frame and remove the bracket (C, **Figure 7**).
   c. Remove the front through bolt (B, **Figure 3**).

25. Remove the lower rear through bolt (C, **Figure 4**) and nut.

26. Once again, check that everything has been disconnected from the engine.

27. Slowly move the engine forward and toward the right-hand side.

28. Slightly lower the engine on the jack and continue to move the engine forward and toward the right-hand side to clear the remaining frame members.

29. Take the engine to a workbench for further disassembly.

30. Install by reversing these removal steps while noting the following:

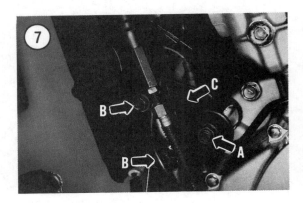

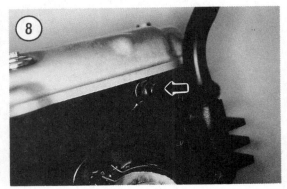

a. Route the air filter drain tube behind the sub-frame mounting bolts and nut and secure with a tie-wrap to keep the tube away from the rear exhaust pipe.

b. Tighten the engine mounting bolts to the torque specifications in **Table 2**.

c. Fill the engine with the recommended type and quantity of oil as described in Chapter Three.

d. Refill the cooling system as described in Chapter Three.

e. Start the engine and check for leaks.

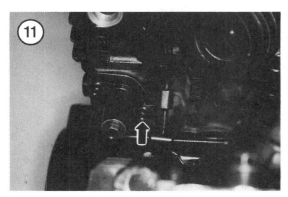

EXTERNAL OIL LINE

Removal

1. Remove the engine as described in this chapter.

2. Remove the union bolt securing the external oil line to the front cylinder head (**Figure 8**) and rear cylinder head (**Figure 9**). Don't lose the sealing washer on each side of the fitting.

3. Remove the front union bolt and oil pressure switch (**Figure 10**) as an assembly securing the external oil line to the crankcase. Don't lose the sealing washer on each side of the fitting.

4. Remove the bolt (**Figure 11**) securing the external oil line to the backside of the front cylinder.

> *NOTE*
> *The bolt (**Figure 12**) securing the external oil line to the alternator cover has had a non-hardening sealant applied to it and may be difficult to loosen.*

5. Remove the bolt (**Figure 12**) securing the external oil pipe to the alternator cover and remove the oil pipe assembly from the engine.

6. Inspect the external oil line assembly (**Figure 13**) for any dents or damage that may restrict oil flow. If damaged in any area, replace the oil line assembly.

Installation

1. Install the external oil line onto the engine, hold it in place and install the bolt (**Figure 11**) securing the external oil line to the cylinder. Tighten this bolt finger-tight at this time.

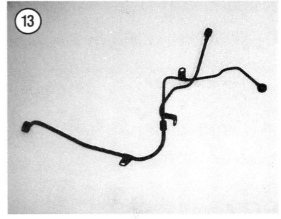

2. At the cylinder heads, install a new sealing washer (**Figure 14**) on each side of the external oil line fitting. Refer to **Figure 8** and **Figure 9**. Install the union bolts through the fittings and tighten to the torque specification listed in **Table 1**.

3. At the front of the crankcase, install a new sealing washer (**Figure 14**) on each side of the external oil line fitting, install the front union and oil pressure switch assembly (**Figure 10**) through the fitting and tighten to the torque specification listed in **Table 1**.

4. Tighten the bolts installed in Step 1 securely.

5. Apply a non-hardening sealant to the threads of the bolt (**Figure 12**) securing the external oil line to the alternator cover. Install the bolt and tighten securely.

6. Install the engine as described in this chapter.

CRANKCASE RIGHT-HAND SIDE COVER

Removal

1. Place the bike on the centerstand on level ground.

2. Drain the engine oil and cooling system as described in Chapter Three.

3. Remove the front exhaust pipe as described under *Exhaust System Removal/Installation* in Chapter Seven.

4. Remove the radiator cover (**Figure 15**).

5. Remove the lower right-hand bolt (**Figure 16**) securing the radiator to the sub-frame.

6. Remove the rear brake pedal assembly (A, **Figure 3**) as described under *Rear Brake Pedal Removal/Installation* in Chapter Twelve.

7. Remove the lower rear bolts (A, **Figure 4**) securing the frame sub-frame to the frame.

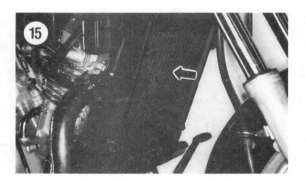

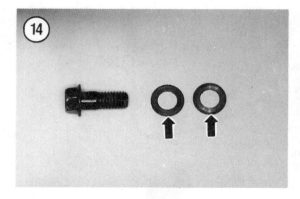

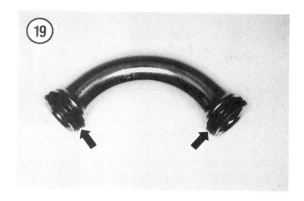

8. Remove the upper front bolts (**Figure 5**) securing the frame sub-frame to the frame.

9. Remove the frame sub-frame (B, **Figure 4**) from the frame.

NOTE
Figure 17 is shown with part of the clutch assembly removed for clarity. It is not necessary to remove the clutch assembly to remove the right-hand cover.

10. Remove the bolts securing the crankcase right-hand cover (A, **Figure 17**).

NOTE
If necessary, use the pry points (B, Figure 17) to work the cover loose from the crankcase.

11. Remove the cover and gasket. Work the coolant pipe free from the fitting on the crankcase (A, **Figure 18**). Don't lose the locating dowels in the crankcase.

12. Remove the coolant pipe from the cover and inspect the O-ring seals (**Figure 19**). Replace the O-rings if they are deteriorated or hard. Do not apply grease to the O-rings.

13. Install by reversing these removal steps while noting the following:

   a. Install the coolant pipe into the cover. Push it down until it bottoms out.

   b. If removed, install the front locating dowel (**Figure 20**) and rear locating dowel (**Figure 21**).

   c. Install a new gasket (**Figure 22**).

   d. Install the cover and insert the coolant pipe into the receptacle in the crankcase. Push the pipe in until it bottoms out.

   e. Install the cover bolts. Apply blue Loctite (No. 242) to the cover bolt (B, **Figure 18**) to the left of the coolant pipe.

   f. Tighten the sub-frame mounting bolts to the torque specifications in **Table 2**.

   g. Fill the engine with the recommended type and quantity of oil as described in Chapter Three.

   h. Refill the cooling system as described in Chapter Three.

   i. Start the engine and check for leaks.

CYLINDER HEAD AND CAMSHAFTS

Camshaft timing on this engine is different from other V-twin engines that are equipped with only 1 camshaft drive chain. Since the Vulcan engine has 2 camshaft drive chains, and an intermediate chain sprocket, all of the timing marks are not visible with the cylinder head installed on the cylinder block.

If the crankshaft *was rotated* after either the front or rear cylinder camshaft has been removed, so that either the front or rear cylinder is no longer at TDC on the compressions stroke, it will be necessary to remove the cylinder head for that specific cylinder to *properly re-time* the camshaft drive chain as described under *Camshaft Drive Chain Guides and Tensioner Assemblies* in this chapter. If the crankshaft *was not rotated* after the camshaft was re-

moved, camshaft installation can be accomplished without removal of the cylinder head.

Front Cylinder Head and Camshafts Removal

Refer to **Figure 23** for this procedure.

1. Remove the engine from the frame as described in this chapter.

2. Remove the external oil line assembly from the engine as described in this chapter.

3. Remove the bolts (A, **Figure 24**) securing the cylinder head cover. Don't lose the washer and rubber grommet in the cylinder cover mounting bolt holes.

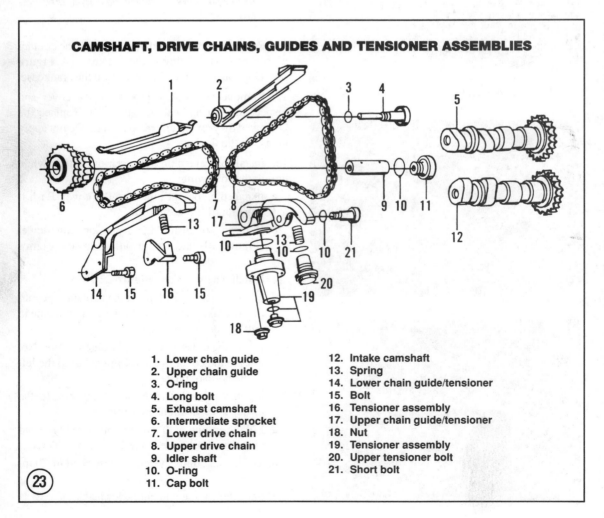

CAMSHAFT, DRIVE CHAINS, GUIDES AND TENSIONER ASSEMBLIES

1. Lower chain guide
2. Upper chain guide
3. O-ring
4. Long bolt
5. Exhaust camshaft
6. Intermediate sprocket
7. Lower drive chain
8. Upper drive chain
9. Idler shaft
10. O-ring
11. Cap bolt
12. Intake camshaft
13. Spring
14. Lower chain guide/tensioner
15. Bolt
16. Tensioner assembly
17. Upper chain guide/tensioner
18. Nut
19. Tensioner assembly
20. Upper tensioner bolt
21. Short bolt

(23)

NOTE
*The front cylinder head cover is **not** equipped with a heat shield.*

4. Remove the cylinder head cover and gasket (B, **Figure 24**).

5. Remove both spark plugs from both cylinder heads as described in Chapter Three. This will make it easier to rotate the engine.

6. Remove the bolts and O-rings (A, **Figure 25**) securing the alternator inner cover (B, **Figure 25**) and remove the cover and O-ring seal.

CAUTION
The next steps will position the front cylinder at top dead center (TDC) on the compression stroke. This is necessary to avoid damage to the camshafts, rocker arms and related parts.

7. Use a 17 mm socket and wrench on the alternator rotor bolt (**Figure 26**). Rotate the engine *counterclockwise*, as viewed from the left-hand side, until the front cylinder is at top dead center (TDC) on the compression stroke (**Figure 27**). Align the "TF" mark on the alternator rotor with the pointer on the alternator cover (**Figure 28**).

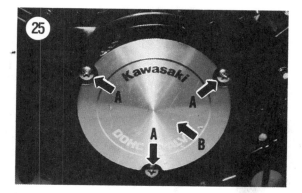

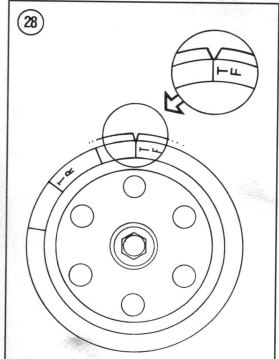

8. With the alternator rotor in this "TF" position, make sure that the index marks (A, **Figure 29**) on the front camshaft sprockets are aligned with the top surface of the cylinder head (B, **Figure 29**).

9. If the camshaft sprocket index marks are not aligned correctly, rotate the engine an additional 360° until the camshaft sprocket index marks are aligned correctly and the "TF" mark on the alternator rotor is still aligned with the pointer on the alternator cover (**Figure 28**).

10. When all marks are aligned the front cylinder is at TDC and the camshaft lobes are facing away from the rocker arms (**Figure 30**).

> *CAUTION*
> *Never partially loosen the camshaft chain tensioner mounting nuts and then retighten the nuts as the tensioner housing may have moved away from the cylinder head mounting surface as well as the camshaft chain. The tensioner pushrod is a non-return type and if the tensioner moves away from the camshaft chain, even the slightest amount, the internal pushrod will move out to take up this new slack. If the tensioner mounting nuts are then retightened with the pushrod extended this additional distance, it will place far greater pressure on the camshaft chain than specified. This increased pressure will lead to camshaft chain and tensioner damage. If the mounting nuts are loosened any amount, the tensioner assembly must be completely removed, the pushrod repositioned, the tensioner reinstalled and the nuts tightened.*

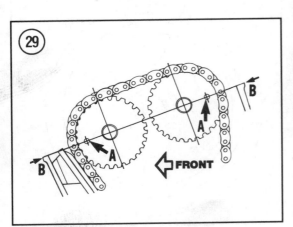

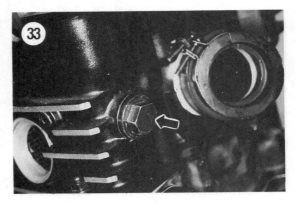

11. On the left-hand side, unscrew and remove the spark plug retainer (**Figure 31**). Use a thick 27 mm nut (A, **Figure 32**)inserted into the opening and 27 mm wrench (B, **Figure 32**), or the Kawasaki special tool (hexagonal wrench, part No. 57001-1210) or equivalent.

12. Remove the camshaft chain upper tensioner spring mounting bolt (**Figure 33**), O-ring seal and spring.

13. Loosen the camshaft chain tensioner cap bolt. It is not necessary to remove the bolt, only loosen it.

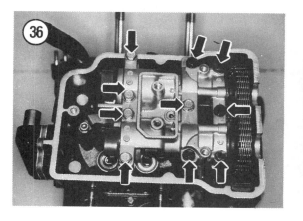

14. Remove the nuts (A, **Figure 34**) securing the camshaft chain tensioner assembly and remove the tensioner assembly and O-ring seal (B, **Figure 34**) from the cylinder block.

15. Remove the Phillips screws and remove the reservoir cover (**Figure 35**) and gasket.

16. Using a crisscross pattern, loosen the camshaft bearing cap mounting bolts (**Figure 36**) in 2-3 steps. Remove all bolts.

17. Remove the camshaft bearing cap. Don't lose the locating dowels.

18. Remove the valve lash adjuster oil filter spring (**Figure 37**).

19. To remove the oil filter from the receptacle in the cylinder head, perform the following:

   a. Place a finger over the oil galley hole to catch the oil filter as it comes out (A, **Figure 38**).

   b. Apply compressed air in short spurts, to the oil galley hole (B, **Figure 38**) and force the oil filter out of the hole.

   c. Discard the oil filter as a new one must be installed during installation.

NOTE
*The exhaust camshaft (A, **Figure 39**) is shorter than the intake camshaft (B, **Figure 39**).*

NOTE
*There is **no identifying groove** on the front cylinder head camshaft sprockets as there is on the rear cylinder camshafts. Make sure to install the correct set of camshafts into the correct cylinder head.*

20. Lift up on the left-hand end of the camshaft, disengage the sprocket from the camshaft upper chain and remove the exhaust camshaft (A, **Figure 40**) then remove the intake camshaft (B, **Figure 40**).

21. Let the camshaft upper chain fall into the cylinder head cavity. It will stop at the intermediate sprocket and will not fall into the crankcase.

22. Remove the camshaft upper chain guide and tensioner as described under *Camshaft Drive Chain Guides and Tensioner Assemblies* in this chapter.

NOTE
The rocker arms and hydraulic lash adjusters can remain in the cylinder head during cylinder head removal.

23. Loosen the cylinder head mounting bolts and nuts in the following order:

  a. The two external 6 mm nuts (**Figure 41**) securing the cylinder head to the cylinder block at the camshaft chain side.

  b. The two internal 6 mm bolts (A, **Figure 42**) securing the cylinder head to the cylinder block in the camshaft chain cavity.

  c. The two external 8 mm nuts securing the cylinder head to the cylinder block at the front (**Figure 43**) and rear (**Figure 44**).

  d. The four internal 10 mm nuts (B, **Figure 42**) securing the cylinder head to the crankcase studs.

24. Remove all bolts and nuts loosened in Step 22.

25. Loosen the cylinder head by tapping around the perimeter with a rubber or soft-faced mallet. If nec-

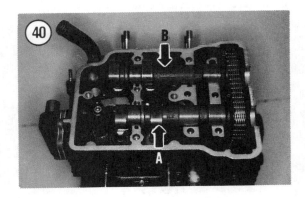

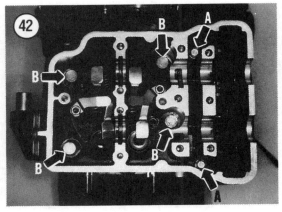

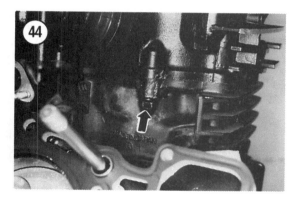

essary, *gently* pry the cylinder head loose with a broad-tipped screwdriver.

26. Pull the cylinder head (**Figure 45**) straight up and off the crankcase studs. Work the camshaft upper chain up through the chain cavity in the cylinder head.

27. Place the cylinder head on a clean surface on the work bench right side up.

CAUTION
If the crankshaft must be rotated with the camshafts removed, pull up on the camshaft upper chain and keep it taut, make certain that the upper camshaft chain is properly meshed onto the intermediate sprocket then rotate the crankshaft. If this step is not followed, the chain may become kinked and damage the camshaft chain, the intermediate sprocket and the crankcase.

28. Inspect the camshafts and cylinder head as described in this chapter.

Front Cylinder Head and Camshafts Installation

NOTE
*Step 1 is only necessary if the crankshaft has been rotated after the front camshafts and cylinder head were removed (front cylinder no longer at TDC on the compression stroke). If the engine has **not** been disturbed, the front cylinder will still be positioned at TDC on the compression stroke and Step 1 is not necessary. Proceed to Step 2.*

1. *If it is necessary* to place the front cylinder at TDC on the compression stroke, refer to *Camshaft Drive Chain Guides and Tensioner Assemblies-Front Cylinder Installation* in this chapter for correct camshaft drive chain timing procedure.

2. If removed, install the locating dowels (A, **Figure 46**) in the cylinder block.

3. Install a new cylinder head gasket (B, **Figure 46**) and make sure all holes are aligned correctly.

4. Carefully slide the cylinder head down the crankcase studs while guiding the camshaft upper chain up through the chain cavity in the cylinder head. Tie a piece of wire to the camshaft upper chain and attach it to the exterior of the engine.

5. Push the cylinder head down until it bottoms out.

6. Install all bolts and nuts securing the cylinder head to the cylinder block and tighten only finger-tight.

7. Tighten the cylinder head mounting bolts and nuts, to the torque specification listed in **Table 2**, in the following order:

   a. The four internal 10 mm nuts (B, **Figure 42**) securing the cylinder head to the crankcase studs. Use a crisscross pattern and tighten in 2-3 steps.

   b. The two external 8 mm nuts securing the cylinder head to the cylinder block at the front (**Figure 43**) and rear (**Figure 44**).

   c. The two internal 6 mm bolts (A, **Figure 42**) securing the cylinder head to the cylinder block in the camshaft chain cavity.

   d. The two external 6 mm nuts (**Figure 41**) securing the cylinder head to the cylinder block at the camshaft chain side.

8. Apply a light coat of molybdenum disulfide grease to the camshaft bearing surfaces in the cylinder head and camshaft bearing cap.

9. Install the camshaft upper chain guide and tensioner as described under *Camshaft Drive Chain Guides and Tensioner Assemblies* in this chapter.

10. Apply a light coat of molybdenum disulfide grease to the bearing surfaces and lobes of the camshaft.

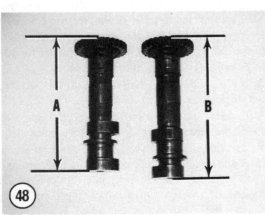

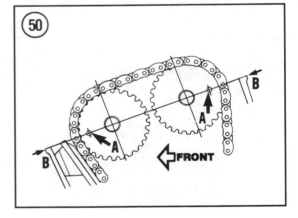

NOTE

*If both sets of camshafts have been removed, be sure to install the correct set of camshafts in the front cylinder head. There is **no** identifying radial groove on the front cylinder head camshaft sprockets (A, **Figure 47**) as there is a radial groove (B, **Figure 47**) on the rear cylinder camshafts.*

11. Untie the wire from the camshaft upper chain.

NOTE

*The exhaust camshaft (A, **Figure 48**) is shorter than the intake camshaft (B, **Figure 48**).*

12. Install the intake camshaft into the cylinder head.

13. Lift up on the camshaft upper chain.

14. Position the intake camshaft so the timing mark on the sprocket is directed *away* from the center of the cylinder head and is aligned with the top surface of the cylinder head (A, **Figure 49**), then mesh it properly with the camshaft upper chain.

15. Install the exhaust camshaft into the cylinder head.

16. Position the exhaust camshaft so the timing mark on the sprocket is directed *away* from the center of the cylinder head and is aligned with the top surface of the cylinder head (B, **Figure 49**).

17. Pull the camshaft upper chain taut over the intake camshaft sprocket and mesh it properly with the exhaust camshaft.

18. After both camshafts have been installed in the cylinder head, check that the timing marks (A, **Figure 50**) on both camshaft sprockets are still aligned with the top surface of the cylinder head (B, **Figure 50**). Readjust if necessary.

19. Install a new valve lash adjuster oil filter (**Figure 51**) and install the spring (**Figure 52**).

20. Make sure the locating dowels (**Figure 53**) are in place in the cylinder head.

21. Install the camshaft bearing cap (**Figure 54**) and bolts. After the bolts are installed, but not tightened, the bolt heads should all stick up above the bearing cap surface the same distance (**Figure 55**). If the bolts are in the wrong location, they should be repositioned.

22. Start in the center and use a crisscross pattern, to tighten the camshaft bearing cap mounting bolts (**Figure 56**) in 2-3 steps. Tighten to the torque specification listed in **Table 2**.
23. Fill the reservoir cavity in the camshaft bearing cap with clean engine oil (**Figure 57**).
24. Make sure the bleeder hole (A, **Figure 58**) in the reservoir cap is not clogged. Clean out if necessary.
25. Install a new gasket (B, **Figure 58**) on the reservoir cover.
26. Install the reservoir cover (**Figure 59**) and the Phillips screws. Tighten the screws securely.

CAUTION
*Do **not** install the camshaft chain tensioner until first repositioning the pushrod. The pushrod **must** be positioned all the way in (**Figure 60**) the housing prior to installation or severe damage will occur to the camshaft chain and the tensioner assembly.*

NOTE
*A small home-made special tool can be used to hold the tensioner pushrod in place during installation. The special tool can be made from a piece of 1.3 mm (0.05 in.) flat stock aluminum. Refer to **Figure 61** for dimensions of the tool.*

27. Reposition the pushrod within the camshaft chain tensioner and install it as follows:
  a. Inspect the housing base O-ring seal (**Figure 62**) and replace if necessary. Make sure it is in place and apply a light coat of clean engine oil to it.
  b. Insert a small thin flat-blade screwdriver (**Figure 63**) into the end of the tensioner assembly

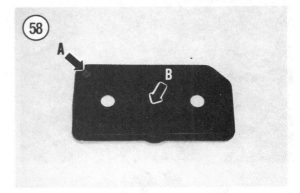

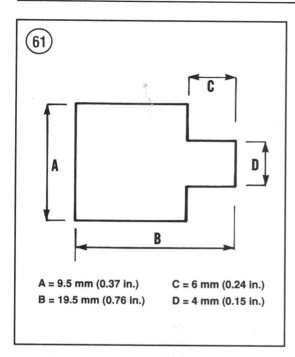

A = 9.5 mm (0.37 in.)   C = 6 mm (0.24 in.)
B = 19.5 mm (0.76 in.)   D = 4 mm (0.15 in.)

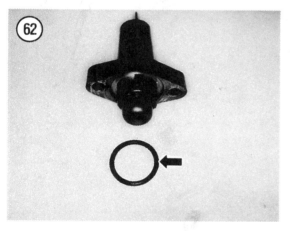

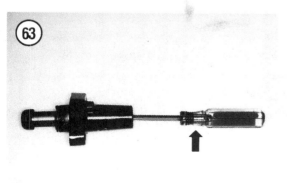

and turn it *clockwise* as viewed from the outer end of the housing. Rotate the screwdriver until the pushrod retracts completely into the housing.

c. Keep the pushrod in the retracted position, remove the screwdriver and insert the small home-made tool into the tensioner (**Figure 64**). This tool will hold the pushrod in the retracted position until the tensioner is completely installed in the cylinder block.

d. Install the tensioner (A, **Figure 65**) onto the cylinder block and push it on until it is against the cylinder block mounting surface.

NOTE
*In B, **Figure 65**, only one of the nuts is visible. Be sure to install and tighten both nuts.*

e. Hold the tensioner tight against the cylinder block, install and tighten both mounting nuts (B, **Figure 65**).

f. Tighten the nuts securely, then remove the special tool (C, **Figure 65**).

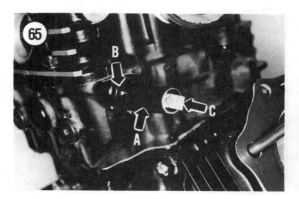

g. Install the O-ring and cap bolt onto the camshaft chain tensioner.

h. Tighten the cap bolt securely.

28. Inspect the camshaft chain upper tensioner O-ring seal (**Figure 66**) and replace if necessary. Make sure it is in place and apply a light coat of clean engine oil.

29. Install the camshaft chain upper tensioner spring (A, **Figure 67**) and the camshaft chain upper tensioner spring mounting bolt and O-ring seal (B, **Figure 67**). Tighten the bolt securely.

30. On the left-hand side, install the spark plug retainer (**Figure 68**). Apply clean engine oil to the O-ring seals (**Figure 69**) prior to installation. Use the same tool set-up used during removal and install the retainer. Tighten securely.

31. Install the alternator inner cover (A, **Figure 70**) and O-ring seal. Make sure O-ring seal (**Figure 71**) is correctly seated in the backside of the outer cover.

32. Be sure to install the small O-rings (**Figure 72**) to the bolts securing the alternator inner cover. If the

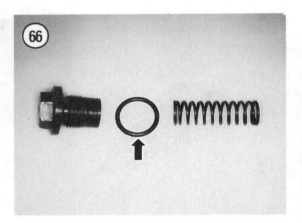

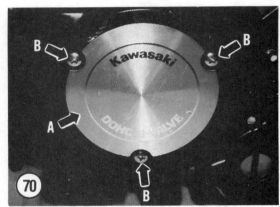

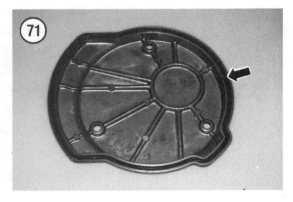

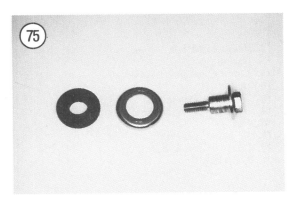

O-rings are left off, there will be an oil leak. Install the bolts (B, **Figure 70**) and tighten securely.

33. Install all 4 spark plugs as described in Chapter Three.

> *NOTE*
> *The front cylinder head cover is **not** equipped with a heat shield.*

34. Inspect the cylinder head cover rubber gasket (**Figure 73**) and replace if necessary.

35. Apply silicone sealant to the rubber gasket end plug receptacles (**Figure 74**) in the cylinder head.

36. Make sure the rubber grommets and washers (**Figure 75**) are in place on the cylinder head cover bolt holes.

37. Install the cylinder head cover (A, **Figure 76**) and bolts (B, **Figure 76**). Tighten the bolts securely.

38. If removed, install a new exhaust manifold gasket (**Figure 77**), then install the exhaust manifold

(A, **Figure 78**). Install the cap flange nuts (B, **Figure 78**) and tighten securely.

39. Install the external oil line assembly from the engine as described in this chapter.

40. Install the engine into the frame as described in this chapter.

Rear Cylinder Head and Camshafts Removal

Refer to **Figure 79** for this procedure.

1. Remove the engine from the frame as described in this chapter.

2. Remove the external oil line assembly from the engine as described in this chapter.

NOTE
*The rear cylinder head cover is equipped with a heat shield (**Figure 80**).*

3. Remove the bolts (A, **Figure 81**) securing the cylinder head cover. Don't lose the washer and rub-

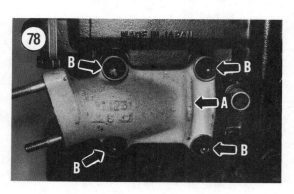

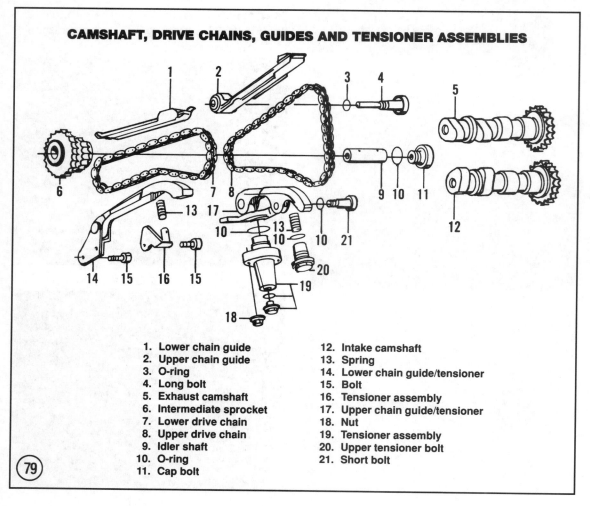

CAMSHAFT, DRIVE CHAINS, GUIDES AND TENSIONER ASSEMBLIES

1. Lower chain guide
2. Upper chain guide
3. O-ring
4. Long bolt
5. Exhaust camshaft
6. Intermediate sprocket
7. Lower drive chain
8. Upper drive chain
9. Idler shaft
10. O-ring
11. Cap bolt
12. Intake camshaft
13. Spring
14. Lower chain guide/tensioner
15. Bolt
16. Tensioner assembly
17. Upper chain guide/tensioner
18. Nut
19. Tensioner assembly
20. Upper tensioner bolt
21. Short bolt

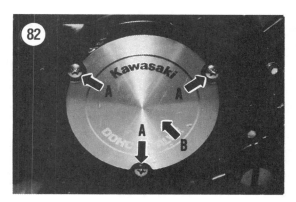

ber grommet in the cylinder cover mounting bolt holes.

4. Remove the cylinder head cover and gasket (B, **Figure 81**).

5. Remove both spark plugs from both cylinder heads as described in Chapter Three. This will make it easier to rotate the engine.

6. Remove the bolts and O-rings (A, **Figure 82**) securing the alternator inner cover (B, **Figure 82**) and remove the cover and O-ring seal.

> *CAUTION*
> *The next steps will position the rear cylinder at top dead center (TDC) on the compression stroke. This is necessary to avoid damage to the camshafts, rocker arms and related parts.*

7. Use a 17 mm socket and wrench on the alternator rotor bolt (**Figure 83**). Rotate the engine *counterclockwise*, as viewed from the left-hand side, until the rear cylinder is at top dead center (TDC) on the compression stroke. Align the "TR" mark on the alternator rotor (**Figure 84**) with the pointer on the alternator cover (**Figure 85**).

8. With the alternator rotor in this "TR" position, make sure that the index marks (A, **Figure 86**) on the rear camshaft sprockets are aligned with the top surface of the cylinder head (B, **Figure 86**).

9. If the camshaft sprocket index marks are not aligned correctly, rotate the engine an additional 360° until the camshaft sprocket index marks are aligned correctly and the "TR" mark on the alternator rotor is still aligned with the pointer on the alternator cover (**Figure 85**).

10. When all marks are aligned, the rear cylinder is at TDC and the camshaft lobes are facing away from the rocker arms (**Figure 87**).

11. Remove the camshaft chain upper tensioner spring mounting bolt and O-ring seal and spring (**Figure 88**).

> *CAUTION*
> *Never partially loosen the camshaft chain tensioner mounting nuts and then retighten the nuts as the tensioner housing may have moved away from the cylinder head mounting surface as well as the camshaft chain. The tensioner pushrod is a non-return type and if the tensioner moves off the camshaft chain, even the slightest amount, the internal pushrod will move out to take up this new slack. If the tensioner mounting nuts are then retightened with the push rod extended this additional distance, it will place far greater pressure on the camshaft chain than specified. This increased pressure will lead to camshaft chain and tensioner damage. If the mounting nuts are loosened any*

> *amount, the tensioner assembly must be completely removed, the pushrod repositioned, the tensioner reinstalled and the nuts tightened.*

12. Loosen the camshaft chain tensioner cap bolt (A, **Figure 89**). It is not necessary to remove the bolt, only loosen it.

> *NOTE*
> *In B, **Figure 89**, only one of the nuts is visible. Be sure to remove both nuts.*

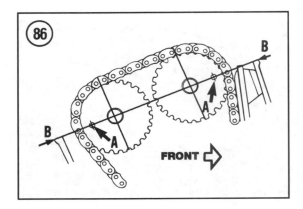

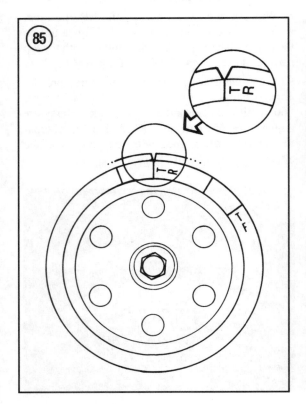

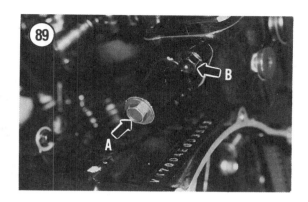

13. Remove the nuts (B, **Figure 89**) securing the camshaft chain tensioner assembly and remove the tensioner assembly and O-ring seal from the cylinder block.

14. On the right-hand side, remove the spark plug retainer (**Figure 90**). Use a thick 27 mm nut (A, **Figure 91**) and wrench (B, **Figure 91**), or the Kawasaki special tool (hexagonal wrench, part No. 57001-1210) or equivalent.

15. Remove the Phillips screws and remove the reservoir cover (A, **Figure 92**).

16. Using a crisscross pattern, loosen the camshaft bearing cap mounting bolts (**Figure 93**) in 2-3 steps. Remove all bolts.

17. Remove the camshaft bearing cap (B, **Figure 92**). Don't lose the locating dowels.

18. Remove the valve lash adjuster oil filter spring (**Figure 94**).

19. To remove the oil filter from the receptacle in the cylinder head, perform the following:

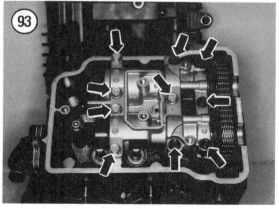

a. Place a finger over the oil galley hole to catch the oil filter as it comes out (A, **Figure 95**).

b. Apply compressed air in short spurts, to the oil galley hole (B, **Figure 95**) and force the oil filter out of the hole.

c. Discard the oil filter as a new one must be installed during assembly.

> *NOTE*
> *The exhaust camshaft (A, **Figure 96**) is shorter than the intake camshaft (B, **Figure 96**).*

> *NOTE*
> *There is an identifying radial groove (**Figure 97**) on the front cylinder head camshaft sprockets. Make sure to install the correct set of camshafts into the correct cylinder head.*

20. Lift up on the right-hand end of the camshaft, disengage the sprocket from the camshaft upper chain and remove the exhaust camshaft (**Figure 98**) then remove the intake camshaft (**Figure 99**).

21. Let the camshaft upper chain fall into the cylinder head cavity. It will stop at the intermediate sprocket and will not fall into the crankcase.

22. Remove the camshaft upper chain guide and tensioner as described under *Camshaft Drive Chain Guides and Tensioner Assemblies* in this chapter.

> *NOTE*
> *The rocker arms and hydraulic lash adjusters can remain in the cylinder head during cylinder head removal.*

23. Loosen the cylinder head mounting bolts and nuts in the following order:

a. The two external 6 mm nuts (**Figure 100**) securing the cylinder head to the cylinder block at the camshaft chain side.

b. The two internal 6 mm bolts (A, **Figure 101**) securing the cylinder head to the cylinder block in the camshaft chain cavity.

c. The two external 8 mm nuts securing the cylinder head to the cylinder block at the front (**Figure 102**) and rear (**Figure 103**).

d. The four internal 10 mm nuts (B, **Figure 101**) securing the cylinder head to the crankcase studs.

24. Remove all bolts and nuts loosened in Step 22.

25. Loosen the cylinder head by tapping around the perimeter with a rubber or soft-faced mallet. If nec-

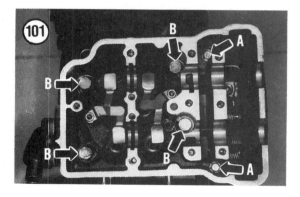

essary, *gently* pry the cylinder head loose with a broad-tipped screwdriver.

26. Pull the cylinder head straight up and off the crankcase studs. Work the camshaft upper chain up through the chain cavity in the cylinder head.

27. Place the cylinder head on a clean surface on the work bench right side up.

> *CAUTION*
> *If the crankshaft must be rotated with the camshafts removed, pull up on the camshaft upper chain and keep it taut, make certain that the upper camshaft chain is properly meshed onto the intermediate sprocket then rotate the crankshaft. If this step is not followed, the chain may become kinked and damage the camshaft chain, the intermediate sprocket and the crankcase.*

28. Inspect the camshafts and cylinder head as described in this chapter.

Rear Cylinder Head and Camshafts Installation

> *NOTE*
> *Step 1 is only necessary if the crankshaft has been rotated after the rear camshafts and cylinder head were removed (front cylinder no longer at TDC on the compression stroke). If the engine has* ***not*** *been disturbed, the rear cylinder will still be positioned at TDC on the compression stroke and Step 1 is not necessary. Proceed to Step 2.*

1. *If it is necessary* to place the rear cylinder at TDC on the compression stroke, refer to *Camshaft Drive*

Chain Guides and Tensioner Assemblies-Front Cylinder Installation in this chapter for correct camshaft drive chain timing procedure.

2. If removed, install the locating dowels (A, **Figure 104**) in the cylinder block.

3. Install a new cylinder head gasket (B, **Figure 104**) and make sure all holes are aligned correctly.

4. Carefully slide the cylinder head down the crankcase studs while guiding the camshaft upper chain up through the chain cavity in the cylinder head. Tie a piece of wire to the camshaft upper chain and attach it to the exterior of the engine.

5. Push the cylinder head down until it bottoms out.

6. Install all bolts and nuts securing the cylinder head to the cylinder block and tighten only finger-tight.

7. Tighten the cylinder head mounting bolts and nuts, to the torque specification listed in **Table 2**, in the following order:

    a. The four internal 10 mm nuts (B, **Figure 101**) securing the cylinder head to the crankcase

studs. Use a crisscross pattern and tighten in 2-3 steps.

    b. The two external 8 mm nuts securing the cylinder head to the cylinder block at the front (**Figure 102**) and rear (**Figure 103**).

    c. The two internal 6 mm bolts (A, **Figure 101**) securing the cylinder head to the cylinder block in the camshaft chain cavity.

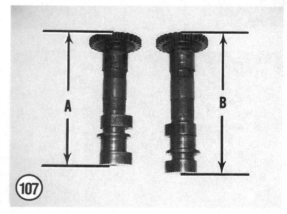

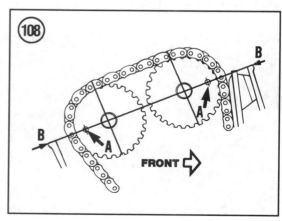

d. The two external 6 mm nuts (**Figure 100**) securing the cylinder head to the cylinder block at the camshaft chain side.

8. Install a new valve lash adjuster oil filter (**Figure 105**) and spring (**Figure 106**).

9. Install the camshaft upper chain guide and tensioner as described under *Camshaft Drive Chain Guides and Tensioner Assemblies* in this chapter.

10. Apply a light coat of molybdenum disulfide grease to the camshaft bearing surfaces in the cylinder head and camshaft bearing cap.

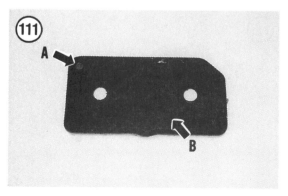

11. Apply a light coat of molybdenum disulfide grease to the bearing surfaces and lobes of the camshaft.

NOTE
*If both sets of camshafts have been removed, be sure to install the correct set of camshafts in the front cylinder head. There is an identifying groove (**Figure 97**) on the rear cylinder head camshaft sprockets.*

NOTE
*The exhaust camshaft (A, **Figure 107**) is shorter than the intake camshaft (B, **Figure 107**).*

12. Install the intake camshaft into the cylinder head.

13. Lift up on the camshaft upper chain.

14. Position the camshaft so the timing mark on the sprocket is directed *away* from the center of the cylinder head and is aligned with the top surface of the cylinder head, then mesh it properly with the camshaft upper chain (**Figure 99**).

15. Install the exhaust camshaft into the cylinder head.

16. Position the camshaft so the timing mark on the sprocket is directed *away* from the center of the cylinder head and is aligned with the top surface of the cylinder head.

17. Pull the camshaft upper chain taut over the intake camshaft sprocket and mesh it properly with the exhaust camshaft (**Figure 98**).

18. After both camshafts have been installed in the cylinder head, check that the timing marks (A, **Figure 108**) on both camshaft sprockets are still aligned with the top surface of the cylinder head (B, **Figure 108**). Readjust if necessary.

19. Make sure the locating dowels (**Figure 109**) are in place in the cylinder head.

20. Install the camshaft bearing cap (B, **Figure 92**) and bolts.

21. Starting in the center of the bearing cap and using a crisscross pattern, tighten the camshaft bearing cap mounting bolts (**Figure 93**) in 2-3 steps. Tighten to the torque specification listed in **Table 2**.

22. Fill the reservoir cavity in the camshaft bearing cap with clean engine oil (**Figure 110**).

23. Make sure the bleeder hole (A, **Figure 111**) in the reservoir cap is not clogged. Clean out if necessary.

24. Install a new gasket (B, **Figure 111**) on the reservoir cover.

25. Install the reservoir cover (A, **Figure 92**) and the Phillips screws. Tighten the screws securely.

CAUTION
*Do **not** install the camshaft chain tensioner until first repositioning the pushrod. The pushrod **must** be positioned all the way in (**Figure 112**) the housing prior to installation or severe damage will occur to the camshaft chain and the tensioner assembly.*

NOTE
A small home-made special tool can be used to hold the tensioner pushrod in

*place during installation. The special tool can be made from a piece of 1.3 mm (0.05 in.) flat stock aluminum. Refer to **Figure 113** for dimensions of the tool.*

26. Reposition the pushrod within the camshaft chain tensioner and install it as follows:

a. Inspect the housing base O-ring seal (**Figure 114**) and replace if necessary. Make sure it is in

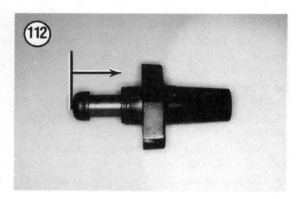

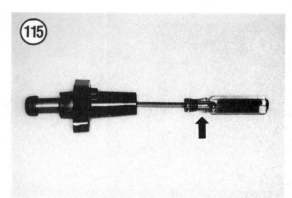

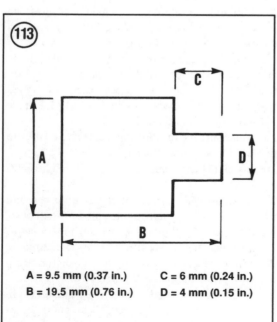

A = 9.5 mm (0.37 in.)   C = 6 mm (0.24 in.)
B = 19.5 mm (0.76 in.)   D = 4 mm (0.15 in.)

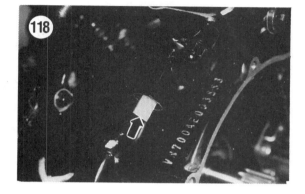

place and apply a light coat of clean engine oil to it.

b. Insert a small thin flat-blade screwdriver (**Figure 115**) into the end of the tensioner assembly and turn it *clockwise* as viewed from the outer end of the housing. Rotate the screwdriver until the pushrod retracts completely into the housing.

c. Keep the pushrod in the retracted position, remove the screwdriver and insert the small home-made tool into the tensioner (**Figure 116**). This tool will hold the pushrod in the retracted position until the tensioner is completely installed in the cylinder block.

d. Install the tensioner (A, **Figure 117**) onto the cylinder block and push it on until it is against the cylinder block mounting surface.

e. Hold the tensioner tight against the cylinder block, install and tighten the mounting nuts (B, **Figure 117**).

f. Tighten the nuts securely, then remove the special tool (**Figure 118**).

g. Install the O-ring (**Figure 119**) and cap bolt onto the camshaft chain tensioner.

h. Tighten the cap bolt (**Figure 88**) securely.

27. Inspect the camshaft chain upper tensioner O-ring seal (**Figure 120**) and replace if necessary. Make sure it is in place and apply a light coat of clean engine oil.

28. Install the camshaft chain upper tensioner spring (A, **Figure 121**) and the camshaft chain upper tensioner spring mounting bolt and O-ring seal (B, **Figure 121**). Tighten the bolt securely.

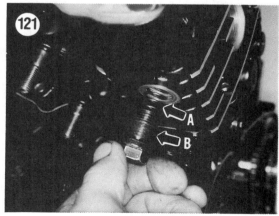

29. On the right-hand side, install the spark plug retainer (**Figure 122**). Apply clean engine oil to the O-ring seals (**Figure 123**) prior to installation. Use the same tool set-up used during removal and install the retainer. Tighten securely.

30. Install the alternator inner cover (A, **Figure 124**) and O-ring seal. Make sure the O-ring seal (**Figure 125**) is correctly seated in the backside of the outer cover.

31. Be sure to install the small O-rings (**Figure 126**) to the bolts securing the alternator inner cover. If the O-rings are left off, there will be an oil leak. Install the bolts and tighten securely.

32. Install all 4 spark plugs as described in Chapter Three.

33. Inspect the cylinder head cover rubber gasket (**Figure 127**) and replace if necessary.

NOTE
*The rear cylinder head cover is equipped with a heat shield (**Figure 128**).*

34. Apply silicone sealant to the end plug receptacles (**Figure 129**) in the cylinder head.

35. Make sure the rubber grommets and washers are in place on the cylinder head cover bolt holes.

36. Install the cylinder head cover (A, **Figure 130**) and bolts (B, **Figure 130**). Tighten the bolts securely.

37. If removed, install a new exhaust manifold gasket (**Figure 131**), then install the exhaust manifold (A, **Figure 132**) and heat shield (B, **Figure 132**). Install the cap flange nuts (**Figure 133**) and tighten securely.

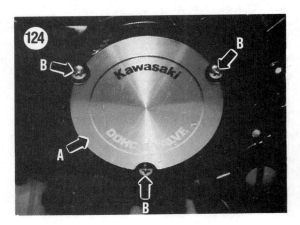

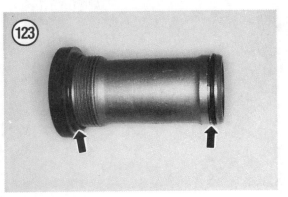

38. Install the external oil line assembly from the engine as described in this chapter.

39. Install the engine into the frame as described in this chapter.

CYLINDER HEAD AND COVER INSPECTION

1. Remove the rocker arms and hydraulic lash adjusters as described in this chapter.

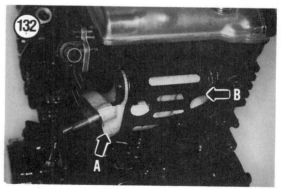

2. Remove all traces of gasket material from the cylinder head-to-cylinder block (**Figure 134**) mating surfaces. Do not scratch the gasket surface.

3. Clean off any silicone sealer residue from the cam bore notches (A, **Figure 135**) on the upper surface of the cylinder head.

4. *Without removing the valves,* remove all carbon deposits from the combustion chamber (A, **Figure 136**) and valve ports with a wire brush. A blunt screwdriver or chisel may be used if care is taken not to damage the head, valves and spark plug threads.

5. Examine the spark plug threads (B, **Figure 136**) in the cylinder head for damage. If damage is minor or if the threads are dirty or clogged with carbon, use a spark plug thread tap to clean the threads following the manufacturer's instructions. If thread damage is severe, refer further service to a dealer or competent machine shop.

6. Inspect the O-ring seals (**Figure 123**) on the spark plug retainer. Replace the O-rings if they are starting to deteriorate or harden.

7. Clean the entire head in solvent after removing carbon from the combustion chamber and the valve port and after repairing the spark plug threaded holes (if required). Blow dry with compressed air.

8. Clean all carbon from the piston crown. Do not remove the carbon ridge from the top of the cylinder bore.

9. Check for cracks in the combustion chamber and exhaust port (A, **Figure 137**). A cracked head must be replaced.

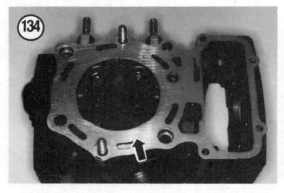

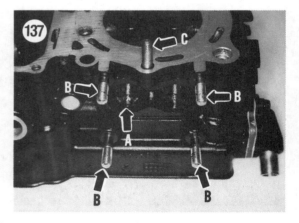

10. Inspect the threads on the exhaust manifold threaded studs (B, **Figure 137**) for damage. Clean up with an appropriate size metric die if necessary. Make sure the studs are tightly secured into the cylinder head.

11. Inspect the camshaft bearing area (B, **Figure 135**) in the cylinder head for damage, wear or burrs. Clean up if damage is minimal; replace cylinder head and cylinder head cover as a set if necessary.

12. Inspect the decorative cooling fins (A, **Figure 138**) for cracks or damage. The fins are minimal but they can still be damaged.

13. Inspect the threads on the short threaded studs for damage. Refer to B, **Figure 138** and C, **Figure 137**. Clean up with an appropriate size metric die if necessary. Make sure the studs are tightly secured into the cylinder head.

14. After the head has been thoroughly cleaned, place a straightedge across the cylinder head/cylinder block gasket surface at several points. Measure the warp by inserting a flat feeler gauge between the straightedge and the cylinder head at several locations (**Figure 139**). Maximum allowable warpage is 0.010 in. (0.25 mm). If warpage exceeds this limit, the cylinder head must be replaced.

15. Inspect the valves and valve guides as described in this chapter.

16. Inspect the exhaust manifolds for cracks or damage. Refer to **Figure 140** for the front manifold and **Figure 141** for the rear manifold. Replace if necessary.

17. Inspect the exhaust manifold studs for damage. Refer to **Figure 142** for the front manifold and **Figure 143** for the rear manifold. Clean up with an appropriate size metric die if necessary.

18. Inspect the rear exhaust manifold heat shield (**Figure 144**) for damage, replace if necessary.

19. Inspect the cylinder head gasket in the area of the camshaft bore cutout fillers (**Figure 145**). These fillers are fragile and may have cracks that would lead to an oil leak. Replace the gasket if necessary.

20. Inspect the camshaft bearing area (**Figure 146**) in the cylinder head cover for damage, wear or burrs. Clean up if damage is minimal. They should not be scored or excessively worn. Replace the cylinder

head and camshaft bearing cap as a set, if the bearing surfaces are worn or scored.

21. Inspect the cylinder head cover (**Figure 147**) for damage, wear or burrs. Clean up damage if it is minimal; replace cylinder head cover and cylinder head as a set if necessary.

22. Install the rocker arms and hydraulic lash adjusters as described in this chapter.

23. Repeat for the other cylinder head.

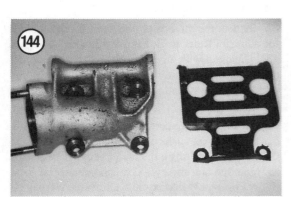

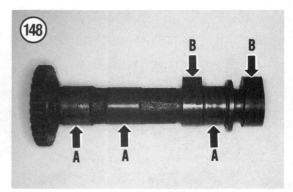

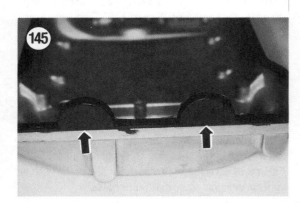

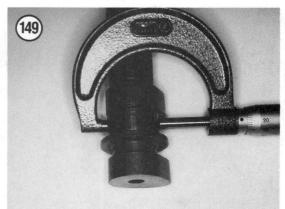

CAMSHAFT INSPECTION

1. Inspect the camshaft bearing journals (A, **Figure 148**) for wear.

2. Measure all camshaft bearing journals (**Figure 149**) with a micrometer. Compare to the dimensions given in **Table 1**. If worn to the service limit or less, the camshaft must be replaced.

3. Check the camshaft lobes (B, **Figure 148**) for wear. The lobes should show no signs of scoring and the edges should be square. Slight damage may be removed with a silicone carbide oilstone. Use No. 100-120 grit stone initially, then polish with a No. 280-320 grit stone.

4. Even though the camshaft lobe surface appears to be satisfactory, with no visible signs of wear, the camshaft lobes must be measured with a micrometer (**Figure 150**). Compare to the dimensions given in **Table 1**. If worn to the service limit or less the camshaft must be replaced.

5. Inspect the camshaft end-float locating boss (**Figure 151**) for wear or damage. If worn or damaged, replace the camshaft.

6. Inspect the camshaft sprocket teeth (**Figure 152**) for wear; replace if necessary.

Camshaft Bearing Clearance Measurement

This procedure requires the use a Plastigage set. The camshaft must be installed into the cylinder head. Before installing the camshaft, wipe all oil residue from the camshaft bearing journals and bearing surfaces in the cylinder head and camshaft bearing cap.

1. Install both camshafts (A, **Figure 153**) into the cylinder head with the lobes facing up. Do not attach the drive sprocket to the camshafts.

2. Make sure the locating dowels (B, **Figure 153**) are in place in the cylinder head.

3. Place a strip of Plastigage material on top of each camshaft center and end bearing journals, parallel to the camshaft.

4. Install the camshaft bearing cap (**Figure 154**).

5. Install the bolts (**Figure 155**) securing the camshaft bearing cap.

6. Tighten the bolts in a crisscross pattern, starting with the center bolts (surrounding the camshaft) and working outward. Tighten in 2-3 stages to the torque specification listed in **Table 2**.

> *CAUTION*
> *Do not rotate the camshafts with the Plastigage material in place.*

7. Loosen the camshaft bearing cap in 2-3 stages in a crisscross pattern, then remove the bolts.

8. Carefully remove the camshaft bearing cap.

9. Measure the width of the flattened Plastigage material at the widest point, according to the manufacturer's instructions.

> *CAUTION*
> *Be sure to remove all traces of Plastigage material from the bearing journals in the cylinder head and camshaft bearing cap. If any material is left in the engine it can plug up an oil control orifice and cause severe engine damage.*

10. Remove *all* Plastigage material from the camshafts.

11. If the oil clearance is greater than specified in **Table 1**, and the camshaft bearing journal outside diameter dimensions were within specification in *Camshaft Inspection*, perform the following:

  a. Remove the camshafts from the cylinder head.

  b. Install the camshaft bearing cap.

  c. Install the bolts securing the camshaft bearing cap.

  d. Tighten the bolts in a crisscross pattern, starting with the center bolts (surrounding the camshaft) and working outward. Tighten in 2-3 stages to the torque specification listed in **Table 2**.

  e. Measure the camshaft bearing inside diameter with a bore gauge (**Figure 156**) at all bearing surface locations (**Figure 157**). Compare the dimensions given in **Table 1**. If worn to the service limit or greater, replace the cylinder head and camshaft bearing cap as a set.

  f. Remove the bolts and the camshaft bearing cap.

ROCKER ARM AND HYDRAULIC LASH ADJUSTER ASSEMBLIES

Removal

> *NOTE*
> *All rocker arms are identical, they all have the same part number. The hydrau-*

lic lash adjusters are also identical, they also having the same part number. It is suggested that the rocker arms and lash adjusters be reinstalled in the same location in the cylinder heads. This is especially true on an engine with high mileage as parts tend to take on a "wear pattern" making it more important that they be reinstalled in the original location in the cylinder heads to reduce the possibility of premature wear.

1. Remove the engine as described in this chapter.

2. Remove the cylinder head and camshafts as described in this chapter.

NOTE
The rocker arm retaining springs are different in length. The short spring is adjacent to the camshaft sprockets.

3. Remove the Allen bolts (A, **Figure 158**) securing the rocker arm retaining springs (B, **Figure 158**). Remove the springs and the rocker arms (**Figure 159**). Keep the rocker arms in the same order so they will be reinstalled in the same location in the cylinder head.

CAUTION
Do not bang or drop the lash adjusters during removal and installation as the internal plunger may be damaged.

4. Use your fingers, *not pliers*, and remove the hydraulic lash adjusters (**Figure 160**) from the cylinder head and store them in an upright position. Keep the lash adjusters in the same order so they will be reinstalled in their original receptacle in the cylinder head.

5. Repeat for the other cylinder head if necessary.

6. Inspect all parts as described in this chapter.

Installation

1. Make sure the hydraulic lash receptacles in the cylinder head are free of dirt and lint (from a shop cloth). They must be completely free of any debris.

2. Fill the hydraulic lash adjuster receptacles in the cylinder head with clean engine oil.

3. Bleed the hydraulic lash adjuster as described in this chapter.

4. Hold the hydraulic lash adjuster upright and coat the exterior of each hydraulic lash adjuster with clean engine oil.

> *NOTE*
> *The hydraulic lash adjusters are identical. Be sure to reinstall them in their original location in the cylinder head. If installing new lash adjusters, they can be installed in any location.*

5. Keep the hydraulic lash adjuster upright and install it into the receptacle in the cylinder head.
6. Install all 4 lash adjusters (**Figure 160**).
7. Coat the rocker arms with clean engine oil.

> *NOTE*
> *The rocker arms are identical. Be sure to reinstall them in their original location in the cylinder head. If installing new rocker arms, they can be installed in any location.*

8. Install each rocker arm onto the hydraulic lash adjuster and the valve stem. Install all 4 rocker arms (**Figure 159**).

> *NOTE*
> *The rocker arm retaining springs are different in length. The short spring must be installed on the set of valves adjacent to the camshaft sprockets.*

9. Install the springs (B, **Figure 158**) and Allen bolts (A, **Figure 158**) securing the rocker arms in place. Tighten the bolts securely.
10. Repeat for the other cylinder head if necessary.
11. Install the cylinder head and camshafts as described in this chapter.
12. Install the engine as described in this chapter.

Rocker Arm Inspection

1. Wash all parts in solvent and thoroughly dry with compressed air.
2. Inspect the rocker arm socket (A, **Figure 161**) where it rides on the hydraulic lash adjuster. If the socket is scratched or unevenly worn, inspect the hydraulic lash adjuster for scoring or damage. Replace the rocker arm if defective as well as the hydraulic lash adjuster if it is damaged.
3. Inspect the rocker arm pad where it rides on the cam lobe (A, **Figure 162**) and where the adjusters

ride on the valve stem (B, **Figure 161**). If the pad is scratched or unevenly worn, inspect the camshaft lobe for scoring, chipping or flat spots. Replace the rocker arm if defective as well as the camshaft if it is damaged.

4. Check the overall condition of the rocker arm for fractures, wear or damage (B, **Figure 162**); replace if necessary.

Hydraulic Lash Adjuster Inspection

> *NOTE*
> *Kawasaki does not provide any new or service limit dimension for the hydrau-*

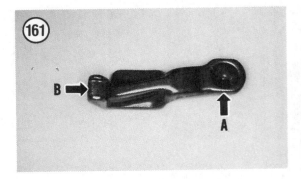

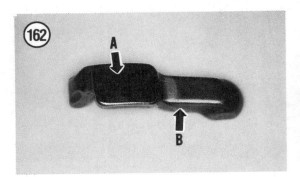

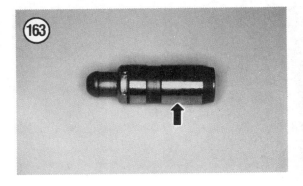

lic lash adjuster outer diameter nor the inner diameter of the lash adjuster receptacle in the cylinder head. If either part shows signs of wear, distortion or damage; replace the worn part(s).

1. Inspect the exterior of the lash adjuster (**Figure 163**) for wear or damage; replace if necessary.

2. Inspect the receptacles in the cylinder head for wear or damage; replace the cylinder head if necessary.

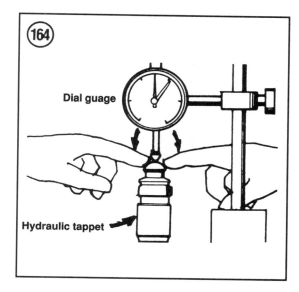

Dial guage

Hydraulic tappet

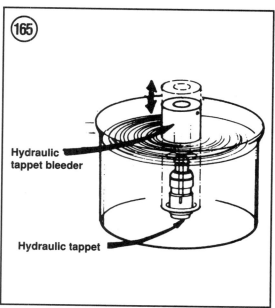

Hydraulic tappet bleeder

Hydraulic tappet

3. Measure the leak-down distance of the lash adjuster as follows:
   a. Bleed the lash adjuster as described in this chapter.
   b. Remove the lash adjuster from the container used for bleeding.
   c. Keep the lash adjuster upright and place it on a flat surface and under a dial gauge.
   d. Zero the dial gauge.
   e. While keeping the lash adjuster upright, try to compress quickly the lash adjuster with your fingers (**Figure 164**).
   f. You should be able to compress the lash adjuster 0-0.2 mm (0-0.0078 in.). If it compresses more than the specified dimension, repeat the bleeding procedure and recheck. If the dimension is still exceeded, the lash adjuster must be replaced.

4. If the lash adjuster is okay, bleed it again prior to installation. After bleeding, keep the lash adjuster upright so the kerosene does not leak out. If the kerosene leaks out, air will enter the high pressure chamber and the lash adjuster must be re-bled.

Hydraulic Lash Adjuster Bleeding

For proper operation, the hydraulic lash adjuster must be free of air in the high pressure chamber. A special Kawasaki tool, Tappet Bleeder (part No. 57001-1200) or an improvised tool set-up may be used.

1. Remove the hydraulic lash adjuster from the cylinder head as described in this chapter.

2. Fill a wide mouth transparent plastic or glass jar with clean kerosene. Fill the jar with enough kerosene so the tappet is completely covered.

> *CAUTION*
> *The lash adjuster must be kept submerged and upright during this procedure.*

3A. If the special tool is used, perform the following:
   a. Place the lash adjuster right side up within the special tool.
   b. Place the special tool and lash adjuster into the jar filled with clean kerosene.
   c. Hold the lash adjuster and special tool upright, push down on the special tool and pump the lash adjuster as shown in **Figure 165**.

d. Continue to pump until air bubbles stop coming from the high pressure chamber in the lash adjuster.

3B. If the special tool is not available, perform the following:

a. Insert a small drift into the hole in the top of the lash adjuster.

b. Place the lash adjuster and small drift into the jar filled with clean kerosene (**Figure 166**).

c. Hold the lash adjuster and small drift upright, push down on the small drift and pump the lash adjuster as shown in **Figure 167**.

d. Continue to pump (**Figure 168**) until air bubbles stop coming from the high pressure chamber in the lash adjuster.

NOTE
The small amount of kerosene left in the high pressure chamber of the lash adjuster will not contaminate the engine's oil. The high pressure chamber must remain filled with the kerosene.

4. Use a pencil magnet (**Figure 169**) and remove the lash adjuster from the jar filled with kerosene and keep the lash adjuster in the *upright position*. If the lash adjuster is laid down on an angle or on its side, air will enter the high pressure chamber and the lash adjuster will have to be bled again. Remove the small drift.

5. Reinstall the lash adjuster into the correct receptacle in the cylinder head as described in this chapter.

6. Repeat for all remaining lash adjusters.

VALVES AND VALVE COMPONENTS

General practice among those who do their own service is to remove the cylinder heads and take them to a machine shop or dealer for inspection and service. Since the cost is relative to the required effort and equipment, this is the best approach even for the experienced mechanics.

This procedure is included for those who chose to do their own valve service.

Refer to **Figure 170** for this procedure.

Valve Removal

1. Remove the cylinder head(s) as described in this chapter.

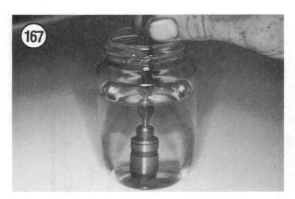

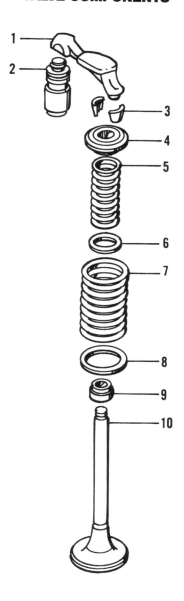

VALVE COMPONENTS

1. Rocker arm
2. Hydraulic lash adjuster
3. Valve keeper
4. Valve spring retainer
5. Inner coil spring
6. Inner coil spring seat
7. Outer coil spring
8. Outer coil spring seat
9. Oil seal
10. Valve

2. Remove the rocker arms and hydraulic lash adjusters as described in this chapter.

CAUTION
To avoid loss of spring tension, do not compress the springs any more than necessary to remove the keepers.

3. Compress the valve springs with a valve compressor tool (**Figure 171**). Remove the valve keepers and release the compression. Remove the valve compressor tool.

4. Remove the valve spring retainer and the outer and inner valve springs.

5. Prior to removing the valve, remove any burrs from the valve stem (**Figure 172**). Otherwise the valve guide will be damaged.

6. Remove the valve.

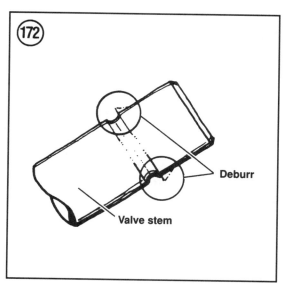

Deburr

Valve stem

7. Remove the oil seal and spring seats from the valve guide.

8. Repeat Steps 3-7 for the remainder of valves requiring service.

9. Mark all parts (**Figure 173**) as they are disassembled so that they will be installed in their same locations. The exhaust valves are adjacent to the exhaust port and the intake valves are located next to the intake pipe.

Valve Inspection

1. Clean the valves with a soft-wire brush and solvent.

2. Inspect the contact surface of each valve (**Figure 174**) for burning or pitting. Unevenness of the contact surface is an indication that the valve is not serviceable. The valve contact surface *cannot* be ground and must be replaced if defective.

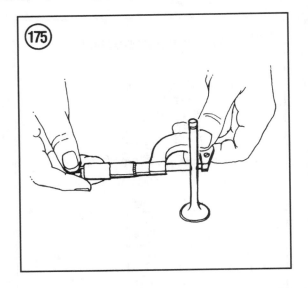

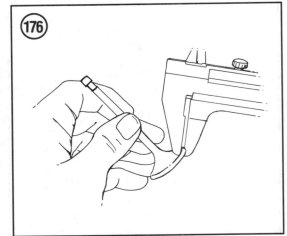

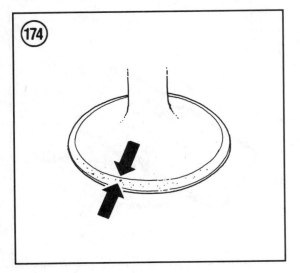

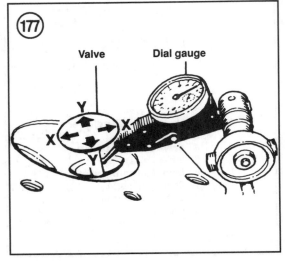

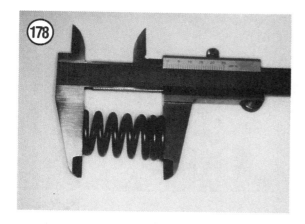

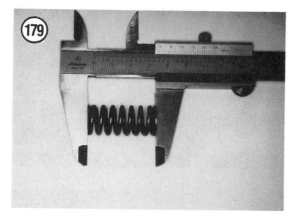

3. Measure each valve stem for wear (**Figure 175**). If worn smaller than the wear limit listed in **Table 1**, the valve must be replaced.

4. Measure each valve seating face for wear (**Figure 176**). If worn beyond the wear limit listed in **Table 1**, the valve must be replaced.

5. Remove all carbon and varnish from each valve guide with a stiff spiral wire brush.

6. To measure valve stem-to-valve guide clearance with the wobble or tilt method, perform the following:

   a. Insert a *new* valve in a guide.

   b. Hold the valve with the head just slightly off the valve seat and rock it sideways in 2 directions, "X" and "Y," perpendicular to each other as shown in **Figure 177**.

   c. If the valve-to-valve guide clearance measured exceeds the limit listed in **Table 1**, replace the valve guide.

7. Measure each valve spring free length with a vernier caliper. Refer to **Figure 178** for the outer spring and **Figure 179** for the inner spring. All should be within the length specified in **Table 1** with no signs of bends or distortion (**Figure 180**). Replace defective springs in pairs (inner and outer).

8. Check the valve spring retainer and valve keepers. If they are in good condition, they may be reused; replace as necessary.

9. Inspect the valve seats (**Figure 181**) in the cylinder head. If worn or burned, they must be reconditioned as described in this chapter.

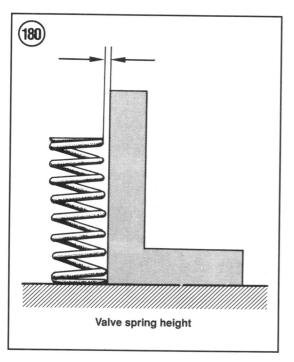

Valve spring height

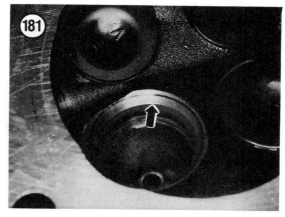

Valve Installation

1. If removed, install a new seal on each valve guide and push it down until it is seated (**Figure 182**).

2. Install the inner spring seat (**Figure 183**) and push it down until it bottoms (**Figure 184**).

3. Install the inner spring seat (**Figure 185**) and push it down until it bottoms (**Figure 186**).

4. Position the valve springs with their closer wound coils (**Figure 187**) facing the cylinder head.

5. Install the inner valve spring (**Figure 188**) and the outer valve spring (**Figure 189**) with their closer wound coils facing the cylinder head.

6. Coat the valve stems with molybdenum disulfide grease. To avoid damage to the valve stem seal, turn the valve slowly while inserting the valve into the cylinder head. Push the valve all the way in until it closes.

7. Position the valve spring retainer with the small shoulder side (**Figure 190**) facing the valve springs and install the valve spring retainer (**Figure 191**) on top of the valve springs.

> *CAUTION*
> *To avoid loss of spring tension, do not compress the springs any more than necessary to install the keepers.*

8. Compress the valve springs with a compressor tool (**Figure 171**).

9. Apply a small amount of cold grease to the valve keeper and install both keepers. Refer to **Figure 192** and **Figure 193**. Make sure the keepers fit snug into the rounded groove in the valve stem.

10. Remove the compression tool.

11. After all springs have been installed, gently tap the end of the valve stem with a soft aluminum or

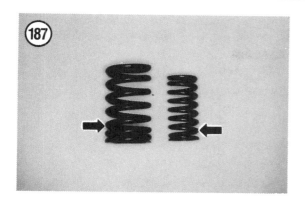

brass drift and hammer. This will ensure that the keepers are properly seated.

12. Repeat for all valve assemblies and for the other cylinder head if necessary.

13. Install the cylinder head(s) as described in this chapter.

Valve Guide Replacement

When valve guides are worn so that there is excessive valve stem-to-guide clearance or valve tip-

4

ping, the guides must be replaced. This job should only be done by a dealer as special tools are required as well as considerable expertise. If the valve guide is replaced; also replace the respective valve.

The following procedure is provided if you choose to perform this task yourself.

> *CAUTION*
> *There **may** be a residual oil or solvent odor left in the oven after heating the cylinder head. If you use a household oven; first check with the person who uses the oven for food preparation to avoid getting into trouble.*

1. If still installed, remove the screws securing the intake pipe (**Figure 194**) onto the cylinder head.

2. If still installed, remove the bolt (A, **Figure 195**) securing the coolant fitting (B, **Figure 195**) to the cylinder head and remove the fitting and O-ring seal.

3. If the air suction reed valve assembly is still installed on the cylinder head, remove it as follows:

    a. Remove the bolts securing the reed valve cover (A, **Figure 196**) to the cylinder head and remove the cover (B, **Figure 196**).

    b. Remove the outer gasket and reed valve (**Figure 197**) from the cylinder head. Discard the gasket.

    c. Remove the inner gasket (**Figure 198**) from the cylinder head. Discard the gasket.

4. The valve guides (**Figure 199**) are installed with a slight interference fit. Place the cylinder head in a heated oven (or on a hot plate). Heat the cylinder head to a temperature between 120-150° C (248-302° F). An easy way to check the proper temperature is to drop tiny drops of water on the cylinder head; if they sizzle and evaporate immediately, the temperature is correct.

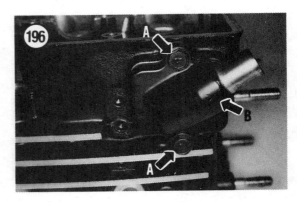

CAUTION
Do not heat the cylinder head with a torch (propane or acetylene)or bring any flame into contact with the cylinder head or valve guide. The direct heat will destroy the case hardening of the valve guide and may warp the cylinder head.

5. Remove the cylinder head from the oven and hold onto it with kitchen pot holders, heavy gloves or heavy shop cloths—*it is very hot.*

6. While heating up the cylinder head, place the new valve guides in a freezer (or refrigerator) if possible. Chilling them will slightly reduce their overall diameter while the hot cylinder head is slightly larger due to heat expansion. This will make valve guide installation much easier.

7. Turn the cylinder head upside down on wood blocks. Make sure the cylinder is properly supported on the wood blocks.

8. From the combustion chamber side of the cylinder head, drive out the old valve guide with a hammer and valve guide arbor (**Figure 200**). Use

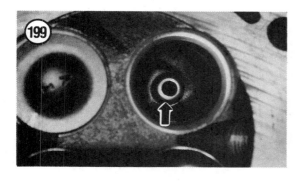

Kawasaki special tool, Valve Guide Arbor (part No. 57001-1021). Remove the special tool.

9. Remove and discard the valve guide. *Never* reinstall a valve guide that has been removed as it is no longer true nor within tolerances.

10. Inspect the valve guide receptacle in the cylinder head for damage. Check for any burrs that may hinder installation of the new valve guide. Carefully remove any burrs.

CAUTION
Failure to apply fresh engine oil to both the valve guide and the valve guide hole in the cylinder head will result in damage to the cylinder head and/or the new valve guide.

11. Apply fresh engine oil to the new valve guide and the valve guide receptacle in the cylinder head.

NOTE
The same tool is used for removal and installation of the valve guide. The same valve guide (same part No.) is used for both intake and exhaust valves.

12. From the top side (valve spring side) of the cylinder head, use Kawasaki special tool, Valve Guide Arbor (part No. 57001-1021) and a hammer to drive in the new valve guide. Drive the guide in until the valve guide shoulder is against the cylinder head, then remove the special tool.

13. After installation, ream the new valve guide as follows:

  a. Use Kawasaki special tool, Valve Guide Reamer (part No. 57001-1079) and thread tap handle (**Figure 201**).

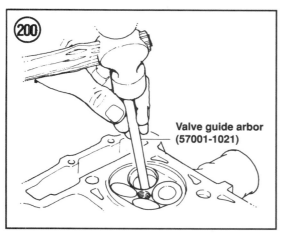

Valve guide arbor
(57001-1021)

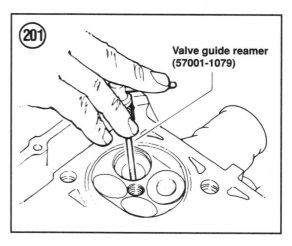

Valve guide reamer
(57001-1079)

b. Apply cutting oil to both the new valve guide and the valve guide reamer.

CAUTION
Always rotate the valve guide reamer clockwise. If the reamer is rotated counterclockwise, damage to a good valve guide will occur.

c. Rotate the reamer *clockwise*. Continue to rotate the reamer and work it down through the entire length of the new valve guide. Apply additional cutting oil during this procedure.

d. Rotate the reamer *clockwise* until the reamer has traveled all the way through the new valve guide.

e. Rotate the reamer *clockwise*, while withdrawing the reamer from the valve guide.

14. If necessary, repeat Steps 1-13 for any other valve guides.

15. Thoroughly clean the cylinder head and valve guides with solvent to wash out all metal particles. Dry with compressed air.

16. Reface the valve seats as described in this chapter.

17. Position the reed valve assembly with the reed stopper side going in first and with the raised end of the stopper facing toward the front of the bike (**Figure 202**).

18. Place a new gasket on each side of the reed valve and install these parts into the receptacle in the cylinder head.

19. Hold these parts in place, position the reed valve cover with the hose fitting facing toward the rear of the bike and install the cover.

20. Install the bolts securing the assembly and tighten securely.

NOTE
*Canadian models omit the red valve assembly. **Only** a blanking plate and gasket are used.*

21. Install the intake pipe. To prevent a vacuum leak, install a new O-ring seal into the groove in the intake pipe. Install the intake pipes and tighten the screws securely.

22. Install a new O-ring seal into the backside of the coolant fitting and install the fitting (B, **Figure 195**) onto the cylinder head. Tighten the bolt (A, **Figure 195**) securely.

Valve Seat Inspection

1. Remove the valves as described in this chapter.

2. An accurate method for testing if the valve closes completely is by using Prussian Blue or machinist's

dye, available from auto parts stores or machine shops. To check the valve seal with Prussian Blue or machines's dye, proceed as follows:

a. Thoroughly clean off all carbon deposits from the valve face with solvent or detergent, then thoroughly dry.

b. Spread a thin layer of Prussian Blue or machinist's dye evenly on the valve face.

c. Moisten the end of a suction cup valve tool (**Figure 203**) and attach it to the valve. Insert the valve into the guide.

d. Using the suction cup tool, tap the valve up and down in the cylinder head. Do *not* rotate the valve or a false indication will result.

e. Remove the valve and examine the impression left by the Prussian Blue or machinist's dye. If the impression left in the dye (on the valve or in the cylinder head) is not even and continuous or the valve seat width (**Figure 204**) is not within specified tolerance listed in **Table 1**, the cylinder head valve seat must be reconditioned.

3. Closely examine the valve seat (**Figure 181**) in the cylinder head. It should be smooth and even with a polished seating surface.

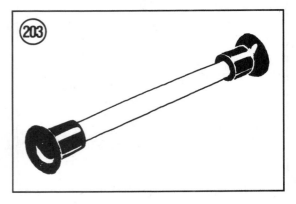

4. If the valve seat is okay, install the valves as described in this chapter.

5. If the valve seat is not correct, recondition the valve seat as described in this chapter.

Valve Seat Reconditioning

Special valve cutter tools and considerable expertise are required to recondition properly the valve

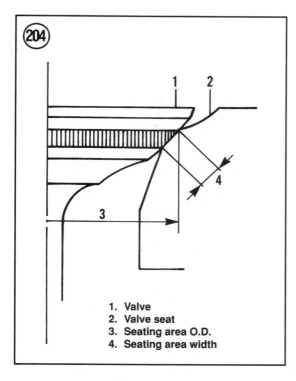

1. Valve
2. Valve seat
3. Seating area O.D.
4. Seating area width

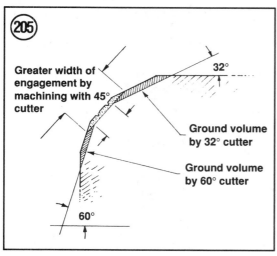

seats in the cylinder heads. You can save considerable money by removing the cylinder heads and taking just the cylinder heads to a dealer or machine shop and have the valve seats ground.

The following procedure is provided if you choose to perform this task yourself.

The following tools will be required:

a. Valve seat cutters (see Kawasaki dealer for part numbers).
b. Vernier caliper.
c. Machinist's blue.
d. Valve lapping stick.

The valve seat for both the intake valves and exhaust valves are machined to the same angles. The valve contact surface is cut to a 45° angle and the area above the contact surface (closest to the combustion chamber) is cut to a 32° angle (**Figure 205**).

1. Install a 45° cutter onto the valve tool and light cut the seat to remove roughness and clean the valve seat with one or two turns (**Figure 205**). See **Figure 206**.

> *CAUTION*
> *Measure the valve seat contact area in the cylinder head after each cut to make sure the contact area is correct and to prevent removing too much material. If too much material is removed, the cylinder head must be replaced.*

2. If the seat is still pitted or burned, turn the 45° cutter additional turns until the surface is clean.

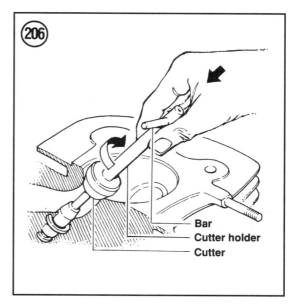

Bar
Cutter holder
Cutter

Refer to the previous CAUTION to avoid removing too much material from the cylinder head.

3. Measure the seat width with a vernier caliper. Record the measurement to refer to when performing the following.

4. Remove the 45° cutter and install the 32° cutter onto the valve tool and lightly cut the seat to remove 1/4 of the existing valve seat.

CAUTION
The 60° cutter removes material quickly. Work carefully and check your progress often.

5. Remove the 32° cutter and install the 60° cutter onto the valve tool and lightly cut the seat to remove the lower 1/4 of the existing valve seat.

NOTE
The 32° and 60° cutters are used to make the 45° seat a consistent width around the entire surface. Differences in seat width create uneven cooling of the valves and can lead to valve warpage. The 32° and 60° cutters are also used to shift the 45° seat up and down, depending on readings taken with machinist's blue.

6. Measure the valve seat with a vernier caliper. If necessary, fit the 45° cutter onto the valve tool and cut the valve seat to the specified seat width listed in **Table 1**.

CAUTION
*Do **not** use any valve lapping compound after the final cut has been made.*

7. Check that the finish has a smooth and velvety surface, it should *not* be shiny or highly polished. The final seating will take place when the engine is first run.

8. Repeat Steps 1-6 for all remaining valve seats.

9. Thoroughly clean the cylinder head and all valve components in solvent or detergent and hot water.

10. Install the valve assemblies as described in this chapter and fill the ports with solvent to check for leaks. If any leaks are present, the valve seats must be inspected for foreign matter or burrs that may be preventing a proper seal.

11. If the cylinder head and valve components were cleaned in detergent and hot water, apply a light coat of engine oil to all bare metal steel surfaces to prevent any rust formations.

CYLINDER BLOCK

Front and Rear Cylinder Block Removal

NOTE
Removal is basically the same for both the front and rear cylinder block. Where differences occur they are noted.

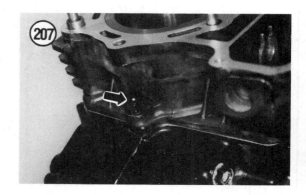

1. Remove the cylinder head and camshafts as described in this chapter.

2. Remove the camshaft chains, intermediate sprocket, guide and tensioner as described under *Camshaft Drive Chain Guides and Tensioner Assemblies* in this chapter.

3A. On the front cylinder block, remove the cap nut (**Figure 207**) at the front of the cylinder block.
3B. On the rear cylinder block, remove the cap nut (**Figure 208**) at the rear of the cylinder block.

4. Remove the nuts (**Figure 209**) located in the camshaft chain cavity of the cylinder block.

CAUTION
Remember the small cooling fins are fragile and may be damaged if tapped or pried too hard. Never use a metal hammer.

5. Loosen the cylinder block (**Figure 210**) by tapping around the perimeter base of the cylinder block with a rubber or soft-faced mallet. If necessary, *gently* pry the cylinder block loose from the crankcase with a broad-tipped screwdriver.

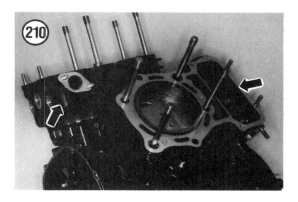

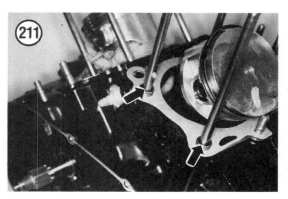

6. Remove the cylinder base gasket and discard it. Don't lose the locating dowels.
7. Place a clean shop cloth into the openings in the crankcase to prevent the entry of foreign matter.
8. Repeat for the other cylinder block.
9. Inspect the cylinder block as described in this chapter.

Front Cylinder Block Installation

1. If used, remove the clean shop cloth from the openings in the crankcase opening.
2. Apply a liberal coat of clean engine oil to the cylinder wall especially at the lower end where the piston will be entering.
3. Also apply clean engine oil to the piston and piston rings. This will make it easier to guide the piston into the cylinder bore.
4. Check that the top surface of the crankcase and the bottom surface of the cylinder are clean prior to installing a new base gasket.
5. If removed, install the locating dowels (**Figure 211**).
6. Install a new cylinder base gasket (**Figure 212**).
7. Make sure the end gaps of the piston rings are *not* lined up with each other—they must be staggered. Lubricate the piston rings and the inside of the cylinder bore with assembly oil or fresh engine oil.

NOTE
*The cylinder blocks are **almost** identical and can accidentally be installed in the wrong location on the crankcase. The camshaft chain tensioner receptacle in the cylinder block **must face toward the***

rear of the crankcase as shown in Figure 213.

8. Position the cylinder block with the camshaft chain tensioner receptacle face toward the rear of the crankcase. Move the cylinder block into position on the crankcase studs.

NOTE
On models so equipped, make sure the rubber plug (A, Figure 214) is in place in the crankcase.

9. Start the cylinder block down over the piston (B, **Figure 214**) while you compress each piston ring with your fingers as it enters the cylinder (**Figure 215**).

10. Slide the cylinder block down (**Figure 216**) until it bottoms out on the crankcase (**Figure 217**).

11. Install the nuts (**Figure 218**) located in the camshaft chain cavity of the cylinder block.

12. Install the cap nut (**Figure 207**) at the front of the cylinder block.

13. Tighten the nuts, installed in Step 11 and Step 12, in 2-3 stages to the torque specification listed in **Table 2**.

14. Install the camshaft chains, intermediate sprocket, guide and tensioner as described under *Camshaft Drive Chain Guides and Tensioner Assemblies* in this chapter.

15. Install the cylinder head and camshafts as described in this chapter.

Rear Cylinder Block Installation

1. If used, remove the clean shop cloth from the openings in the crankcase opening.

2. Apply a liberal coat of clean engine oil to the cylinder wall especially at the lower end where the piston will be entering.

3. Also apply clean engine oil to the piston and piston rings. This will make it easier to guide the piston into the cylinder bore.

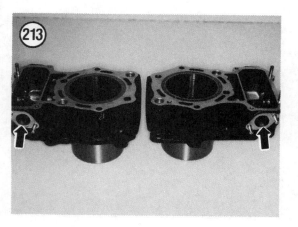

4. Check that the top surface of the crankcase and the bottom surface of the cylinder are clean prior to installing a new base gasket.

5. If removed, install the locating dowels (**Figure 219**).

6. Install a new cylinder base gasket.

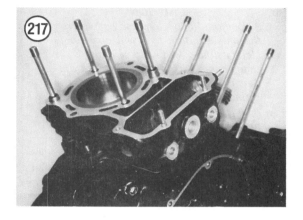

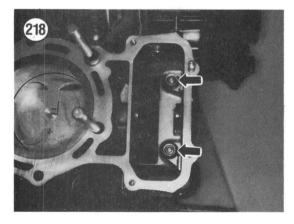

7. Make sure the end gaps of the piston rings are *not* lined up with each other—they must be staggered. Lubricate the piston rings and the inside of the cylinder bore with assembly oil or fresh engine oil.

NOTE
*The cylinder blocks are **almost** identical and can accidentally be installed in the wrong location on the crankcase. The camshaft chain tensioner receptacle in the cylinder block **must face toward the rear of the crankcase** as shown in Figure 213.*

8. Position the cylinder block with the camshaft chain tensioner receptacle (A, **Figure 220**) facing toward the rear of the crankcase. Move the cylinder block into position on the crankcase studs (B, **Figure 220**).

9. Start the cylinder block down over the piston and compress each piston ring with your fingers as it enters the cylinder.

10. Slide the cylinder block down until it is against the crankcase (**Figure 210**).

11. Install the nuts (**Figure 209**) located in the camshaft chain cavity of the cylinder block.

12. Install the cap nut (**Figure 208**) at the rear of the cylinder block.

13. Tighten the nuts, installed in Step 11 and Step 12, in 2-3 stages to the torque specification listed in **Table 2**.

14. Install the camshaft chains, intermediate sprocket, guide and tensioner as described under *Camshaft Drive Chain Guides and Tensioner Assemblies* in this chapter.

15. Install the cylinder head and camshafts as described in this chapter.

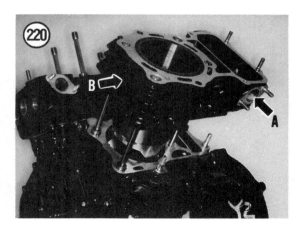

Cylinder Block
Inspection

1. Soak old cylinder head gasket material from the cylinder using solvent. Refer to **Figure 221** and **Figure 222**. Use a broad-tipped *dull* chisel and gently scrape off all gasket residue. Do not gouge the sealing surface as oil, coolant and air leaks will result.

2. Measure the cylinder bore with a cylinder gauge (**Figure 223**) or inside micrometer at the points "A," "B" and "C" shown in **Figure 224**.

3. Measure in 2 axes—in line with the piston-pin and at 90° to the pin. If the taper or out-of-round is 0.004 in. (0.10 mm) or greater, the cylinder must be rebored to the next oversize and a new piston and rings installed. Rebore both cylinders even if only one is worn.

NOTE
The new pistons should be obtained before the cylinders are rebored so that the pistons can be measured; slight manufacturing tolerances must be taken into account to determine the actual size and working clearance. Piston-to-cylinder wear limit is listed in **Table 1**.

NOTE
The maximum wear limit of the cylinder is listed in **Table 1**. *If the cylinder is worn to this limit, it must be replaced. Never rebore a cylinder if the finished rebore diameter will be this dimension or greater.*

4. If the cylinders are not worn past the service limit, thoroughly check the bore surface (**Figure 225**) for scratches or gouges. If damaged in any way, the cylinder will require boring and reconditioning.

5. If the cylinders require reboring, remove all dowel pins from the cylinders and take them to a dealer or machine shop for service.

6. After the cylinders have been serviced, perform the following:

CAUTION
A combination of soap and hot water is the only solution that will completely clean cylinder walls. Solvent and kerosene cannot wash fine grit out of cylinder crevices. Any grit left in the cylinders will act as a grinding compound and cause premature wear to the new rings.

a. Wash each cylinder bore with hot soapy water. This is the only way to clean the cylinders of the fine grit material left from the bore and honing procedure.

b. Also wash out any fine grit material from the cooling cores surrounding each cylinder.

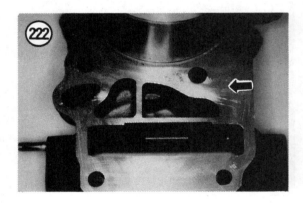

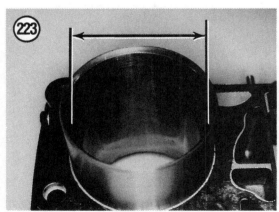

should *not* show any traces of grit or debris. If the rag is the slightest bit dirty, the wall is not thoroughly cleaned and must be rewashed.

d. After the cylinder is cleaned, lubricate the cylinder walls with clean engine oil to prevent the cylinder liners from rusting.

7. Inspect the small cooling fins for cracks or damage.

8. Repeat for the other cylinder block.

CAMSHAFT, DRIVE CHAINS, GUIDES AND TENSIONER ASSEMBLIES

The Vulcan engine's four camshafts are driven by a complex system of chains and sprockets that must be installed correctly for the valves to open at precise times. Each of the two cylinders is equipped with two camshafts. One camshaft operates two exhaust valves and the other operates the two inlet valves. If any of the camshaft drive chains or sprockets is incorrectly installed, the engine will probably not run and damage is likely, even if it does not start.

The camshaft drive system includes four drive chains, ten sprockets and eight timing marks. All of the timing marks must be carefully and accurately

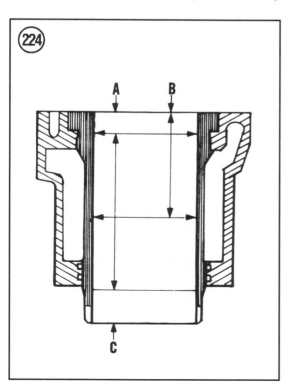

aligned when assembling. Because the intermediate sprockets have an uneven number of teeth, the timing mark on the intermediate sprocket will align infrequently. The timing marks on the crankshaft and the camshaft sprockets will, however, align every other crankshaft revolution in a conventional manner. It is imperative that the following removal and installation procedures be followed as described.

Front Cylinder Removal

Refer to **Figure 226** for this procedure.

1. Remove the front cylinder camshafts as described in this chapter.

2. Remove the alternator rotor as described under *Alternator Removal/Installation* in Chapter Eight.

3. Remove the short bolt and washer (**Figure 227**) securing the camshaft upper guide/tensioner and remove the upper guide/tensioner (**Figure 228**).

4. Remove the long bolt and washer (**Figure 229**) securing the camshaft upper chain guide and remove the upper guide (**Figure 230**).

5. Remove the front cylinder head as described in this chapter.

6. Remove the 2 bolts (A, **Figure 231**) securing the lower chain guide/tensioner assembly.

7. Remove the upper bolt (B, **Figure 231**) securing the chain tensioner and spring assembly, remove the chain tensioner and spring assembly (A, **Figure 232**).

8. Remove the lower chain guide/tensioner assembly (B, **Figure 232**).

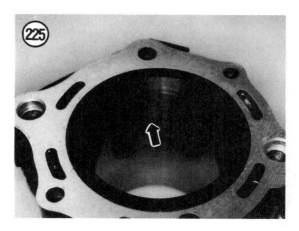

CAMSHAFT, DRIVE CHAINS, GUIDES AND TENSIONER ASSEMBLIES

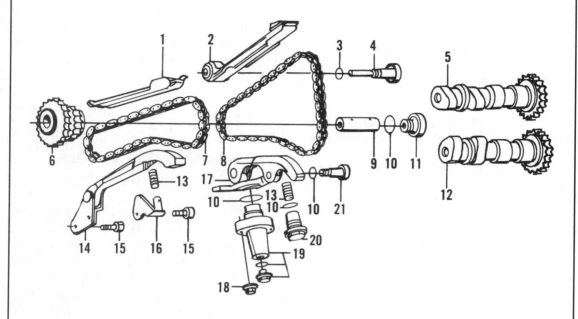

1. Lower chain guide
2. Upper chain guide
3. O-ring
4. Long bolt
5. Exhaust camshaft
6. Intermediate sprocket
7. Lower drive chain
8. Upper drive chain
9. Idler shaft
10. O-ring
11. Cap bolt
12. Intake camshaft
13. Spring
14. Lower chain guide/tensioner
15. Bolt
16. Tensioner assembly
17. Upper chain guide/tensioner
18. Nut
19. Tensioner assembly
20. Upper tensioner bolt
21. Short bolt

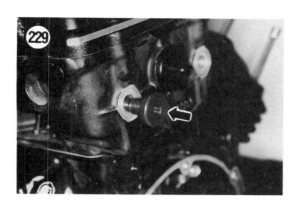

8. Remove the lower chain guide/tensioner assembly (B, **Figure 232**).

9. Remove the bolt and washer (A, **Figure 233**) securing the camshaft lower chain guide (B, **Figure 233**).

10. Remove the intermediate sprocket idler shaft cap bolt (**Figure 234**).

11. Screw a 6 mm bolt (A, **Figure 235**) into the end of the idler shaft (B, **Figure 235**).

4

12. Hold onto the camshaft upper chain (A, **Figure 236**) and withdraw the idler shaft (B, **Figure 236**).

13. Push the lower chain guide (C, **Figure 236**) up and out of its receptacle in the crankcase. Remove the guide out through the cylinder block chain cavity.

14. Disengage the lower chain from the crankshaft drive sprocket (D, **Figure 236**).

15. Carefully pull the camshaft upper chain, intermediate sprocket and lower chain from the chain cavity in the cylinder block and crankcase. Remove the chains and sprocket assembly (**Figure 237**).

16. Inspect all parts as described in this chapter.

17. Remove the front cylinder block as described in this chapter.

Front Cylinder
Installation

1. Install the front cylinder block (A, **Figure 238**) as described in this chapter.

2. Rotate the engine until the front piston is at TDC (B, **Figure 238**).

CAUTION
The alignment of the index marks in Step 3 are critical as they serve as the bench mark for the alignment of all the remaining index marks in this procedure. If these alignment marks are incorrect, the remainder of the procedure will be wrong and will result in incorrect camshaft timing that will lead to expensive engine damage.

3. Make sure the crankshaft sprocket tooth index mark (A, **Figure 239**) is aligned with the crankcase

raised index mark (B, **Figure 239**). If necessary, slightly rotate the crankshaft slightly in either direction until alignment is correct.

4. Apply a light coat of molybdenum disulfide grease to the idler shaft and inner surface of the intermediate sprocket.

NOTE
Position the camshaft lower chain with the link plate white paint index marks facing out.

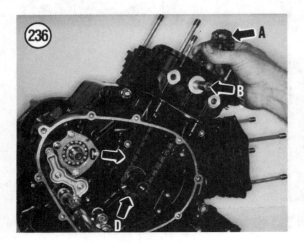

CAUTION
*When counting to the 38th link on the lower chain, be sure to count down on the **right-hand side** of the chain. If the counting is done on the left-hand side, the camshaft timing will be **incorrect**— leading to expensive engine damage.*

NOTE
If the white paint index marks are no longer visible on the lower chain, re-mark the chain yourself. Lay the chain

*out on a flat surface and straighten-it out. Mark the side plate of any link, any link is okay to start with, and establish this as the 1st link. Paint a white mark on this link's side plate. Count down the **right-hand side** of the chain until the **38th link** is located. Paint a white mark on this link's side plate.*

5. The camshaft lower chain has one white paint index mark on one link plate, referred to as the 1st link and another white paint index mark on the 38th link plate. These two marks are used for timing the camshaft lower chain.

NOTE
*The camshaft lower and upper chains have different widths. The upper chain is narrow (A, **Figure 240**) and must be installed onto the correct side of the intermediate sprocket (B, **Figure 240**). The lower chain is wide (C, **Figure 240**) and must be installed onto the correct side of the intermediate sprocket (D, **Figure 240**).*

6. Position the intermediate sprocket index mark straight up at 12 o'clock position.

7. Install the camshaft lower chain (A, **Figure 241**) onto the intermediate sprocket inner teeth and align the 38th link index mark (B, **Figure 241**) with the index mark on the intermediate sprocket (C, **Figure 241**).

8. Install the camshaft upper chain onto the outer sprocket teeth (D, **Figure 241**). There are no index marks on the upper chain.

9. Partially install the intermediate sprocket idler shaft into the cylinder block (A, **Figure 242**). Push it in until it is flush with the inner surface of the chain cavity outer wall. If the shaft is pushed in too far, it will interfere with the installation of the intermediate sprocket in the next step.

CAUTION
Do not allow the lower chain and inter-mediate sprocket to shift during instal-lation in Step 9. The timing mark alignment of the upper chain-to-inter-mediate sprocket established in Step 7 must remain aligned. The alignment cannot be accidentally changed during installation, otherwise camshaft timing will be incorrect.

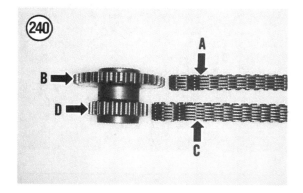

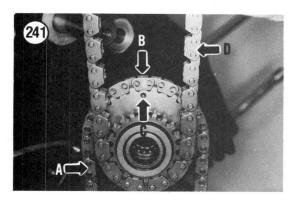

10. Carefully lower the camshaft lower chain and intermediate sprocket through the camshaft chain cavity in the cylinder block and the crankcase (B, **Figure 242**).

11. Carefully guide the lower end of the lower chain around the end of the crankshaft (A, **Figure 243**).

12. Install the camshaft lower chain onto the crankshaft sprocket. Align the index mark on the camshaft lower chain's 1st link with the index mark on the crankshaft sprocket (**Figure 244**).

13. Check that the index mark on the intermediate sprocket is still at the 12 o'clock position (**Figure 245**).

14. Push the idler sprocket shaft (B, **Figure 243**) in until it bottoms.

15. Make sure the O-ring is in place on the idler shaft cap bolt. Install the cap bolt (**Figure 234**) and tighten securely.

16. With the camshaft lower chain in place on the crankshaft sprocket and the intermediate sprocket in place in the cylinder block, refer to **Figure 246** and make sure all timing marks are properly aligned (**Figure 247**). Readjust if necessary.

NOTE
The camshaft lower guides are marked with a "F" (front cylinder) and "R" (rear cylinder). Be sure to install the one marked with the "F" mark.

17. From the top, insert the camshaft lower guide down through the cylinder block and crankcase. Push it down until it bottoms in the receptacle of the crankcase (**Figure 248**).

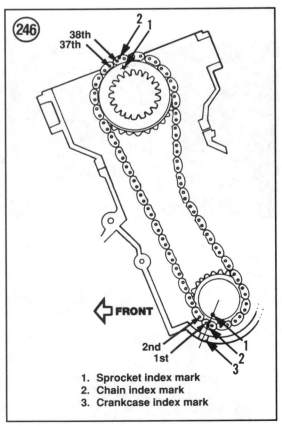

1. Sprocket index mark
2. Chain index mark
3. Crankcase index mark

18. Apply blue Loctite (No. 242) to the retaining bolt. Install the retaining bolt and washer (A, **Figure 233**) and tighten securely.

19. From the bottom, install the camshaft chain rear guide/tensioner up through the chain cavity in the crankcase and cylinder block (**Figure 249**). Align the bolt holes, but do not install the bolts at this time, the assembly will stay in place without the bolts.

20. Compress the spring on the tensioner and insert a piece of stiff wire (an old carburetor jet needle will work) in the shaft hole to hold the spring in this compressed position (**Figure 250**).

21. Install the tensioner spring assembly (A, **Figure 251**) up into place on the backside of the tensioner and align the mounting hole.

22. Apply blue Loctite (No. 242) to the tensioner spring mounting bolt. Install the bolt (B, **Figure 251**) and tighten securely.

23. Remove the piece of stiff wire, or jet needle, (C, **Figure 251**) from the tensioner assembly.

24. Apply blue Loctite (No. 242) to the rear guide/tensioner mounting bolts. Install the bolts (**Figure 252**) and tighten securely.

4

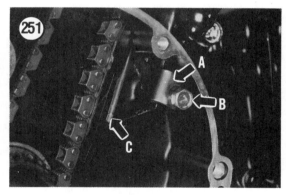

25. After the lower guide and lower guide/tensioner assemblies are installed, refer to **Figure 253** to confirm that all parts are installed correctly.

26. Install the cylinder head as described in this chapter. Do not install the camshafts at this time.

27. The square mounting boss (A, **Figure 254**) on the lower end of the upper chain guide must index properly into the grooves in the cylinder block.

28. Install the upper chain guide (B, **Figure 254**) into the cylinder head and push it down into the locating grooves in the cylinder block.

29. Make sure the O-ring (**Figure 255**) is in place on the long bolt. Install the long bolt (**Figure 256**) and tighten to the torque specification listed in **Table 2**.

30. The square mounting boss on the lower end of the upper chain guide/tensioner must index properly into the grooves in the cylinder block.

31. Partially install, then slightly rotate the upper chain guide/tensioner (**Figure 257**) to start it into the chain cavity, then straighten it out and guide it down into the cylinder block (**Figure 258**).

32. Insert the lower end of the metal arm into the receptacle created by the upper end of the lower chain guide and the crankcase. Align the bolt hole.

33. Make sure the O-ring (**Figure 259**) is in place on the short bolt. Install the short bolt (**Figure 260**) and tighten to the torque specification listed in **Table 2**.

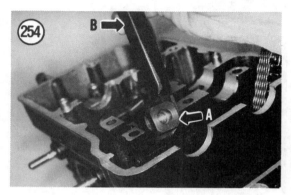

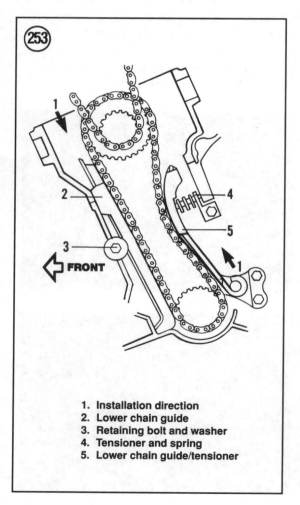

1. Installation direction
2. Lower chain guide
3. Retaining bolt and washer
4. Tensioner and spring
5. Lower chain guide/tensioner

(257)

(258)

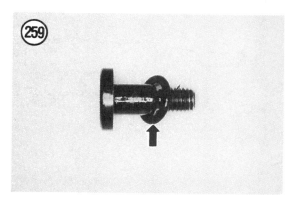

(259)

(260)

34. After the upper guide and upper guide/tensioner assemblies are installed, refer to **Figure 261** to confirm that all parts are installed correctly.

35. Install the front cylinder camshafts as described in this chapter. Do not perform Step 1 since the front cylinder is already located at TDC on the compression stoke.

36. After the cylinder head and camshafts are installed, refer to **Figure 262** and make sure the cam-

4

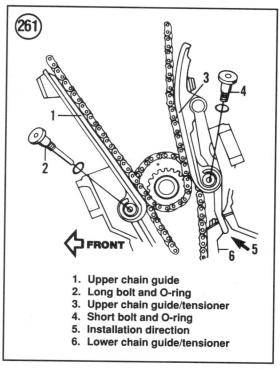

(261)

1. Upper chain guide
2. Long bolt and O-ring
3. Upper chain guide/tensioner
4. Short bolt and O-ring
5. Installation direction
6. Lower chain guide/tensioner

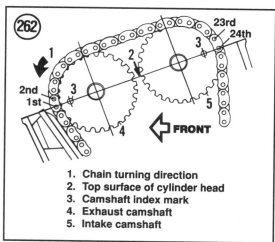

(262)

1. Chain turning direction
2. Top surface of cylinder head
3. Camshaft index mark
4. Exhaust camshaft
5. Intake camshaft

shaft index marks are still correctly aligned with the top surface of the cylinder head. Also make sure the chain link numbers correspond correctly.

37. Install the alternator as described in Chapter Eight.

Rear Cylinder
Removal

Refer to **Figure 263** for this procedure.

1. Remove the rear cylinder head camshafts as described in this chapter.

2. Remove the clutch, including the outer housing, as described under *Clutch Removal/Installation* in Chapter Five.

3. Remove the primary drive gear as described in this chapter.

4. Remove the long bolt and washer (**Figure 264**) securing the camshaft upper chain guide and remove the upper guide (**Figure 265**).

5. Remove the short bolt and washer (**Figure 266**) securing the camshaft upper guide/tensioner and remove the upper guide/tensioner (**Figure 267**).

6. Remove the rear cylinder head as described in this chapter.

7. Remove the 2 bolts (A, **Figure 268**) securing the lower chain guide/tensioner assembly.

8. Remove the upper bolt (B, **Figure 268**) securing the chain tensioner and spring assembly, remove the chain tensioner and spring assembly.

9. Remove the lower chain guide/tensioner assembly.

10. Remove the intermediate sprocket idler shaft cap bolt (**Figure 269**).

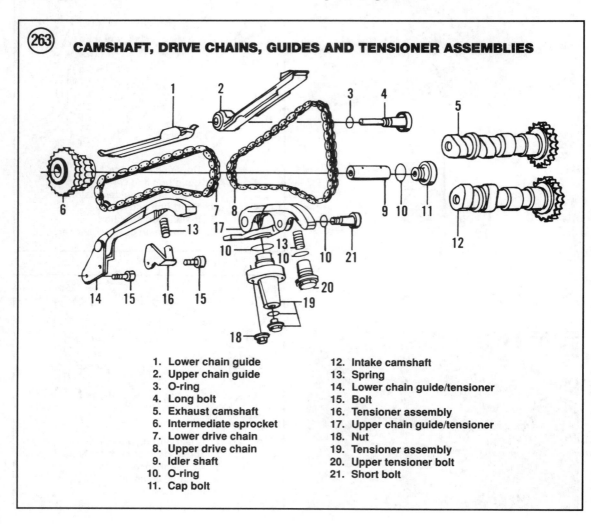

263

CAMSHAFT, DRIVE CHAINS, GUIDES AND TENSIONER ASSEMBLIES

1. Lower chain guide
2. Upper chain guide
3. O-ring
4. Long bolt
5. Exhaust camshaft
6. Intermediate sprocket
7. Lower drive chain
8. Upper drive chain
9. Idler shaft
10. O-ring
11. Cap bolt
12. Intake camshaft
13. Spring
14. Lower chain guide/tensioner
15. Bolt
16. Tensioner assembly
17. Upper chain guide/tensioner
18. Nut
19. Tensioner assembly
20. Upper tensioner bolt
21. Short bolt

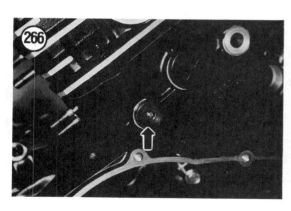

11. Screw a 6 mm bolt (A, **Figure 270**) into the end of the idler shaft (B, **Figure 270**).

12. Hold onto the camshaft upper chain and withdraw the idler shaft (B, **Figure 270**).

13. Push the lower chain guide up and out of its receptacle in the crankcase. Remove the guide out through the cylinder block chain cavity.

14. Disengage the lower chain from the crankshaft drive sprocket.

4

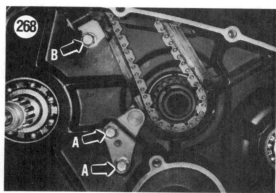

15. Carefully pull the camshaft upper chain, intermediate sprocket and lower chain from the chain cavity in the cylinder block and crankcase. Remove the chains and sprocket assembly.

16. Inspect all parts as described in this chapter.

17. Remove the cylinder block as described in this chapter.

Rear Cylinder
Installation

1. Install the rear cylinder block as described in this chapter.

2. Rotate the engine 305° *counterclockwise*, as viewed from the left-hand side of the engine, until the rear piston is at TDC on the compression stroke.

> *CAUTION*
> *The alignment of the index marks in Step 3 are critical as they serve as the bench mark for the alignment of all the remaining index marks in this procedure. If these alignment marks are incorrect, the remainder of the procedure will be wrong and will result in incorrect camshaft timing that will lead to expensive engine damage.*

3. Make sure the crankshaft sprocket tooth index mark (A, **Figure 271**) is aligned with the crankcase raised index mark (B, **Figure 271**). If necessary, slightly rotate the crankshaft in either direction until alignment is correct.

4. Apply a light coat of molybdenum disulfide grease to the idler shaft and inner surface of the intermediate sprocket.

> *NOTE*
> *Position the camshaft lower chain with the link plate white paint index marks facing out.*

> *CAUTION*
> *When counting to the 38th link on the lower chain, be sure to count down on the **left-hand side** of the chain. If the counting is done on the right-hand side, the camshaft timing will be **incorrect**— leading to expensive engine damage.*

> *NOTE*
> *If the white paint index marks are no longer visible on the lower chain, re-*

*mark the chain yourself. Lay the chain out on a flat surface and straighten it out. Mark the side plate of any link, any link is okay to start with, and establish this as the 1st link. Paint a white mark on this link's side plate. Count down the **left-hand side** of the chain until the **38th link** is located. Paint a white mark on this link's side plate.*

5. The camshaft lower chain has one white paint index mark on one link plate, referred to as the 1st

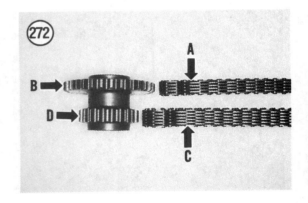

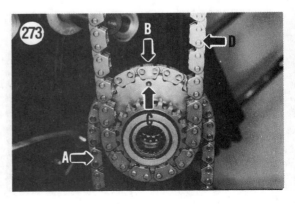

link and another white paint index mark on the 38th link plate. These two marks are used for timing the camshaft lower chain.

NOTE
*The camshaft lower and upper chains have different widths. The upper chain is narrow (A, **Figure 272**) and must be installed onto the correct side of the intermediate sprocket (B, **Figure 272**).*

*The lower chain is wide (C, **Figure 272**) and must be installed onto the correct side of the intermediate sprocket (D, **Figure 272**).*

6. Position the intermediate sprocket index mark straight up at 12 o'clock position.

7. Install the camshaft lower chain (A, **Figure 273**) onto the intermediate sprocket inner teeth and align the 38th link index mark (B, **Figure 273**) with the index mark on the intermediate sprocket (C, **Figure 273**).

8. Install the camshaft upper chain onto the outer sprocket teeth (D, **Figure 273**). There are no index marks on the upper chain.

9. Partially install the intermediate sprocket idler shaft into the cylinder block. Push it in until it is flush with the inner surface of the chain cavity outer wall. If the shaft is pushed in too far, it will interfere with the installation of the intermediate sprocket in the next step.

CAUTION
Do not allow the lower chain and intermediate sprocket to shift during installation in Step 9. The timing mark alignment of the upper chain-to-intermediate sprocket established in Step 7 must remain aligned. The alignment cannot be accidentally changed during installation, otherwise camshaft timing will be incorrect.

10. Carefully lower the camshaft lower chain and intermediate sprocket through the camshaft chain cavity in the cylinder block and the crankcase.

11. Carefully guide the lower end of the lower chain around the end of the crankshaft.

12. Install the camshaft lower chain onto the crankshaft sprocket. Align the index mark on the camshaft lower chain's 1st link with the index mark on the crankshaft sprocket (**Figure 274**).

13. Check that the index mark on the intermediate sprocket is still at the 12 o'clock position (**Figure 275**).

14. Push the idler sprocket shaft in until it bottoms out (**Figure 276**).

15. Make sure the O-ring is in place on the idler shaft cap bolt. Install the cap bolt (**Figure 269**) and tighten securely.

16. With the camshaft lower chain in place on the crankshaft sprocket and the intermediate sprocket in

place in the cylinder block, refer to **Figure 277** and make sure all timing marks are properly aligned. Readjust if necessary.

NOTE
The camshaft lower guides are marked with a "F" (front cylinder) and "R" (rear cylinder). Be sure to install the one marked with the "R" mark.

17. From the top, insert the camshaft lower guide down through the rear cylinder block and crankcase (**Figure 278**). Push it down until it bottoms in the receptacle of the crankcase (**Figure 279**).

18. From the bottom, install the camshaft chain rear guide/tensioner up through the chain cavity in the crankcase and cylinder block (**Figure 280**). Align the bolt holes.

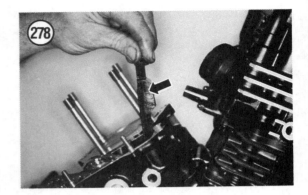

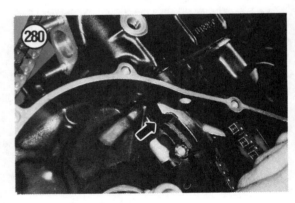

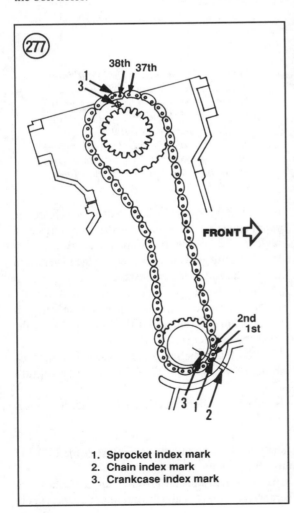

1. Sprocket index mark
2. Chain index mark
3. Crankcase index mark

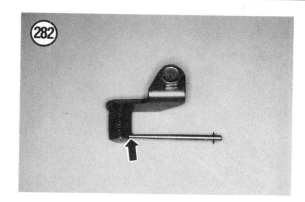

19. Apply blue Loctite (No. 242) to the rear guide/tensioner mounting bolts. Install the bolts (**Figure 281**) and tighten securely.

20. Compress the spring on the tensioner and insert a piece of stiff wire (an old carburetor jet needle will work) in the shaft hole to hold the spring in this compressed position (**Figure 282**).

21. Install the tensioner spring assembly up into place on the backside of the tensioner and align the mounting hole.

22. Apply blue Loctite (No. 242) to the tensioner spring mounting bolt. Install the bolt (A, **Figure 283**) and tighten securely.

23. Remove the piece of stiff wire, or jet needle, (B, **Figure 283**) from the tensioner assembly.

24. After the lower guide and lower guide/tensioner assemblies are installed, refer to **Figure 284** to confirm that all parts are installed correctly.

25. Install the rear cylinder head as described in this chapter. Do not install the camshafts at this time.

26. The square mounting boss (A, **Figure 285**) on the lower end of the upper chain guide/tensioner must index properly into the grooves in the cylinder block.

27. Slightly rotate the rear upper chain guide/tensioner (B, **Figure 285**) to start it into the chain cavity, then straighten it out and guide it down into the cylinder block (**Figure 286**).

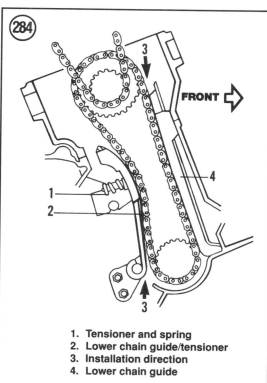

1. Tensioner and spring
2. Lower chain guide/tensioner
3. Installation direction
4. Lower chain guide

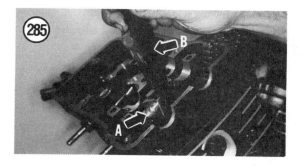

28. Insert the lower end of the metal arm into the receptacle created by the upper end of the lower chain guide and the crankcase. Align the bolt hole.

29. Make sure the O-ring (**Figure 287**) is in place on the short bolt. Install the short bolt (**Figure 288**) and tighten to the torque specification listed in **Table 2**.

30. The square mounting boss (A, **Figure 289**) on the lower end of the upper chain guide must index properly into the grooves in the cylinder head.

31. Install the upper chain guide (B, **Figure 289**) into the cylinder head and push it down into the locating grooves in the cylinder block

32. Make sure the O-ring (**Figure 290**) is in place on the long bolt. Install the long bolt (**Figure 291**) and tighten to the torque specification listed in **Table 2**.

33. After the upper guide and upper guide/tensioner assemblies are installed, refer to **Figure 292** to confirm that all parts are installed correctly.

34. Install the rear cylinder camshafts as described in this chapter. Do not perform Step 1 since the rear cylinder is already located at TDC on the compression stoke.

35. After the rear cylinder head and camshafts are installed, refer to **Figure 293** and make sure the camshaft index marks are still correctly aligned with the top surface of the cylinder head. Also make sure the chain link numbers correspond correctly.

36. Install the primary drive gear as described in this chapter.

37. Install the clutch, including the outer housing, as described under *Clutch Removal/Installation* in Chapter Five.

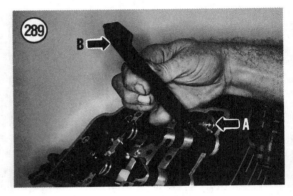

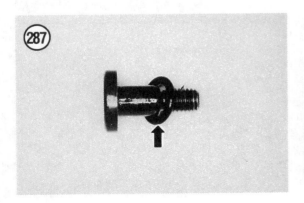

Camshaft Chain, Chain Guides and Guide/Tensioner Assemblies Inspection

NOTE
The 20-pin inspection specification relates to both the camshaft upper and lower chains and for both the front and rear cylinders.

1. Lay each camshaft chain on a workbench and stretch a 20-pin segment as shown in **Figure 294**. Measure the 20 pins with a vernier caliper at several points around the chain. Repeat for all chains. Replace the chain(s) if the length of 20 pins exceeds the service limit in **Table 1**.

2. Inspect both the upper (A, **Figure 295**) and lower (B, **Figure 295**) chains for wear or damage, replace if necessary. If either chain is worn, also inspect the sprocket(s) the chain rides on as they may also be damaged and in need of replacement.

3. Inspect the teeth (**Figure 296**) on the intermediate sprocket for missing teeth, wear or damage.

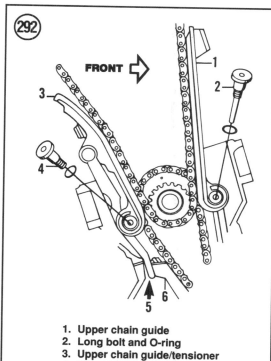

1. Upper chain guide
2. Long bolt and O-ring
3. Upper chain guide/tensioner
4. Short bolt and O-ring
5. Installation direction
6. Lower chain guide/tensioner

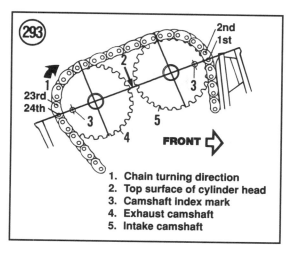

1. Chain turning direction
2. Top surface of cylinder head
3. Camshaft index mark
4. Exhaust camshaft
5. Intake camshaft

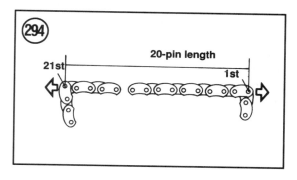

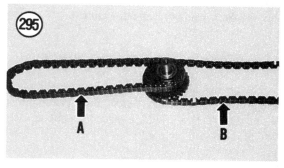

4. Inspect the needle bearings at each end of the intermediate sprocket for wear or damage. Refer to **Figure 297** and **Figure 298**. The needle bearings cannot be replaced, and if damaged the sprocket assembly must be replaced.

5. Inspect the intermediate sprocket idler shaft (**Figure 299**) for wear, scoring or damage. Insert the idler shaft into the sprocket (**Figure 300**) and rotate it. Check for roughness or binding. Replace the worn part(s).

6. Inspect the chain sliding surfaces (**Figure 301**) of chain guides and guide/tensioners for wear or damage. Replace the worn part(s).

7. Inspect the mounting and/or pivot areas (**Figure 302**) of chain guides and guide/tensioners for wear or damage. Replace the worn part(s).

8. Make sure the E-clip (**Figure 303**) is in place and secure on the guide/tensioners pivot points.

9. Inspect the camshaft chain tensioner adjuster body for wear or damage (A, **Figure 304**). Kawasaki does not provide any service specifications for the tensioner adjuster assembly.

10. Make sure the ratchet (B, **Figure 304**) operates correctly.

11. Inspect the O-ring seal (C, **Figure 304**) for hardness or deterioration, replace if necessary.

12. If any part of the tensioner adjuster body or ratchet is worn or damaged, replace the entire assembly. Replacement parts are not available.

PISTONS AND PISTON RINGS

The pistons are made of an aluminum alloy and the piston pins are made of steel. Each piston pin is a precision fit and is held in place by a clip at each end of the piston pin bore.

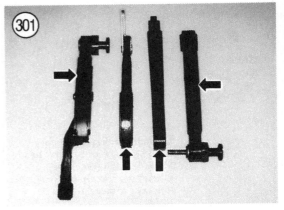

Piston
Removal/Installation

1. Remove the cylinder head and cylinder block as described in this chapter.

2. Stuff clean shop cloths into the cylinder bore crankcase openings (**Figure 305**) to prevent objects from falling into the crankcase.

3. Lightly mark the top of the pistons with an "F" (front) or "R" (rear) so they will be installed into the correct cylinder. Also mark an arrow (**Figure 306**) indicating the direction of the piston in the engine.

4. If necessary, remove the piston rings as described in this chapter.

5. Before removing the piston, hold the rod tightly and rock the piston as shown in **Figure 307**. Any

4

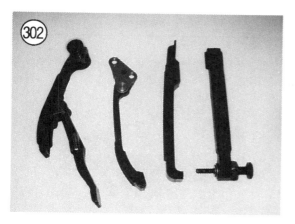

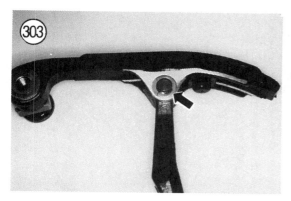

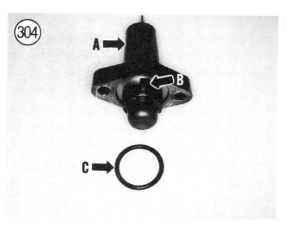

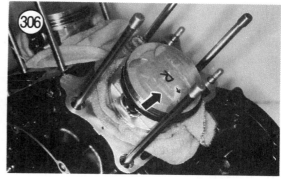

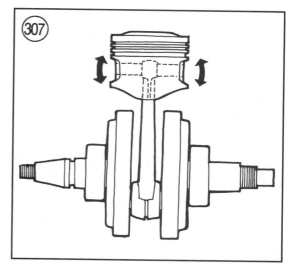

rocking motion (do not confuse with the normal sliding motion) indicates wear on the piston pin, piston pin bore or connecting rod small-end bore (more likely a combination of these). Mark the piston and pin so that they will be reassembled into the same set.

6. Remove the clips from each side of the piston pin bore with a small screwdriver, scribe or needlenose pliers (**Figure 308**). Hold your thumb over one edge of the clip when removing it to prevent the clip from springing out.

7. Use a proper size wooden dowel or socket extension and push out the piston pin.

CAUTION
Be careful when removing the pin to avoid damaging the connecting rod. If it is necessary to gently tap the pin to remove it, be sure that the piston is properly supported so that lateral shock is not transmitted to the connecting rod lower bearing.

8. If the piston pin is difficult to remove, heat the piston and pin with a butane torch. The pin will probably push right out. Heat the piston to only about 140° F (60° C), i.e., until it is too warm to touch, but not excessively hot. If the pin is still difficult to push out, use a homemade tool as shown in **Figure 309**.

9. Lift the piston off the connecting rod and inspect it as described in this chapter.

10. If the piston is going to be left off for some time, place a piece of foam insulation tube over the end of the rod to protect it.

11. Apply molybdenum disulfide grease to the inside surface of the connecting rod piston pin bore.

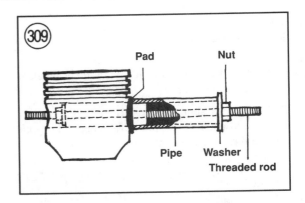

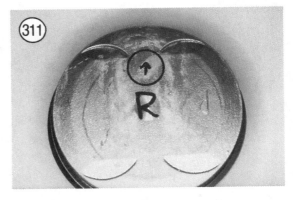

12. Oil the piston pin with assembly oil or fresh engine oil and install it in the piston until its end extends slightly beyond the inside of the boss (**Figure 310**).

13. Correctly position the piston-to-connecting rod as follows:

a. Refer to arrow mark (**Figure 311**) made during disassembly and install the piston with the arrow toward the front of the engine.

b. If the pistons were not marked, or new pistons are being installed, position the piston with the "arrow" mark on the crown pointing toward the *exhaust valve side* of the cylinder.

14. Place the piston over the connecting rod.

15. Line up the piston pin with the hole in the connecting rod. Push the piston pin through the connecting rod and into the other side of the piston until it is even with the piston pin clip grooves.

> *CAUTION*
> *If it is necessary to tap the piston pin into the connecting rod, do so gently with a block of wood or a soft-faced hammer. Make sure you support the piston to prevent the lateral shock from being transmitted to the connecting rod lower bearing.*

> *NOTE*
> *In the next step, install the clips with the gap away from the cutout in the piston (**Figure 312**).*

16. Install *new* piston pin clips (**Figure 308**) in both ends of the pin boss. Make sure they are seated in the grooves in the piston.

17. Check the installation by rocking the piston back and forth around the pin axis and from side to side along the axis. It should rotate freely back and forth but not from side to side.

18. Install the piston rings as described in this chapter.

19. Repeat Steps 1-18 for the other piston.

Piston Inspection

> *NOTE*
> *Kawasaki does not provide service dimensions for the piston pin O.D. or the piston pin bore I.D. in the piston.*

1. Carefully clean the carbon from the piston crown (**Figure 313**) with a chemical remover or with a soft scraper. Do not remove or damage the carbon ridge around the circumference of the piston above the top ring. If the piston, rings and cylinder are found to be dimensionally correct and can be reused, removal of the carbon ring from the top of the piston or the carbon ridge from the top of the cylinder will promote excessive oil consumption.

> *CAUTION*
> *Do not wire brush the piston skirts or ring lands. The wire brush removes aluminum and increases piston clearance. It also rounds the corners of the ring lands, which results in decreased support for the piston rings.*

2. Examine each ring groove for burrs, dented edges and wide wear. Pay particular attention to the top compression ring groove as it usually wears more than the other grooves.

3. If damage or wear indicates that piston replacement is required, select a new piston as described under *Piston Clearance Measurement* in this chapter.

4. Oil the piston pin and install it in the connecting rod (**Figure 314**). Slowly rotate the piston pin and

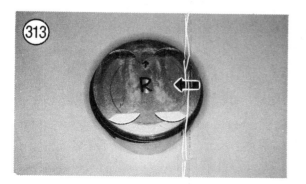

check for radial and axial play (**Figure 315**). If any play exists, the piston pin should be replaced, providing the rod bore is in good condition.

5. Check the oil control holes in the piston for carbon or oil sludge buildup. Refer to **Figure 316** and **Figure 317**. Clean the holes with a small diameter drill bit and blow out with compressed air.

6. Check the piston skirt for galling and abrasion which may have been caused by piston seizure. If light galling is present, smooth the affected area with No. 400 emery paper and oil or a fine oilstone. However, if galling is severe or if the piston is deeply scored, replace it.

7. Inspect the grooves (**Figure 318**) in the piston pin bore on each side of the piston. If either groove is damaged, replace the piston.

8. If damage or wear indicates that piston replacement is required, select a new piston as described under *Piston Clearance Measurement* in this chapter.

9. Inspect the piston pin (**Figure 319**) for chrome flaking or cracks. Replace if necessary.

Piston Clearance Measurement

1. Make sure the piston and cylinder walls are clean and dry.

2. Measure the inside diameter of the cylinder bore at a point 1/2 in. (13 mm) from the upper edge with a bore gauge.

3. Measure the outside diameter of the piston across the skirt (**Figure 320**) at right angles to the piston

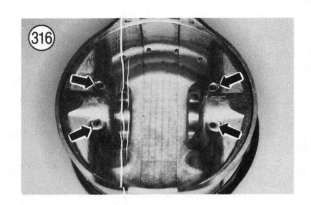

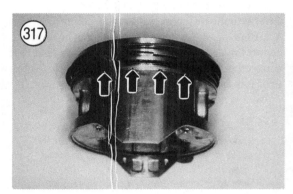

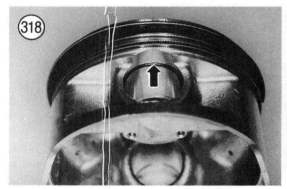

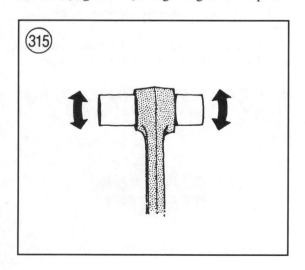

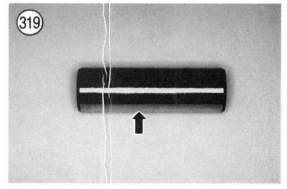

pin. Measure at a distance 5 mm (0.20 in.) up from the bottom of the piston skirt.

4. Subtract the measured diameter of the piston from the cylinder diameter and compare to the dimension listed in **Table 1**. If clearance is excessive, the piston should be replaced and the cylinder should be rebored to the next oversize. Purchase the new piston first; measure its diameter and add the specified clearance to determine the proper cylinder bore diameter.

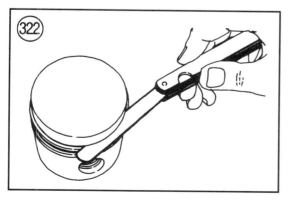

Piston Ring
Removal/Installation

> *WARNING*
> *The edges of all piston rings (**Figure 321**) are very sharp. Be careful when handling them to avoid cutting your fingers.*

1. Measure the side clearance of each ring in its groove with a flat feeler gauge (**Figure 322**) and compare to dimensions given in **Table 1**. If the clearance is greater than specified, the rings must be replaced. If the clearance is still excessive with the new rings, the piston must also be replaced.

2. Remove the old rings with a ring expander tool (**Figure 323**) or by spreading the ends with your thumbs just enough to slide the ring up over the piston (**Figure 324**). Repeat for the remaining rings.

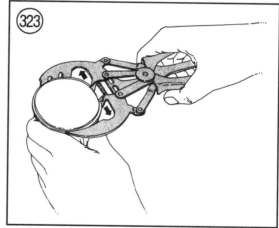

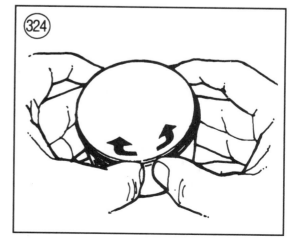

3. Carefully remove all carbon buildup from the ring grooves with a broken piston ring (**Figure 325**).

4. Inspect the grooves carefully for burrs, nicks or broken and cracked lands. Recondition or replace the piston if necessary.

5. Check the end gap of each ring. To check the ring, insert the ring, one at a time, into the bottom of the

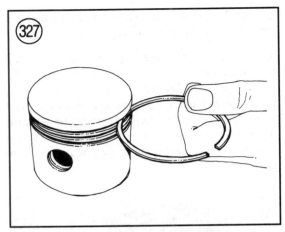

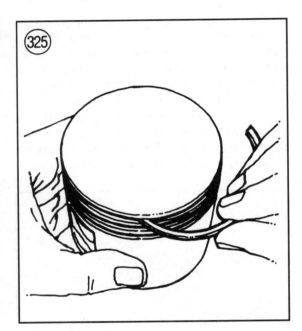

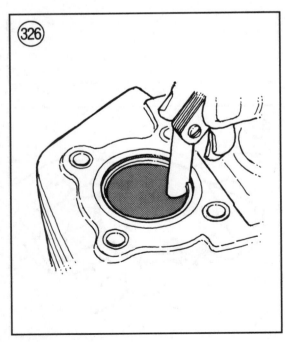

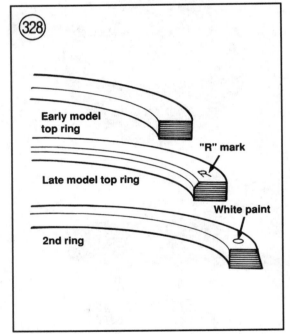

Early model top ring

Late model top ring

"R" mark

White paint

2nd ring

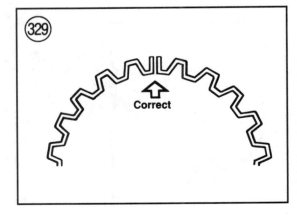

Correct

cylinder bore and push it in about 20 mm (5/8 in.) with the crown of the piston to ensure that the ring is square in the cylinder bore. Measure the gap with a flat feeler gauge (**Figure 326**) and compare to dimensions in **Table 1**. If the gap is greater than specified, the rings should be replaced. When installing new rings, measure their end gap in the same manner as for old ones. If the gap is less than specified, carefully file the ends with a fine-cut file until the gap is correct.

6. Roll each ring around its piston groove as shown in **Figure 327** to check for binding. If there is any binding, reclean the ring groove with solvent as there may still be a carbon or oil sludge buildup that was

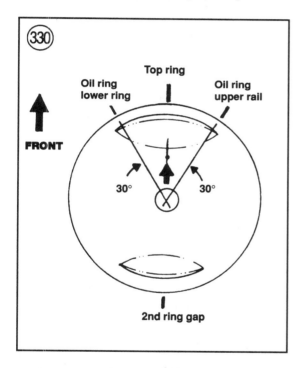

not previously removed. After cleaning with solvent, reclean the groove with a broken piston ring (**Figure 325**).

7. Install the rings in the order shown in **Figure 328**.

8. Install the piston rings—first, the bottom oil control ring assembly, then the middle, then the top ring—by carefully spreading the ends with your thumbs and slipping the rings over the top of the piston. The piston rings must be installed with the manufacturer's mark or paint mark toward the top of the piston. Install the rings as follows:

   a. Install the oil control ring expander first and make sure the ends of the ring butt together as shown in **Figure 329**. The ends must not overlap.

   b. Install the lower steel rail then the upper steel rail.

   c. The second ring is not symmetrical and must be installed as shown in **Figure 328**.

   d. On early models, the top ring is symmetrical and can be installed either way. On later models the top ring is not symmetrical and must be installed as shown in **Figure 328**.

9. Make sure the rings are seated completely in their grooves all the way around the piston and that the ends are distributed around the piston as shown in **Figure 330**. Be sure that the ring gaps are not aligned with each other when installed in the cylinder.

10. If new rings were installed, measure the side clearance of each ring in its groove with a flat feeler gauge (**Figure 322**) and compare to dimensions given in **Table 1**.

11. After the rings are installed, apply clean engine oil to the rings. Rotate the rings several complete revolutions in their respective grooves. This will assure proper oiling when the engine is first started after after piston service.

OIL PUMP

Removal/Installation

1. Remove the engine from the frame and disassemble the crankcase as described in this chapter.

2. Remove the crankshaft assembly as described in this chapter.

3. Remove the circlip (A, **Figure 331**) securing the oil pump driven sprocket (B, **Figure 331**).

4. Remove the driven sprocket and oil pump drive chain as an assembly. Slide the balancer shaft (A,

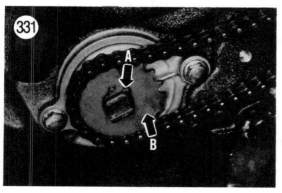

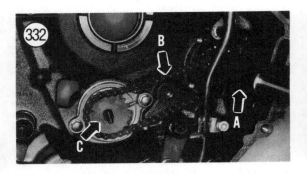

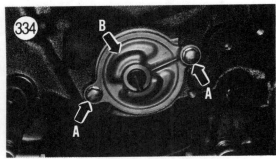

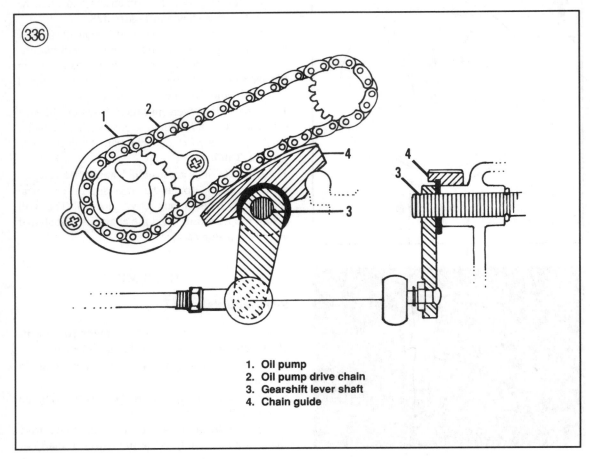

1. Oil pump
2. Oil pump drive chain
3. Gearshift lever shaft
4. Chain guide

Figure 332) out of its bearing in the left-hand crankcase half along with the oil pump drive chain (B, **Figure 332**) and driven sprocket (C, **Figure 332**).

5. Remove the sprocket from the drive chain, remove the drive chain (A, **Figure 333**) from the balancer shaft (B, **Figure 333**) and leave the balancer shaft resting in the crankcase.

NOTE
The oil pump mounting screws have had a locking agent applied to them during installation and may be difficult to loosen.

6. Use an impact driver and loosen the oil pump mounting screws (A, **Figure 334**). Remove the screws.

7. Remove the oil pump assembly (B, **Figure 334**) and O-ring from the crankcase. Hold the *open end* of the oil pump up so the rotors will not fall from the body.

8. Install by reversing these removal steps while noting the following:

a. If the oil pump was disassembled, prime it with clean engine oil.

b. Make sure the O-ring seal (**Figure 335**) is in place on the oil pump body prior to installation.

c. Position the sprocket circlip with the sharp side edge facing away from the oil pump and install the circlip. Make sure it seats correctly in the shaft groove.

d. Apply blue Loctite (No. 242) to the oil pump mounting screws prior to installation and install the screws. Tighten the screws securely.

e. On 1987-on models, make sure the oil pump chain guide is in place and positioned correctly above the gearshift lever shaft as shown in **Figure 336**.

Disassembly/Inspection/Assembly

Refer to **Figure 337** for this procedure.

1. Remove the driveshaft, dowel pin, inner rotor and outer rotor from the pump body.

2. Clean all parts in solvent and dry with compressed air.

3. Inspect the oil pump body (A, **Figure 338**) for cracks or bore damage. If worn or damaged, replace the oil pump body.

4. Inspect the oil pump mounting bosses (B, **Figure 338**) for fractures or damage. If damaged, replace the oil pump body.

5. Inspect the driveshaft for wear or damage. If worn or damaged, replace the driveshaft.

6. Make sure the dowel pin is a tight fit in the driveshaft. If loose replace the worn part.

7. Inspect the inner and outer rotors (**Figure 339**) for wear, abrasion or damage. If either is damaged

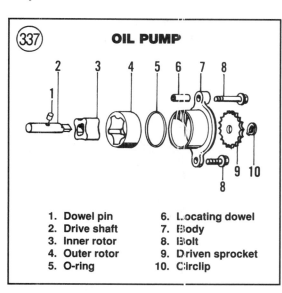

OIL PUMP

1. Dowel pin
2. Drive shaft
3. Inner rotor
4. Outer rotor
5. O-ring
6. Locating dowel
7. Body
8. Bolt
9. Driven sprocket
10. Circlip

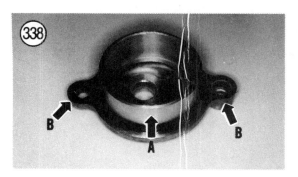

replace both rotors as a pair. They cannot be replaced separately.

8. Install the outer rotor, inner rotor and driveshaft into the oil pump body.

9. Check the clearance between the inner and outer rotors with a flat feeler gauge (**Figure 340**). If the clearance is greater than the service limit in **Table 1**, replace the rotors as a set.

10. Check the clearance between the outer rotor and the oil pump body with a flat feeler gauge (**Figure 341**). If the clearance is greater than the service limit in **Table 1**, refer to the following steps and measure the outer diameter of the outer rotor and the inner diameter of the oil pump body to see which part is worn.

11. Measure the outer diameter of the outer rotor with a micrometer (**Figure 342**) or vernier caliper. If worn to the service limit listed in **Table 1** or less, replace the rotors as a set.

12. Measure the inner diameter of the oil pump body with an inside micrometer, vernier caliper or small bore gauge (**Figure 343**). If worn to the service limit listed in **Table 1** or greater, replace the oil pump body.

13. Check the rotor side clearance with a straightedge and flat feeler gauge (**Figure 344**). If the clearance is greater than the service limit in **Table 1**, replace the oil pump assembly.

14. Inspect the teeth on the driven gear. Replace the driven gear if the teeth are damaged or any are missing. If the gear is damaged, inspect the drive chain as it may also be damaged. Replace the chain if necessary.

15. Remove the inner rotor, outer rotor, driveshaft and the dowel pin from the body.

16. Coat all parts with clean engine oil.

17. Install the outer rotor into the oil pump body (**Figure 345**).

18. Position the inner rotor with the groove for the dowel pin facing up and install the inner rotor into the outer rotor (**Figure 346**).

19. Install the dowel pin (A, **Figure 347**) into the drive shaft.

20. Position the driveshaft with the flat tab going in first and install the drive shaft into the inner rotor (B, **Figure 347**). Make sure the dowel pin is properly seated into the inner rotor groove.

21. If removed, install the O-ring (**Figure 335**) onto the oil pump body.

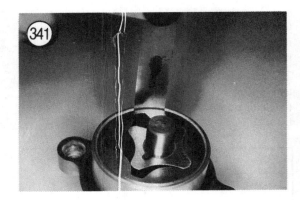

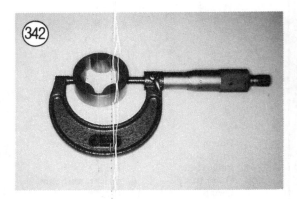

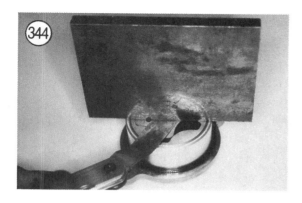

PRIMARY DRIVE GEAR

Removal

1. Remove the crankcase right-hand side cover as described in this chapter.

2A. If the clutch assembly is still in place, perform the following:

    a. Stuff a shop cloth or copper penny (A, **Figure 348**) between the clutch outer housing gear and the primary drive gear. This will prevent the gear from rotating while loosening the bolt.

    b. Loosen the primary drive gear bolt (B, **Figure 348**).

2B. If the clutch assembly is removed, perform the following:

    a. If still in place, remove the piston from one of the connecting rods.

    b. Insert a 1/2 in. drive socket extension or round drift through the small end of the connecting rod.

CAUTION
*Use only a **round** extension or drift in sub-step 2Bc. Any other shape could cause damage to the connecting rod piston pin hole surface.*

    c. Rotate the crankshaft until the extension or round drift, in the connecting rod, is resting on the top surface of the crankcase.

    d. Loosen the primary drive gear bolt (B, **Figure 348**).

    e. Remove the socket extension or drift from the connecting rod.

3. Remove the flange bolt and the washer (A, **Figure 349**).

4. Slide the primary drive gear (B, **Figure 349**) off the end of the crankshaft.

5. Don't lose the Woodruff key (**Figure 350**) from the crankshaft. It is not necessary to remove it unless it is loose.

6. Inspect all components as described in this chapter.

Installation

1. If removed, install the Woodruff key (**Figure 350**) in the slot in the crankshaft.

2. Align the keyway in the gear with the Woodruff key and install the primary drive gear (B, **Figure 349**).

3. Install the bolt and washer (A, **Figure 349**).

4. Use the same tool set-up (**Figure 351**) used in Step 2 to prevent the crankshaft from rotating while tightening the bolt.

5. Tighten the primary drive gear bolt to the torque specification listed in **Table 2**.

6. Install the crankcase right-hand side cover as described in this chapter.

Inspection

> *NOTE*
> *If the primary drive gear teeth are damaged, inspect the gear teeth on the clutch outer housing (**Figure 352**) as they may also be damaged and require replacement.*

1. Inspect the primary drive gear (**Figure 353**) for chipped or missing teeth, wear or damage. Replace the gear if necessary.

2. Check the keyway (**Figure 354**) for wear or damage, replace the gear if necessary.

BALANCER ASSEMBLY
AND STARTER GEARS

The balancer system eliminates the vibration normally associated with a large displacement twin

using a common crankpin. The engine and frame are designed to be compatible with this balancer system. If the balancer system is eliminated it will result in major fatigue and failure to engine and frame components. Do *not* eliminate this feature.

CAUTION
Any applicable manufacturer's warranty will be voided if the balancer system is modified, disconnected or removed.

Removal

Refer to the following illustrations for this procedure:

    a. **Figure 355**: balancer gear assembly.

    b. **Figure 356**: starter clutch gears.

1. Remove the engine from the frame as described in this chapter.

2. Remove the crankcase right-hand side cover as described in this chapter.

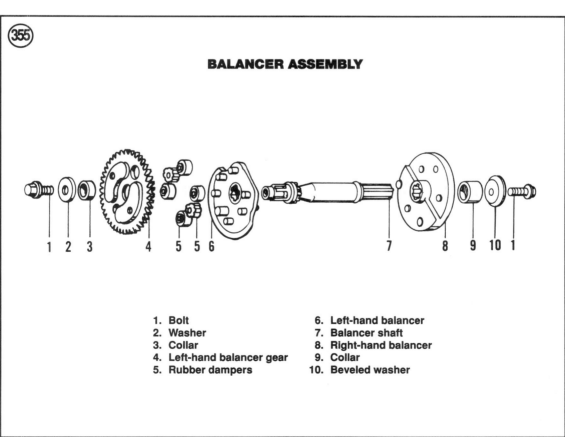

BALANCER ASSEMBLY

1. Bolt
2. Washer
3. Collar
4. Left-hand balancer gear
5. Rubber dampers
6. Left-hand balancer
7. Balancer shaft
8. Right-hand balancer
9. Collar
10. Beveled washer

3. Remove the alternator rotor as described under *Alternator Rotor Removal/Installation* in Chapter Eight.

4. To remove the left-hand balancer, perform the following:

a. Place a socket and wrench on the right-hand balancer bolt (A, **Figure 357**) to keep the balancer shaft from rotating while loosening the left-hand bolt.

CAUTION
*The left-hand balancer bolt has **left-hand** threads. Turn the wrench **clockwise** to loosen the left-hand bolt (**Figure 358**).*

b. Loosen the bolt (A, **Figure 359**) securing the balancer gear and left-hand balancer.

c. Remove the bolt (A, **Figure 359**), washer (B, **Figure 359**) and collar (**Figure 360**).

d. Slide the balancer gear and left-hand balancer assembly (**Figure 361**) off the balancer shaft.

5. On 750 cc models, remove the washer from the starter idle gear.

6. To remove the right-hand balancer and starter gear, perform the following:

a. Install the clutch holder tool onto the starter gear to prevent the gear from turning while loosening the bolt.

b. Loosen the starter gear bolt (A, **Figure 357**).

c. Remove the bolt and beveled washer (B, **Figure 357**).

d. Slide the starter driven gear (**Figure 362**) off the balancer shaft.

e. Remove the needle bearing (**Figure 363**) and collar (**Figure 364**).

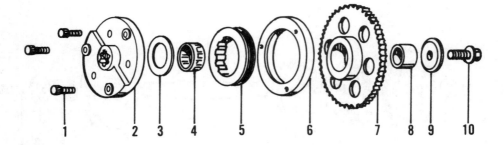

STARTER CLUTCH GEARS

1. Allen bolt
2. Right-hand balancer
3. Copper washer
4. Needle bearing
5. One-way clutch
6. Starter coupling
7. Starter driven gear
8. Collar
9. Beveled washer
10. Bolt

f. Remove the copper washer (**Figure 365**).

g. Slide the right-hand balancer and starter clutch assembly (**Figure 366**) off the balancer shaft.

7. Remove the starter idler gear and washer (**Figure 367**) from the crankcase.

8. Inspect all parts as described in this chapter.

Inspection

1. Separate the left-hand balancer (A, **Figure 368**) from the left-hand balancer gear (B, **Figure 368**).

2. Inspect the 6 rubber dampers (**Figure 369**) for wear or deterioration. Replace as a set if any require replacement.

3. Inspect the 6 posts (**Figure 370**) on the left-hand balancer for wear or damage. Replace if necessary.

4. Inspect the left-hand balancer gear (**Figure 371**) for worn, chipped or missing teeth. Replace if necessary.

5. Inspect the inner splines in the right-hand balancer (**Figure 372**) and the left-hand balancer (**Figure 373**) for wear or damage. Replace if necessary.

6. Inspect the outer splines on the balancer shaft for wear or damage. Replace if necessary.

7. Inspect the starter idle gear (**Figure 374**) for wear or damage. Replace if necessary.

8. Inspect the starter driven gear (A, **Figure 375**) and the mating gear on the idle gear (B, **Figure 375**) for worn, chipped or missing teeth. Replace the gear(s) if necessary.

9. Inspect the starter driven gear outer surface (**Figure 376**) where it rides on the one-way clutch. If the surface is damaged, replace the gear.

10. Inspect the starter driven gear inner surface (**Figure 377**) where it rides on the needle bearing. If the surface is damaged, replace the gear.

11. Inspect the needle bearing (**Figure 378**) for wear or damage. It must rotate freely with no binding, replace if necessary.

12. Inspect the inner and outer surfaces of the collar for wear or damage. Insert the collar into the needle bearing (**Figure 379**) and rotate it. It should rotate freely with no binding. Replace the collar if necessary.

13. Inspect the rollers (**Figure 380**) of the one-way clutch for burrs, wear or damage. To remove the one-way from the balancer, perform the following:

    a. Remove the Allen bolts (**Figure 381**) securing the one-way clutch (A, **Figure 382**) and coupling (B, **Figure 382**) to the right-hand balancer and remove both parts.

    b. Install the one-way clutch (A, **Figure 382**) with the flanged side facing the right-hand balancer, then install the coupling (B, **Figure 382**).

    c. Apply red Loctite (No. 271) to the Allen bolt threads prior to installation. Install the bolts (**Figure 381**) and tighten to the torque specification listed in **Table 2**.

14. Assemble the left-hand balancer gear onto the left-hand balancer as follows:

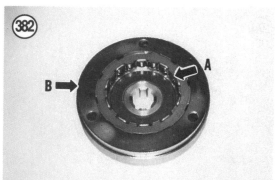

a. Make sure all 6 rubber dampers (A, **Figure 383**) are in place.

> *CAUTION*
> *The balancer and balancer gear must be assembled together correctly. If assembled incorrectly, the balance weight will be 180° out of alignment resulting in **severe engine vibration** that will lead to internal engine damage.*

b. Position the balancer locating pin (B, **Figure 383**) so it will be inserted into the *smaller diameter hole* of the balancer gear (C, **Figure 383**).

c. Install the balancer onto balancer gear and push them together.

d. Make sure the balancer locating pin is indexed correctly into the balancer gear *smaller diameter hole* (**Figure 384**). This alignment is necessary to ensure proper balancer operation.

Installation

Refer to the following illustrations for this procedure:

a. **Figure 355**: balancer assembly.

b. **Figure 356**: starter clutch gears.

> *CAUTION*
> *Both balancer assemblies must be properly aligned and installed onto the balancer shaft in order to operate correctly. If either balancer is installed incorrectly it will result in **severe engine vibration** leading to internal engine damage. Be sure to follow all alignment steps in this procedure to ensure proper installation of all components.*

1. Make sure the washer (**Figure 385**) is in place on the backside of the starter idler gear and install the starter idler gear (**Figure 367**) onto the crankcase.

2. To install the right-hand balancer and starter gear, perform the following:

> *CAUTION*
> *For the right-hand balancer to operate correctly, the index mark on the right-hand balancer (**Figure 386**) must be aligned with the index mark on the balancer shaft (**Figure 387**).*

a. Align the right-hand balancer index mark (A, **Figure 388**) with the balancer shaft index mark (B, **Figure 388**) and slide the right-balancer onto the shaft (**Figure 366**). Recheck the index marks to ensure proper alignment.

b. Install the copper washer (**Figure 365**) and center it.

c. Install the collar (**Figure 364**) and needle bearing (**Figure 363**). Make sure the collar fits into the center of the copper washer.

d. Slide the starter driven gear (**Figure 362**) onto the needle bearing on the balancer shaft. Push the gear on until it bottoms out.

e. Position the beveled washer with the beveled side going on first and install the washer (B, **Figure 357**).

f. Apply blue Loctite (No. 242) to the bolt threads prior to installation.

g. Install the bolt (A, **Figure 357**).

h. Use the same tool set-up used during removal to prevent the gear from turning while tightening the bolt.

i. Tighten the bolt to the torque specification listed in **Table 2**.

3. On 750 cc models, install the washer onto the starter idle gear.

4. To install the left-hand balancer, perform the following:

a. Align the left-hand balancer index mark with the balancer shaft index mark and slide the left-balancer onto the shaft. Recheck the index marks to ensure proper alignment (**Figure 389**).

b. Install the collar (**Figure 390**) and push it in until it bottoms (**Figure 360**).

c. Apply blue Loctite (No. 242) to the bolt threads prior to installation.

d. Install the bolt (A, **Figure 391**).

e. Use the same tool set-up used during removal to prevent the gear from turning while tightening the bolt.

CAUTION
*The left-hand balancer bolt has **left-hand** threads. Turn the wrench **counter-clockwise** (B, Figure 391) to tighten the left-hand bolt.*

f. Tighten the bolt to the torque specification listed in **Table 2**.

5. Install the alternator rotor as described in Chapter Eight.

6. Install the crankcase right-hand side cover as described in this chapter.

7. Install the engine into the frame as described in this chapter.

FRONT BEVEL GEAR ASSEMBLY

Removal

NOTE
The front bevel gear assembly can be removed with the engine installed in the

frame. This procedure is shown with the engine removed for clarity.

1. Place the bike on the centerstand on level ground.

2. Place a drain pan under the front bevel gear case as some engine oil may drain out when the case is removed.

3. Disconnect the lower end of the clutch cable from the clutch release lever as described in Chapter Five.

4. Using a criss-cross pattern, loosen then remove the bolts (**Figure 392**) securing the front bevel gear assembly to the crankcase.

5. Carefully remove the front bevel gear assembly and gasket from the crankcase and separate the splines from the universal joint on the drive shaft. Discard the gasket.

6. Hold onto the damper cam follower and spring so they will not fall out of the open end of the front bevel gear assembly.

7. Don't lose the locating pin in the crankcase.

8. Inspect the components as described in this chapter.

Installation

1. Make sure the clutch rod (A, **Figure 393**) is still in place in the crankcase.

2. Apply a light coat of molybdenum disulfide grease to the ramps on the damper cam (B, **Figure 393**) and the damper cam follower (**Figure 394**).

3. If removed, install the locating dowels (C, **Figure 393**) in the crankcase.

4. Install a new gasket (D, **Figure 393**).

5. If removed, install the spring (**Figure 395**) and the damper cam follower (**Figure 394**).

6. Hold onto the damper cam follower and spring so they will not fall out during installation.

7. Install the front bevel gear assembly onto the crankcase while aligning the splines with the universal joint on the drive shaft.

8. Properly mesh the ramps on the damper cam with the damper cam follower.

9. Slowly push the front bevel gear assembly onto the receptacle in the crankcase.

10. Apply blue Loctite (No. 242) to the 95 mm bolts securing the front bevel gear case bolts prior to installation. Install the bolts (**Figure 392**).

11. Tighten the bolts finger-tight until they are snug against the gear assembly case. Due to the internal spring pressure, there will be a 5 mm (0.20 in.) gap (**Figure 396**) between the housing and the mating surface of the crankcase. This is normal.

12. Tighten the front bevel gear housing bolts (**Figure 392**) and tighten in a criss-cross pattern to the torque specification listed in **Table 2**.

NOTE
Make sure the transmission is in neutral.

13. Rotate the rear wheel to make sure the universal joint and front bevel gear assembly are rotating properly. If not, correct the problem at this time.

14. Connect the lower end of the clutch cable onto the clutch release lever as described in Chapter Five.

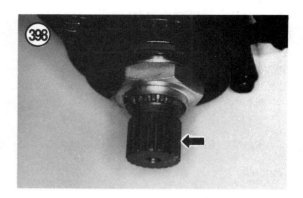

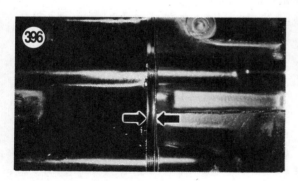

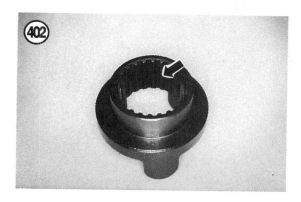

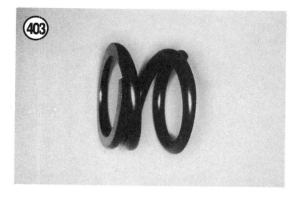

15. Adjust the clutch cable as described in Chapter Three.

16. Check the oil level in the engine as described in Chapter Three, add oil if necessary.

Inspection

Special tools are required to disassemble the front bevel gear assembly. If any service procedures are required, refer this type of work to a Kawasaki dealer.

1. Inspect for chipped or missing teeth on the gears (**Figure 397**).

2. Inspect the driven gear assembly splines (**Figure 398**) for wear or damage. If damaged, both the drive and driven gears must be replaced as a set. Also check the inner splines (**Figure 399**) of the universal joint as they may also be damaged.

3. Make sure the driven gear shaft retaining nut is still staked in place (**Figure 400**).

4. Inspect the drive gear assembly splines (**Figure 401**) for wear or damage. If damaged, also check the inner splines (**Figure 399**) of the cam follower (**Figure 402**) as they may also be damaged.

5. Inspect the cam follower spring (**Figure 403**) for wear, cracks or damage and replace if necessary.

6. Inspect the cam follower ramps (**Figure 404**) for wear or damage. If the ramps are damaged, inspect the ramps on the damper cam follower (**Figure 405**) attached to the end of the transmission countershaft. If worn or damaged, it should also be replaced as described in this chapter.

CRANKCASE

Service to the lower end requires that the crankcase assembly be removed from the motorcycle frame and disassembled (split).

Disassembly

1. Remove the engine as described in this chapter.

2. Remove the following exterior assemblies from the crankcase assembly:

    a. Cylinder head, cylinder block assemblies and pistons: this chapter.

    b. Camshaft drive chains, guides and tensioners: this chapter.

    c. Alternator: Chapter Eight.

d. Balancer assembly: Chapter Eight.

e. Front bevel gear assembly: this chapter.

f. Oil filter: Chapter Three.

g. External shift mechanism: Chapter Six.

h. Clutch: Chapter Five.

i. Starter motor: Chapter Eight.

j. Neutral switch: Chapter Eight.

k. Oil pressure switch: Chapter Eight.

3. If still in place, remove the primary drive gear Woodruff key (**Figure 406**) from the crankshaft taper.

4. Shift the transmission into gear.

5. Un-stake the nut (**Figure 407**) securing the damper cam to the end of the transmission countershaft.

6. Loosen, then remove the nut (**Figure 408**) securing the damper cam.

7. Remove the washer (**Figure 409**) and remove the damper cam (**Figure 410**) from the end of the transmission countershaft.

8. Remove the bolt and bearing retainer (**Figure 411**).

9. Remove the clutch pushrod (A, **Figure 412**) and the pushrod retainer (B, **Figure 412**).

10. Remove the bolts securing the oil filter plate (**Figure 413**) and remove the plate and the large and small O-ring seals.

11. Turn the crankcase on its side with the right-hand side facing up.

12. On the right-hand side, loosen the 4 bolts by 1/2 turn in a crisscross pattern, then remove the bolts. Make sure all 4 bolts are removed. Refer to **Figure 414**, **Figure 415** and **Figure 416**.

13. Turn the crankcase over with the left-hand side facing up.

14. Starting with the 6 mm bolts along the bottom and rear of the crankcase. Refer to **Figure 417** and **Figure 418**. Don't forget the 2 bolts (**Figure 419**) in the deep recesses at the rear. Loosen all bolts by 1/2

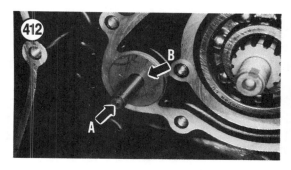

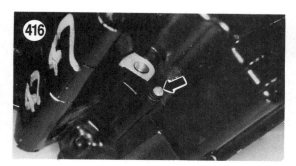

turn in a crisscross pattern, then remove the 6 mm bolts. Make sure all 8 bolts are removed.

15. Next, loosen the three 10 mm bolts (**Figure 420**) by 1/2 turn, then remove the 10 mm bolts. Make sure all 3 bolts are removed.

16. Turn the crankcase back over so the right-hand side is facing up.

> *CAUTION*
> *If it is necessary to pry the crankcase apart, do it very carefully only at the pry points located at the front and rear. Be careful that you do not mar and damage the gasket surfaces. If the surface is damaged, the cases will leak and must be replaced as a set. They cannot be repaired.*

17. Carefully tap around the perimeter of the crankcase with a plastic mallet (do not use a metal hammer) to help separate the 2 case halves. Separate the case halves by pulling the right-hand crankcase up and off the left-hand case half.

18. After removing the right-hand crankcase half, the transmission and crankshaft assemblies should stay with the left-hand crankcase. Check the right-hand crankcase to make sure no transmission shims are stuck to the bearings. If found, reinstall them immediately in their original positions.

19. Remove the oil filter adapter bolt and O-ring (**Figure 421**).

20. If loose, remove the 2 small dowel pins (**Figure 422**) from the left-hand crankcase half. If the pins are secure in their receptacles, do not remove them.

21. Remove the transmission, shift forks and shift drum assemblies from the left-hand crankcase half as described in Chapter Five in this section of the manual.

22. Remove the oil pump and drive chain as described in this chapter.

23. Remove the crankshaft assembly as described in this chapter.

Inspection

The following procedure may require the use of some highly specialized and expensive measuring instruments. If such instruments are not readily available, have the measurements performed by a dealer or qualified machine shop.

1. Remove all old sealant residue material from both crankcase mating surfaces.

2. Soak with solvent any old cylinder block gasket material that may be stuck to the top surface where the cylinder blocks attach. Use a broad-tipped *dull* chisel and gently scrape off all gasket residue. Do not gouge the sealing surfaces as oil and air leaks will result.

3. On the inside surface of the left-hand crankcase half, remove the bolts securing the oil pipes (**Figure 423**) and remove the oil pipes and the O-ring seals.

4. On the left-hand crankcase half, remove the bolts securing the oil pipe (**Figure 424**) and remove the oil pipe and O-ring seal.

5. On the exterior of the left-hand crankcase, remove the screws (A, **Figure 425**) securing the oil pipe (B, **Figure 425**) and remove the oil pipe and O-ring seals.

6. On the exterior of the left-hand crankcase, remove the single countersunk screw (A, **Figure 426**) and 2 round head screws (B, **Figure 426**) securing the oil passage cover (C, **Figure 426**) and remove the cover and gasket. Discard the gasket.

7. Remove the oil pressure relief valve (**Figure 427**) from the left-hand crankcase half.

8. Remove the circlip securing the water pump driveshaft and remove the driveshaft from the right-hand crankcase half.

9. Thoroughly clean the inside and outside of both crankcase halves with cleaning solvent. Dry with compressed air. Make sure there is no solvent residue left in either part as it will contaminate the new engine oil.

10. Make sure the crankcase studs (**Figure 428**) are tight.

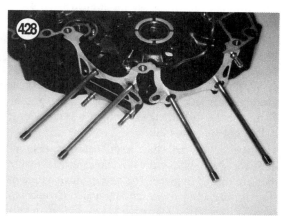

11. Check all studs (**Figure 429**) and threaded holes for stripping, cross-threading or deposit buildup. Threaded holes should be blown out with compressed air as dirt buildup in the bottom of a hole may prevent the bolt from being torqued properly. Replace damaged bolts and washers.

12. Inspect machined surfaces for burrs, cracks or other damage. Repair minor damage with a fine-cut file or oilstone.

13. Make sure that all oil passages throughout both crankcase halves are clean.

14. Make sure the oil passages in the oil pump receptacle (**Figure 430**) are clear with no sludge build-up.

15. Apply a light coat of engine oil to the bearing surfaces to prevent any rust formation.

16. Inspect the threads of the oil filter adaptor bolt. Clean off with a wire brush if necessary. If the threads are damaged, clean them up with an appropriate size metric thread die.

17. Inspect the crankcase bearings as described in this chapter.

18. Make sure the oil control holes are clear. Clean out with a piece of wire and compressed air.

19. Install all items removed during this inspection process.

20. Install new O-ring seals on the oil pipes prior to installation. Tighten the bolts securely.

Crankcase Bearings
Inspection

1. After cleaning the crankcase halves in cleaning solvent and drying with compressed air, lubricate the bearings with engine oil.

2. With your fingers, rotate the transmission bearing inner races (**Figure 431**) and the balancer shaft bearing inner race (**Figure 432** and **Figure 433**) while checking for play or roughness. Replace the bearing(s) if it is noisy or if it does not spin smoothly.

3. With your fingers, rotate the front bevel gear bearing inner race (**Figure 434**) and check for play or roughness. Replace the bearing if it is noisy or if it does not spin smoothly.

4. Inspect the crankshaft main bearings (**Figure 435**) for wear (bluish tint) or damage. Make sure they are locked in place. The bearing inside dimension is measured as described under *Crankshaft Bearing and Oil Clearance Measurement* in this

chapter. If the bearings are damaged or worn, have them replaced.

Crankcase Bearings Replacement

Crankshaft main bearings

The crankshaft main bearings are removed and installed from the crankcase halves with a hydraulic

press and special tools. After the new bearings are installed, they must be honed.

To avoid damage to a costly set of crankcase halves, this procedure should be entrusted to a Kawasaki dealer or machine shop. Improper removal and installation of the bearings could result in costly crankcase damage.

Bearings other than crankshaft main bearings

1. On bearings equipped with retainers, perform the following:

NOTE
The bearing retainer screws had a locking agent applied to the threads during installation and may be difficult to remove. To avoid damage or "rounding" off of the screw head, use the recommended tool in this procedure.

a. Use an impact driver with the appropriate size bit and loosen the screws securing the bearing retainers.
b. Remove the screws and retainers.

CAUTION
*If you use a household oven, first check with the person who uses the oven for food preparation to avoid getting into trouble, because there **may** be a residual oil or solvent odor left in the oven after heating the crankcase.*

2. Heat the crankcase to approximately 205-257° F (95-125° C) in an oven or on a hot plate. Do not attempt bearing removal by heating the crankcases with a torch as this type of localized heating may warp the cases.
3. Wear a pair of gloves for protection while removing the case from the oven and placing it on wood blocks for support.
4. Drive the bearing out with a suitable size drift placed on the outside bearing race. A large socket also works well for bearing removal.
5. Install new crankcase bearings by reversing the removal steps, noting the following:
a. Installation of the bearings is easier if the bearings are first placed in a freezer for approximately 30 minutes. Reheat the crankcase half and install the cold bearing by driving it squarely into position. If the bearing cocks in its

bore, remove it and reinstall. It may be necessary to refreeze the bearing and reheat the case half.

b. Lubricate the bearing races with clean engine oil after installation.

c. On bearings with retainers, install the retainer, apply red Loctite (No. 271) to the screw threads prior to installation. Install the screws and tighten with an impact driver and appropriate bit.

Assembly

1. Prior to installation, all rotating parts should be coated with assembly oil or engine oil.
2. Place the left-hand crankcase on wood blocks.
3. Install the shift drum, shift forks and transmission assemblies as described in Chapter Five.
4. Install the crankshaft as described in this chapter. Make sure the connecting rods (A, **Figure 436**) are positioned correctly within the connecting rod and piston openings (B, **Figure 436**) in the crankcase.
5. If removed, install the 2 small dowel pins (**Figure 422**) into the left-hand crankcase half.
6. Apply oil to the transmission shafts, crankshaft and balancer shaft bearing surfaces to make installation easier.
7. Clean the crankcase mating surfaces of both halves with aerosol electrical contact cleaner and wipe dry with a lint-free cloth.
8. Make sure both crankcase half sealing surfaces are perfectly clean and dry.

NOTE
Use a black silicone sealant, ThreeBond No. 1207, or equivalent gasket sealer. If using an equivalent, avoid thick and hard-setting materials.

9. Apply a light coat of gasket sealer to the sealing surfaces of the left-hand half. Make the coating as thin as possible.
10. Install the oil filter adapter bolt (**Figure 421**).
11. Align the right-hand crankcase bearings with the left-hand assembly. Join both halves and tap together lightly with a plastic mallet—do not damage the cases by using a metal hammer.

CAUTION
The crankcase halves should fit together without force. If the crankcase

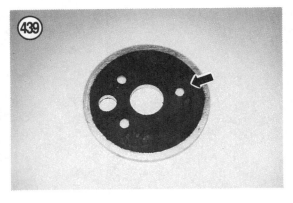

halves do not fit together, do not attempt to pull them together with the crankcase bolts. Separate the crankcase halves and investigate the cause of the interference. If the transmission shafts were disassembled, recheck to make sure that a gear is not installed backwards. Do not risk damage by trying to force the cases together.

12. Turn the crankcase over with the left-hand side facing up.

NOTE
Install all bolts in the crankcase half so that all bolt heads protrude up from the

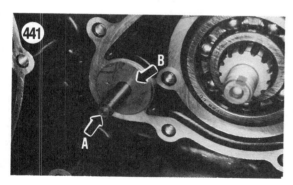

surface of the crankcase the same amount. If a bolt is installed in the wrong location, remove the bolt and insert it in the correct hole.

13. First tighten the three 10 mm bolts (**Figure 420**) securely in two stages.

14. Then tighten the 6 mm bolts along the bottom and rear of the crankcase. Refer to **Figure 417** and **Figure 418**. Don't forget the 2 bolts (**Figure 419**) in the deep recesses at the rear. Tighten the bolts securely in a crisscross pattern in two stages.

15. Turn the crankcase on its side with the right-hand side facing up.

16. Install and tighten the 4 bolts. Refer to **Figure 414**, **Figure 415** and **Figure 416**. Tighten the bolts securely in a crisscross pattern in two stages.

17. Install new O-ring seals (**Figure 437**) on the oil filter adapter bolt and inlet hole.

18. After the crankcase halves are assembled, and the bolts tightened, apply a light coat of the same sealant used in Step 9 to the cylinder block sealing surface where the 2 crankcase halves join near the oil filter plate (**Figure 438**). Perform this step at both cylinder block sealing surface areas on the crankcase assembly.

19. Install a new gasket (**Figure 439**) onto the backside of the oil filter plate. Install the plate (**Figure 440**) and the bolts and tighten securely.

20. Apply a light coat of molybdenum disulfide grease to the ends of the clutch pushrod and install the pushrod (A, **Figure 441**) and the pushrod retainer (B, **Figure 441**).

21. Position the bearing retainer with the shoulder side (**Figure 442**) going in first. Install the bearing retainer and bolt (**Figure 443**). Tighten the bolt securely.

22. Shift the transmission into gear.

23. Install the damper cam (**Figure 444**) onto the end of the transmission countershaft.

24. Install the washer (**Figure 445**).

25. Install a new damper cam nut (**Figure 446**) and tighten to the torque specification listed in **Table 2**.

26. Use a hammer and chisel and stake the damper cam nut (**Figure 447**) into the groove in the end of the transmission countershaft.

27. Install the following exterior assemblies onto the crankcase assembly:

   a. Oil pressure switch: Chapter Eight.

   b. Neutral switch: Chapter Eight.

   c. Starter motor: Chapter Eight.

   d. Clutch: Chapter Five.

   e. External shift mechanism: Chapter Six.

   f. Oil filter: Chapter Three.

   g. Starter clutch assembly: Chapter Eight.

   h. Balancer assembly: Chapter Eight.

   i. Front bevel gear assembly: this chapter.

   j. Alternator: Chapter Eight.

   k. Camshaft drive chains, guides and tensioners: this chapter.

   l. Pistons, cylinder block and cylinder head assemblies: this chapter.

28. Install the engine as described in this chapter.

CRANKSHAFT AND CONNECTING RODS

Removal/Installation

1. Split the crankcase as described in this chapter.

2. Remove the crankshaft assembly (**Figure 448**) from the left-hand crankcase half.

3. Remove the connecting rod cap bolt nuts and separate the rods from the crankshaft.

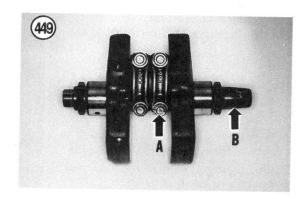

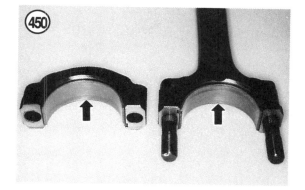

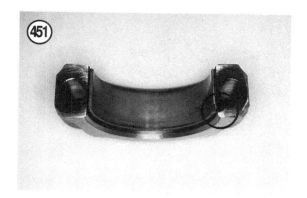

NOTE
*The rear cylinder connecting rod (A, **Figure 449**) is located on the left-hand portion of the crankpin adjacent to the tapered end (B, **Figure 449**) of the crankshaft.*

4. Mark each rod and cap as a set. Also mark them with a "F" (front) and "R" (rear) to indicate from which cylinder they were removed.

5. If the inserts are going to be removed, mark each rod cap and bearing insert so that they can be reinstalled in their original position.

CAUTION
If the old bearings are reused, they must be installed in their exact positions.

6. If removed, install the bearing inserts (**Figure 450**) into each connecting rod and cap. Make sure they are locked in place correctly (**Figure 451**).

7. Lubricate the bearings and crank pins with molybdenum disulfide grease.

8. Position the connecting rod and cap with the I.D. code number (**Figure 452**) facing toward the *rear* of the engine.

9. The rear cylinder connecting rod (A, **Figure 449**) is located on the left-hand portion of the crankpin adjacent to the tapered end (B, **Figure 449**) of the crankshaft.

10. Install the caps and tighten the caps nuts (**Figure 453**) evenly, in 2 stages, to the torque specification listed in **Table 2**.

NOTE
*When installing the crankshaft, make sure the connecting rods (A, **Figure 436**) are positioned correctly within the connecting rod and piston openings (B,*

Figure 436) in the crankcase. Continue to check this alignment until the crankshaft is completely installed.

11. Install the crankshaft with the tapered end in the left-hand crankcase (**Figure 448**).

12. Assemble the crankcase as described in this chapter.

Connecting Rod Inspection

1. Check each rod and cap for obvious damage such as cracks and burrs.

2. Check the connecting rod small end for wear or scoring.

3. Insert the piston pin into the connecting rod (**Figure 454**) and rotate it to check for looseness or roughness. Replace the defective part.

4. Take the rods to a machine shop and have them checked for twisting and bending.

5. Examine the bearing inserts (**Figure 450**) for wear, scoring or burning. They can be reused if in good condition. Check the back of each insert before it is discarded to see if an undersize is marked on the back. A previous owner may have installed under-size bearings.

6. Inspect the connecting rod threaded studs (**Figure 455**) for wear or damaged threads. Clean up with an appropriate size metric die. If damage is severe, replace the connecting rod.

7. Check bearing clearance as described in this chapter.

Connecting Rod Bearing and Oil Clearance Measurement

CAUTION
If the old bearings are to be reused, be sure that they are installed in their exact original locations.

1. Wipe bearing inserts and crank pins clean. Install bearing inserts in rod and cap (**Figure 450**).

2. Place a piece of Plastigage on one crankpin parallel to the crankshaft.

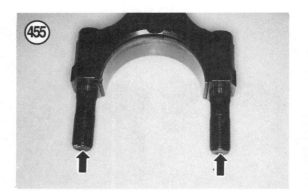

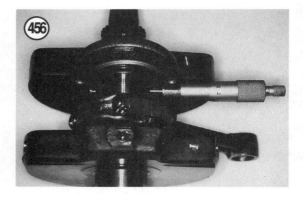

3. Install rod, cap and nuts, then tighten the nuts to the torque specification listed in **Table 2**.

CAUTION
Do not rotate crankshaft while Plastigage is in place.

4. Remove nuts and the rod cap.

5. Measure width of flattened Plastigage according to the manufacturer's instructions. Measure at both ends of the strip. A difference of 0.001 in. (0.025 mm) or more indicates a tapered crankpin; the crank-

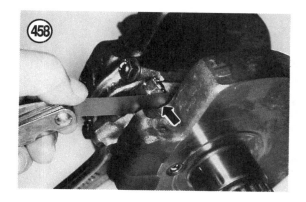

shaft must be reground or replaced. Use a micrometer and measure the crankpin OD (**Figure 456**) to get an exact journal dimension.

6. If the crankpin taper is within tolerance, determine the bearing clearance with the same strip of Plastigage. Correct bearing clearance is specified in **Table 1**. Remove the Plastigage strips.

7. If the bearing clearance is greater than specified, use the following steps for new bearing selection.

8. The connecting rods and caps either have a mark (**Figure 452**) or are not marked at all.

9. The crankshaft may have a mark (**Figure 457**) at the counterbalancer or may be unmarked.

10. Refer to **Table 3**, select new bearings by cross-referencing the connecting rod journal I.D. code in the vertical column with the crankpin O.D. code number in the horizontal column. Where the columns intersect, the new bearing color is indicated. **Table 3** gives the bearing color.

11. After new bearings have been installed, recheck clearance with Plastigage. If the clearance is out of specifications, either the connecting rod or the crankshaft is worn beyond the service limit. Refer the engine to a dealer or qualified specialist.

Connecting Rod Side Clearance Measurement

1. With both connecting rods attached to the crankshaft, insert a flat feeler gauge between the counterweight and the connecting rod big end (**Figure 458**).

2. The specified side clearance is listed in **Table 1**.

3. If the clearance is out of specification, replace the connecting rods and recheck the side clearance. If the clearance is still out of specification, replace the crankshaft assembly.

Crankshaft Inspection

1. Clean crankshaft thoroughly with solvent. Clean oil holes (**Figure 459**) with rifle cleaning brushes; flush thoroughly and dry with compressed air. Lightly oil all journal surfaces immediately after cleaning to prevent rust.

2. Inspect the connecting rod journals (A, **Figure 460**) and the main bearing journals (B, **Figure 460**) for scratches, ridges, scoring, nicks, etc.

3. If the surfaces of all bearing journals appear to be satisfactory, measure the main bearing journals with

a micrometer (**Figure 461**) and check for out-of-roundness and taper.

4. Inspect the camshaft chain sprocket on the right-hand end (**Figure 462**) and on the left-hand end (A, **Figure 463**). If it is worn or damaged, the crankshaft must be replaced.

5. Inspect the taper (B, **Figure 463**) where the alternator rotor is installed on the left-hand end. If it is worn or damaged, the crankshaft must be replaced.

6. Inspect the Woodruff key and slot on each end of the crankshaft for wear or damage. The key must fit tight in the slot to secure the Woodruff key. If necessary, replace the Woodruff key. If the new key still does not fit in securely, the crankshaft should be replaced.

7. Measure the overall length of the crankshaft web (**Figure 464**) with a vernier caliper. Compare to the dimension listed in **Table 1**. If worn to the service limit or less, replace the crankshaft.

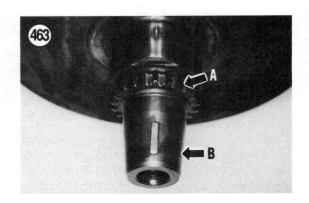

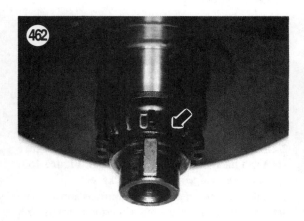

4

Crankshaft Bearing and Oil Clearance Measurement

1. Wipe bearing inserts in the crankcase and the main bearing journals clean.

2. Use a micrometer and measure the main journal OD (**Figure 461**) at two places. Write these dimensions down.

3. Use a bore gauge and measure the main journal insert ID (**Figure 465**) at two places (**Figure 466**). Write these dimensions down.

4. To select the proper bearing insert number, subtract the crankshaft OD (Step 2) from the main journal insert ID (Step 3). 5. The oil clearance specification is listed in **Table 1**. If the clearance is out of specifications, either the crankshaft or the bearing insert is worn beyond the service limit.

NOTE
The main bearings are removed and installed with a hydraulic press and special tools. After new bearings have been installed, they must be honed to a specific dimension. To avoid damage to a costly set of crankcase halves, this procedure should be entrusted to a Kawasaki dealer or machine shop. Improper removal and installation of the bearings could result in severe crankcase damage.

BREAK-IN

Following cylinder servicing (boring, honing, new rings, etc.) and major lower end work, the engine should be broken-in just as if it were new. The performance and service life of the engine depends greatly on a careful and sensible break-in. For the first 500 miles, no more than one-third throttle should be used and speed should be varied as much as possible within the one-third throttle limit. Prolonged, steady running at one speed, no matter how moderate, is to be avoided, as is hard acceleration.

Following the 500-mile service, increasingly more throttle can be used but full throttle should not be used until the motorcycle has covered at least 1,000 miles and then it should be limited to short bursts until 1,500 miles have been logged.

The mono-grade oils recommended for break-in and normal use provide a superior bedding pattern for rings and cylinders than do multi-grade oils. As a result, piston ring and cylinder bore life are greatly increased. During this period, oil consumption will be higher than normal. It is therefore important to frequently check and correct the oil level. At no time, during break-in or later, should the oil level be allowed to drop below the bottom line on the inspection window; if the oil level is low, the oil will overheat causing insufficient lubrication and increased wear.

500-Mile Service

It is essential that the oil and filter be changed after the first 500 miles. In addition, it is a good idea to change the oil and filter at the completion of break-in (about 1,500 miles) to ensure that all of the particles produced during break-in are removed from the lubrication system. The small added expense may be considered a smart investment that will pay off in increased engine life.

Table 1 ENGINE SPECIFICATIONS

	Specification	Wear limit
General		
Type and number of cylinders	V-2 cylinder, DOHC, liquid cooled	
Bore × stroke		
700 cc	82.0 × 66.2 mm (3.2 × 2.6 in.)	
750 cc	84.9 × 66.2 mm (3.34 × 2.6 in.)	
(continued)		

Table 1 ENGINE SPECIFICATIONS (continued)

	Specification	Wear limit
General (continued)		
Displacement		
700 cc	699 ml	
	(42.6 cu. in.)	
750 cc	749 ml	
	(45.71 cu. in.)	
Compression ratio	10.3:1	
Compression pressure	890-1,370 kPa	
	(129-199 psi)	
Camshaft		
Cam lobe height		
Intake	33.450-33.558 mm	33.350 mm
	(1.3169-1.3212 in.)	(1.313 in.)
Exhaust	33.139-33.247 mm	33.039 mm
	(1.3046-1.3089 in.)	(1.301 in.))
Journal O.D.	26.959-26.980 mm	26.93 mm
	(1.0614-1.0622 in.)	(1.0602 in.)
Bearing I.D.	27.000-27.021 mm	27.08 mm
	(1.0629-1.0638 in.)	(1.0661 in.)
Journal oil clearance	0.020-0.062 mm	0.150 mm
	(0.0007-0.0024 in.)	(0.0059 in.)
Chain 20 link length		
Upper and lower chain	127.0-127.4 mm	128.9 mm
	(5.000-5.016 in.)	(5.075 in.)
Cylinder head distortion	–	0.05 mm (0.002 in.)
Cylinder head cover distortion	–	0.05 mm (0.002 in.)
Valves and valve springs		
Valve stem O.D.		
Intake	5.475-5.490 mm	–
	(0.2155-0.2161 in.)	
Exhaust	5.455-5.470 mm	–
	(0.2147-0.2153 in.)	
Valve stem bend	–	0.05 mm (0.002 in.)
Valve guide I.D.	5.500-5.512 mm	–
Intake and exhaust	(0.2165-0.2170 in.)	
Valve stem-to-guide clearance (wobble method)		
Intake	0.020-0.080 mm	0.22 mm
	(0.0007-0.0031 in.)	(0.008 in.)
Exhaust	0.07-0.13 mm	0.27 mm
	(0.0027-0.0051 in.)	(0.011 in.)
Valve seating surface:		
Outside diameter		
Intake	30.9-31.3 mm	–
	(0.1216-0.1224 in.)	
Exhaust	26.9-27.1 mm	–
	(0.1059-0.1067 in.)	
Width		
Intake and exhaust	0.5-1.0 mm	–
	(0.0196-0.039 in.)	
Valve seat cutting angle	32, 45, 60 degrees	
Valve spring free length		
Inner	35.9 mm (1.413 in.)	33.8 mm (1.33 in.)
Outer	41.5 mm (1.634 in.)	39.4 mm (1.55 in.)
Hydraulic lash adjuster	0-0.2 mm (0-0.0078 in.)	0.2 mm (0.0078 in.)
leak down distance		

(continued)

Table 1 ENGINE SPECIFICATIONS (continued)

	Specification	Wear limit
Cylinders		
Bore		
700 cc	82.000-82.012 mm	82.10 mm
	(3.2283-3.2288 in.)	(3.2322 in.)
750 cc	84.900-84.912 mm	85.000 mm
	(3.3425-3.3429 in.)	(3.3464 in.)
Cylinder/piston clearance	0.043-0.070 mm	–
	(0.0016-0.0027 in.)	
Out-of-round	–	0.05 mm (0.002 in.)
Pistons		
Outer diameter		
700 cc	81.942-81.957 mm	81.800 mm
	(3.2226-3.2266 in.)	(3.2205 in.)
750 cc	84.842-84.857 mm	84.700 mm
	(3.3402-3.3408 in.)	(3.3346 in.)
Piston ring groove width		
Top	1.02-1.04 mm	1.12 mm
	(0.040-0.041 in.)	(0.044 in.)
Piston rings		
Number per piston		
Compression	2	–
Oil control	1	–
Ring thickness		
Top and second	0.97-0.99 mm	1.08 mm
	(0.0381-0.0389 in.)	(0.042 in.)
Ring/groove clearance		
Top	0.03-0.07 mm	0.17 mm
	(0.0012-0.0027 in.)	(0.0067 in.)
Second	0.02-0.06 mm	0.16 mm
	(0.0007-0.0023 in.)	(0.0063 in.)
Ring end gap		
Top and second	0.25-0.45 mm	0.75 mm
	(0.009-0.018 in.)	(0.029 in.)
Connecting rods		
Big end side clearance	0.16-0.46 mm	0.70 mm
	(0.006-0.018 in.)	(0.027 in.)
Big end oil clearance	0.026-0.054 mm	0.09 mm
	(0.0010-0.0021 in.)	(0.0035 in.)
Big end bore I.D.		
Marking: None	46.000-46.010 mm	–
	(1.8110-1.8114 in.)	
Marking: "1"	46.011-46.020 mm	–
	(1.8114-1.8118 in.)	
Crankshaft		
Crankpin O.D.		
Marking: None	42.984-42.992 mm	–
	(1.6923-1.6925 in.)	
Marking: "1"	42.993-43.000 mm	–
	(1.6926-1.6929 in.)	
Main bearing journal O.D.	42.984-43.00 mm	42.96 mm
	(1.6923-1.6929 in.)	(1.691 in.)
Runout	0.2 mm (0.0078 in.)	0.75 mm (0.0295 in.)
Side clearance	0.05-0.55 mm	0.75 mm
	(0.0019-0.0216 in.)	(0.0295 in.)

(continued)

Table 1 ENGINE SPECIFICATIONS (continued)

	Specification	Wear limit
Crankshaft (continued)		
Web length	96.85-96.95 mm (3.8129-3.8169 in.)	96.6 mm (3.803 in.)
Crankcase		
Main bearing journal bore I.D.	43.025-43.041 mm (1.6938-1.6945 in.)	43.09 mm (1.6964 in.)
Oil pump		
Outer rotor-to-inner rotor clearance	less than 0.12 mm (0.0047 in.)	0.20 mm (0.0078 in.)
Outer rotor-to-body clearance	0.15-0.21 mm (0.005-0.008 in.)	0.30 mm (0.0118 in.)
Outer rotor O.D.	40.53-40.56 mm (1.5956-1.5968 in.)	40.45 mm (1.5925 in.)
Pump body I.D.	40.71-40.74 mm (1.6027-1.6039 in.)	40.80 mm (1.6063 in.)
Rotor side clearance	0.02-0.07 mm (0.0007-0.0027 in.)	0.12 mm (0.00472 in.)
Drive chain slack	8-10 mm (0.3149-0.3937 in.)	13 mm (0.5118 in.)

Table 2 ENGINE TIGHTENING TORQUES

Item	N·m	ft-.lb.
Engine mounting bolts and nuts		
Front mounting bracket bolts	24	17.5
Right-hand side bracket bolts	24	17.5
Sub-frame bolts and nuts	44	33
Through bolts and nuts	44	33
Cylinder head cover bolts	9.8	87 in.-lb.
Camshaft bearing cap bolts	12	8.5
Cylinder head bolts	12	8.5
Cylinder head-to-crankcase stud nuts		
6 mm		
Preliminary	6.9	5
Final	15	11
10 mm		
Preliminary	25	18
Final	39	29
Cylinder head-to-cylinder nuts	8-12	6-8.5
6 mm		
Preliminary	8.8	6.5
Final	15	11
8 mm		
Preliminary	18	13
Final	25	18
Spark plug retainer	12	8.5
Exhaust manifold cap nuts	25	18
Cylinder block		
Cap nuts	25	18
Nuts	25	18
Upper chain guide bolts	24	17.5
Upper chain guide tensioner bolt	15	11
Connecting rod cap nuts	46	34
Oil pressure relief valve	15	11
(continued)		

Table 2 ENGINE TIGHTENING TORQUES (continued)

Item	N·m	ft-.lb.
Oil pressure switch bolt	20	14.5
Oil screen/drain bolt	18	13
Right-hand balancer bolt	69	51
Left-hand balancer bolt	69	51
External oil line bolt	12	8.5
Starter one-way clutch Allen bolts	34	25
Damper cam nut	120	88.5
Front bevel gear case bolt	12	8.5

Table 3 CONNECTING ROD BEARING SELECTION

Con. rod big end bore diameter marking	Crankpin diameter marking	Bearing insert size color	Part No.
O	1	black	13034-1058
None	None	black	13034-1058
O	None	blue	13034-1057
None	1	brown	13034-1059

CHAPTER FIVE

CLUTCH

This chapter provides complete service procedures for the clutch and clutch release mechanism.

The clutch is a wet multi-plate type which operates immersed in the engine oil. It is mounted on the right-hand end of the transmission main shaft. The inner clutch hub is splined to the main shaft and the outer housing can rotate freely on the main shaft. The outer housing is geared to the crankshaft. The clutch pushrod operates in a channel in the transmission main shaft.

The clutch release mechanism is cable operated and requires routine adjustment that is covered in this chapter. Movement of the release mechanism located on the left-hand side of the engine is transmitted to the clutch located on the right-hand side by a pushrod that rides within the channel in the transmission mainshaft.

Specifications for the clutch are listed in **Table 1**. **Table 1** and **Table 2** are located at the end of this chapter.

CLUTCH

Removal/Disassembly

The clutch assembly can be removed with the engine in the frame. All clutch components, with the exception of the outer housing, can be removed by just removing the clutch cover (**Figure 1**). If removal of the clutch outer housing is required, the engine right-hand crankcase cover must be removed.

This procedure is shown with the engine removed and partially disassembled for clarity.

Refer to **Figure 2** for this procedure.

1. Drain the engine oil as described under *Engine Oil and Filter Change* in Chapter Three.
2. Shift the transmission into gear.
3. Remove the exhaust system for the front cylinder as described under *Exhaust System Removal/Installation* in Chapter Seven.
4. Remove the bolts securing the clutch cover (**Figure 3**). Remove the clutch cover and gasket. If necessary, use a broad-tipped screwdriver and carefully pry the cover away from the crankcase cover.
5. Using a crisscross pattern, loosen the clutch bolts (**Figure 4**).

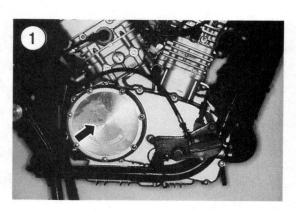

CLUTCH ASSEMBLY

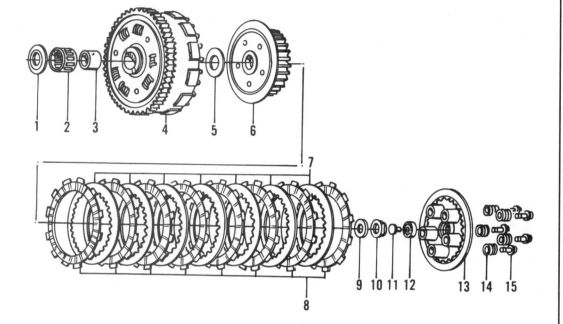

1. Thrust washer
2. Needle bearing
3. Bushing
4. Outer housing
5. Thrust washer
6. Clutch hub
7. Clutch disc
8. Friction plate
9. Washer
10. Nut
11. Push piece
12. Ball bearing
13. Pressure plate
14. Spring
15. Bolt

6. Remove the bolts.

7. Remove the clutch springs (**Figure 5**) and the pressure plate (**Figure 6**). Don't lose the clutch push piece in the backside of the pressure plate.

8. Remove the friction discs and clutch plates.

9. If necessary, remove the clutch pushrod from the transmission shaft.

> *CAUTION*
> *Do not clamp the special tool too tight as it may damage the grooves in the clutch hub.*

10. Attach a special tool such as the "Grabbit" (**Figure 7**) to the clutch hub to keep it from turning in the next step.

11. Loosen and then remove the clutch locknut (**Figure 8**) and washer (**Figure 9**).

12. Remove the special tool from the clutch hub.

13. Remove the clutch hub (**Figure 10**).

14. Remove the thrust washer (**Figure 11**).

15. If the clutch housing is going to be removed, perform the following:

a. Remove right-hand crankcase cover (**Figure 12**) as described under *Right-hand Crankcase Cover Removal/Installation* in Chapter Four.

> *CAUTION*
> *The needle bearing and bushing may stay with the clutch outer housing when it is removed. Do not drop the bearing or bushing after the outer housing is removed.*

b. Remove the clutch outer housing (**Figure 13**) from the transmission shaft.

c. If still in place, remove the needle bearing (**Figure 14**) and bushing (**Figure 15**) from the transmission shaft.

d. Remove the thrust spacer (**Figure 16**) from the transmission shaft.

Inspection

Refer to **Table 1** for clutch specifications.

1. Clean all clutch parts in petroleum-based solvent such as kerosene and thoroughly dry with compressed air.

2. Measure the free length of each clutch spring as shown in **Figure 17**. Compare to the specifications listed in **Table 1**. Replace any springs that have sagged to the service limit or less.

3. Measure the thickness of each friction disc at several places around the disc as shown in **Figure 18**. Compare to the specifications listed in **Table 1**. Replace any friction disc that is worn to the service limit or less.

4. Check the friction discs (**Figure 19**) and clutch plates (**Figure 20**) for surface damage from heat or lack of oil. Replace any disc and plate that is damaged in any way.

5. Check the friction discs (**Figure 21**) and the clutch plates (**Figure 22**) for warpage with a flat feeler gauge on a surface plate such as a piece of plate glass. Compare to the specifications listed in **Table 1**. Replace any plate that is warped to the service limit or more.

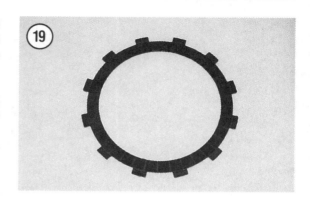

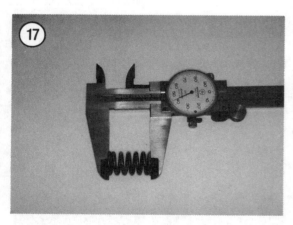

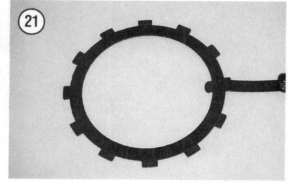

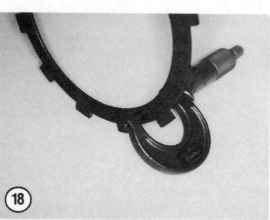

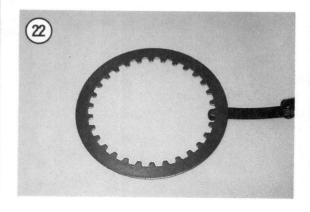

NOTE
If any of the friction discs, clutch plates or clutch springs require replacement, you should consider replacing all of them as a set to retain maximum clutch performance.

6. Inspect the slots (**Figure 23**) and reinforcement ribs (**Figure 24**) in the clutch outer housing for cracks, nicks or galling where they come in contact with the friction disc tabs. If any severe damage is evident, the housing must be replaced.

7. Inspect the driven gear teeth (**Figure 25**) on the clutch outer housing for damage. Remove any small nicks with an oilstone. If damage is severe, the clutch outer housing must be replaced.

8. Inspect the damper springs (**Figure 26**). If they are sagged or broken, the housing must be replaced.

9. Inspect the outer grooves (**Figure 27**) and studs (**Figure 28**) in the clutch hub. If either show signs of wear or galling, the clutch hub should be replaced.

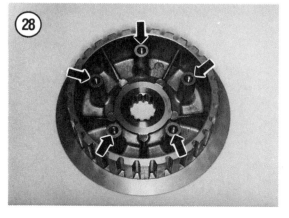

10. Inspect the inner splines (**Figure 29**) in the clutch hub for damage. Remove any small nicks with an oilstone. If damage is severe, the clutch hub must be replaced.

11. Inspect the spring receptacles (**Figure 30**) and inner grooves (A, **Figure 31**) in the clutch pressure plate for wear or damage. Replace the clutch pressure plate if necessary.

12. Check the inner surface (**Figure 32**) of the clutch outer housing, where the needle bearing rides, for signs of wear or damage. Replace the clutch outer housing if necessary.

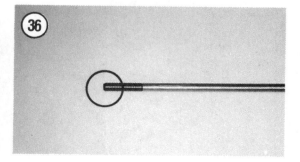

13. Check the needle bearing (**Figure 33**). Make sure it rotates smoothly with no signs of wear or damage. Replace if necessary.

14. Check the inner and outer surfaces of the bushing (**Figure 34**) for signs of wear or damage. Replace if necessary.

15. Install the bushing into the needle bearing, rotate the bushing (**Figure 35**) and check for wear. Replace parts as necessary.

16. Check the clutch push piece (B, **Figure 31**) for wear or damage. Replace if necessary.

17. Check the clutch push piece bearing (C, **Figure 31**). Make sure it rotates smoothly with no signs of wear or damage. Replace if necessary.

18. Inspect the clutch push rod for bending by rolling it on a surface plate or piece of plate glass. Kawasaki does not provide service information for this component, but if the rod is bent or deformed in any way it must be replaced. Otherwise, it may hang up in the channel inside the transmission shaft, causing erratic clutch operation.

19. Inspect each end (**Figure 36**) of the clutch push rod for wear or damage. Replace if necessary.

Assembly/Installation

Refer to **Figure 37** for this procedure.

5

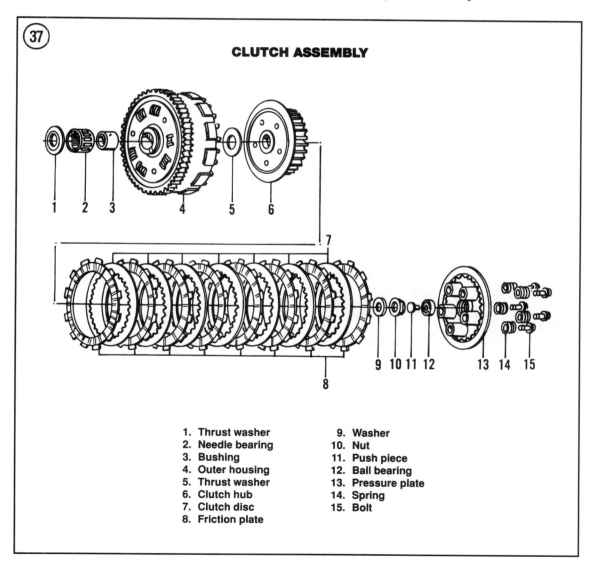

CLUTCH ASSEMBLY

1. Thrust washer
2. Needle bearing
3. Bushing
4. Outer housing
5. Thrust washer
6. Clutch hub
7. Clutch disc
8. Friction plate
9. Washer
10. Nut
11. Push piece
12. Ball bearing
13. Pressure plate
14. Spring
15. Bolt

1. If the clutch housing was removed, perform the following:
   a. Position the thrust spacer with the chamfered side (**Figure 38**) going on first, toward the engine. Install the thrust spacer (**Figure 16**) onto the transmission shaft.
   b. Install the bushing (**Figure 15**) onto the transmission shaft.
   c. Apply a good coat of clean engine oil to the needle bearing and install the needle bearing (**Figure 14**) onto the transmission shaft.
   d. Install the clutch outer housing (**Figure 13**) onto the needle bearing on the transmission shaft.
   e. Install the right-hand crankcase cover as described in Chapter Four.
2. Install the thrust washer (**Figure 11**).
3. Install the clutch hub (**Figure 10**).
4. Install the washer (**Figure 9**) and new clutch locknut (**Figure 8**).

> *CAUTION*
> *Do not clamp the special tool on too tight as it may damage the grooves in the clutch hub.*

5. Attach a special tool such as the "Grabbit" (**Figure 7**) to the clutch hub to keep it from turning in the next step.

6. Tighten the locknut to the torque specification listed in **Table 2**.

7. Remove the special tool from the clutch hub.

8. If removed, apply a light coat of molybdenum disulfide grease to the clutch pushrod and install the clutch pushrod onto the transmission shaft. Push the pushrod in until it stops.

NOTE
On some early models, the grooves cut into the friction discs radiate at an angle out from the center. On these models,

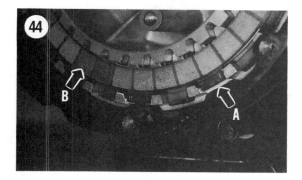

position the friction discs so the groove runs toward the center in the direction of the clutch hub rotation (counterclockwise as viewed from the right-hand side).

NOTE
If new friction discs and clutch plates are being installed, apply new engine oil to all surfaces to avoid having the clutch lock up when used for the first time.

NOTE
The clutch outer housing has 2 sets of grooves that accept the tangs of the frictions discs. The main grooves (A, Figure 39) are reinforced while the secondary grooves (B, Figure 39) are not. All friction discs except the last friction disc are to be installed into the **main grooves**. *The last friction disc is to be installed into the* **secondary grooves**.

9. First install a friction disc (A, **Figure 40**) onto the clutch hub with the friction disc tangs going into the *main grooves* (B, **Figure 40**).

10. Install a clutch plate (**Figure 41**) onto the clutch hub, then a friction disc (**Figure 42**).

11. Continue to install the clutch plates and friction discs, alternating them until all are installed except for the last friction disc. All of these friction disc tangs go into the main grooves.

12. Position the *last* friction disc so the tangs (A, **Figure 43**) go into the *secondary grooves* (B, **Figure 43**) and install this friction disc (A, **Figure 44**). The last item installed is this friction disc (B, **Figure 44**).

13. If removed, install the clutch push piece (B, **Figure 31**) into the backside of the pressure plate.

14. Install the clutch pressure plate (**Figure 6**).

15. Install the springs (**Figure 5**) and bolts.

16. Using a crisscross pattern, tighten the clutch bolts (**Figure 4**) to the torque specification listed in **Table 2**.

17. Position the clutch cover gasket with the triangle mark (**Figure 45**) located at the top and install the gasket.

18. Position the clutch cover with the indicator mark (**Figure 46**) located at the bottom and install the cover.

NOTE
If the clutch cover bolts are to be reused, apply a non-permanent locking agent

(blue Loctite No. 242) to the threads prior to installation. If new bolts are being installed, the locking agent is not necessary.

19. Install the clutch cover bolts and tighten securely.

20. Install the exhaust system for the front cylinder as described in Chapter Seven.

21. Refill the engine oil as described under *Engine Oil and Filter Change* in Chapter Three.

CLUTCH RELEASE MECHANISM

The clutch release mechanism is located in the front bevel gear case assembly. The release mechanism assembly can be removed with the front bevel case installed on the engine with the engine in the frame. This procedure is shown with the front bevel case removed from the engine for clarity.

Removal

Refer to **Figure 47** for this procedure.

1. Place the bike on the centerstand on level ground.

2. At the clutch lever on the handlebar, loosen the clutch cable locknut (A, **Figure 48**) and turn the

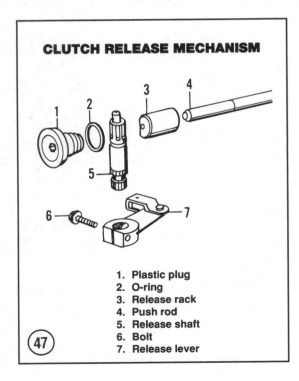

CLUTCH RELEASE MECHANISM

1. Plastic plug
2. O-ring
3. Release rack
4. Push rod
5. Release shaft
6. Bolt
7. Release lever

adjuster (B, **Figure 48**) in all the way to allow maximum slack in the clutch cable.

3. Place a drain pan under the alternator cover on the left-hand side. Some engine oil may drain out during this procedure.

4. Disconnect the lower end of the clutch cable from the release lever (**Figure 49**).

NOTE
The following steps are shown with the engine removed from the frame and the front bevel gear case removed from the

crankcase for clarity. It is not necessary to remove the engine nor separate the bevel gear case for this procedure.

5. Remove the bolt and washer (**Figure 50**) securing the clutch release shaft in the front bevel gear case.

CAUTION
*In Step 6, insert the 5 mm Allen wrench **all the way** into the relatively soft plastic plug until it bottoms. If the Allen wrench is only partially inserted into the opening and then pressure applied to loosen the plug, the opening will "round off" making removal very difficult.*

6. Use a 5 mm Allen wrench and carefully unscrew the plastic plug (**Figure 51**).

7. Rotate the release shaft *counterclockwise*, as viewed from the bottom, and withdraw the release rack (**Figure 52**) from the front bevel gear housing opening.

8. Withdraw the release shaft from the front bevel gear housing until it stops at the oil seal lip (**Figure 53**).

NOTE
If the oil seal is to be replaced, there is no need to use the oil seal guide in Step 9.

9. Insert a special tool, oil seal guide (part No. 57001-261) into the oil seal on the release shaft to protect the oil seal.

10. Carefully pull the release shaft from the front bevel gear housing and remove it.

Installation

Refer to **Figure 47** for this procedure.

1. Position the oil seal guide (part No. 57001-261) and install the release lever into the bevel gear case.

2. Rotate the release shaft until the release lever is about parallel with the surface of the front bevel case (A, **Figure 54**).

3. Install the release rack (B, **Figure 54**) into the front bevel gear housing opening.

4. Rotate the release shaft and lever back and forth to make sure the rack moves freely with no binding.

5. Rotate the release shaft *counterclockwise* (as viewed from the bottom) until the release rack

moves down into the receptacle in the front bevel gear case.

6. Align the lever gap (A, **Figure 55**) with the raised rib on the case (B, **Figure 55**).

7. Install the plastic plug (**Figure 51**). Use a 5 mm Allen wrench and tighten the plastic plug securely. Refer to previous NOTE regarding the Allen wrench.

8. Make sure the sealing washer (**Figure 56**) is in place on the bolt and install the bolt securing the pivot shaft in the front bevel gear case. It may be necessary to *slightly* move the pivot shaft in and out (**Figure 57**) in order to align the pivot groove shaft with the bolt. Tighten the bolt securely.

9. Recheck that the lever gap (A, **Figure 58**) is aligned with the raised rib on the front bevel gear case (B, **Figure 58**).

10. Adjust the clutch as described under *Clutch Adjustment* in this chapter.

11. Start the engine and check the oil level, add oil if necessary.

Inspection

1. Inspect the teeth on the release shaft and release rack (**Figure 59**) for wear or damage. If either is severely damaged, replace both parts as a set.

2. Inspect the oil seal and needle bearing (**Figure 60**) in the front bevel gear case. Replace if necessary.

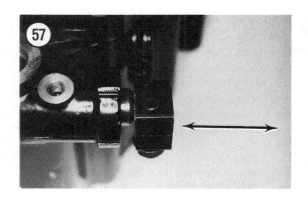

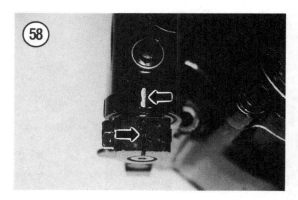

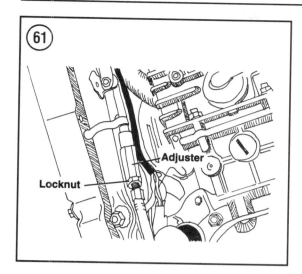

Figure 61

Locknut — Adjuster

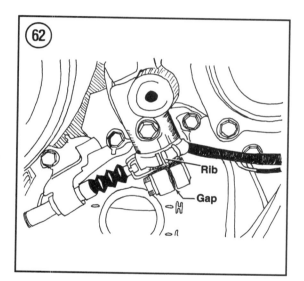

Figure 62

Rib — Gap

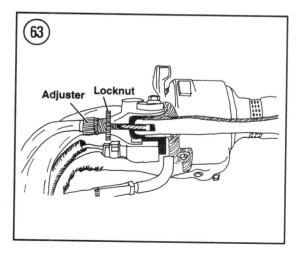

Figure 63

Adjuster — Locknut

Clutch Adjustment

1. Locate the cable adjuster in the approximate center of the clutch cable. See **Figure 61**.

2. Loosen the adjuster locknut and turn the adjuster in fully to provide the maximum play in the clutch cable.

3. Next, turn the clutch release lever (on the engine) in its normal direction of rotation until the clutch just begins to release. The clutch is just beginning to release when the clutch release lever becomes hard to move. With the clutch release lever in this position, the gap in the lever should be directly below the rib on the bevel gearcase boss. See **Figure 62**. If not, remove the bolt securing the release lever to the release shaft and reposition the lever on the shaft as necessary.

4. At the clutch lever on the handlebar, loosen the clutch cable locknut (**Figure 63**) just enough to permit the adjuster to turn freely. Then, turn the adjuster out so a 5-6 mm clearance is present between the adjuster and locknut.

5. At the adjuster in the center of the clutch cable (**Figure 61**), turn the adjusting nut as required to remove all play in the clutch cable, then tighten the locknut.

6. Last, turn the adjuster (**Figure 63**) at the handlebar mounted clutch lever to obtain 2-3 mm freeplay in the lever, measured as shown in **Figure 64**. When the correct freeplay is present, tighten the locknut.

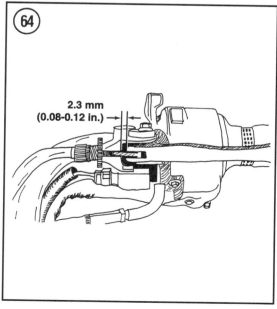

Figure 64

2.3 mm
(0.08-0.12 in.)

5

Table 1 CLUTCH SPECIFICATIONS

Item	Standard	Wear limit
Friction disc	2.9-3.1 mm (0.114-0.122 in.)	2.8 mm (0.110 in.)
Friction disc and clutch plate warpage	less than 0.2 mm	0.3 mm (0.0118 in.)
Clutch spring free length	33.0-34.2 mm (1.29-1.35 in.)	32.6 mm (1.28 in.)

Table 2 CLUTCH TIGHTENING TORQUES

Item	N·m	ft.-lb.
Clutch locknut	130	95.8
Clutch spring bolts	9	6.6

CHAPTER SIX

TRANSMISSION AND GEARSHIFT MECHANISMS

This chapter provides complete service procedures for the transmission shaft assemblies and the external and the internal shift mechanism.

Table 1 and **Table 2** are located at the end of this chapter.

EXTERNAL GEARSHIFT MECHANISM

The external gearshift ratchet mechanism is located on the left-hand side of the crankcase. To remove the external and internal shift mechanism (shift drum and shift forks), it is necessary to remove the engine and split the crankcase as described in Chapter Four.

The gearshift lever shaft is subject to a lot of abuse. If the bike has been in a hard spill, the gearshift lever may have been hit and the gearshift lever shaft bent. It is very hard to straighten the shaft without subjecting the crankcase halves to abnormal stress where the shaft enters the crankcase. If the shaft is bent enough to prevent it from being withdrawn from the crankcase, there is little recourse but to cut the shaft off very close to the crankcase. It is much cheaper in the long run to replace the shaft than risk damaging a very expensive crankcase assembly.

Removal

NOTE
The external shift mechanism cover and the gear position lever are the only com-

ponents that can be removed with the engine in the frame. For removal of all other parts, the crankcase must be disassembled.

Refer to **Figure 1** for this procedure.

1. Remove the engine as described under *Engine Removal/Installation* in Chapter Four.
2. Remove the bolts securing the external shift mechanism cover (**Figure 2**) and remove the cover and gasket. Don't lose the locating dowels in the crankcase.
3. Remove the bolt (A, **Figure 3**) securing the gear position lever (B, **Figure 3**) and remove the lever and spring.
4. From the left-hand side of the shift lever shaft, remove the following:
   a. Slide off the outer washer (**Figure 4**).
   b. Remove the outer circlip (**Figure 5**).
   c. Remove the inner circlip (A, **Figure 6**).
   d. Slide off the inner washer (B, **Figure 6**).
5. Disassemble the crankcase as described under *Crankcase Disassembly* in Chapter Four.
6. Loosen the nut (**Figure 7**) securing the change lever to the change lever shaft.

NOTE
On 1987 and later models, there is an oil pump drive chain guide located above the shift lever shaft. Remove it along with the shift lever shaft in the next step.

7. Remove the nut (A, **Figure 8**) and remove the change lever (B, **Figure 8**) and the shift lever shaft assembly (C, **Figure 8**) from the inner surface of the left-hand crankcase. See information regarding a *bent shift lever shaft* in the introductory paragraph of this procedure.

8. Withdraw the change lever shaft (**Figure 9**) from the outer surface of the left-hand crankcase.

Inspection

1. Inspect the return spring on the change lever shaft assembly. If broken or weak, it must be replaced.

2. Inspect the gearshift shaft assembly for bending, wear or other damage; replace if necessary.

3. Inspect the roller (**Figure 10**) on the gear position lever for wear or damage; replace if necessary.

Installation

1. Install the change lever shaft (**Figure 9**) into the outer surface of the left-hand crankcase. Properly index the return spring onto the locating stud and push it in until it bottoms out. Have an assistant hold the change lever shaft assembly in position.

2A. On 1985-1986 models, install the change lever (B, **Figure 8**) and the shift lever shaft assembly (C, **Figure 8**) into the inner surface of the left-hand crankcase. Position the change lever so the lever notch aligns with the crankcase index mark (D, **Figure 8**). Push it in until it bottoms.

2B. On 1987 and later models, perform the following:

   a. Partially install the change lever and the shift lever shaft assembly into the inner surface of the left-hand crankcase.

   b. Install the oil pump drive chain guide onto the shift lever and index it onto the lever.

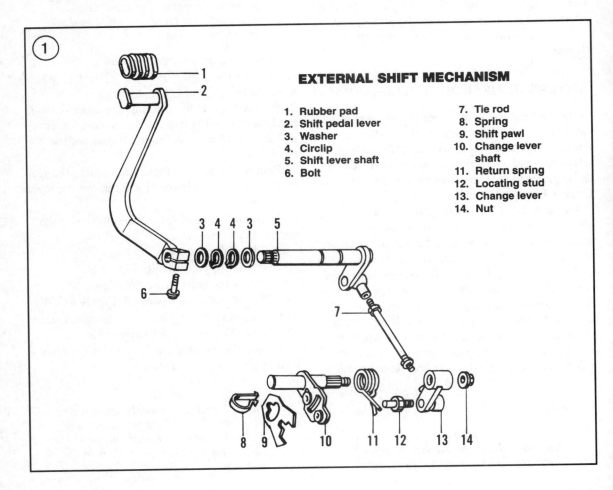

(1)

EXTERNAL SHIFT MECHANISM

1. Rubber pad
2. Shift pedal lever
3. Washer
4. Circlip
5. Shift lever shaft
6. Bolt
7. Tie rod
8. Spring
9. Shift pawl
10. Change lever shaft
11. Return spring
12. Locating stud
13. Change lever
14. Nut

6

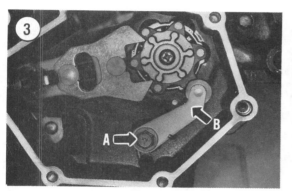

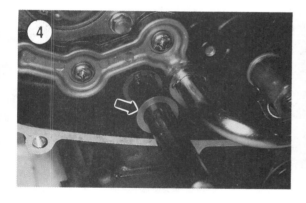

c. Push the shift lever assembly the rest of the way into the crankcase and correctly locate the guide under the drive chain. Position the change lever so the lever notch aligns with the crankcase index mark (D, **Figure 8**). Push it in until it bottoms out.

3. Install the nut (**Figure 7**) and tighten securely.

4. Assemble the crankcase as described in Chapter Four.

5. Install the following onto the left-hand side of the shift lever shaft:

a. Slide on the inner washer (B, **Figure 6**). Push it on all the way.

b. Install the inner circlip (**Figure 11**). Make sure it is correctly seated in the groove.

c. Install the outer circlip (**Figure 5**). Make sure it is correctly seated in the groove.

d. Slide on the outer washer (**Figure 12**). Push it on all the way.

6. Partially install the gear position lever (A, **Figure 13**) and spring (B, **Figure 13**). Insert the spring into the hole in the crankcase and install the bolt part way.

7. After the bolt is partially threaded into the hole, move the gear position lever into place (B, **Figure 3**), then tighten the bolt securely (A, **Figure 3**).

8. Make sure the locating dowels (**Figure 14**) are in place in the crankcase.

9. Install a new gasket (**Figure 15**) and the external shift mechanism cover (**Figure 2**). Install the bolts and tighten securely.

10. Install the engine as described in Chapter Four.

TRANSMISSION AND INTERNAL SHIFT MECHANISM

To gain access to the transmission and internal shift mechanism, it is necessary to remove the en-

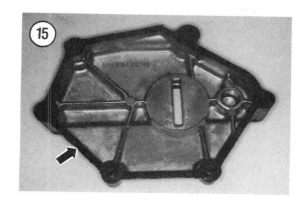

gine and disassemble the crankcase as described in Chapter Four.

The internal shift mechanism is removed along with the transmission shaft assemblies except for the shift drum. The shift drum can be removed after the transmission assemblies are removed.

Refer to **Table 1** at the end of the chapter for transmission and gearshift mechanism specifications.

Removal/Installation

1. Remove the engine and disassemble the crankcase as described under *Crankcase Disassembly* in Chapter Four.

2. Remove the crankshaft assembly (**Figure 16**).

3. Remove the shift fork shaft (**Figure 17**).

4. Remove the bolts (A, **Figure 18**) securing the shift drum bearing retainer and remove the retainer (B, **Figure 18**).

5. Move the shift fork cam pin followers out of mesh with the shift drum.

6. Remove the shift drum (**Figure 19**).

> *NOTE*
> *The right-hand and left-hand shift forks are identical (same Kawasaki part Nos.), but should be reinstalled in the same location during assembly. Mark them for identification with a "L-H" and "R-H" as soon as they are removed from the crankcase.*

7. Remove the shift forks from the transmission assemblies.

8. Remove the mainshaft (A, **Figure 20**) and countershaft (B, **Figure 20**) as an assembly. Don't lose

the 2 loose washers on the left-hand end of the mainshaft assembly.

9. Inspect the transmission shaft assemblies as described in this chapter.

10. Inspect the internal shift components as described in this chapter.

NOTE
Coat all bearing surfaces with assembly oil prior to installation.

CAUTION
Hold onto the 2 washers on the left-hand end of the mainshaft during installation with your fingers. They must remain in place during installation of the transmission shaft assemblies.

11. Install the mainshaft (A, **Figure 20**) and countershaft (B, **Figure 20**) transmission assemblies as an assembly. Push both shaft assemblies all the way down until they bottom.

NOTE
Install the shift forks with their cast-in marks (Nos. 25 and 26) facing down toward the left-hand crankcase half.

NOTE
*Position the left- and right-hand shift forks with the longer side of the boss (**Figure 21**) facing away from the left-hand crankcase half. Position the center shift fork as shown in **Figure 22**.*

12. Insert the left-hand shift fork (A, **Figure 23**) into the countershaft.

13. Insert the center shift fork (B, **Figure 23**) into the mainshaft.

14. Insert the right-hand shift fork (C, **Figure 23**) into the countershaft.

15. Position the shift forks so the cam pin followers will mesh properly with the shift drum.

16. Install the shift drum (**Figure 19**) into the left-hand crankcase half. Push it in until it bottoms out.

17. Install the shift drum bearing retainer (B, **Figure 18**).

18. If the retainer screws are to be reused, apply blue Loctite (No. 242) to the threads prior to installation. If new screws are used, the locking agent is not required.

19. Tighten the screws (A, **Figure 18**) securely.

20. Move each shift fork so the cam pin follower is meshed properly with the shift drum. Make sure all 3 followers are meshed properly (**Figure 24**).

21 Align the shift fork shaft holes and install the shift fork (**Figure 25**). Push it in until it bottoms (**Figure 17**).

22. After both transmission assemblies and the internal shift mechanism are installed, perform the following:

a. Shift both shafts into NEUTRAL. Hold onto the mainshaft and rotate the countershaft. The

countershaft should rotate freely. If it does not, shift the gear that is engaged so that both shafts are in NEUTRAL.

b. Rotate both shaft assemblies by hand. Make sure there is no binding. This is the time to find that something may be installed incorrectly—not after the crankcase is completely assembled.

23. Reassemble the crankcase and install the engine as described in Chapter Four.

Transmission
Preliminary Inspection

After the transmission shaft assemblies have been removed from the crankcase, clean and inspect the assemblies prior to disassembling them. Place the assembled shaft into a large can or plastic bucket and thoroughly clean with a petroleum based solvent such as kerosene and a stiff brush. Dry with compressed air or let it sit on rags to drip dry. Repeat for the other shaft assembly.

NOTE
Don't lose the 2 loose washers on the end of the mainshaft. They are not held in place and may slide off the end of the shaft into the bucket.

1. Visually inspect the components of the transmission for excessive wear after they have been cleaned. Any burrs, pitting or roughness on the teeth of a gear will cause wear on the mating gear. Minor roughness can be cleaned up with an oilstone but there's little point in attempting to remove deep scars.

NOTE
Defective gears should be replaced. A good procedure is to replace the mating gear on the other shaft even though it may not show as much wear or damage.

2. Carefully check the engagement dogs. If any are chipped, worn, rounded or missing, the affected gear must be replaced.

3. Rotate the transmission bearings (**Figure 26**) in both crankcase halves by hand. Check for roughness, noise and radial play. Any bearing that is suspect should be replaced as described in this chapter.

4. If the transmission shafts are satisfactory and are not going to be disassembled, apply assembly oil or

engine oil to all components and reinstall them in the crankcase as described in this chapter.

NOTE
If disassembling a used, well run-in (high mileage) transmission for the first time by yourself, pay particular attention to any additional shims that may have been added by a previous owner. These may have been added to take up the tolerance of worn components and must be reinstalled in the same position since the shims and adjoining gear(s) have developed a wear pattern. If new

parts are going to be installed, these shims may be eliminated. This is something you will have to determine upon reassembly.

**Transmission
Service Notes**

1. A divided container, such as a restaurant type egg carton can be used to help maintain correct alignment and positioning of the parts. As you remove a part from the shaft, set it in the depressions in the same position from which it was removed. Refer to

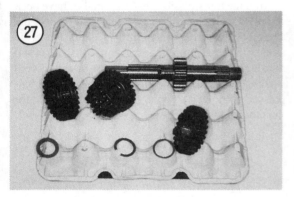

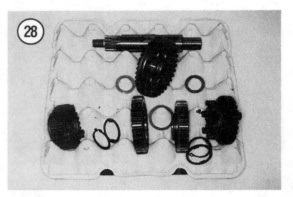

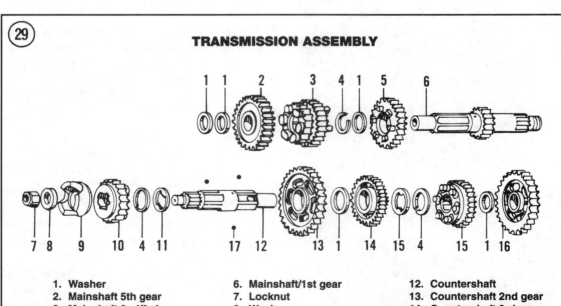

TRANSMISSION ASSEMBLY

1. Washer
2. Mainshaft 5th gear
3. Mainshaft 2nd/3rd combination gear
4. Circlip
5. Mainshaft 4th gear
6. Mainshaft/1st gear
7. Locknut
8. Washer
9. Damper cam
10. Countershaft 5th gear
11. Splined washer
12. Countershaft
13. Countershaft 2nd gear
14. Countershaft 3rd gear
15. Countershaft 4th gear
16. Countershaft 1st gear
17. Steel balls

Figure 27 for the mainshaft and **Figure 28** for the countershaft. This is an easy way to remember the correct relationship of all parts.

2. The circlips are a tight fit on the transmission shafts. It is recommended to replace all circlips during reassembly.

3. Circlips will turn and fold over making removal and installation difficult. To ease replacement, open the circlips with a pair of circlip pliers while at the same time holding the back of the circlip with a pair of pliers and remove them. Repeat for installation.

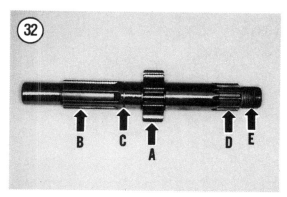

Mainshaft
Disassembly/Inspection

Refer to **Figure 29** for this procedure.
1. If not cleaned in the *Preliminary Inspection* sequence, place the assembled shaft into a large can or plastic bucket and thoroughly clean with solvent and a stiff brush. Dry with compressed air or let it sit on rags to dry.
2. Slide both washers off the left-hand end of the shaft.
3. Slide off the 5th gear.
4. Slide off the 2nd/3rd combination gear.
5. Remove the circlip and slide off the washer.
6. Slide off the 4th gear.
7. Check each gear for excessive wear, burrs, pitting, or chipped or missing teeth (A, **Figure 30**). Make sure the lugs (A, **Figure 31**) on the gears are in good condition.
8. Check the gear inner splines (B, **Figure 31**) for excessive wear or damage. Replace the gear if necessary.
9. Check the inner bearing surface (B, **Figure 30**) for excessive wear or damage. Replace the gear if necessary.
10. Inspect the circlips and splined washers for bending wear or damage. Replace if necessary.
11. Inspect the shift fork groove and any oil control holes. Make sure the oil holes are clear.
12. Inspect the shift fork-to-gear clearance as described under *Internal Gearshift Mechanism* in this chapter.

NOTE
Defective gears should be replaced. It is a good idea to replace the mating gear on the countershaft even though it may not show as much wear or damage.

NOTE
The 1st gear (A, Figure 32) is part of the mainshaft. If the gear is defective, the mainshaft must be replaced.

13. Make sure that all gears and bushings slide smoothly on the mainshaft splines.

NOTE
It is recommended that all circlips be replaced every time the transmission is disassembled to ensure proper gear alignment. Do not expand a circlip more than necessary to slide it over the shaft.

14. Inspect the splines (B, **Figure 32**) and, the circlip groove (C, **Figure 32**) of the mainshaft. If any are damaged, the shaft must be replaced.

15. Inspect the clutch hub splines (D, **Figure 32**) and clutch nut threads (E, **Figure 32**) of the mainshaft. If any splines are damaged, the shaft must be replaced. If the threads have burrs or have minor damage, clean with a proper size metric thread die. If thread damage is severe, the shaft must be replaced.

Mainshaft Assembly

1. Apply a light coat of clean engine oil to all sliding surfaces prior to installing any parts.

2. Position the 4th gear with the engagement dog side going on last and install the 4th gear (**Figure 33**).

3. Slide on the washer (A, **Figure 34**) and the circlip (B, **Figure 34**). Make sure the circlip is seated correctly in the mainshaft groove (**Figure 35**).

4. Position the 2nd/3rd combination gear with the larger diameter gear (**Figure 36**) going in first and install the gear (**Figure 37**).

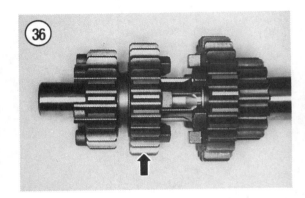

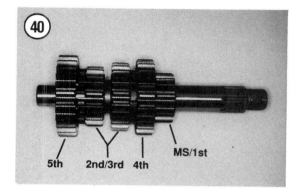

5th   2nd/3rd   4th   MS/1st

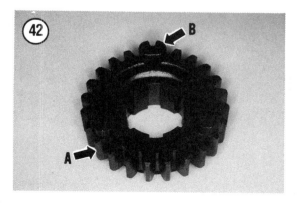

5. Position the 5th gear with the flush side going on last and install the 5th gear (**Figure 38**).

6. Install both washers (**Figure 39**).

7. Refer to **Figure 40** for correct placement of all gears. Make sure the circlip is correctly seated in the mainshaft groove.

8. Make sure each gear properly engages the adjoining gear where applicable.

Countershaft
Disassembly/Inspection

Refer to **Figure 29** for this procedure.

1. If not cleaned in the *Preliminary Inspection* sequence, place the assembled shaft into a large can or plastic bucket and thoroughly clean with solvent and a stiff brush. Dry with compressed air or let it sit on rags to dry.

2. Slide off the 1st gear and washer.

NOTE
*The 4th gear is retained on the countershaft with 3 loose **small** steel balls (**Figure 41**) that ride in the small receptacles in the raised splines of the shaft. These balls perform the function of a positive neutral finder mechanism.*

NOTE
*Perform Step 3 over the work bench and over a small box or pan to catch the **small** steel balls that will fall out when the 4th gear is removed from the shaft.*

3. Remove the 4th gear as follows:
   a. Hold the transmission shaft vertical with the 4th gear facing up.
   b. Hold onto the 3rd gear with one hand and quickly spin the 4th gear and shaft assembly while pulling up on the 4th gear.
   c. Remove the 4th gear and 3 *small* steel balls.

4. Remove the circlip and slide off the splined washer.

5. Slide off the 3rd gear and washer.

6. Slide off the 2nd gear.

7. Slide the 5th gear from the other end of the shaft.

8. Remove the circlip and slide off the splined washer.

9. Check each gear for excessive wear, burrs, pitting, or chipped or missing teeth (A, **Figure 42**). Make sure the lugs (B, **Figure 42**) on the gears are in good condition.

10. Inspect the inner splines (**Figure 43**) for wear or damage. Replace if necessary.

11. Check the inner bearing surface (**Figure 44**) for excessive wear or damage. Replace the gear if necessary.

12. Inspect the circlips and splined washers for bending wear or damage. Replace if necessary.

13. Inspect the shift fork groove (A, **Figure 45**) and any oil control holes (B, **Figure 45**). Make sure the oil holes are clear.

14. Inspect the shift fork-to-gear clearance as described under *Internal Gearshift Mechanism* in this chapter.

NOTE
Defective gears should be replaced. It is a good idea to replace the mating gear on the mainshaft even though it may not show as much wear or damage.

15. Make sure that all gears slide smoothly on the countershaft splines.

NOTE
It is recommended that all circlips be replaced every time the transmission is disassembled to ensure proper gear alignment. Do not expand a circlip more than necessary to slide it over the shaft.

16. Inspect the splines (A, **Figure 46**) and circlip grooves (B, **Figure 46**) of the countershaft. If any are damaged, the shaft must be replaced.

17. Inspect the damper cam splines (C, **Figure 46**) and damper cam retaining nut threads (D, **Figure 46**) of the countershaft. If any of the splines are damaged, the shaft must be replaced. If the threads have burrs or have minor damage, clean with a proper size metric thread die.

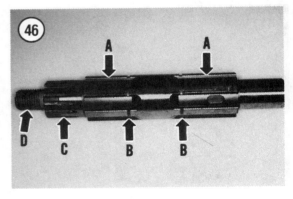
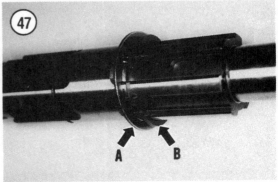

Countershaft Assembly

1. Apply a light coat of clean engine oil to all sliding surfaces prior to installing any parts.

2. Slide on the splined washer (A, **Figure 47**) and install the circlip (B, **Figure 47**). Make sure the circlip (**Figure 48**) is correctly seated in the countershaft groove.

> *CAUTION*
> *Do **not** use grease to hold the 3 small steel balls in place within the receptacles in the 4th gear. If grease is used, the positive neutral finder mechanism will malfunction.*

3. Apply a light coat of clean engine oil to the 3 receptacles within the 4th gear.

4. Install the 4th gear as follows:
   a. Hold the 4th gear horizontal with the shift fork groove facing down.
   b. Install the 3 steel balls (**Figure 49**) into the 4th gear (**Figure 50**).
   c. Hold the transmission shaft vertical.
   d. Align the 4th gear so the 3 *small* steel balls are aligned with the 3 receptacles in the raised splines on the shaft.
   e. Slowly push the 4th gear onto the shaft until the steel balls fall into the receptacles in the shaft. Carefully move the 4th gear back and forth (**Figure 51**) on the shaft to make sure the steel balls are correctly seated.

5. Position the 3rd gear with the long shoulder side going on last and slide the 3rd gear on (A, **Figure 52**).

6. Slide the washer on (B, **Figure 52**).

7. Position the 2nd gear with the long shoulder side (**Figure 53**) going on last and slide the 2nd gear on (**Figure 54**).

8. Slide on the splined washer (A, **Figure 55**) and install the circlip (B, **Figure 55**). Make sure the circlip (**Figure 56**) is correctly seated in the counter-shaft groove.

9. Position the 5th gear with the shift fork groove going on last and install the 5th gear (**Figure 57**).

10. Install the washer (**Figure 58**) against the 4th gear at the other end of the shaft.

11. Position the 1st gear with the flush side going on last and slide the 1st gear on (**Figure 59**).

12. Slide the 2 washers on (**Figure 60**).

13. Refer to **Figure 61** for correct placement of all gears. Make sure all circlips are correctly seated in the countershaft grooves.

14. After both transmission shafts have been assembled, mesh the 2 assemblies together in the correct position (**Figure 62**). Check that all gears properly engage. This is your last check prior to installing the shaft assemblies into the crankcase; make sure they are correctly assembled.

Internal Gearshift Mechanism Inspection

Refer to **Figure 63** for this procedure.

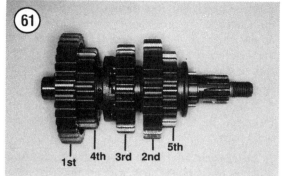

1st 4th 3rd 2nd 5th

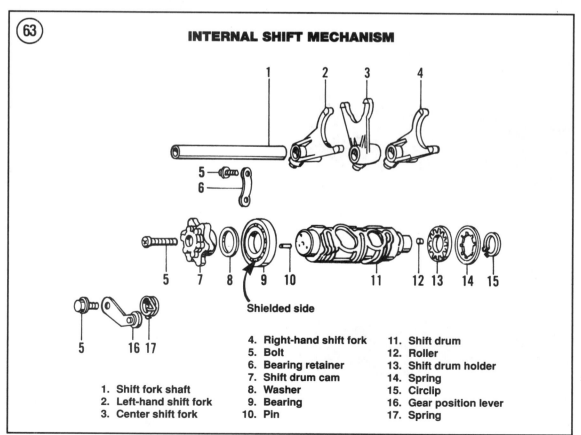

INTERNAL SHIFT MECHANISM

Shielded side

1. Shift fork shaft
2. Left-hand shift fork
3. Center shift fork
4. Right-hand shift fork
5. Bolt
6. Bearing retainer
7. Shift drum cam
8. Washer
9. Bearing
10. Pin
11. Shift drum
12. Roller
13. Shift drum holder
14. Spring
15. Circlip
16. Gear position lever
17. Spring

6

1. Inspect each shift fork for signs of wear or cracking. Check for any arc-shaped wear or burned marks on the fingers of the shift forks. This indicates that the shift fork has come in contact with the gear. The fork fingers have become excessively worn and the fork must be replaced.

2. Check the bore of each shift fork and the shift fork shaft for burrs, wear or pitting. Replace any worn parts.

3. Install each shift fork onto its shaft and make sure it moves freely on the shaft with no binding.

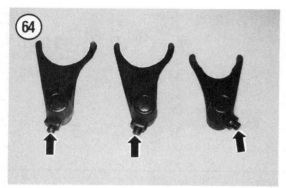

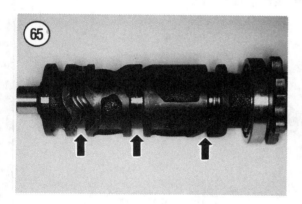

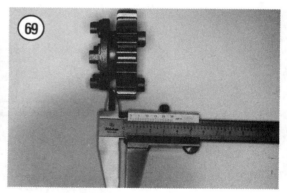

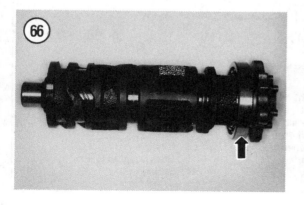

4. Check the cam pin followers (**Figure 64**) on each shift fork that rides in the shift drum for wear or damage. Replace the shift fork(s) as necessary.

5. Roll the shift fork shaft on a flat surface such as a piece of plate glass and check for any bends. If the shaft is bent, it must be replaced.

6. Check the grooves in the shift drum (**Figure 65**) for wear or roughness. If any of the groove profiles have excessive wear or damage, replace the shift drum.

7. Check the shift drum bearing (**Figure 66**). Make sure it operates smoothly with no signs of wear or damage. If damaged, replace it.

8. Check the shift drum cam ramps (**Figure 67**) for wear or roughness. If any of the ramps have excessive wear or damage, replace the shift drum cam (**Figure 68**).

CAUTION
It is recommended that marginally worn shift forks be replaced. Worn forks can cause the transmission to slip out of gear, leading to more serious and expensive damage.

9. Measure the width of the shift fork groove in the gears with a vernier caliper as shown in **Figure 69**. Compare to the specifications listed in **Table 1**.

10. Measure the width of the gearshift fork fingers with a micrometer (**Figure 70**). Replace the shift fork(s) worn to the service limit listed in **Table 1**.

11. Measure the outer diameter of the gearshift fork guide pins with a micrometer. Replace the shift fork(s) worn to the service limit listed in **Table 1**.

6

Table 1 TRANSMISSION AND GEARSHIFT SPECIFICATIONS

Item	Specifications	Wear limit
Shift fork groove in gear	5.05-5.15 mm (0.198-0.203 in.)	5.3 mm (0.208 in.)
Shift fork finger thickness	4.9-5.0 mm (0.193-0.197 in.)	4.8 mm (0.189 in.)
Shift fork guide pin O.D.	5.9-6.0 mm (0.232-0.236 in.)	5.8 mm (0.228 in.)
Shift fork groove width	6.05-6.20 mm (0.238-0.244 in.)	6.3 mm (0.248 in.)
Transmission gear ratios		
1st gear	2.250 (36/16):1	
2nd gear	1.600 (32/20):1	
3rd gear	1.230 (32/26):1	
4th gear	1.000 (26/26):1	
5th gear	0.857 (22/28):1	
Primary reduction ratio	2.428 (85/35)	
Final reduction ratio		
U.S. and Canadian models	2.522 (37/10)	
All other models	2.454 (36/10)	

Table 2 TRANSMISSION TIGHTENING TORQUES

Item	N·m	ft.-lb.
Damper cam nut	120	88.5

CHAPTER SEVEN

FUEL, EMISSION CONTROL AND EXHAUST SYSTEMS

The fuel system consists of the fuel tank, the shutoff valve, 2 carburetors and a separate air filter assembly for each carburetor. The exhaust system consists of 2 exhaust pipes and 2 mufflers.

The emission controls consist of the "Evaporative Emission Control System" equipped on California models and the "Clean Air System" equipped on both California and Switzerland models.

This chapter includes service procedures for all parts of the fuel system and exhaust system. Air filter service is covered in Chapter Three.

Carburetor specifications are covered in **Table 1** located at the end of this chapter.

> *NOTE*
> *Where differences occur relating to the United Kingdom (U.K.) models they are identified. If there is no (U.K.) designation relating to a procedure, photo or illustration it is identical to the United States (U.S.) models.*

CARBURETOR OPERATION

For proper operation, a gasoline engine must be supplied with fuel and air mixed in proper proportions by weight. A mixture in which there is an excess of fuel is said to be rich. A lean mixture is one which contains insufficient fuel. A properly adjusted carburetor supplies the proper mixture to the engine under all operating conditions.

Each carburetor consists of several major systems. A float and float valve mechanism maintain a constant fuel level in the float bowls. The pilot system supplies fuel at low speeds. The main fuel system supplies fuel at medium and high speeds. A starter (choke) system supplies the very rich mixture needed to start a cold engine.

CARBURETOR SERVICE

Major carburetor service (removal and cleaning) should be performed at the intervals indicated in

Table 1 in Chapter Three or when poor engine performance, hesitation and little or no response to mixture adjustment is observed. Alterations in jet size, throttle slide cutaway, and changes in jet needle position, etc., should be attempted only if you're experienced in this type of "tuning" work; a bad guess could result in costly engine damage or, at least, poor performance. If, after servicing the carburetor and making the adjustments described in this chapter, the bike does not perform correctly (and assuming that other factors affecting performance are correct, such as ignition component condition, etc.), the bike should be checked by a dealer or a qualified performance tuning specialist.

CARBURETOR ASSEMBLY

Removal/Installation

Remove the 2 carburetors and throttle cable assembly that is attached to both carburetors as an assembled unit.

1. Remove the seat as described under *Seat Removal/Installation* in Chapter Thirteen.

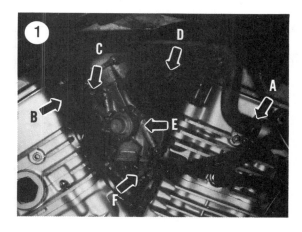

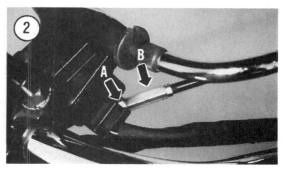

2. Remove the fuel tank as described in this chapter.
3. Disconnect the battery negative lead as described in Chapter Three.
4. Remove both right- and left-hand frame head side covers as described in Chapter Thirteen.

NOTE
Steps 5-9 are necessary so the rear portion of the air filter surge tank can be raised for carburetor removal.

5. On California models, disconnect the charcoal canister purge hose from the air filter surge tank.
6. Remove both air filter housings as described in this chapter.
7. Remove the thermostat housing as described under *Thermostat and Housing Removal/Installation* in Chapter Nine. After the thermostat housing is removed, remove the short hose still attached to the front cylinder head.
8. Remove the bolts securing the coolant filler neck assembly and remove the assembly.
9. On California and Switzerland models, disconnect the right-hand air hose (A, **Figure 1**) from the front cylinder head.
10. Disconnect the vent hose (B, **Figure 1**) from each carburetor. Move the hose out of the way.
11. To disconnect the upper end of the choke cable, perform the following:
   a. Loosen the locknut (A, **Figure 2**) and turn the adjuster (B, **Figure 2**) all the way in to allow maximum slack in the choke cable.
   b. Remove the cable sheath out of the cable bracket on the front carburetor.
   c. Disconnect the choke cable end from the plunger lever (C, **Figure 1**) at the rear carburetor.
12. Loosen the clamp screws on the cable clamps securing the surge tank ducts to the surge tank and to the carburetors.
13. Lift up on the rear of the surge tank and remove both surge tank ducts (D, **Figure 1**).

NOTE
The front cylinder carburetor-to-cylinder head rubber boot is to remain attached to the cylinder head during carburetor assembly removal.

14. Loosen the *carburetor side screw only* of the front cylinder carburetor-to-cylinder head rubber

boot. This rubber boot will stay with the cylinder head,

15. Loosen the *cylinder head side screw only* on the rear cylinder carburetor-to-cylinder head rubber boot. This rubber boot will come off with the carburetor assembly.

16. Slowly move the carburetor assembly (E, **Figure 1**) partially up and out of right-hand side of the frame area, then perform the following:

   a. Loosen the locknuts and turn the adjusters all the way in to allow maximum slack in both throttle cables.

   b. Disconnect the throttle cables from the from the throttle wheel (F, **Figure 1**).

17. Carefully remove the carburetor assembly and attached cables out of the frame. Take the assembly to a workbench for disassembly and cleaning.

18. Insert clean lint-free cloths into the intake ports in the cylinder heads to prevent the entry of foreign matter.

19. Install by reversing these removal steps while noting the following:

   a. The carburetor-to-cylinder head rubber boots are marked with a "F" (front cylinder head) and "R" (rear cylinder head).

   b. Make sure the front carburetor-to-cylinder head rubber boot is in place on the cylinder head and that the boot projection is aligned with the mark on the cylinder head inlet pipe. Align if necessary and tighten the clamping screw.

   c. If removed, install the rear carburetor-to-cylinder head rubber boot onto the rear carburetor. Align the rubber boot to the carburetor as shown with the projection over toward the outside by about 15 mm (0.60 in.). Tighten the clamping screw securing the rubber boot to the carburetor.

   d. After the carburetor assembly is installed, make sure the projection on the rear carburetor-to-cylinder head rubber boot is aligned with the projection on the cylinder head inlet pipe. Realign if necessary and tighten the clamping screws securely.

   e. Make sure the screws on the clamping bands are tight to avoid a vacuum loss and possible valve damage due to a lean fuel mixture.

   f. The surge tank ducts are marked with a "F" (front cylinder head) and "R" (rear cylinder head).

   g. Align the surge tank duct notch with the projection on the surge tank and install the ducts into the surge tank.

   h. Insert the carburetor vent hoses (A, **Figure 3**) into the right-hand air filter housing (**Figure 4**). Do not insert the vent hose too deep into the receptacle (B, **Figure 3**) in the housing (C, **Figure 3**).

   i. Adjust the throttle cable as described under *Throttle Cable Adjustment* in Chapter Three.

   j. Adjust the choke cable as described under *Choke Cable Adjustment* in Chapter Three.

CARBURETOR SERVICE

The front and rear carburetor are attached to a common float chamber. It is necessary to remove the carburetor(s) from the float chamber for disassembly, cleaning and inspection.

Separation

Refer to the following illustrations for this procedure:

   a. **Figure 5**: carburetor body components.

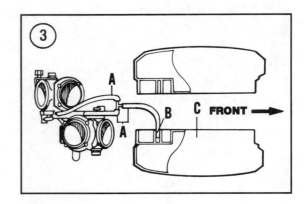

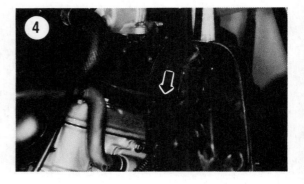

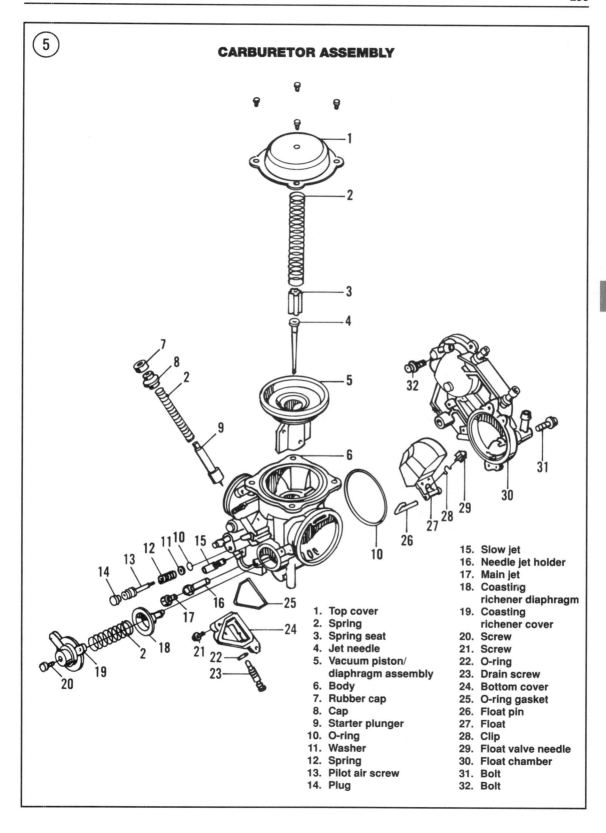

CARBURETOR ASSEMBLY

1. Top cover
2. Spring
3. Spring seat
4. Jet needle
5. Vacuum piston/
   diaphragm assembly
6. Body
7. Rubber cap
8. Cap
9. Starter plunger
10. O-ring
11. Washer
12. Spring
13. Pilot air screw
14. Plug
15. Slow jet
16. Needle jet holder
17. Main jet
18. Coasting
    richener diaphragm
19. Coasting
    richener cover
20. Screw
21. Screw
22. O-ring
23. Drain screw
24. Bottom cover
25. O-ring gasket
26. Float pin
27. Float
28. Clip
29. Float valve needle
30. Float chamber
31. Bolt
32. Bolt

7

⑥

CARBURETOR LINKAGE AND HOSES

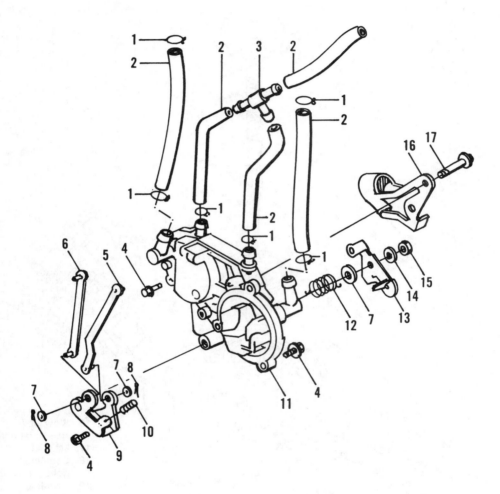

1. Hose clamp	9. Throttle lever
2. Hose	10. Spring
3. T-fitting	11. Float chamber
4. Screw	12. Spring
5. Rear carburetor throttle link	13. Throttle lever
	14. Washer
6. Front carburetor throttle link	15. Nut
	16. Throttle cable bracket
7. Plastic washer	17. Bolt
8. Cotter pin	

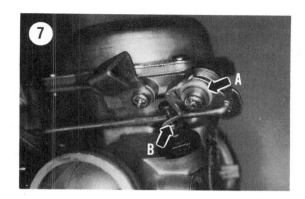

b. **Figure 6**: float chamber and linkage components.

It is recommended to disassemble only one carburetor at a time to prevent accidental interchange of parts.

1. On the front carburetor, perform the following:
   a. Remove the screw securing the starter plunger rod bracket (A, **Figure 7**).
   b. Disconnect the bracket (B, **Figure 7**) from the starter plunger.
   c. Disconnect the starter plunger rod from the bracket and remove the rod, bracket and spring from the rear carburetor.

2. On the rear carburetor, perform the following:
   a. Remove the screw, metal washer and plastic washer securing the starter plunger rod bracket (A, **Figure 8**) and spring assembly.
   b. Disconnect the bracket (B, **Figure 8**) from the starter plunger.
   c. Disconnect the starter plunger rod from the bracket and remove the rod and bracket from the rear carburetor.

3. Remove the cotter pin and plastic washer (A, **Figure 9**) securing the throttle link (B, **Figure 9**) to the carburetor to be removed. Discard the cotter pin as a new one must be installed.

4. Remove the screw (A, **Figure 10**) securing the throttle adjust knob and bracket (B, **Figure 10**) to the coasting richener cover. Move the throttle adjust knob, cable and bracket out of the way.

5. Remove the 3 screws (**Figure 11**) securing the carburetor body to the float chamber.

6. Disconnect the throttle link from the carburetor throttle lever and separate the carburetor body from the float chamber.

7. Disassemble the carburetor as described in this chapter.

8. Make sure the O-ring (**Figure 12**) is in place on the float chamber.

9. Position the throttle link so its pin (A, **Figure 13**) will align with the pin hole (B, **Figure 13**) on the carburetor body.

10. Install the carburetor body onto the float chamber.

11. Push the carburetor body into place on the float chamber until it bottoms out. Make sure the O-ring stayed in place during assembly.

12. Install the 3 screws (**Figure 11**) securing the carburetor body to the float chamber. Tighten the screws securely.

13. Insert a screwdriver blade (A, **Figure 14**) under the throttle link and push the throttle link and pin (B, **Figure 14**) into place on the carburetor throttle lever pin hole and hold the link in place (B, **Figure 9**).

14. Install the plastic washer onto the pin and install a new cotter pin (A, **Figure 9**). Bend the ends of the cotter pin over completely so it will not fall out. Move the throttle link back and forth to check for proper operation. It must move freely with no binding.

15. Position the starter arm (**Figure 15**) in the correct location between the 2 carburetor bodies.

NOTE
*First attach the starter plunger rod to the **rear carburetor** then the front carburetor.*

16. On the rear carburetor, perform the following:
   a. Connect the bracket (B, **Figure 8**) onto the starter plunger.

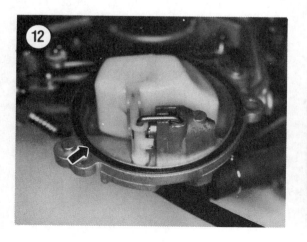

   b. Connect the starter plunger rod onto the bracket and install the screw (A, **Figure 8**). Tighten the screw securely.

   c. Slowly move the rod back and forth and make sure the bracket moves the starter plunger up and down smoothly.

17. On the front carburetor, perform the following:

   a. Connect the starter plunger rod (A, **Figure 16**) into the hole in the starter plunger rod bracket (B, **Figure 16**).

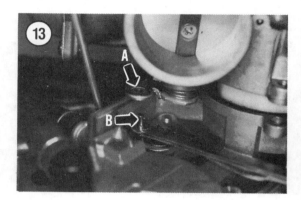

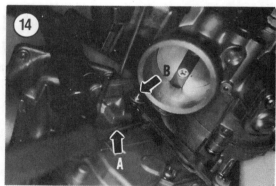

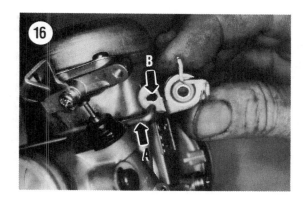

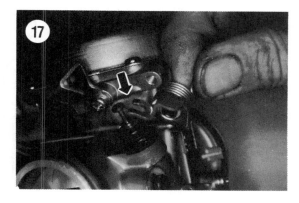

b. Hook the bracket fork under the starter plunger (**Figure 17**).

c. Use pliers and wind the spring *counterclockwise* as viewed from the front to place the spring under tension.

d. Move the bracket into position and hook the spring behind the boss (**Figure 18**) on the carburetor body. The spring must be located as shown in order to maintain the tension applied in sub-step 17 c.

e. Install the plastic washer (**Figure 19**), then the metal washer (A, **Figure 20**) and screw (B, **Figure 20**). Tighten the screw securely.

f. Recheck and make sure the spring is still located behind the boss on the carburetor (**Figure 18**).

g. Slowly move the rod back and forth and make sure both brackets move the starter plungers up and down smoothly.

Disassembly

Refer to **Figure 5** for this procedure.

1. Unscrew and remove the starter plunger assembly (**Figure 21**).

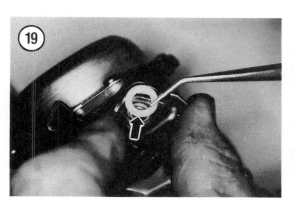

2. Remove the screws (A, **Figure 22**) securing the top cover and remove the cover (B, **Figure 22**).

3. Remove the spring and spring seat from the vacuum piston/diaphragm assembly (A, **Figure 23**).

4. Remove the vacuum piston/diaphragm assembly and jet needle from the carburetor (B, **Figure 23**).

5. Turn the vacuum piston/diaphragm assembly over and remove the jet needle and spring seat.

6. Remove the screw(s) securing the coasting richener valve cover and remove the cover (**Figure 24**).

7. Remove the spring (**Figure 25**) and the diaphragm (**Figure 26**) from the carburetor.

8. Remove the screws (A, **Figure 27**) securing the bottom cover and remove the bottom cover (B, **Figure 27**) and O-ring seal.

9. Unscrew the main jet (**Figure 28**) and the needle jet holder (**Figure 29**).

10. Unscrew the slow jet (**Figure 30**).

11. Remove the O-ring seal (**Figure 31**) from the bottom cover.

12. Remove the drain screw (**Figure 32**) from the bottom cover.

13. From the float chamber, perform the following:

   a. Use a small screwdriver or awl and carefully pry the float pin (A, **Figure 33**) free from the float chamber.

   b. Remove the float pin from the mounting boss.

c. Remove the float (B, **Figure 33**) and needle valve assembly.

NOTE
*Further disassembly is neither necessary nor recommended. If throttle shaft (**Figure 34**) or butterfly (**Figure 35**) is*

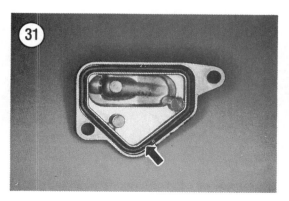

*damaged, take the carburetor body
and/or float chamber to a dealer for
replacement.*

14. Clean and inspect all parts as described under
Cleaning and Inspection in this chapter.

Assembly

1. Into the float chamber perform the following:
   a. Make sure the needle valve (**Figure 36**) is still
   in place on the float arm.
   b. Install the float and needle valve into place
   (**Figure 37**).
   c. Install the pivot pin (**Figure 38**). Press down on
   the pivot pin only in the area of the mounting
   boss (**Figure 39**) to avoid bending the pivot pin.
   d. After the pivot pin is installed, make sure the
   float pivots freely on the pin to ensure proper
   fuel flow.

2. Screw the starter plunger assembly (**Figure 21**)
into place and tighten securely.

3. Install the slow jet (**Figure 30**) and tighten securely.

4. Install the needle jet holder (**Figure 29**) and
tighten securely.

5. Install the main jet (**Figure 28**) and tighten securely.

6. Install the drain screw (**Figure 32**) into the bottom cover and tighten securely.

7. Install a new O-ring seal (**Figure 31**) into the
bottom cover. Make sure it seats completely.

8. If removed, install the small O-ring seal (**Figure
40**) into the coasting richener valve groove in the
carburetor body.

9. Install the coasting valve diaphragm (**Figure 26**)
onto the carburetor.

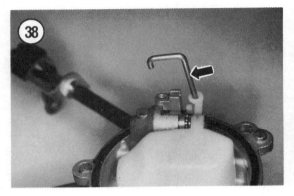

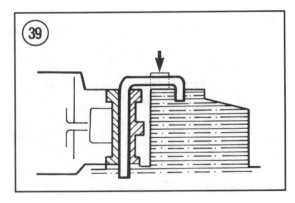

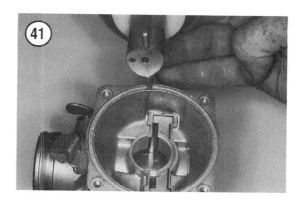

10. Install the spring (**Figure 25**) onto the diaphragm.

11. Install the coasting richener valve cover (**Figure 24**) and install only the 1 screw shown. Tighten the screw securely. The other screw will be installed later in this procedure.

12. Correctly position the vacuum piston/diaphragm assembly (**Figure 41**) and install it into the carburetor body (**Figure 42**).

13. Install the jet needle (**Figure 43**) into the vacuum piston/diaphragm assembly. Make sure the jet needle is correctly positioned in the recess (**Figure 44**) in the top of the vacuum piston/diaphragm assembly.

14. Install the spring (A, **Figure 45**) onto the spring seat (B, **Figure 45**) with the open end going in first.

15. Align the ribs of the spring seat with the grooves in the raised boss in the vacuum piston/diaphragm assembly and install the spring and spring seat assembly (**Figure 46**). When correctly aligned, the spring seat will *not* block the hole in the base of the vacuum piston/diaphragm assembly. This hole must remain open to provide for proper vacuum piston/diaphragm assembly operation.

7

16. Install the top cover onto the spring. Locate the spring into the receptacle in the top cover (**Figure 47**).

17. Install the top cover (B, **Figure 22**) and screws (A, **Figure 22**). Tighten the screws securely.

18. Insert your finger into the carburetor venturi and slowly push the vacuum piston/diaphragm assembly up in the carburetor body. It should move up freely and the spring should push the assembly back down.

19. After the carburetor has been disassembled, the idle speed should be adjusted and the carburetors synchronized as described in Chapter Three.

Cleaning and Inspection

1. Thoroughly clean and dry all parts. Kawasaki does not recommend the use of a caustic carburetor cleaning solvent. Instead, clean carburetor parts in a petroleum based solvent. Then rinse in clean water.

2. Allow the carburetor to dry thoroughly before assembly and blow dry with compressed air. Blow out the jets and needle jet holder with compressed air.

3. Inspect the float chamber O-ring seal (**Figure 48**) and all other O-ring seals. O-ring seals tend to become hardened after prolonged use and heat and therefore lose their ability to seal properly.

> *CAUTION*
> *If compressed air is not available, allow the parts to air dry or use a clean lint-free cloth. Do **not** use a paper towel to dry carburetor parts, as small paper particles may plug openings in the carburetor body or jets.*

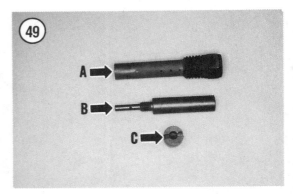

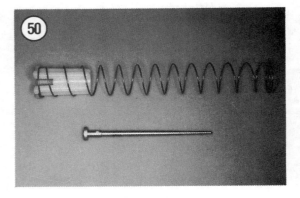

CAUTION
*Do **not** use a piece of wire to clean them as minor gouges in the jet can alter flow rate and upset the fuel/air mixture.*

4. Make sure the holes in the needle jet (A, **Figure 49**), slow jet (B, **Figure 49**) and main jet (C, **Figure 49**) are clear. Clean out if they are plugged in any way. Replace the needle jet and/or jets if you cannot unplug the holes.

5. Examine the jet needle, spring and spring seat (**Figure 50**) for wear or damage.

6. Make sure the diaphragm (**Figure 51**) is not torn or cracked. Replace any damaged or worn parts.

7. Inspect the piston valve (**Figure 52**) portion of the vacuum piston/diaphragm assembly for wear or damage. Replace the assembly if necessary.

8. Inspect the piston valve grooves (**Figure 53**) portion of the carburetor body for wear or damage. If damaged, replace the carburetor assembly.

9. Inspect the float (**Figure 54**) for deterioration or damage. If the float is suspected of leakage, place it in a container of non-caustic solution and push it down. If the float sinks or if bubbles appear (indicating a leak); replace the float assembly.

10. Inspect the end of the float valve (**Figure 55**) and seat (**Figure 56**) in the float chamber for wear or damage; replace either or both parts if necessary.

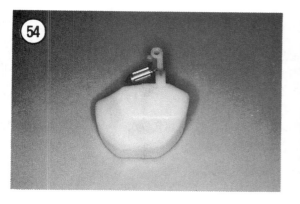

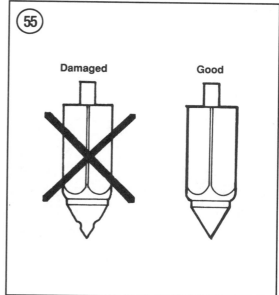

11. Inspect the coasting richener diaphragm (A, **Figure 57**) for tears or cracks. Replace any damaged or worn parts.

12. Inspect the coasting richener diaphragm cover (B, **Figure 57**) for damage. Make sure the opening (**Figure 58**) in the cover is open. Clean out if it is plugged in any way.

13. Make sure all openings in the carburetor body are clear. Refer to **Figure 59**, **Figure 60**, **Figure 61** and **Figure 62**. Clean out if they are plugged in any way.

14. Inspect the choke plunger (A, **Figure 63**) and spring (B, **Figure 63**) for wear or damage. Replace if necessary.

15. Inspect all interconnecting linkage for wear, looseness or damage; replace as necessary. Refer to **Figure 64** and **Figure 65**. Make sure all linkage moves smoothly with no binding or hesitation.

16. Make sure all cotter pins (**Figure 66**) are in place and that the ends are bent over completely.

17. Make sure the idle adjust screw and cable assembly (**Figure 67**) rotate smoothly. Lubricate the cable if necessary.

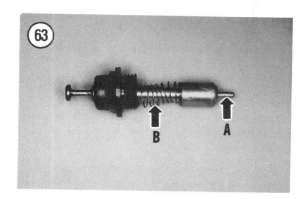

CARBURETOR ADJUSTMENTS

Fuel Level Inspection

The fuel level must be checked with the carburetor assembly installed on the engine. This inspection *cannot* be performed with the carburetor assembly removed.

1. Place the bike on the centerstand on level ground. The bike must be in a true vertical position or the reading will be false.

2. Attach a piece of suitable size clear vinyl tubing to the drain outlet fitting (A, **Figure 68**) on the carburetor bottom cover (A, **Figure 69**).

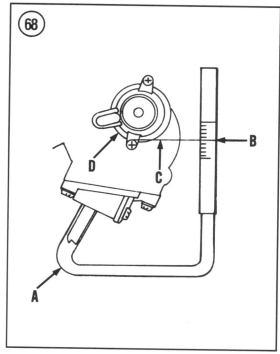

7

3. Connect the Kawasaki special tool, Fuel Level Gauge (part No. 57001-1017) to the end of the vinyl tubing.

4. Hold the fuel level gauge in a vertical position next to the carburetor body. Position the "Zero" line (B, **Figure 68**) on the fuel level gauge several millimeters higher than the upper edge of the lower mounting screw (C, **Figure 68**) on the coasting enrichener cover (D, **Figure 68**).

5. Turn the fuel shutoff valve on the fuel tank to the ON or RES position. Disconnect the vacuum line from the valve and attach a hand held vacuum pump to the valve. Apply a vacuum to allow the fuel to flow in the next step.

6. Unscrew the carburetor drain screw (B, **Figure 69**) several turns to allow fuel to enter the fuel level gauge. Wait until the fuel level in the gauge settles.

> *NOTE*
> *Do **not** lower the "Zero" line on the fuel level gauge below the upper edge of the coasting richener lower mounting screw. If the fuel level gauge lowered, then raised again, the fuel within the fuel level gauge will be "slightly higher" than the actual fuel level, resulting in a false reading.*

7. Keep the gauge vertical, slowly lower the fuel level gauge until the "Zero" line (B, **Figure 68**) is even with the upper edge of the coasting richer cover mounting screw (C, **Figure 68**). Record the fuel level in the gauge for this carburetor.

8. Disconnect the vacuum pump from the shutoff valve and reconnect the vacuum hose.

9. Turn the fuel shutoff valve on the fuel tank to the OFF position.

10. Tighten the carburetor drain screw and drain the fuel in the gauge and hose into a container. Dispose of the fuel properly.

11. Repeat Steps 2-10 for the other carburetor and record the fuel level reading.

12. The correct fuel level reading is as follows:
   a. Front carburetor: 0.8 mm (0.03 in.) below to 1.2 mm (0.047 in.) above the upper edge of the lower mounting screw.
   b. Rear carburetor: 1.2 mm (0.047 in.) below to 0.8 mm (0.03 in.) above the upper edge of the lower mounting screw.

13. If the fuel level is incorrect, adjust it as described under *Fuel Level Adjustment* in this chapter.

Fuel Level Adjustment

The carburetor assembly has to be removed and partially disassembled for this adjustment.

1. Remove the carburetor assembly as described in this chapter.

2. Separate the carburetor(s) from the float chamber as described under *Carburetor Separation* in this chapter.

3. Hold the float chamber almost vertical so the spring loaded rod in the float valve needle makes contact with the tangs on the float, but is not pushing it down.

4. Check that the float mating edge is between the chamber ribs as shown in **Figure 70**.

5. If the float height is incorrect, bend the float tang (**Figure 71**) a very slight amount until the float edge is between the chamber ribs.

6. Repeat for the other carburetor if necessary.

7. Assemble the carburetor(s) onto the float chamber as described in this chapter.

8. Install the carburetor assembly as described in this chapter.

> *NOTE*
> *If the float tang cannot be adjusted sufficiently to achieve the correct fuel level in the carburetor, either the float and/or the float valve may be faulty. Replace either of these parts as necessary.*

9. Repeat the *Fuel Level Inspection* in this chapter to verify the float tang was adjusted correctly.

10. Repeat this procedure if necessary.

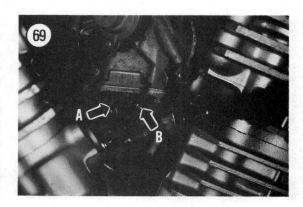

Rejetting The Carburetors

Do not try to solve a poor running engine problem by rejetting the carburetors if all of the following conditions hold true:

a. The engine has held a good tune in the past with the standard jetting.

b. The engine has not been modified.

c. The motorcycle is being operated in the same geographical region under the same general climatic conditions as in the past.

d. The motorcycle was and is being ridden at average highway speeds.

If those conditions all hold true, the chances are that the problem is due to a malfunction in the carburetor or in another component that needs to be adjusted or repaired. Changing carburetor jet size probably won't solve the problem. Rejetting the carburetors may be necessary if any of the following conditions hold true:

a. Non-standard type of air filter elements are being used.

b. A non-standard exhaust system is installed on the motorcycle.

c. Any of the top end components in the engine (pistons, camshafts, valves, compression ratio, etc.) have been modified.

d. The motorcycle is in use at considerably higher or lower altitudes or in a considerably hotter or colder climate than in the past.

e. The motorcycle is being operated at considerably higher speeds than before and changing to colder spark plugs does not solve the problem.

f. Someone has previously changed the carburetor jetting.

g. The motorcycle has never held a satisfactory engine tune.

If it is necessary to re-jet the carburetors, check with a dealer or motorcycle performance tuner for recommendations as to the size of jets to install for your specific situation.

If you do change the jets, do so only one size at a time. After rejetting, test ride the bike and perform a spark plug test; refer to *Reading Spark Plugs* in Chapter Three.

FUEL SYSTEM CLEANLINESS INSPECTION

1. Place the bike on the centerstand on level ground.
2. Attach a piece of suitable size clear vinyl tubing to the drain outlet fitting (A, **Figure 69**) on both carburetor bottom covers.
3. Place the loose ends in a *clean* transparent container.

70

15°-20°

1. Float tang
2. Float valve
3. Float mating edge
4. Chamber ribs
5. Float chamber body

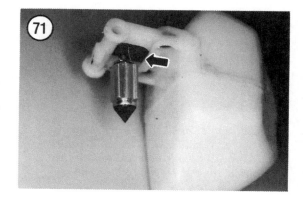
71

4. Turn the fuel shutoff valve on the fuel tank to the ON or RES position. Disconnect the vacuum line from the valve and attach a hand held vacuum pump to the valve. Apply a vacuum to allow the fuel to flow in the next step.

5. Unscrew the bottom cover drain screw (B, **Figure 69**), on each carburetor, several turns and drain both carburetor float bowls.

6. Turn the fuel shutoff valve on the fuel tank to the OFF position.

7. Disconnect the vacuum pump from the shutoff valve and reconnect the vacuum hose.

8. Tighten the carburetor drain screws and disconnect the tubing.

9. Inspect the spent fuel for water, rust and other contaminates. If water is present in the fuel it will be in a layer by itself below the fuel. Dispose of this fuel properly.

10. Water in the fuel usually is a result of water contaminated gasoline or from a leaking fuel filler cap that has allowed moisture to enter the fuel system.

11. Rust particles also may have also come from contaminated gasoline or from an internally rusted fuel tank.

12. If water and/or rust is present in the fuel system it must be corrected as soon as possible.

13. Remove the carburetors, disassemble and clean them to remove all contaminates. Make sure all jets are clear.

14. Remove the fuel shutoff valve from the fuel tank as described in this chapter and clean the integral fuel filter.

15. Remove the fuel tank and the fuel filler cap as described in this chapter. Inspect the fuel tank for rust accumulations and check the filler cap for any possible leaks. Have the fuel tank cleaned to remove the rust and correct any possible fuel filler cap leaks.

THROTTLE CABLE REPLACEMENT

This procedure describes the replacement of the throttle cables from the throttle grip to the carburetor assembly.

NOTE
The throttle "pull" cable is shorter than the "push" cable. Also the "pull" cable has a cable guide attached to it at the carburetor end. Do not confuse one cable from the other during installation.

1. Remove the seat as described under *Seat Removal/Installation* in Chapter Thirteen.

2. Remove the fuel tank as described in this chapter.

3. Disconnect the battery negative lead as described in Chapter Three.

4. At the throttle grip, loosen both throttle cable locknuts (A, **Figure 72**). Turn the adjusters (B, **Figure 72**) to achieve the maximum amount of slack in both throttle cables.

5. Remove the screws securing the right-hand switch assembly (C, **Figure 72**) together and separate the switch halves.

6. Disengage the throttle cable from the throttle grip.

7. Remove the throttle cable from the upper half of the right-hand switch assembly.

8. At the carburetor assembly, loosen the throttle cable locknuts at the throttle wheel. Turn the adjuster to achieve the maximum amount of slack in the throttle cable.

9. Disengage the throttle cables from the throttle wheel.

NOTE
The piece of string attached in the next step will be used to pull the new throttle cables back through the frame so they will be routed in exactly the same position as the old ones were.

10. Tie a piece of heavy string or cord (approximately 3 ft. [1 m long]) to the carburetor assembly end of both throttle cables. Wrap this end with masking or duct tape. Tie the other end of the string to the frame in the adjacent area.

11. At the throttle grip end of the cable, carefully pull the cables (and attached string) out through the

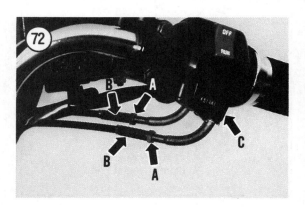

frame. Make sure the attached string follows the same path as the cable through the frame.

12. Remove the tape and untie the string from the old cables.

13. Lubricate the new cables as described under *Control Cable* in Chapter Three.

14. Tie the string to both new throttle cables and wrap it with tape.

15. Carefully pull the string back through the frame routing the new cables through the same path as the old cables.

16. Remove the tape and untie the string from the cables and the frame.

17. Attach both throttle cables to the throttle wheel and temporarily tighten the locknuts on the cable adjusters.

18. Insert the throttle cables into the upper half of the right-hand switch assembly.

19. Engage the throttle cables into the receptacles in the throttle grip.

20. Install the upper half and install the screws securing the right-hand switch assembly (C, **Figure 72**) together.

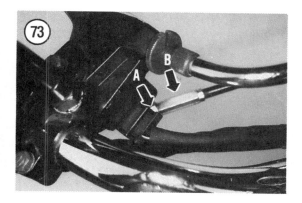

21. Connect the battery negative lead as described in Chapter Three.

22. Install the fuel tank as described in this chapter.

23. Install the seat as described in Chapter Thirteen.

24. Adjust the throttle cables as described under *Throttle Cable Adjustment* in Chapter Three.

25. Test ride the bike slowly at first and make sure the throttle is operating correctly.

CHOKE CABLE REPLACEMENT

This procedure describes the replacement of the choke cable from the choke lever at the left-hand hand grip to the carburetor assembly.

1. Remove the seat as described under *Seat Removal/Installation* in Chapter Thirteen.

2. Remove the fuel tank as described in this chapter.

3. Disconnect the battery negative lead as described in Chapter Three.

4. At the choke lever on the left-hand handlebar, loosen the choke cable locknut (A, **Figure 73**). Turn the adjuster (B, **Figure 73**) to achieve the maximum amount of slack in the choke cable.

5. Remove the screws securing the left-hand switch assembly (**Figure 74**) together to gain access to the choke cable end. Separate the switch assembly.

6. Remove the screw on the cable bracket and disconnect the choke cable from the choke lever assembly.

7. At the carburetor assembly, disengage the choke cable from the starter plunger.

NOTE
The piece of string attached in the next step will be used to pull the new choke cable back through the frame so it will be routed in exactly the same position as the old one was.

8. Tie a piece of heavy string or cord (approximately 3 ft. [1 m long]) to the carburetor assembly end of the choke cable. Wrap this end with masking or duct tape. Tie the other end of the string to the frame in the adjacent area.

9. At the choke lever end of the cable, carefully pull the cable (and attached string) out through the frame. Make sure the attached string follows the same path as the cable through the frame.

10. Remove the tape and untie the string from the old cable.

7

11. Lubricate the new cable as described under *Control Cable* in Chapter Three.

12. Tie the string to the new choke cable and wrap it with tape.

13. Carefully pull the string back through the frame routing the new cable through the same path as the old cables.

14. Remove the tape and untie the string from the cable and the frame.

15. Attach the choke cable to the starter plunger.

16. Connect the choke cable onto the choke lever assembly and install the mounting screw on the cable bracket. Tighten securely.

17. Install the upper half and install the screws securing the left-hand switch assembly (**Figure 74**) together.

18. Connect the battery negative lead as described in Chapter Three.

19. Install the fuel tank as described in this chapter.

20. Install the seat as described in Chapter Thirteen.

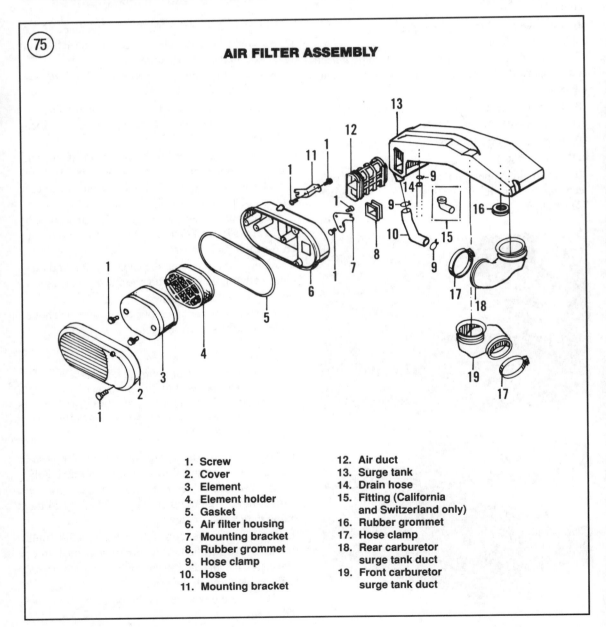

AIR FILTER ASSEMBLY

1. Screw
2. Cover
3. Element
4. Element holder
5. Gasket
6. Air filter housing
7. Mounting bracket
8. Rubber grommet
9. Hose clamp
10. Hose
11. Mounting bracket
12. Air duct
13. Surge tank
14. Drain hose
15. Fitting (California and Switzerland only)
16. Rubber grommet
17. Hose clamp
18. Rear carburetor surge tank duct
19. Front carburetor surge tank duct

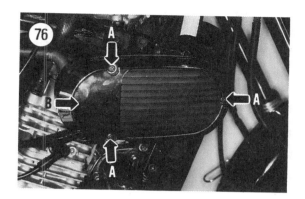

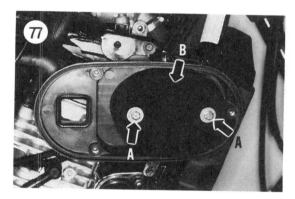

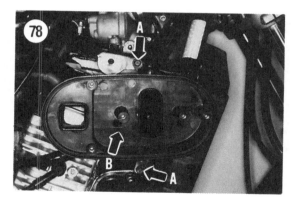

21. Adjust the choke cable as described under *Throttle Cable Adjustment* Chapter Three.
22. Test ride the bike slowly at first and make sure the throttle is operating correctly.

AIR FILTER

Air Filter Housing
Removal/Installation

Refer to **Figure 75** for this procedure.
1. Remove the screws (A, **Figure 76**) securing the air filter cover and remove the cover (B, **Figure 76**).
2. Remove the 2 bolts and washers (A, **Figure 77**) securing the air filter element assembly (B, **Figure 77**) to the air filter housing and remove the element assembly from the housing.
3. Remove the 2 bolts (A, **Figure 78**) securing the air filter housing (B, **Figure 78**) to the surge tank and its air duct.
4. Remove the air filter housing.
5. If necessary, repeat for the other air filter housing.
6. Install by reversing these removal steps while noting the following:
    a. Make sure the air duct is seated correctly against the surge tank (**Figure 79**).
    b. Make sure the air filter housing is seated correctly against the surge tank air duct (**Figure 80**).
    c. Refer to Chapter Three and clean the air filter elements prior to installing them in the housings.

Surge Tank
Removal/Installation

Refer to **Figure 75** for this procedure.

1. Remove the engine as described under *Engine Removal/Installation* in Chapter Four.
2. Pull the surge tank down and out of the frame.
3. Install by reversing these removal steps.

FUEL TANK

Removal/Installation

Refer to **Figure 81** for this procedure.

1. Remove the seat as described under *Seat Removal/Installation* in Chapter Thirteen.

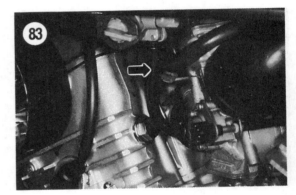

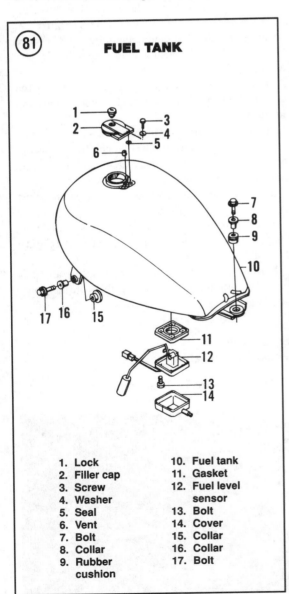

81

FUEL TANK

1. Lock	10. Fuel tank
2. Filler cap	11. Gasket
3. Screw	12. Fuel level
4. Washer	sensor
5. Seal	13. Bolt
6. Vent	14. Cover
7. Bolt	15. Collar
8. Collar	16. Collar
9. Rubber	17. Bolt
cushion	

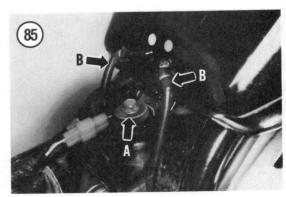

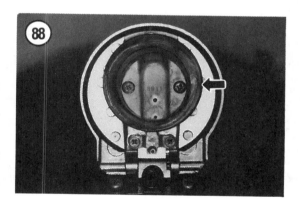

7

2. Disconnect the battery negative lead as described in Chapter Three.

3. Turn the fuel shutoff valve to the OFF position (**Figure 82**).

4. Disconnect the fuel line (**Figure 83**) from the fitting on each side of the fuel shutoff valve. Plug the end of the line with a golf tee to prevent the entry of foreign matter and prevent any loss of any residual fuel in the line.

5. Disconnect the vacuum line from the fitting on the fuel shutoff valve. Plug the end of the line with a golf tee to prevent the entry of foreign matter.

6. Remove the flange bolt (**Figure 84**) securing the front of the fuel tank on each side.

7. Remove the flange bolt (A, **Figure 85**) securing the rear of the fuel tank.

8. Pull the fuel tank partially up at the rear.

9. Disconnect the electrical connector from the fuel level sensor.

10. On California models, disconnect the evaporative emission system vent lines (B, **Figure 85**) from the fuel tank.

11. Lift up and pull the tank to the rear and remove the fuel tank from the frame.

12. Inspect the fuel tank mounting tabs (**Figure 86**) for cracks or damage.

13. Open the fuel filler cap (**Figure 87**) and inspect the cap gasket (**Figure 88**). Replace if it has started to deteriorate or harden.

14. Make sure the breather hole (**Figure 89**) is clear. If the hole is clogged, replace the filler cap.

15. Install by reversing these removal steps while noting the following:

  a. Make sure the rubber cushion and metal collar (**Figure 90**) are in place in each mounting area on the frame.

b. Make sure the fuel line (**Figure 83**) is secure on the fuel valve.

c. Turn the fuel shutoff valve to the ON position (**Figure 91**), start the engine and check for fuel leaks.

FUEL SHUTOFF VALVE AND FILTER

Removal/Installation

Refer to **Figure 92** for this procedure.

> *WARNING*
> *Some fuel may spill in the following procedure. Work in a well-ventilated area at least 50 feet from any sparks or flames, including gas appliance pilot lights. Do not allow anyone to smoke in*

the area. Keep a B:C rated fire extinguisher handy.

1. Remove the fuel tank as described in this chapter.

2. Place a blanket or several towels on the work bench to protect the surface of the fuel tank.

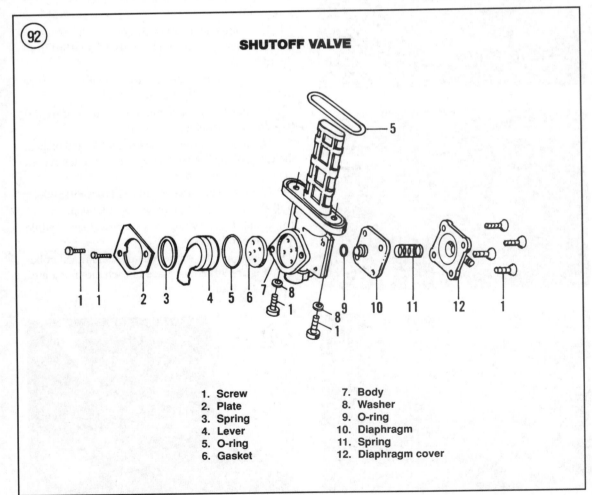

SHUTOFF VALVE

1. Screw
2. Plate
3. Spring
4. Lever
5. O-ring
6. Gasket
7. Body
8. Washer
9. O-ring
10. Diaphragm
11. Spring
12. Diaphragm cover

3. Drain the fuel from the tank into a clean sealable container.

4. Turn the fuel tank on its side (**Figure 93**) with the fuel shutoff valve side up.

5. Remove the bolts and Nylon washers (A, **Figure 94**) securing the shutoff valve to the fuel tank and remove the valve (B, **Figure 94**).

6. After removing the valve, insert the corner of a lint-free cloth into the opening in the tank to prevent the entry of foreign matter or tape it closed.

7. Inspect the shutoff valve mounting O-ring; replace if necessary.

8. Clean the filter portion of the valve with a medium soft toothbrush and blow out with compressed air. If the filter is broken in any area or starting to deteriorate, replace the shutoff valve. The filter is an integral part of the shutoff valve and cannot be replaced separately.

9. To replace the gasket and O-ring, perform the following:

   a. Remove the screws securing the plate and remove the plate, spring, lever, O-ring and the gasket.

b. Inspect the gasket and/or O-ring for deterioration or damage, replace as necessary.

10. To inspect the diaphragm, perform the following:

   a. Remove the screws securing the diaphragm cover.

   b. Remove the diaphragm cover, spring and diaphragm.

   c. Inspect the diaphragm for deterioration or damage, replace if necessary.

11. Install by reversing these removal steps while noting the following:

   a. Be sure to use Nylon washers under the valve mounting bolts. Do not substitute a metal washer as they will not seal the bolts sufficiently resulting in a fuel leak.

   b. Pour a small amount of gasoline in the tank after installing the valve and check for leaks. If a leak is present, solve the problem immediately—do not reinstall the fuel tank with a leaking valve.

FUEL LEVEL SENSOR

Removal/Installation

Refer to **Figure 81** for this procedure.

1. Remove the fuel tank as described in this chapter.

2. Place a blanket or several towels on the work bench to protect the surface of the fuel tank.

3. Drain the fuel from the tank into a clean sealable container.

4. Turn the fuel tank on its side.

5. Remove the cover (**Figure 95**).

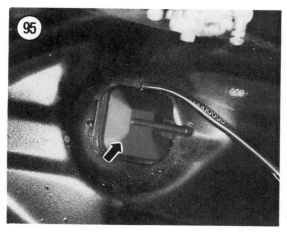

6. Remove the screws securing the fuel level sensor (**Figure 96**) to the base of the fuel tank.

7. Carefully withdraw the fuel level sensor from the opening in the fuel tank. Do not bend the arm or damage the float during removal.

8. Remove the gasket from the fuel tank.

9. Move the float and arm up and down and check for binding. The arm must move freely to give an accurate reading of the fuel level in the tank. If the arm does not move freely, replace the assembly.

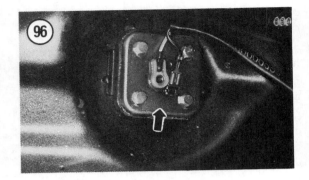

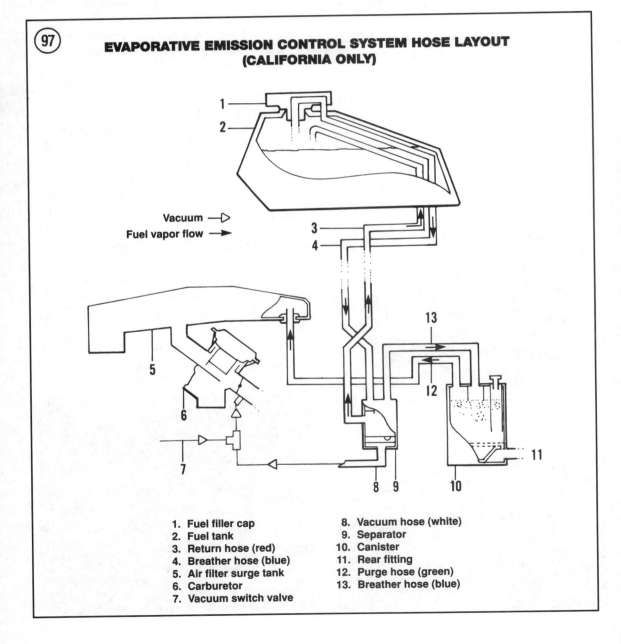

EVAPORATIVE EMISSION CONTROL SYSTEM HOSE LAYOUT (CALIFORNIA ONLY)

Vacuum ⟶ ▷
Fuel vapor flow ⟶

1. Fuel filler cap
2. Fuel tank
3. Return hose (red)
4. Breather hose (blue)
5. Air filter surge tank
6. Carburetor
7. Vacuum switch valve
8. Vacuum hose (white)
9. Separator
10. Canister
11. Rear fitting
12. Purge hose (green)
13. Breather hose (blue)

10. Install by reversing these removal steps while noting the following:

    a. Install a new gasket between the fuel tank and the sensor.

    b. Tighten the mounting screws securely.

    c. Pour a small amount of gasoline in the tank after installing the sensor and check for leaks. If a leak is present, solve the problem immediately—do not reinstall the fuel tank with a leaking sensor.

CRANKCASE BREATHER SYSTEM (U.S. ONLY)

To comply with air pollution standards, all models are equipped with a closed crankcase breather system. The system routs the engine combustion gases into the air filter surge tank where they are burned in the engine.

Inspection/Cleaning

Make sure the hose clamps at each end of both hose are tight. Check the hose for deterioration and replace as necessary.

Open the end of the drain tube attached to each air filter surge tank and drain out all residue. This cleaning procedure should be done more frequently if a considerable amount of riding is done at full throttle or in the rain.

EVAPORATIVE EMISSION CONTROL SYSTEM (CALIFORNIA MODELS ONLY)

To comply with the California Air Resources Board, an evaporative emission control system is installed on all models sold in California.

Fuel vapor from the fuel tank is routed into a charcoal canister. This vapor is stored when the engine is not running. When the engine is running, these vapors are drawn through a purge hose, into the air filter surge tank and into the carburetors to be burned. **Figure 97** is a basic schematic layout of the system. **Figure 98** shows the hose routing and components of the system.

All components within the system require no routing maintenance but all hoses and fitting should be inspected as indicated in **Table 1** in Chapter Three. Make sure all hose clamps are tight. Check all hoses for deterioration and replace as necessary.

Prior to removing the hoses from any of the parts of this system, mark the hose and the fitting with a piece of masking tape and identify where the hose

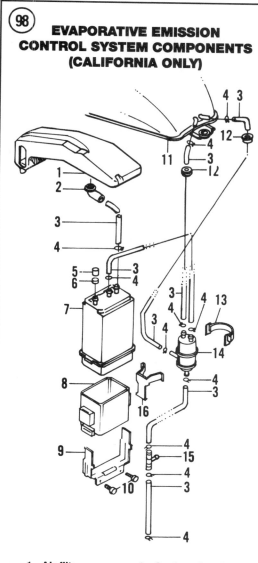

(98) EVAPORATIVE EMISSION CONTROL SYSTEM COMPONENTS (CALIFORNIA ONLY)

1. Air filter surge tank
2. Elbow fitting
3. Hose
4. Hose clamp
5. Cap
6. Band
7. Canister
8. Canister holder
9. Canister bracket
10. Bolts
11. Fuel tank
12. Rubber grommet
13. Mounting strap
14. Separator
15. T-fitting
16. Separator mounting bracket

goes. There are so many vacuum hoses on these models it can be very confusing where each one is supposed to be attached. If the hoses are incorrectly routed, the system will not operate correctly.

Separator and Charcoal Canister Removal/Installation

> *NOTE*
> *This procedure is shown with the rear wheel and swing arm removed for clarity in order to better see the components. It is not necessary to remove either component for this procedure.*

1. Remove the cooling system reservoir tank as described under *Reservoir Tank Removal/installation* in Chapter Nine.

> *NOTE*
> *Prior to removing the hoses from the separator and the charcoal canister, mark the hose and the fitting with a piece of masking tape and identify where the hose goes.*

2. Unhook the rubber strap and remove the separator (A, **Figure 99**) from the mounting bracket. Remove the separator from the bracket and disconnect the hoses from it.

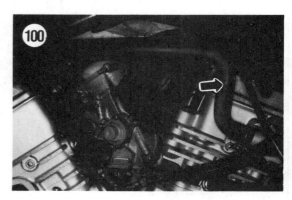

3. Carefully pull the charcoal canister and the rubber holder (B, **Figure 99**) from the mounting bracket. Remove the canister from the bracket and disconnect the hoses from it.

4. If necessary, remove the screws securing the canister mounting bracket (C, **Figure 99**) to the frame and remove the bracket.

5. Install by reversing these removal steps while noting the following:

   a. Be sure to install the hoses to their correct fitting on the charcoal canister and the separator.
   b. Make sure the hoses are not kinked, twisted or in contact with any sharp surfaces.

Inspection

1. Remove the separator and canister as described in this chapter.
2. Inspect the separator and the canister for cracks or damage.

3. If there is any type of exterior damage; replace the separator and/or canister.

CLEAN AIR SYSTEM (CALIFORNIA AND SWITZERLAND MODELS)

Air Suction Valve and Hose Assembly Removal/Installation

1. Remove the seat as described under *Seat Removal/Installation* in Chapter Thirteen.

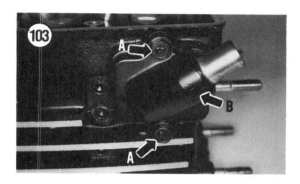

2. Disconnect the fresh air hoses from both cylinder heads. Refer to **Figure 100** for the front cylinder head or **Figure 101** for the rear cylinder head.
3. Carefully disconnect the air hose from the elbow fitting on the air filter surge tank.
4. Disconnect the vacuum line (**Figure 102**) from the fitting on the rear carburetor.
5. Remove the vacuum switch and hose assembly from the engine and frame.
6. Inspect all hoses for deterioration or damage, replace as necessary.
7. Install by reversing these removal steps while noting the following:
   a. Make sure the elbow fitting on the air filter surge tank is securely in place.
   b. Make sure the nozzle is in place in the surge tank end of the air hose. If loose, apply an adhesive, reinstall the nozzle down into the hose by 10 mm (0.40 in.).
   c. Install all hoses onto their correct fittings without being flattened or kinked. They must be unobstructed to allow maximum air flow.
   d. Make sure all hose clamps are on tight.

Air Suction Reed Valve Removal/Inspection/Installation

The air suction reed valve assembly is attached to each cylinder head. The reed valve allows fresh air to flow from the air filter surge tank into the exhaust port and also blocks any air from returning from the exhaust port to the surge tank.
1. Disconnect the fresh air hoses from both cylinder heads. Refer to **Figure 100** for the front cylinder head or **Figure 101** for the rear cylinder head.

NOTE
The following steps are shown with the cylinder head removed from the engine for clarity. It is not necessary to remove the cylinder head for this procedure.

2. Remove the bolts securing the reed valve cover (A, **Figure 103**) to the cylinder head and remove the cover (B, **Figure 103**).
3. Remove the outer gasket and reed valve (**Figure 104**) from the cylinder head. Discard the gasket.
4. Remove the inner gasket (**Figure 105**) from the cylinder head. Discard the gasket.
5. Inspect the reed valve assembly for visible signs of wear, distortion or damage. Check for signs of

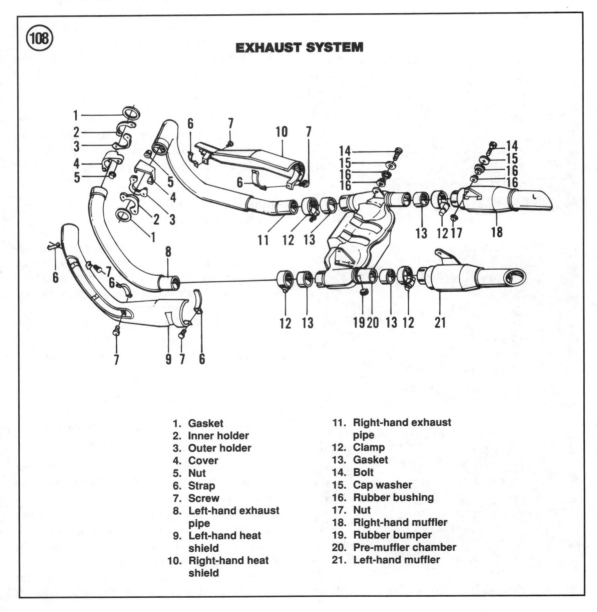

EXHAUST SYSTEM

1. Gasket
2. Inner holder
3. Outer holder
4. Cover
5. Nut
6. Strap
7. Screw
8. Left-hand exhaust pipe
9. Left-hand heat shield
10. Right-hand heat shield
11. Right-hand exhaust pipe
12. Clamp
13. Gasket
14. Bolt
15. Cap washer
16. Rubber bushing
17. Nut
18. Right-hand muffler
19. Rubber bumper
20. Pre-muffler chamber
21. Left-hand muffler

cracks, metal fatigue, distortion or foreign matter damage.

6. Replacement parts are not available for the reed valve assembly. If there is any doubt about the condition of the reed valve, replace it along with both gaskets.

NOTE
Make sure all parts of the reed valve are clean and free of any small dirt particles or lint from a shop cloth as they may cause a small amount of distortion in the reed plate. Any dirt that may be stuck between the reed valve and the stopper will keep the reed valve from opening completely.

7. Make sure the air inlet opening (**Figure 106**) in the cylinder head is open. Clean out if necessary.
8. Position the reed valve assembly with the reed stopper side going in first and with the raised end of the stopper facing toward the front of the bike (**Figure 107**).
9. Place a new gasket on each side of the reed valve and install these parts into the receptacle in the cylinder head.
10. Hold these parts in place, position the reed valve cover with the hose fitting facing toward the rear of the bike and install the cover.
11. Install the bolt securing the assembly and tighten securely.
12. Install the air hose onto the fitting on the reed valve cover. Make sure the hose clamp is secure.
13. Repeat for the other reed valve if necessary.

Air Suction Valve
Testing

When the throttle is open or during normal riding conditions, the air suction valve should remain open and allow air to flow.

During engine braking with the throttle closed the valve should close, not allowing any air to flow.
1. Remove the air suction valve and hose assembly as described in this chapter.
2. Leave all of the hoses attached to the air suction valve for this test.
3. Attach a hand operated vacuum pump and gauge to the vacuum line going to the air suction valve.

NOTE
For this test, blow through the air inlet hose (larger diameter) and hold your hand over the air outlet hose(s) (smaller diameter).

4. Apply vacuum and check the valve operation as follows:
   a. At low vacuum, the valve should allow air to flow through to the reed valve. Blow through the inlet hose and it should flow out through the outlet hoses.
   b. Increase vacuum to 39-47 kPa (11.51-13.88 in. Hg). Blow through the inlet hose and the air should stop or *not* flow out through the outlet hoses.
5. If the air suction valve fails either of these tests, replace the valve.

EXHAUST SYSTEM

The exhaust system is a vital performance component and frequently, because of its design, it is a vulnerable piece of equipment. Check the exhaust system for deep dents and fractures and repair or replace them immediately. Check the exhaust system frame mounting flanges for cracks or fractures. Check the cylinder head mounting flanges for tightness. A loose exhaust pipe connection can rob the engine of power.

Exhaust Pipe and Muffler
(Right-hand Side)
Removal/Installation

Refer to **Figure 108** for this procedure.
1. Remove the 2 lower screws (A, **Figure 109**) securing the muffler cover clamps.
2. Remove the clamps and the right-hand muffler cover (B, **Figure 109**).
3. Loosen the clamping bolt (A, **Figure 110**) securing the muffler to the pre-muffler chamber.

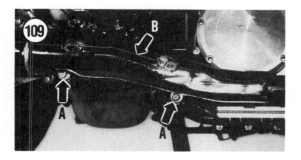

4. Remove the bolt, cap washer and nut (B, **Figure 110**) securing the muffler to the footpeg bracket.

5. Pull the muffler (C, **Figure 110**) straight out of the pre-muffler chamber and remove the muffler from the pre-muffler chamber and frame.

6. Remove the nuts (A, **Figure 111**) securing the exhaust pipe, cover and both holders to the cylinder head. Remove the cover (B, **Figure 111**) and holders (**Figure 112**) from the threaded studs on the cylinder head exhaust port.

7. Loosen the clamping bolt securing the exhaust pipe to the pre-muffler chamber.

8. Loosen the bolts and nuts securing the pre-muffler chamber and the exhaust pipe to the footpeg bracket. By loosening these bolts and nuts, removal of the exhaust pipe is much easier.

9. Carefully pull the exhaust pipe out from the cylinder head studs, then pull the exhaust pipe forward and out of the pre-muffler. Remove the exhaust pipe from the engine and frame.

10. Install by reversing these removal steps while noting the following.

    a. Inspect the gasket where the exhaust pipe joins the pre-muffler chamber; replace as necessary.

    b. Install a new gasket where the exhaust pipe joins the cylinder head exhaust port (**Figure 113**).

    c. Tighten the exhaust pipe cylinder head nuts first to minimize exhaust leaks at the cylinder head. Tighten the nuts securely.

    d. Tighten the bolt securing the pre-muffler chamber to the footpeg bracket first then tighten the clamping bolt where the exhaust pipe joins the pre-muffler. Tighten the bolts securely.

    e. Tighten the bolt securing the muffler to the footpeg bracket. Tighten the bolt securely.

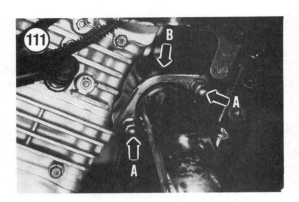

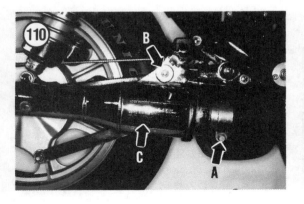

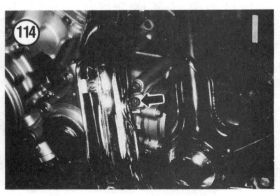

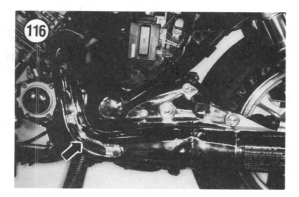

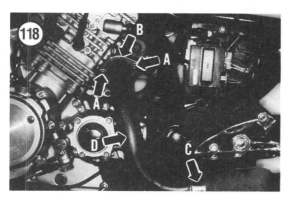

f. After installation is complete, start the engine and make sure there are no exhaust leaks.

**Exhaust Pipe and Muffler
(Left-hand Side)
Removal/Installation**

Refer to **Figure 108** for this procedure.

1. Remove the front bolt (**Figure 114**) and the 2 lower screws (**Figure 115**) securing the muffler cover clamps.

2. Remove the clamps and the left-hand muffler cover (**Figure 116**).

3. Loosen the clamping bolt (A, **Figure 117**) securing the muffler to the pre-muffler chamber.

4. Remove the bolt, cap washer and nut (B, **Figure 117**) securing the muffler to the footpeg bracket.

5. Pull the muffler (C, **Figure 117**) straight out of the pre-muffler chamber and remove the muffler from the pre-muffler and frame.

6. Remove the nuts (A, **Figure 118**) securing the exhaust pipe, cover and both holders to the cylinder head. Remove the cover (B, **Figure 118**) and holders from the threaded studs on the cylinder head exhaust port.

7. Loosen the clamping bolt securing the exhaust pipe (C, **Figure 118**) to the pre-muffler chamber.

8. Loosen the bolts and nuts securing the pre-muffler chamber and the exhaust pipe to the footpeg bracket. By loosening these bolts and nuts, removal of the exhaust pipe is much easier.

9. Carefully pull the exhaust pipe (D, **Figure 118**) out from the cylinder head studs, then pull the exhaust pipe forward and out of the pre-muffler chamber. Remove the exhaust pipe from the engine and frame.

10. Install by reversing these removal steps while noting the following.

 a. Inspect the gasket where the exhaust pipe joins the pre-muffler chamber; replace as necessary.

 b. Install a new gasket where the exhaust pipe joins the cylinder head exhaust port.

 c. Tighten the exhaust pipe cylinder head nuts first to minimize exhaust leaks at the cylinder head. Tighten the nuts securely.

 d. Tighten the bolt securing the pre-muffler chamber to the footpeg bracket first then tighten the clamping bolt where the exhaust pipe joins the pre-muffler. Tighten the bolts securely.

e. Tighten the bolt securing the muffler to the footpeg bracket. Tighten the bolt securely.

f. After installation is complete, start the engine and make sure there are no exhaust leaks.

Pre-muffler Chamber
Removal/Installation

Refer to **Figure 108** for this procedure.

1. Remove the exhaust pipes and mufflers from each side as described in this chapter.

2. Remove the bolt and cap washer (A, **Figure 119**) on each side securing the pre-muffler chamber to the frame.

3. Pull the pre-muffler chamber (B, **Figure 119**) straight down and out of the frame.

4. Install by reversing these removal steps while noting the following.

a. Make sure the rubber bushings are still in place on the footpeg bracket.

b. Tighten the bolts securing the pre-muffler chamber to the footpeg securely.

c. After installation is complete, start the engine and make sure there are no exhaust leaks.

Table 1 CARBURETOR SPECIFICATIONS

| | U.S. & Canadian Models | |
	1985 700 cc	1985 750 cc
Carburetor type	Keihin CVK34	Keihin CVK34
Main jet No.	135	132
Main air jet	(100)	(100)
Jet needle		
Front	N27H	N27J
Rear	N27M	N27K
Needle clip position	fixed	fixed
Pilot jet	38	38
Pilot air jet	(95)	(95)
Pilot screw (turns out)	–	1 5/8
Starter jet	(52)	(52)
Fuel level	see text	see text
Float height	see text	see text
	(continued)	

Table 1 CARBURETOR SPECIFICATIONS (continued)

U.S. & Canadian Models		
	1986 750 cc	1987-1994 750 cc
Carburetor type	Keihin CVK34	Keihin CVK34
Main jet No.	132	132
Main air jet	(100)	(100)
Jet needle (U.S.)		
Front	N27U	N53A
Rear	N27V	N53B
Jet needle (Canadian)		
Front	N27J	N53A
Rear	N27K	N53B
Needle clip position	fixed	fixed
Pilot jet	38	38
Pilot air jet	(95)	(95)
Pilot screw (turns out)		
U.S.	1 5/8	1 5/8
Canadian	1 5/8	2
Starter jet	(52)	(52)
Fuel level	see text	see text
Float height	see text	see text

European Models		
	1985 750 cc	1986 750 cc
Carburetor type	Keihin CVK34	Keihin CVK34
Main jet No.	135	108 (G & W)*
		110 all other
Main air jet	(100)	(100)
Jet needle		
Front	N27J	N31F
Rear	N27K	N31F
Needle clip position	fixed	fixed
Pilot jet	38	38
Pilot air jet	(95)	(95)
Pilot screw (turns out)	1 5/8	1 5/8
Starter jet	(52)	(52)
Fuel level	see text	see text
Float height	see text	see text

(continued)

7

Table 1 CARBURETOR SPECIFICATIONS (continued)

	European Models	
	1987 750 cc	1988-1992 750 cc
Carburetor type	Keihin CVK34	Keihin CVK34
Main jet No.	105 (W)	132
	110 all other	
Main air jet	(100)	(100)
Jet needle		
Front	N31F	N60D (W)*
	–	N31F all other
Rear	N31F	N60D (W)*
	–	N31F all other
Needle clip position	fixed	fixed
Pilot jet	38	38
Pilot air jet	(95)	(95)
Pilot screw (turns out)	1 5/8	1 5/8
Starter jet	(52)	(52)
Fuel level	see text	see text
Float height	see text	see text

	European Models
	1993-1994 750 cc
Carburetor type	Keihin CVK34
Main jet No.	110
Main air jet	(100)
Jet needle	
Front	N31F
Rear	N31F
Needle clip position	fixed
Pilot jet	38
Pilot air jet	(95)
Pilot screw (turns out)	1 1/2
Starter jet	(52)
Fuel level	see text
Float height	see text

* G = West German models, W = Switzerland models

ELECTRICAL SYSTEM

This chapter contains test and service procedures for electrical and ignition components. Information regarding the battery and spark plugs are covered in Chapter Three.

The electrical system includes the following systems:

a. Charging system.
b. Ignition system.
c. Starting system.
d. Lighting system.
e. Directional signal system.
f. Switches.
g. Various electrical components.

Tables 1-5 are located at the end of this chapter.

NOTE
Where differences occur relating to the United Kingdom (U.K.) models they are identified. If there is no (U.K.) designa-

tion relating to a procedure, photo or illustration, it is identical to the United States (U.S.) models.

NOTE
*Most motorcycle dealers and parts suppliers will not accept the return of any electrical part. When testing electrical components, three general requirements to make are: (1) that you follow the test procedures as described in this chapter; (2) that your test equipment is working properly; and (3) that you are familiar with the test equipment and its operation. If a test result shows that a component is defective, have a Kawasaki dealer **retest** the component to verify your test results prior to purchasing the new part.*

ELECTRICAL CONNECTORS

The Kawasaki Vulcan is equipped with many electrical components, connectors and wires. Corrosion-causing moisture can enter these electrical connectors and cause poor electrical connections leading to component failure. Troubleshooting an electrical circuit with one or more corroded electrical connectors can be time-consuming and frustrating.

When attaching electrical connectors, pack them with a dielectric grease compound. Dielectric grease is especially formulated for sealing and waterproofing electrical connectors and will not interfere with the current flow through the electrical connectors. Use only this compound or an equivalent designed for this specific purpose. Do *not* use a substitute that may interfere with the current flow within the electrical connector. Do *not* use silicone sealant.

After cleaning both the male and female connectors, make sure they are thoroughly dry. Using this dielectric compound, pack the interior of one of the connectors prior to connecting. Pack one of the connector halves with dielectric grease compound before joining the 2 connector halves. On multi-pin connectors, pack the male side and on single-wire connectors, pack the female side. Use a good-size glob so that it will squish out when the two halves are pushed together. For best results, the compound should fill the entire inner area of the connector. On multi-pin connectors, also pack the backside of both the male and female side with the compound to prevent moisture from entering the backside of the connector. After the connector is fully packed, wipe the excessive compound from the exterior.

Get into the practice of cleaning and sealing all electrical connectors every time they are unplugged. This may prevent a breakdown on the road and also save you time when troubleshooting a circuit.

Always make sure all ground connections are free of corrosion and are tight at various locations on the bike.

BATTERY NEGATIVE TERMINAL

Some of the component replacement procedures and some of the test procedures in this chapter require disconnecting the battery negative (–) lead as a safety precaution.

1. Place the bike on the centerstand on level ground.

2. Remove the seat as described under *Seat Removal/Installation* in Chapter Thirteen.

3. Remove the bolt and disconnect the battery negative (**Figure 1**) cable from the terminal.

4. Reach into the battery case and move the negative lead out of the way so it will not accidentally make contact with the battery negative terminal.

> *CAUTION*
> *Make sure that system is not shorted before permanently attaching the negative (ground) lead to the battery.*

5. Connect the battery negative lead to the battery negative terminal and tighten the bolt securely.

6. Install the seat as described in Chapter Thirteen.

CHARGING SYSTEM

The charging system consists of the battery, alternator and a solid-state voltage regulator/rectifier (**Figure 2**).

Alternating current generated by the alternator is rectified to direct current. The voltage regulator maintains constant voltage to the battery and electrical loads (lights, ignition, etc.) regardless of engine speed and load.

A malfunction in the charging system generally causes the battery to remain undercharged. To prevent damage to the alternator and the regulator/rectifier when testing and repairing the charging system, note the following precautions:

1. Always disconnect the negative battery cable, as described in this chapter, before removing a component from the charging system.

2. When it is necessary to charge the battery, remove the battery from the motorcycle and recharge it as described in Chapter Three.

3. Inspect the physical condition of the battery. Look for bulges or cracks in the case, leaking electrolyte or corrosion build-up.

4. Check the wiring in the charging system for signs of chafing, deterioration or other damage.

5. Check the wiring for corroded or loose connections. Clean, tighten or reconnect as required.

Leakage Test

Perform this test prior to performing the output test to determine if some electrical component is remaining on and draining the battery.

1. Turn the ignition switch OFF.

2. Disconnect the battery negative (–) lead (**Figure 1**).

> *CAUTION*
> *Before connecting the ammeter into the circuit in Step 3, set the meter to its*

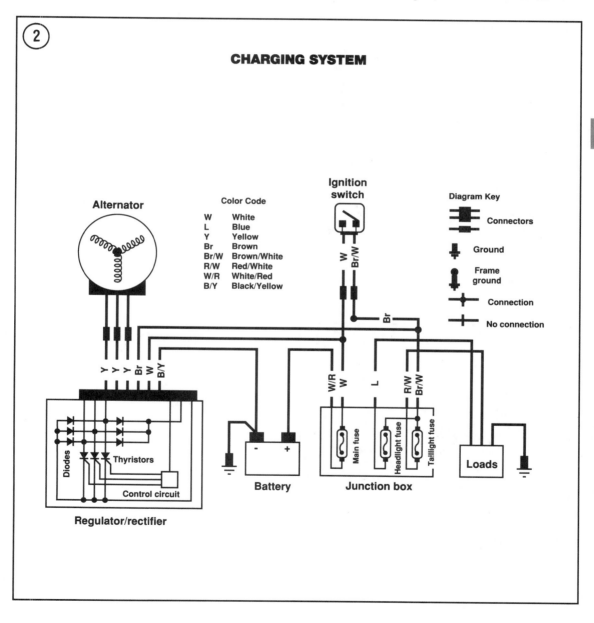

8

CHARGING SYSTEM

highest amperage scale. This will prevent a large current flow from damaging the meter or blowing the meter's fuse, if so equipped.

3. Connect an ammeter between the battery negative (–) lead and the negative (–) terminal of the battery (**Figure 3**).

4. If indicated amperage is low, the ammeter can be switched from its highest to a lower amperage scale. The ammeter should read less than 1.2 mA.

5. Any indicated drain in the system will eventually discharge the battery, but more than 1.2 mA is considered excessive.

6. Some probable causes of excessive drain are a short circuit in the electrical system or a load (light, radio, etc.) is turned ON.

> *NOTE*
> *The radiator fan is connected to the battery regardless of the position of the ignition switch. If the radiator fan runs continuosly, check Cooling Fan Thermo Switch as described in this chapter.*

7. Disconnect the ammeter and reconnect the battery negative lead.

Charging System Output Voltage Test

Whenever a charging system problem is suspected, make sure the battery is fully charged and in good condition before going any further. Clean and test the battery as described in Chapter Three. Make sure all electrical connectors are tight and free of corrosion.

1. Start the engine and let it reach normal operating temperature. Shut off the engine and place it on the centerstand on level ground.

2. Remove the seat as described under *Seat Removal/Installation* in Chapter Thirteen.

3. Start the engine and let it idle.

4. On models other than U.S. and Canadian, turn the headlight ON.

5. Connect a 0-20 DC voltmeter positive (+) test lead to the battery positive terminal connector and the voltmeter negative (–) test lead to the negative terminal (**Figure 4**).

6. Increase and then decrease engine speed and observe the voltmeter needle movement. The voltmeter should read *nearly* battery voltage (14-15 volts), then as engine speed increases the voltage reading should also rise. Note the readings.

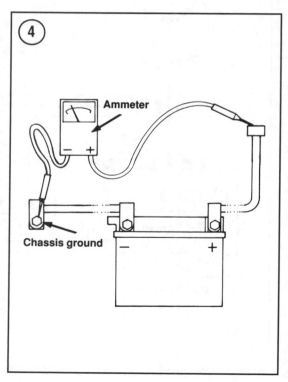

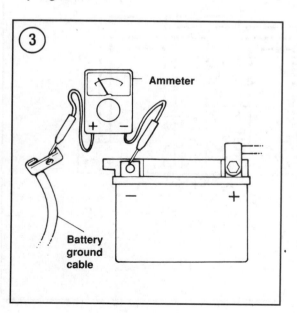

7A. On U.S. and Canadian models, refer to *Headlight Bulb and Lens Replacement* in this chapter and disconnect the electrical connector (**Figure 5**) from the backside of the bulb.

7B. On models other than U.S. and Canadian, turn the headlight OFF.

8. Increase and then decrease engine speed and observe the voltmeter needle movement. The voltmeter should read battery voltage (14-15 volts), then as engine speed increases the voltage reading should also rise but stay within the specified range of 14-15 volts. Note the readings.

9. If the voltage readings are much higher than specified, the voltage regulator/rectifier is probably faulty. Test the voltage regulator/rectifier resistance values as described under *Voltage Regulator/Rectifier Resistance Value Inspection* in this chapter.

10. If the voltage readings do not rise as engine speed increases, then the voltage regulator/rectifier is faulty or the alternator output is insufficient for the electrical load requirement. Test the voltage regulator/rectifier resistance values as described under *Voltage Regulator/Rectifier Resistance Value Inspection* in this chapter.

11. After the test is completed, perform the following:

   a. Shut OFF the engine.

   b. Disconnect the voltmeter.

   c. Install the seat.

   d. Replace the voltage regulator/rectifier if necessary.

Charging System Output Current Test

Whenever a charging system problem is suspected, make sure the battery is fully charged and in good condition before going any further. Clean and test the battery as described in Chapter Three. Make sure all electrical connectors are tight and free of corrosion.

1. Start the engine and let it reach normal operating temperature. Shut off the engine.

2. Remove the seat as described under *Seat Removal/Installation* in Chapter Thirteen.

3. Connect a portable tachometer following the manufacturer's instructions.

4. Remove the frame left-hand side cover.

5. Unhook the fuse panel cover (**Figure 6**) and remove the cover.

6. Remove the 2 top fuses; the headlight fuse (A, **Figure 7**) and the taillight fuse (B, **Figure 7**). This will reduce the load on the charging system to only that required for the ignition system.

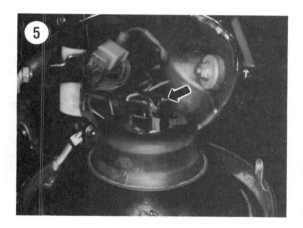

7. Attach an ammeter capable of measuring 20A DC to the battery cable according to the tool manufacturer's instructions (**Figure 8**).

8. After the engine has run for a while, the amperage should drop as the battery returns to full charge after restarting the engine.

9. If the amperage does not drop, and the battery is fully charged, then the voltage regulator/rectifier is faulty. Test the voltage regulator/rectifier resistance values as described under *Voltage Regulator/Rectifier Resistance Value Inspection* in this chapter.

10. After the test is completed, perform the following:

   a. Shut OFF the engine.
   b. Disconnect the ammeter and tachometer.
   c. Reconnect the battery positive (+) lead.
   d. Install the seat.
   e. Install both fuses, install the fuse panel cover and the frame side cover.
   f. Replace the voltage regulator/rectifier if necessary.

VOLTAGE REGULATOR/RECTIFIER

Resistance Value Inspection

If the voltage regulator/rectifier fails either the output voltage and/or output current test, then the voltage regulator/rectifier should be tested for an internal short or open.

1. Start the engine and let it reach normal operating temperature. Shut off the engine.

2. Remove the frame left-hand side cover.

3. Disconnect the 6-pin electrical connector (**Figure 9**) containing 6 wires (3 yellow, 1 brown, 1 white and 1 black/yellow) from the voltage regulator/rectifier.

NOTE
In Step 4 connect the ohmmeter test leads to the voltage regulator/rectifier electrical connector terminals.

4. Use an ohmmeter set at R × 100 and check continuity between each of the voltage regulator/rectifier terminals. Refer to **Figure 10** for terminal identification and to **Figure 11** for test lead placement and specified resistance readings.

5. If any of the resistance readings are higher than specified, there is an open in the unit. If any of the resistance readings are lower than specified, there is a short in the unit.

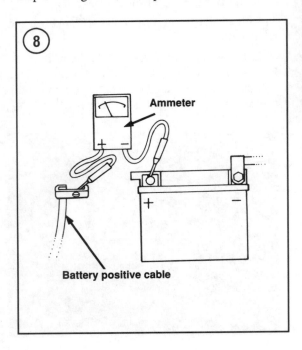

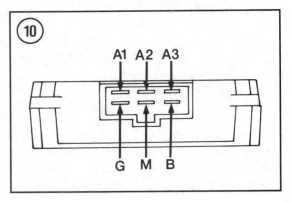

6. If the voltage regulator/rectifier fails any portion of this test, the unit is faulty and must be replaced as described in this chapter.

Removal/Installation

The voltage regulator/rectifier is mounted to the bottom surface of the battery case.

1. Place the bike on the centerstand on level ground.

2. Disconnect the battery negative (–) lead as described in this chapter.

3. Remove the frame left-hand side cover.

4. Disconnect the 6-pin electrical connector (A, **Figure 12**) containing 6 wires (3 yellow, 1 brown, 1 white and 1 black/yellow) from the voltage regulator/rectifier.

NOTE
Removal can be accomplished by two different methods and this is your choice depending on what components may have already been removed from the bike for other service procedures. Both procedures are quite extensive and it's really "mechanics' choice" on which components you want to remove.

5A. Remove the battery case as described under *Battery Case Removal/Installation* in this chapter.

5B. Remove the exhaust system pre-muffler as described under *Exhaust System* in Chapter Seven.

6. Remove the bolts securing the voltage regulator/rectifier (B, **Figure 12**) to the bottom surface of the battery case.

7. Install by reversing these removal steps while noting the following:

    a. Tighten the mounting bolts securely.

    b. Make sure all electrical connections are tight and free of corrosion.

    c. Connect the battery negative (–) lead.

ALTERNATOR

The alternator is a form of electrical generator in which a magnetized field called a rotor revolves around a set of stationary coils called a stator assembly. As the rotor revolves, alternating current is induced in the stator coils. The current is then rectified to direct current and is used to operate the electrical systems on the motorcycle and to keep the battery charged. The rotor is permanently magnetized.

Rotor Testing

The rotor is permanently magnetized and cannot be tested except by replacing it with a known good one. The rotor can lose magnetism from old age or a sharp hit. If defective, the rotor must be replaced; it cannot be re-magnetized.

(11)

REGULATOR/RECTIFIER RESISTANCE

Range ×100Ω	Meter (+) Lead Connection			
Terminal	B	M	G	A1,2,3
B		∞	∞	∞
M	10 kΩ ~ ∞		10 kΩ ~ ∞	10 kΩ ~ ∞
G	0.4 ~ 2 kΩ	1 ~ 5 kΩ		0.2 ~ 0.6 kΩ
A1,2,3	0.2 ~ 0.6 kΩ	∞	∞	*

(left axis label: Meter (–) Lead Connection)

*Any meter reading among A1, A2 and A3 should indicate infinity.

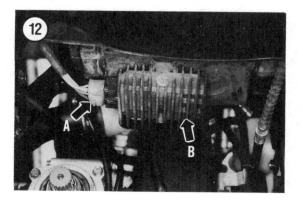

Stator Testing

1. Remove the frame left-hand side cover.

2. Start the engine and let it reach normal operating temperature. Shut off the engine.

3. Disconnect all 3 of the alternator's individual yellow wire electrical connectors located in front of the battery case (**Figure 13**).

4. Use an ohmmeter set at R × 1 and check continuity between each yellow terminal on the alternator stator side of the connector. The specified resistance is listed in **Table 3**.

5. Replace the stator assembly if any yellow terminal shows no continuity (infinite resistance) to any other yellow terminal. This would indicate an open in the stator coil winding.

6. Use an ohmmeter set at R × 1 and check continuity from each yellow terminal on the alternator stator side of the connector and to ground.

7. Replace the stator assembly if any yellow terminal shows continuity (indicated resistance) to ground. This would indicate a short with the stator coil winding.

NOTE
Prior to replacing the stator assembly, check the electrical wires to and within the electrical connector for any opens or poor connections.

8. If the stator assembly fails either of these tests, it must be replaced as described in this chapter.

9. If the stator checks okay, reconnect all 3 yellow individual connectors. Make sure they are free of corrosion and are tight.

10. Install the frame left-hand side cover.

Stator Assembly
Removal

Refer to **Figure 14** for this procedure.

1. Remove the engine as described under *Engine Removal/Installation* in Chapter Four.

2. Remove the external oil line assembly as described under *External Oil Line Removal/Installation* in Chapter Four.

3. Remove the 3 bolts and small O-rings (A, **Figure 15**) securing the inner cover. Remove the inner cover (B, **Figure 15**) and O-ring seal.

4. Remove the bolts securing the outer cover. Remove the outer cover (**Figure 16**) and gasket. Don't lose the locating dowels or the outer washer on the shift lever shaft.

5. Place several shop cloths on the workbench to protect the finish of the alternator inner cover. Turn the alternator inner cover upside down on these cloths.

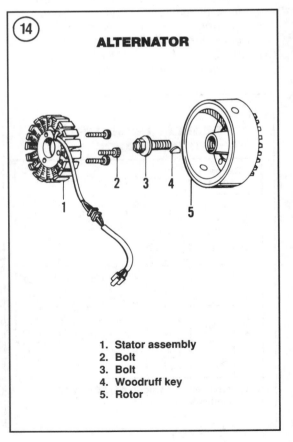

(14)

ALTERNATOR

1. Stator assembly
2. Bolt
3. Bolt
4. Woodruff key
5. Rotor

(13)

6. Remove the screws (A, **Figure 17**) securing the stator assembly (B, **Figure 17**) to the alternator inner cover.

> *NOTE*
> *The upper rubber grommet contains the ignition signal generator electrical wires, the lower grommet contains the alternator stator electrical wires.*

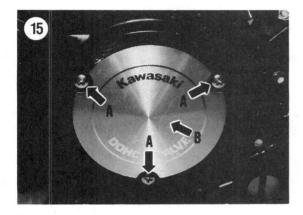

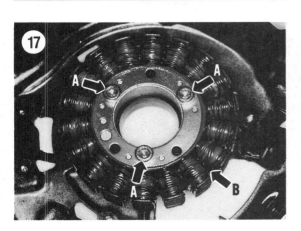

7. Carefully pull both rubber grommets (**Figure 18**) and electrical wires loose from the cover.
8. Remove the stator assembly from the cover.

Stator Assembly
Installation

1. Install the stator assembly in the inner cover.
2. First install the lower grommet containing the alternator stator electrical wires. Then install the upper rubber grommet containing the ignition signal generator electrical wires.
3. Make sure both rubber grommets (**Figure 18**) are installed correctly in the cover. Push them down until they seat tightly in the cover groove.
4. Apply blue Loctite (No. 242) to the stator bolt threads prior to installation. Install the stator bolts (A, **Figure 17**) and tighten to the torque specification listed in **Table 1**.
5. If removed, install the washer (**Figure 19**) onto the gearshift shaft.

8

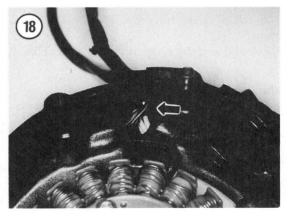

6. If removed, install the locating dowels (A, **Figure 20**), then install a new gasket (B, **Figure 20**).

NOTE
Do not install the single bolt that holds the external oil line to the inner cover at this time.

7. Install the outer cover (**Figure 16**) and bolts. Install the electrical cable clamp under the bolt as shown in **Figure 21** and the clutch cable bracket under the bolt shown in **Figure 22**.

8. Tighten the bolts in a crisscross pattern in 2-3 stages. Tighten the bolts securely.

9. Be sure to install the small O-rings (**Figure 23**) onto the bolts securing the inner cover. If the O-rings are left off, there will be an oil leak.

10. Make sure the perimeter O-ring seal (**Figure 24**) is correctly seated in the backside of the outer cover.

11. Install the inner cover (B, **Figure 15**) and O-ring seal. Make sure O-ring seal is correctly seated in the backside of the outer cover. Install the bolts (A, **Figure 15**) and tighten securely in a crisscross pattern.

12. Install the external oil line as described in Chapter Four.

13. Install the engine as described in Chapter Four.

Rotor
Removal/Installation

Refer to **Figure 14** for this procedure.

1. Remove the alternator stator assembly as described in this chapter.

2. Place a copper penny or washer between the alternator rotor gear and the left-hand balancer gear where they mesh at the upper portion of the gears. This will prevent the alternator rotor from turning in the next step.

3. Loosen, then remove the alternator rotor 17 mm bolt (**Figure 25**). Remove the penny or washer.

CAUTION
Don't try to remove the rotor without a puller; any attempt to do so will ultimately lead to some form of damage to the engine and/or rotor. Many aftermarket pullers are available from motorcycle dealers or mail order houses. The cost of one of these pullers is low and it makes an excellent addition to any mechanic's tool box. If you can't buy or

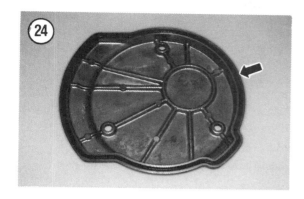

borrow one, have the dealer remove the rotor.

4. Install the rotor removal tool, Kawasaki special tool (part No. 57001-1099 or -1216), or equivalent (A, **Figure 26**) onto the threads of the rotor. Screw it on until it stops against the end of the crankshaft.

5. Place a copper penny or washer between the alternator rotor gear and the left-hand balancer gear where they mesh at the lower portion of the gears. This will prevent the alternator rotor from turning in the next step.

6. Turn the rotor remover tool (A, **Figure 26**) with an open-end wrench. Turn the tool until the rotor disengages from the crankshaft taper. Remove the penny.

NOTE
If the rotor is difficult to remove, strike the end of the puller (not the rotor as it would be damaged) with a hammer a few times. This will usually break it loose.

CAUTION
If normal rotor removal attempts fail, do not force the puller as the threads may be stripped from the rotor causing expensive damage. Take the bike to a dealer and have the rotor removed.

7. Remove the rotor (B, **Figure 26**) from the crankshaft, then unscrew the rotor puller from the rotor.

8. Inspect the inside of the rotor (**Figure 27**) for small bolts, washers or other metal "trash" that may have been picked up by the magnets. These small metal bits can cause severe damage to the alternator stator assembly.

9. Inspect the rotor keyway (**Figure 28**) for wear or damage. If damage is severe, replace the rotor.

8

10. Install by reversing these removal steps while noting the following:

   a. Use an aerosol electrical contact cleaner and clean all oil residue from the crankshaft taper where the rotor slides onto it and the matching tapered surface of the rotor. This is to assure a good tight fit of the rotor onto the crankshaft.

   b. If removed, install the Woodruff key in the crankshaft slot and center it.

> *CAUTION*
> *The alignment between the alternator rotor and the left balancer gear is necessary for proper synchronization of the balance shaft assembly with the engine. The balancer shaft system eliminates the vibration normally associated with large displacement V-twins.*

> *CAUTION*
> *Any applicable manufacturer's warranty will be voided if the balancer system is modified or eliminated.*

   c. Align the Woodruff key slot in the rotor with the key on the crankshaft and partially install the rotor onto the crankshaft.

   d. Rotate the left balancer gear and align the index line mark on the rotor (A, **Figure 29**) with the punch mark or index line on the left balancer gear (B, **Figure 29**).

   e. After alignment is correct, push the rotor the rest of the way onto the crankshaft until it stops. Make sure the index marks on the rotor and left balancer gear are still aligned, if not; remove the rotor and realign the 2 parts.

   f. Tighten the rotor bolt (**Figure 25**) to the torque specification listed in **Table 1**.

TRANSISTORIZED IGNITION SYSTEM

The Kawasaki Vulcan is equipped with a solid-state ignition system, a solid-state system that uses no mechanical parts such as cams or breaker points and requires no routine maintenance. The ignition circuit is shown in **Figure 30**.

The ignition signal generation consists of a single raised tab on the alternator rotor and two pickup coils, attached to the alternator inner cover next to the alternator stator coil assembly. As the alternator rotor is turned by the crankshaft, the raised tab pass by the pickup coils and signal is sent to the I.C.

ignitor unit. This signal turns the I.C. ignitor unit transistor alternately ON and OFF. As the transistor is turned ON and OFF, the current passing through the primary windings of the ignition coil, is also turned ON and OFF. Thus it induces the secondary current in the ignition coil's secondary windings and produces the current necessary to fire the spark plugs (2 per cylinder).

Transistorized Ignition System Precautions

Certain measures must be taken to protect the ignition system. Instantaneous damage to the semiconductors in the system will occur if the following precautions are not observed.

1. Never connect the battery backwards. If the battery polarity is wrong, damage will occur to the voltage regulator/rectifier, I.C. ignitor unit and alternator stator assembly.

2. Do not disconnect the battery when the engine is running. A voltage surge will occur which will damage the voltage regulator/rectifier and possibly burn out light bulbs.

3. Never disconnect any of the electrical connections while the engine is running.

4. Keep all connections between the various ignition system units clean and tight. Be sure that the wiring connectors are pushed together firmly to help keep out moisture. Also pack the connectors with dielectric compound as described at the beginning of this chapter.

5. Do not substitute another type of ignition coil.

6. Most components are mounted within a rubber vibration isolator. Always be sure that the isolator is in place when installing the units in the system.

7. Prior to inspection or troubleshooting the ignition system, check the battery charge as described under

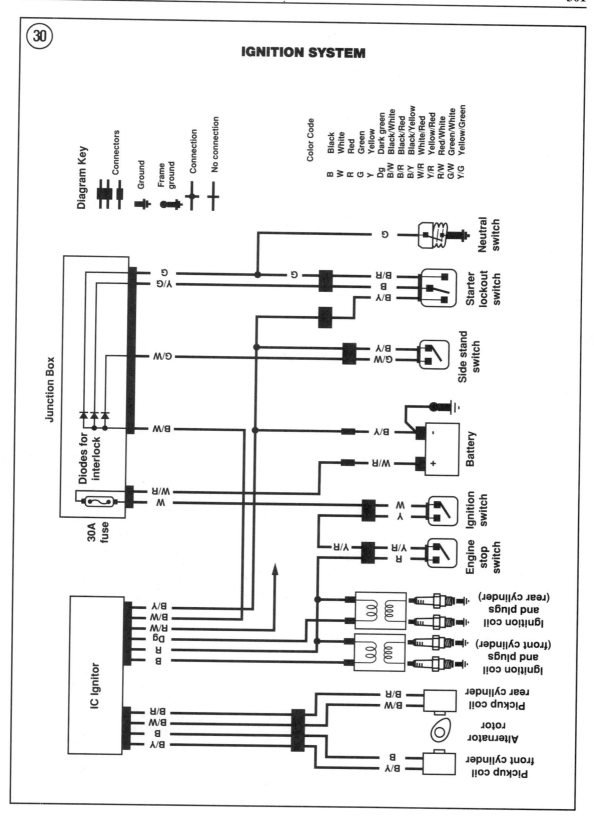

8

Battery in Chapter Three. For best test results, the battery must be fully charged (12.0 volts or higher). A lower voltage reading will result with different and inaccurate test readings.

8. Do *not* turn the engine over unless *all* spark plugs are installed in the cylinder head or grounded against the engine.

Troubleshooting

Problems with the transistorized ignition system are indicated by either a weak spark or no spark at all. Refer to **Table 2**. Refer to **Table 3** for ignition component specifications.

Pickup Coil Testing

1. Remove the frame left-hand side cover.
2. Disconnect pickup coils 4-pin electrical connector (**Figure 31**) containing 4 wires (1 black/yellow, 1 black, 1 black/white and 1 black/red).
3. Set the ohmmeter to R × 1000 and zero the test leads.
4. Check the resistance between the following wires in the pickup coil side of the 4-pin electrical connector.
   a. *Front cylinder:* between the black/yellow and black terminals.
   b. *Rear cylinder:* between the black/white and black/red terminals.
   The specified resistance is listed in **Table 3**.
5. If the resistance shown is less than specified, there is a short; if there is more than specified, the coil has an open. In either case the pickup coil assembly must be replaced as described in this chapter.
6. Set the ohmmeter to its highest setting and zero the test leads.
7. Check the resistance between each of the 4 wires in the pickup coil side of the 4-pin electrical connector and chassis ground. Any meter reading less than infinity indicates a short and the pickup coil assembly must be replaced as described in this chapter.
8. If the pickup coils check out okay, reconnect the electrical connector. Make sure the electrical connector is free of corrosion and is tight.
9. Install the frame cover.

Pickup Coil Assembly
Removal/Installation

1. Perform Steps 1-5 of *Alternator Stator Removal* in this chapter.
2. Remove the screws securing the pickup coil assemblies (A, **Figure 32**) to the alternator inner cover.
3. Cut the plastic tie wrap (B, **Figure 32**) securing the wires to the outer case.
4. Carefully pull the upper rubber grommet as it contains the ignition signal generator electrical wires. Leave the lower grommet in place as it contains the alternator stator electrical wires.
5. Carefully remove the assemblies from the cover.
6. Install new pickup coil assemblies and tighten the screws securely.
7. Be sure to route the pickup coil wiring harness onto the inside cover rib and secure them with a new plastic tie wrap as shown in **Figure 33**. This is necessary to prevent the wires from coming in contact with the alternator rotor when the engine is running.
8. Perform Steps 5-13 of *Alternator Stator Installation* in this chapter.

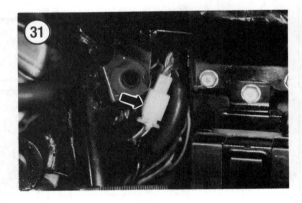

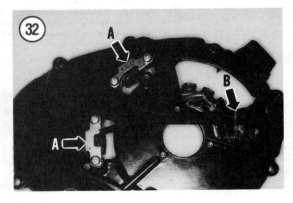

Ignition Coil

The ignition coil is a form of transformer which develops the high voltage required to jump the spark plug gap. The only maintenance required is that of keeping the electrical connections clean and tight and occasionally checking to see that the coils are mounted securely.

If the condition of the coil(s) is doubtful, there are several checks which may be made.

Performance Test

> *NOTE*
> *The spark plug must ground against a piece of bare metal on the engine or frame. If necessary on early models, carefully scrape away some of the engine paint.*

First as a quick check of coil condition, disconnect the high voltage lead from the spark plug. Remove one of the spark plugs (**Figure 34**) from one of the cylinder heads as described under *Spark Plugs* in

Chapter Three. Connect a new or known good spark plug to the high voltage lead and place the spark plug base on a good ground like the engine cylinder head. Position the spark plug so you can see the electrodes.

> *WARNING*
> *If it is necessary to hold the high voltage lead, do so with an insulated pair of pliers. The high voltage generated by the signal generator could produce serious or fatal shocks.*

Turn the engine over with the starter. If a fat blue spark occurs, the coil is in good condition; if not proceed as follows. Make sure that you are using a known good spark plug for this test. If the spark plug used is defective, the test results will be incorrect.

Reinstall the spark plug in the cylinder head and connect the high voltage lead.

Resistance Test

> *NOTE*
> *In order to get accurate resistance measurements, the coil must be warm (minimum temperature is 20° C/68° F). If possible, start the engine and let it warm up to normal operating temperature. If the engine will not start, warm the ignition coils with a portable hair dryer.*

1. Remove the fuel tank as described under *Fuel Tank Removal/Installation* in Chapter Seven.
2. Remove the frame left-hand side cover.
3. Disconnect the battery negative lead as described in this chapter.
4. Disconnect all ignition coil wires (including the spark plug leads from the spark plugs) before testing.

> *NOTE*
> *In Step 5 and Step 6, the resistance specification is not as important as the fact that there is continuity between the terminals. If the ignition coil windings are in good condition, the resistance values will be close to those specified.*

5. Set the ohmmeter to R × 1 and zero the test leads.
6. Measure the primary coil resistance between the primary wire terminals on top of the ignition coil

(**Figure 35**). The specified resistance value is listed in **Table 3**.

7. Remove the spark plug cap off of each lead.

8. Set the ohmmeter to R × 1k and zero the test leads.

9. Measure the secondary coil resistance between the 2 spark plug leads (**Figure 36**). The specified resistance value is listed in **Table 3**.

10. Repeat Steps 5-10 for the other ignition coil.

11. If the coil resistance does not meet (or come close to) either of these specifications, the coil must be replaced. If the coil exhibits visible damage, it should be replaced as described in this chapter.

12. If the coil(s) checks out okay, reconnect all ignition coil wires to the ignition coil.

13. Install the fuel tank as described in Chapter Seven.

14. Install the frame left-hand side cover.

Ignition Coil
Removal/Installation

1. Remove the fuel tank as described under *Fuel Tank Removal/Installation* in Chapter Seven.

2. Remove the frame left-hand side cover.

3. Disconnect the battery negative lead as described in this chapter.

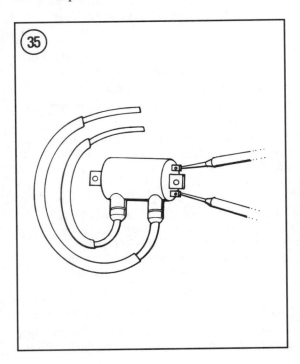

4. Disconnect the primary leads (A, **Figure 37**) from the ignition coil.

5. Disconnect the high voltage lead (B, **Figure 37**) from the spark plug.

6. Remove the bolts (C, **Figure 37**) securing the ignition coil to the frame and remove the coil.

7. If necessary, repeat Steps 4-6 for the other ignition coil.

8. Install by reversing these removal steps. Make sure all electrical connections are free of corrosion and are tight.

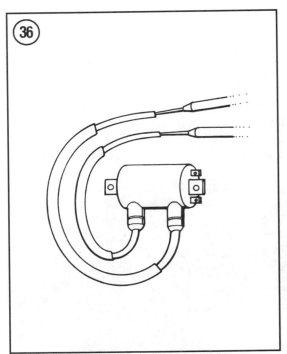

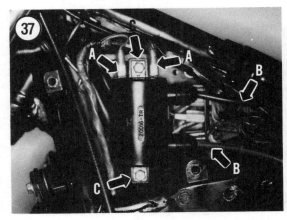

I.C. Ignitor Unit

Complete testing of the I.C. ignitor unit requires a special Kawasaki multimeter (Hand Tester, part No. 57001-983) and should be tested by a Kawasaki dealer service department. This test procedure is provided if you are able to procure this piece of test equipment and choose to perform this test yourself.

NOTE
Do not perform this test procedure with an ohmmeter other than that specified in this procedure. The use of another meter may show different readings, leading to the wrong diagnosis of a problem that may or may not exist within the I.C ignitor unit.

The dealer will either test the ignitor unit with the special tool or perform a "remove and replace" test to see if the ignitor unit is faulty. This type of "R/R" test is expensive for an individual to perform. Remember if you purchase a new I.C. ignitor unit and it does *not* solve your particular ignition system problem, you *cannot* return the I.C. ignitor unit for a refund. Most motorcycle dealers will *not* accept returns on any electrical component since they could be damaged internally even though they look okay externally.

Make sure all connections between the various components are clean and tight. Be sure that the wiring connectors are pushed together firmly and packed with a dielectric compound to help keep out moisture.

Performance Test

1. Remove the fuel tank as described under *Fuel Tank Removal/Installation* in Chapter Seven.
2. Remove the frame right-hand side cover.
3. Disconnect the high voltage lead (**Figure 38**) from one of the spark plugs. Remove the spark plug from the cylinder head as described under *Spark Plugs* in Chapter Three.

NOTE
The spark plug must ground against a piece of bare metal on the engine or frame. If necessary, carefully scrape away some of the paint to reach bare metal.

4. Connect a new or known good spark plug to the high voltage lead and place the spark plug base on a good ground like the engine cylinder head cover. Position the spark plug so you can see the electrodes.

WARNING
If it is necessary to hold the high voltage lead, do so with an insulated pair of pliers. The high voltage generated by the ignitor unit could produce serious or fatal shocks.

5. Turn the engine over rapidly with the starter and check for a spark. If there is a fat blue spark, the ignitor unit is working properly.
6. If a weak spark or no spark is obtained and the pickup coils and ignition coils are okay, test the I.C. ignitor yourself or have it tested by a Kawasaki dealer.
7. Reinstall the spark plug and connect the high voltage lead onto the spark plug.
8. If all of the ignition components are okay, then check the following:
   a. Check for an open or short in the wire harness between each component in the system.
   b. Again, make sure all connections between the various components are clean and tight. Be sure that the wiring connectors are pushed together firmly to help keep out moisture.

Resistance Test

1. Remove the fuel tank as described under *Fuel Tank Removal/Installation* in Chapter Seven.
2. Remove the frame right-hand side cover.

3. Disconnect the battery negative lead as described in this chapter.

4. Disconnect the 6-pin and 4-pin electrical connectors (**Figure 39**) from the I.C. ignitor.

5. Set the ohmmeter to R × 10 and zero the test leads.

6. Check the resistance between the indicated wire terminals in the I.C. ignitor side of the 6-pin and 4-pin electrical connector.

7. Refer to **Figure 40** for terminal identification and to **Figure 41** for test lead placement and specified resistance readings.

8. If any of the resistance readings are higher than specified, there is an open in the unit. If any of the resistance readings are lower than specified, there is a short in the unit.

9. If the I.C. ignitor unit fails any portion of this test, the unit is faulty and must be replaced as described in this chapter.

10. If the I.C. ignitor checks out okay, reconnect the 6-pin and 4-pin electrical connectors to the I.C. ignitor unit (**Figure 39**). Make sure the electrical connectors are free of corrosion and are tight.

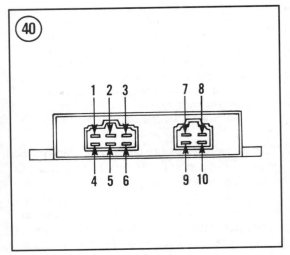

④① IC IGNITOR INTERNAL RESISTANCE

Terminal Number	Tester (+) Lead Connection									
	1	2	3	4	5	6	7	8	9	10
1		∞	∞	∞	∞	∞	–	–	–	–
2	G		F	G	G	F	–	–	–	–
3	C	F		C	E	A	–	–	–	–
4	∞	∞	∞		∞	∞	–	–	–	–
5	F	G	E	F		E	–	–	–	–
6	B	F	A	B	E		–	–	–	–
7	–	–	–	–	–	–		D	D	D
8	–	–	–	–	–	–	D		D	D
9	–	–	–	–	–	–	D	D		D
10	–	–	–	–	–	–	D	D	D	

(Tester (−) Lead Connection)

Value (kΩ)	
∞	Infinity
A	0.9 – 1.7
B	2 – 4
C	3.6 – 6
D	4 – 6
E	8.5 – 15
F	14 – 26
G	24 – 50

11. Connect the battery negative lead as described in this chapter.

12. Install the frame right-hand side cover.

13. Install the fuel tank as described in Chapter Seven.

Ignitor Unit Replacement

1. Disconnect the 6-pin and 4-pin electrical connectors (**Figure 39**) from the I.C. ignitor.

2. Remove the battery case as described in this chapter.

3. Remove the flange bolts securing the ignitor unit to the backside of the case.

4. Remove the ignitor unit.

5. Install a new ignitor unit onto the battery case and tighten the bolts securely.

6. Install the battery case as described in this chapter.

7. Make sure all electrical connectors are free of corrosion and are tight.

STARTER SYSTEM

The starter system includes an ignition switch, a starter switch, clutch interlock switch, side stand interlock switch, starter relay, battery and starter motor as shown in **Figure 42**. Each component of this system is covered separately in this chapter

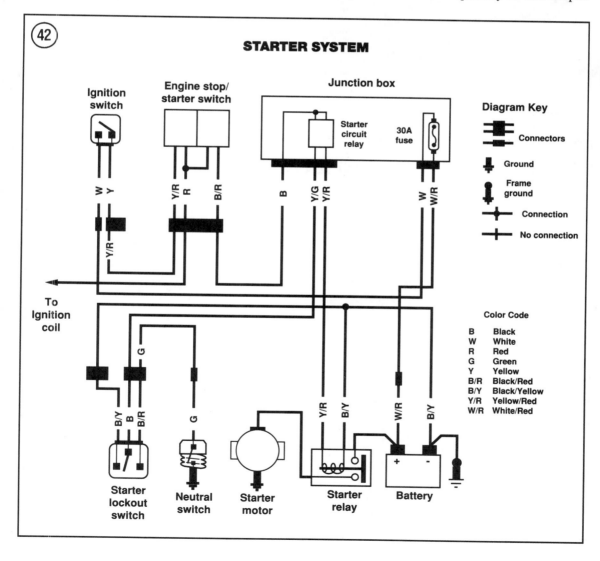

8

except for the battery that is covered in Chapter Three and the starter clutch and gears that are covered in Chapter Four.

ELECTRIC STARTER

Removal/Installation

1. Drain the engine oil as described under *Engine Oil and Filter Change* in Chapter Three.

2. Disconnect the battery negative (–) lead as described in this chapter.

3. Slide back the rubber boot (A, **Figure 43**) on the electrical cable connector.

4. Remove the nut and disconnect the starter electrical motor cable from the starter motor.

5. Remove the 2 bolts (B, **Figure 43**) securing the starter motor to the crankcase.

NOTE
There is an interference fit between the starter motor mounting bosses and the

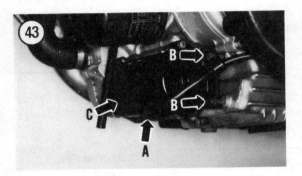

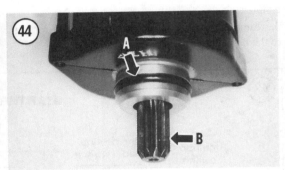

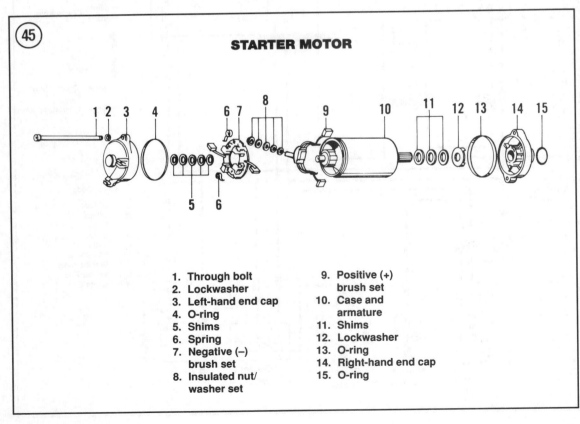

STARTER MOTOR

1. Through bolt
2. Lockwasher
3. Left-hand end cap
4. O-ring
5. Shims
6. Spring
7. Negative (–) brush set
8. Insulated nut/ washer set
9. Positive (+) brush set
10. Case and armature
11. Shims
12. Lockwasher
13. O-ring
14. Right-hand end cap
15. O-ring

*crankcase. After the 2 mounting bolts are removed, the starter motor **cannot** be easily removed from the crankcase without force. This necessitates the use of the plastic faced mallet in the next step.*

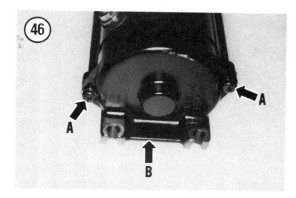

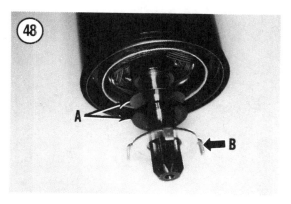

6. Use a soft-faced or plastic-faced mallet and gently tap on the case of the starter motor to dislodge it from the crankcase boss.

7. Pull the starter motor toward the left-hand side to disengage it from the idle gears. Remove the starter motor (C, **Figure 43**) from the opening in the crankcase.

8. Inspect the starter motor as described in this chapter.

9. Install by reversing these removal steps while noting the following:
   a. Make sure the O-ring seal (A, **Figure 44**) is in place on the end of the end case and apply a light coat of clean engine oil to it prior to installing it in the crankcase.
   b. If the starter motor gear will not mesh properly, slightly rotate the gear and try again until alignment is correct.
   c. Push the starter motor all the way in until it bottoms against the crankcase surface.
   d. Refill the engine with the recommended type and quantity of engine oil as described in Chapter Three.
   e. Start the engine and check for proper operation.

Preliminary Inspection

The overhaul of a starter motor is best left to a specialist. This procedure shows how to detect a defective starter.

Inspect the O-ring seal (A, **Figure 44**). O-ring seals tend to harden after prolonged use and heat and therefore lose their ability to seal properly. Replace as necessary.

Inspect the gear (B, **Figure 44**) for chipped or missing teeth. If damaged, the starter assembly must be replaced.

Disassembly

Refer to **Figure 45** for this procedure.

1. Remove the case through-bolts and lockwashers (A, **Figure 46**).

2. Remove the right-hand end cap (**Figure 47**) from the case.

NOTE
*Write down the number of shims (A, **Figure 48**) used on the shaft next to the right-hand end cap.*

3. Slide the lockwasher (A, **Figure 49**) and shims (B, **Figure 49**) from the armature shaft.

4. Remove the left-hand end cap (B, **Figure 46**) from the case.

NOTE
*Write down the number of shims (**Figure 50**) used on the shaft next to the commutator and next to the left-hand end cap.*

5. Slide the shims (**Figure 51**) from the armature shaft.

6. Partially remove the negative (–) brush holder (A, **Figure 52**) from the case. Disengage the positive (+) brushes (B, **Figure 52**) from the negative brush holder, then remove the negative brush holder.

7. Withdraw the armature coil assembly (**Figure 53**) from the case.

NOTE
*Before removing the nuts, washers and O-ring (**Figure 54**), write down their description and order. They must be re-installed in the same order to insulate this set of brushes from the case.*

8. If necessary, remove the nut, washers and O-ring (A, **Figure 55**) securing the brush positive (+) brush set and remove the set (B, **Figure 55**).

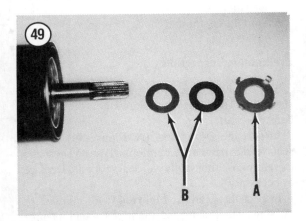

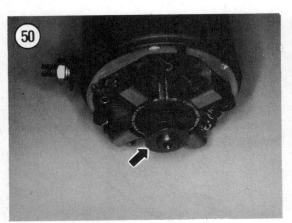

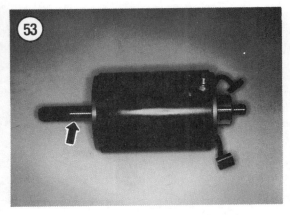

Do not immerse the wire windings in the case or the armature coil in solvent as the insulation may be damaged. Wipe the windings with a cloth lightly moistened with solvent and thoroughly dry.

9. Clean all grease, dirt and carbon from all components.

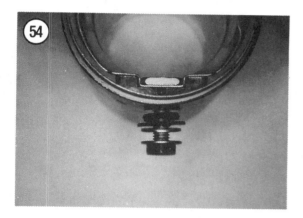

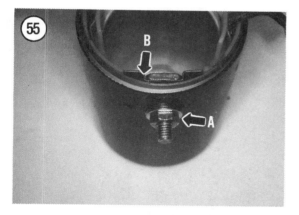

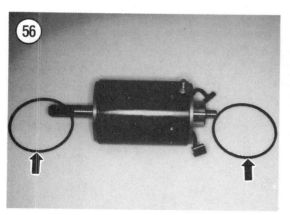

10. Inspect the starter motor components as described in this chapter.

Assembly

Refer to **Figure 45** for this procedure.

NOTE
In the next step, install all parts in the same order as noted during disassembly. This is essential in order to insulate the positive (+) set of brushes from the case.

1. If removed, install the positive (+) brush holder (B, **Figure 55**), O-ring, washers and nut (A, **Figure 55**). Tighten the nut securely.
2. Position the armature coil assembly so the armature end is installed into the case where the positive (+) brush set is located. Insert the armature coil assembly (**Figure 53**) into the end of the case.
3. If removed, install the O-ring seal (**Figure 56**) onto each end of the case. Apply a light coat of clean engine oil to the O-rings.

NOTE
*In order to ease the installation of the brush assemblies onto the commutator, carefully pull the brush spring off the backside of the brush and insert a small plastic or metal washer (**Figure 57**) between the brush and the spring. This will keep the spring pressure off the brush and the brushes will remain retracted in their holders.*

4. Partially install the negative (–) brush holder (A, **Figure 52**) onto the armature. Carefully insert the

8

positive (+) brush electrical wires through the slots in the negative (–) brush holder (A, **Figure 58**). Make sure they are correctly routed so they will not get pinched during final assembly.

5. Insert the positive brushes onto their holders and install the washer (B, **Figure 58**) as described in the previous Note.

6. Align the locating tab (C, **Figure 58**) on the negative (–) brush holder with the locating notch (D, **Figure 58**) in the left-case and push the holder assembly into place.

NOTE
*In the next step, install the exact same number of shims (**Figure 51**) as noted during disassembly. This is necessary to maintain the correct amount of armature end play.*

7. Slide the shims (**Figure 51**) onto the armature shaft.

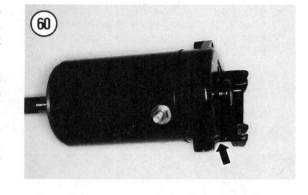

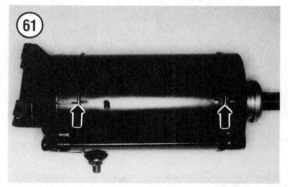

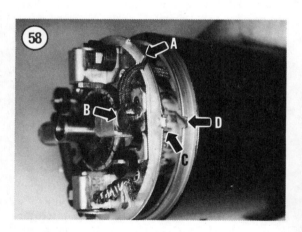

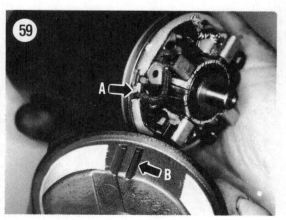

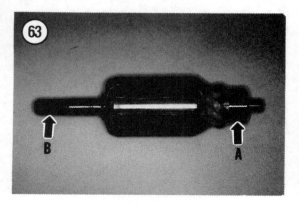

8. Align the raised tab (A, **Figure 59**) on the negative (–) brush holder with the locating notch (B, **Figure 59**) in the left-hand end cap and install the left-hand end cap (**Figure 60**).

NOTE
In the next step, install the exact same number of shims (B, Figure 49) as noted during disassembly. This is necessary to maintain the correct amount of armature end play.

9. Slide the shims (A, **Figure 48**) and lockwasher (B, **Figure 48**) onto the shaft.

10. Install the right-hand end cap (**Figure 47**). Slightly rotate it back and forth to make sure the

lockwasher is seated correctly in the right-hand end cap.

11. Align the alignment marks on the end caps with the case (**Figure 61**).

12. Apply a small amount of blue Loctite No. 242 to the case through-bolt threads prior to installation. Install the case through-bolts and lockwashers (A, **Figure 46**), then tighten securely.

Inspection

1. Measure the length of each brush (**Figure 62**) with a vernier caliper. If the length is 8.5 mm (0.33 in.) or less for any one of the brushes, both brush sets must be replaced as a pair. The brush sets cannot be replaced individually.

2. Inspect the commutator (A, **Figure 63**). The mica should be just below the surface of the copper bars. On a worn commutator, the mica and copper bars may be worn to the same level (**Figure 64**). If necessary, have the commutator serviced by a dealer or electrical repair shop.

3. Inspect the commutator copper bars (**Figure 65**) for discoloration. If a pair of bars are discolored, grounded armature coils are indicated.

4. Use an ohmmeter and perform the following:
   a. Check for continuity between the commutator bars (**Figure 66**); there should be continuity (indicated resistance) between any two of the bars.

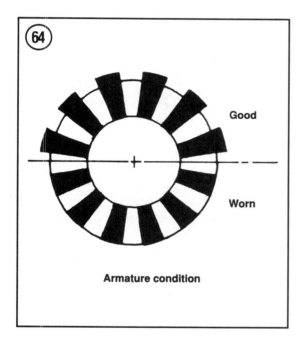

Good

Worn

Armature condition

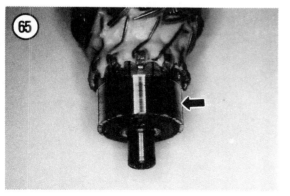

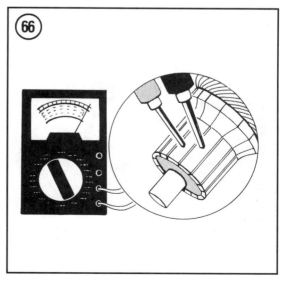

b. Check for continuity between the commutator bars and the shaft (**Figure 67**); there should be *no* continuity (infinite resistance).

c. If the unit fails either of these tests, the starter assembly must be replaced. The armature cannot be replaced individually.

5. Use an ohmmeter and perform the following:

a. Check for continuity between the starter cable terminal and the starter case; there should be no continuity.

b. Check for continuity between the starter cable terminal and the brush wire terminal; there should be continuity.

c. If the unit fails either of these tests, the starter assembly must be replaced. The case/field coil assembly cannot be replaced individually.

6. Inspect the oil seal (A, **Figure 68**) and needle bearing (B, **Figure 68**) in the right-hand end cap for wear, damage or deterioration. Neither part is available as a replacement part. If either is damaged, replace the right-hand end cap.

7. Inspect the left-hand end cap for wear or damage, replace if necessary.

8. Inspect the left-hand end cap bushing (**Figure 69**) for wear or damage. The bushing is not available as a replacement part. If either is damaged, replace the left-hand end cap.

9. Inspect the case assembly for wear or damage. Make sure the field coils (**Figure 70**) are bonded securely in place. If damaged or any field coils are loose, replace the case assembly.

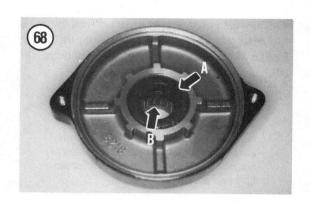

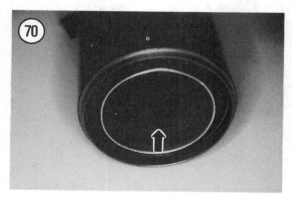

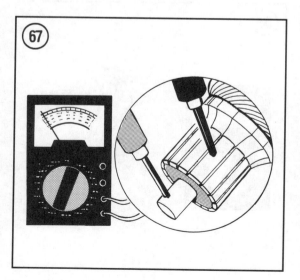

10. Inspect the positive (+) brush holder (**Figure 71**) assembly for wear or damage; replace any damaged parts.

11. Inspect the negative (–) brush holder and brush springs (**Figure 72**) assembly for wear or damage. The springs are the only replacement parts available for this assembly.

12. Inspect the gear splines (B, **Figure 63**) on the armature coil assembly for wear or damage. If damage is severe, replace the starter motor assembly.

STARTER RELAY

Testing

1. Remove the seat and frame right-hand side cover as described in Chapter Thirteen.

2. Shift the transmission into neutral.

> *CAUTION*
> *Because the battery positive (+) lead at the starter relay is connected directly to the battery, even when the ignition switch is OFF, do **not** allow the end of the lead to touch any part of the bike*

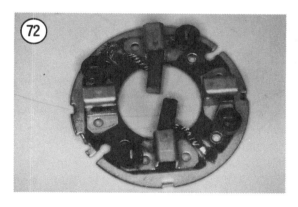

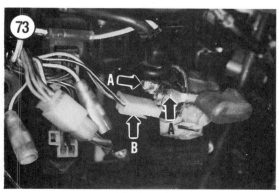

during the following procedure—this would result in a short.

3. Move the rubber boots back off the electrical connectors on top of the starter relay.

4. Remove the nuts and washers and disconnect the starter motor lead and the battery positive (+) cable (A, **Figure 73**) from the starter relay.

5. Position the switches in the following positions in order to run this test correctly:

   a. Ignition switch: ON.

   b. Engine stop switch: RUN.

   c. Neutral switch: ON (transmission in neutral).

   d. Starter button: ON.

6. Set the ohmmeter to R × 1 and zero the test leads.

7. Connect the ohmmeter between the relay large terminals, press the start button and observe the following:

   a. If the relay makes a *single* clicking sound and the meter reads zero resistance, the relay is good.

   b. If the relay clicks, but the meter reads a value greater than zero, the relay is defective and must be replaced.

   c. If the relay does not click, the relay is defective and must be replaced.

8. If the relay checks out okay, install all electrical wires to the relay and to the large terminals. Tighten the nuts securely. Make sure the electrical connectors are on tight and that the rubber boot is properly installed to keep out moisture.

9. If the relay is faulty, replace it as described in this chapter.

10. Install the seat and frame right-hand side cover.

Removal/Installation

1. Remove the seat and frame right-hand side cover as described in Chapter Thirteen.

2. Remove the nuts and washers and disconnect the starter motor lead and the battery positive (+) cable (A, **Figure 73**) from the starter relay.

3. Disconnect the relay coil wire 2-pin electrical connector (B, **Figure 73**) containing 2 wires (1 yellow/red, 1 black/yellow) from the harness.

4. Pull the rubber isolator from the mounting tab on the frame.

5. Withdraw the relay from the rubber isolator and install a new one.

8

6. Replace by reversing these removal steps while noting the following:

   a. Install all electrical wires to the relay. Tighten the nuts securely.

   b. Make sure the electrical connectors are on tight and that the rubber boots are properly installed (**Figure 74**) to keep out moisture.

LIGHTING SYSTEM

The lighting system consists of a headlight, taillight/brakelight, directional lights, indicator lights

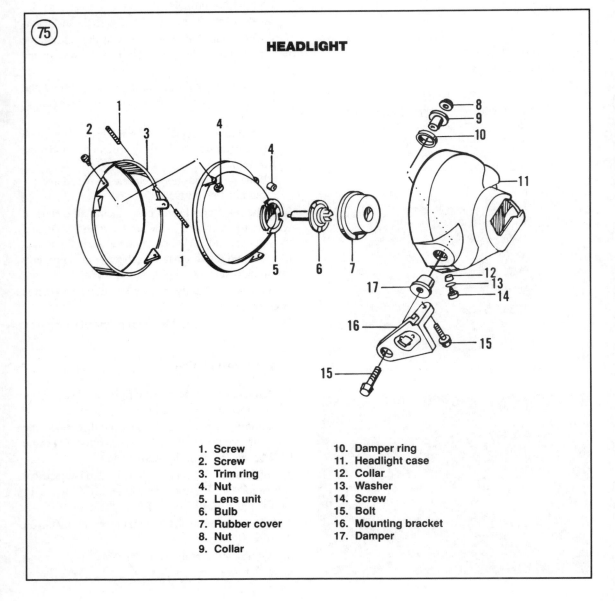

HEADLIGHT

1. Screw	10. Damper ring
2. Screw	11. Headlight case
3. Trim ring	12. Collar
4. Nut	13. Washer
5. Lens unit	14. Screw
6. Bulb	15. Bolt
7. Rubber cover	16. Mounting bracket
8. Nut	17. Damper
9. Collar	

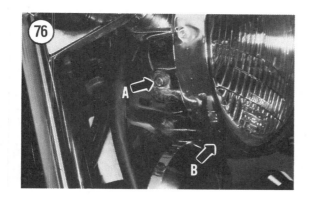

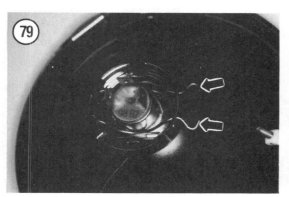

and meter illumination lights. **Table 4** lists replacement bulbs for these components.

Always use the correct wattage bulb as indicated in this section. The use of a larger wattage bulb will give a dim light and a smaller wattage bulb will burn out prematurely.

Headlight Bulb and Lens Replacement

Refer to **Figure 75** for this procedure.

1. Remove the mounting screw, lockwasher and collar (A, **Figure 76**), from each side, at the bottom of the headlight case.

2. Pull the bottom of the headlight trim ring (B, **Figure 76**) out to disengage it from the retaining tab at the top of the headlight case. Remove the trim ring and headlight lens unit assembly from the case.

3. Disconnect the electrical connector (**Figure 77**) from the backside of the bulb.

4. Remove the rubber cover (**Figure 78**) from the back of the headlight lens unit.

8

> *CAUTION*
> *Carefully read all instructions shipped with the replacement quartz bulb. Do not touch the bulb glass with your fingers because any traces of skin oil on the quartz halogen bulb will drastically reduce bulb life. Clean any traces of oil from the bulb with a cloth moistened in alcohol or lacquer thinner.*

5. Squeeze the ends of the retaining clip together (**Figure 79**) and release the clip from the lens unit.

6. Remove the light bulb (**Figure 80**) and replace with a new bulb (**Figure 81**).

7. To remove the headlight lens unit, perform the following:

a. Remove the adjustment screw (A, **Figure 82**).

b. Remove the screws, washers and spacers (B, **Figure 82**) that secure the lens unit to the trim ring. Remove the trim ring (C, **Figure 82**) from the lens unit (D, **Figure 82**).

8. Install by reversing these removal steps while noting the following.

a. If the headlight lens unit was removed, position it with the "TOP" mark on the lens facing up, then install the trim ring.

b. Install the rubber cover with the flat portion (**Figure 78**) facing down.

c. Make sure the electrical connector (**Figure 77**) is on tight and that the rubber cover is properly installed to keep out moisture.

d. Be sure to install collar (**Figure 83**) on the mounting screw. Do not overtighten the screw as the plastic headlight case mounting area may fracture.

e. Adjust the headlight as described in this chapter.

**Front Position Light
Bulb Replacement
(U.K.Models)**

1. Reach up under the headlight case and remove the socket/bulb and electrical connector from the headlight case.

2. Remove the bulb from the socket.

3. Replace the bulb and install the socket assembly.

**Headlight Case
Removal/Installation**

1. Remove the headlight bulb and lens assembly from the headlight case as described in this chapter.

2. Disconnect the electrical wire connectors (A, **Figure 84**) located inside the headlight case.

3. Remove the bolts and nuts (B, **Figure 84**) securing the headlight case to the mounting brackets.

4. Partially remove the case assembly and withdraw the wires from the opening in the back of the case (C, **Figure 84**).

5. Remove the case from the brackets.

6. Install by reversing these removal steps while noting the following:

a. Make sure the collar and rubber damper are in place in the mounting hole on each side of the headlight case.

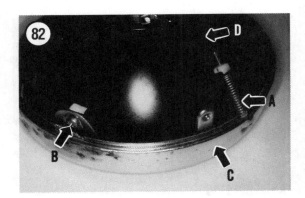

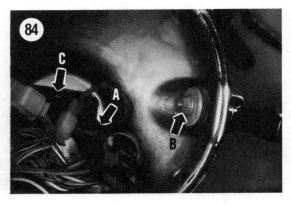

b. Do not overtighten the nuts as the plastic headlight case mounting area may fracture.

c. Adjust the headlight as described in this chapter.

Headlight Adjustment

Adjust the headlight horizontally and vertically
according to Department of Motor Vehicle regulations in your area.

Turn the screws on the bottom of the trim ring,
until the aim is correct.

To adjust the headlight horizontally, turn the right-
hand adjust screw (A, **Figure 85**). Turning the screw
clockwise moves the headlight beam toward the
left-hand side of the road.

NOTE
*It is **not** necessary to loosen the headlight case mounting bolts and nuts for
vertical adjustment. The case will move
within the rubber dampers around the
bolts.*

To adjust the headlight vertically, firmly hold onto
the headlight case and move it up or down until
adjustment is correct. If necessary, slightly loosen
the mounting bolt (B, **Figure 85**), then retighten
after adjustment is complete.

Taillight/Brake Light
Bulb Replacement

Refer to **Figure 86** for this procedure.

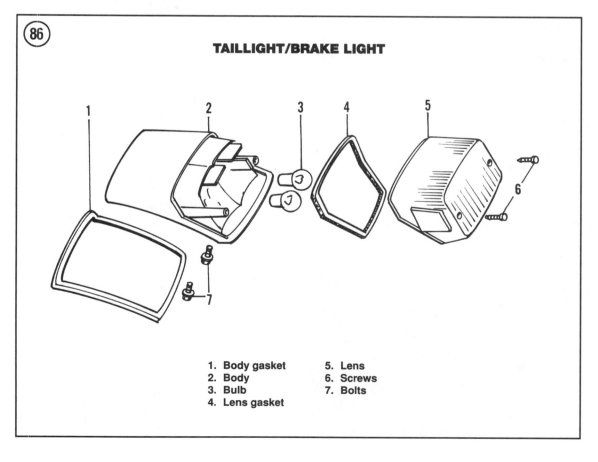

TAILLIGHT/BRAKE LIGHT

1. Body gasket
2. Body
3. Bulb
4. Lens gasket
5. Lens
6. Screws
7. Bolts

1. Remove the screws (A, **Figure 87**) securing the lens and remove the lens and gasket (B, **Figure 87**).

2. Wash out the inside and outside of the lens with a mild detergent and wipe dry.

3. Inspect the lens gasket (A, **Figure 88**) and replace it if damaged or deteriorated.

4. Push in and turn the bulb (A, **Figure 89**) counterclockwise to remove the bulb(s).

5. Carefully wipe off the reflector surface (B, **Figure 89**) behind the bulb with a soft cloth.

6. Replace the bulb (**Figure 90**) and install the lens and gasket; do not over-tighten the screws as the lens may crack.

Taillight/Brake Light Body Removal/Installation

Refer to **Figure 86** for this procedure.

1. Remove the taillight/brake light lens, gasket and bulb from the body as described in this chapter.

2. Disconnect the 3-pin electrical connector for the taillight/brake light assembly.

3. From the under side of the rear fender, remove the screws securing the taillight/brake light body (B, **Figure 88**) to the rear fender and remove the body and gasket.

4. Install by reversing these removal steps while noting the following:

   a. Replace the body gasket if it is starting to harden or deteriorate.

   b. Make sure the electrical connector is tight and free of corrosion.

License Plate Light Bulb Replacement

Refer to **Figure 91** for this procedure.

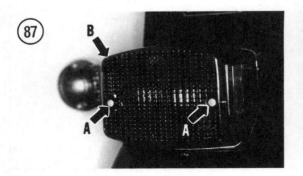

1. Remove the screws securing the bulb cover/lens assembly (**Figure 92**) from the body on the license plate bracket and remove the bulb cover/lens assembly.

2. Wash out the inside of the bulb cover/lens with a mild detergent and wipe dry.

3. Inspect the sealing surface of the damper and body and replace if damaged or deteriorated.

4. Push in and turn the bulb (**Figure 93**) counterclockwise and remove the bulb.

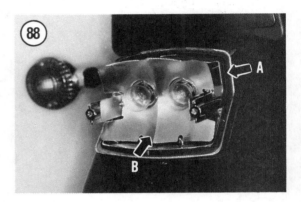

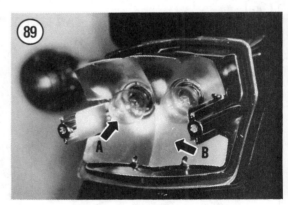

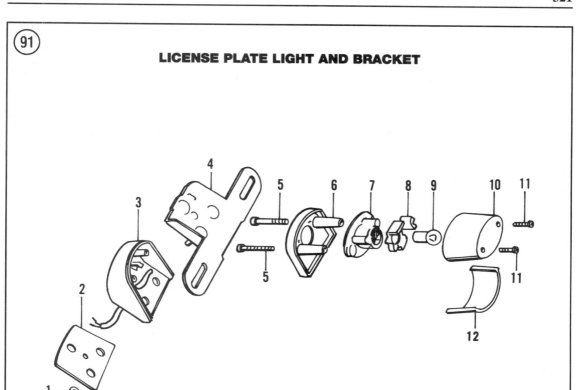

LICENSE PLATE LIGHT AND BRACKET

1. Nut
2. Bracket base gasket
3. Bracket base
4. Bracket
5. Bolt
6. Body
7. Damper
8. Reflector
9. Bulb
10. Bulb cover
11. Screw
12. Lens

8

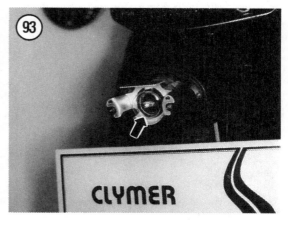

5. Replace the bulb (**Figure 94**) and install the bulb cover/lens assembly; do not over-tighten the screws as the bulb cover/lens may crack.

License Plate Light Assembly
Removal/Installation

Refer to **Figure 91** for this procedure.

1. Remove the license plate bulb cover/lens and bulb as described in this chapter.

2. Disconnect the 2 individual electrical connectors for the license light assembly.

3. From the under side of the rear fender, remove the nuts securing the license plate light body and bracket (**Figure 95**) to the rear fender and remove the assembly and gasket.

4. Install by reversing these removal steps while noting the following:

   a. Replace the gasket if it is starting to harden or deteriorate.

   b. Make sure the electrical connectors are tight and free of corrosion.

Directional Signal Light
Bulb Replacement

1. Remove the screws securing the lens (**Figure 96**) and remove the lens.

2. Push in and turn the bulb (A, **Figure 97**) counter-clockwise to remove the bulb.

3. Wash out the inside and outside of the lens with a mild detergent and wipe dry.

4. Carefully wipe off the reflector surface (B, **Figure 97**) behind the bulb with a soft cloth.

5. Inspect the lens gasket (**Figure 98**) and replace it if damaged or deteriorated.

6. Replace the bulb (**Figure 99**) and install the lens and gasket. Be sure to install the small plastic washer

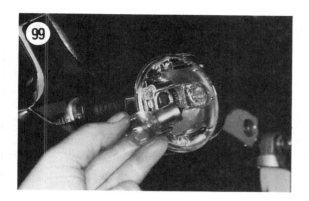

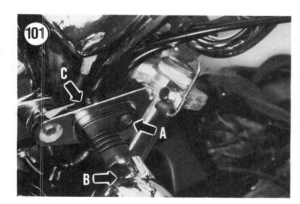

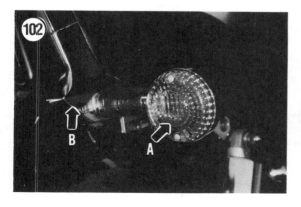

(**Figure 100**) on the lens mounting screws; do not over-tighten the screws as the lens may crack.

Directional Signal Light Assembly Removal/Installation

1. Disconnect the 2 (or 3) individual electrical connectors for the directional signal light assembly.
2. Remove the screw (A, **Figure 101**) securing the front directional signal light assembly (B, **Figure 101**) to the headlight mounting bracket (C, **Figure 101**).
3. Remove the screw securing the rear directional signal light assembly (A, **Figure 102**) to the rear fender stay (B, **Figure 102**).
4. Carefully pull the electrical wires out through the opening in the mounting surface and remove the assembly. Don't lose the collar in the directional signal light assembly mounting hole.
5. Install by reversing these removal steps. Make sure the electrical connectors are tight and free of corrosion.

8

Meter Illumination Light and Indicator Light Replacement

NOTE
This procedure covers replacement of the speedometer, tachometer and indicator bulbs. Perform only the steps necessary for the removal of the bulbs that require replacement.

CAUTION
During this procedure, do not place the meter assembly upside down or on its side for any length of time as the meter(s) will malfunction.

1. Remove the meter assembly (**Figure 103**) as described in this chapter.

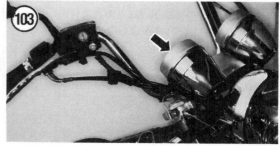

CAUTION
In the following steps, do not allow the meter assembly to remain upside-down any longer than necessary as the needle damping fluid will leak out and render the meters useless.

2. Remove the screw securing the cover to the speedometer assembly and remove the cover.

3. Remove the screw securing the cover to the tachometer assembly and remove the cover.

4. Carefully pull the defective lamp holder/electrical wire assembly from the backside of the speedometer, tachometer or indicator light housing.

5. Pull the bulb straight out of the holder and replace the defective bulb.

NOTE
If a new bulb will not work, check the wire connections for loose or broken wires. Also check the bulb socket for corrosion. Replace as necessary.

6. Push the lamp socket/electrical wire assembly back into the backside of the speedometer, tachometer or indicator light housing. Make sure it is completely seated to prevent the entry of water and moisture.

7. If removed, make sure the cover O-ring seal is in place and install the cover onto the speedometer or tachometer housing. Tighten the screw securely.

8. Install the meter assembly as described in this chapter.

SWITCHES

Switches can be tested for continuity with an ohmmeter (see Chapter One) or a test light at the switch connector plug by operating the switch in each of its operating positions and comparing results with the switch operation. For example, **Figure 104** shows a continuity diagram for a typical ignition switch. It shows which terminals should show con-

(104) IGNITION SWITCH CONNECTIONS

	BR/W	W	Y	BL	R	W/BK	O/G
Off, Lock							
On	●———	●———	●	●———	●	●———	●
P(Park)			●———	●		●———	●

(105) ENGINE STOP SWITCH CONNECTIONS

	R	Y/R
Off		
Run	●———	●

(106) SIDESTAND SWITCH CONNECTIONS

	BK/Y or BR*	G/W
When sidestand is up	●———	●
When sidestand is down		

*U.S. and Canada

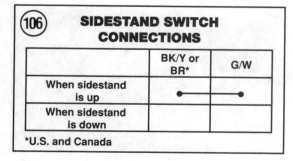

(107) STARTER LOCKOUT SWITCH CONNECTIONS

	BK/Y	Y/G	LG
When clutch lever is pulled in	●———	●	
When clutch lever is released		●———	●

(108) STARTER BUTTON CONNECTIONS

	BK/R	BK/R or R*
Free		
Push on	●———	●

*U.S. and Canada

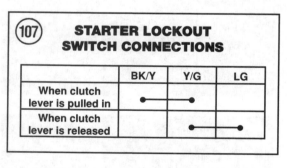

109 HEADLIGHT SWITCH CONNECTIONS (U.K.)

	R/W	R/BL	BL	BL/Y
Off				
■	•———	———•		
On	•———	———•	•———	———•

110 FRONT BRAKE LIGHT SWITCH CONNECTIONS

	BK	BK
When brake lever is pulled on	•———	———•

111 REAR BRAKE LIGHT SWITCH CONNECTIONS

	BR	BL
When brake pedal is pushed down	•———	———•

112 DIMMER SWITCH CONNECTIONS (U.S. and Canada)

	BL/Y	BL/O	R/Y	R/BK
Hi	•————	——————	—————	———•
		•————	———•	
Lo	•————	——————	———•	
		•————	—————	———•

113 DIMMER SWITCH CONNECTIONS (U.K.)

	R/BK	BL/Y	R/Y
Hi	•————	———•	
Lo		•————	———•

tinuity when the ignition switch is in a given position.

When the ignition switch is in the PARK position, there should be continuity between the white and red terminals and between the white/black and orange/green terminals. This is indicated by the line on the continuity diagram. An ohmmeter connected between these 2 terminals should indicate little or no resistance and a test lamp should light. When the ignition switch is OFF, there should be no continuity between any of the terminals.

Testing

If the switch or button doesn't perform properly, replace it. Refer to the following figures when testing the switches:

  a. Ignition switch: **Figure 104**.
  b. Engine stop switch and start switch: **Figure 105**.
  c. Sidestand switch: **Figure 106**.
  d. Starter lockout switch (clutch): **Figure 107**.
  e. Starter button switch: **Figure 108**.
  f. Headlight switch (U.K.): **Figure 109**.
  g. Front brake switch: **Figure 110**.
  h. Rear brake switch: **Figure 111**.
  i. Dimmer switch (U.S. & Canada): **Figure 112**.
  j. Dimmer switch (U.K.): **Figure 113**.
  k. Hazard switch (U.S. & Canada): **Figure 114**.
  l. Passing button switch (U.K.): **Figure 115**.

114 HAZARD SWITCH CONNECTIONS (U.S. and Canada)

	GY	O/G	G
Off ■			
On	•———	———•———	———•

115 PASSING BUTTON CONNECTIONS (U.K.)

	BL	R/BK
Free		
Push on	•———	———•

m. Directional signal switch: **Figure 116**.

n. Oil pressure switch: **Figure 117**.

o. Horn switch: **Figure 118**.

p. Neutral indicator switch: **Figure 119**.

When testing switches, note the following:

a. First check the fuses as described under *Fuses* in this chapter.

b. Check the battery as described under *Battery* in Chapter Three; charge the battery to the correct state of charge, if required.

c. Disconnect the negative (–) cable from the battery, as described in this chapter, if the switch connectors are not disconnected in the circuit.

CAUTION
Do not attempt to start the engine with the battery negative (–) cable disconnected or you will damage the wiring harness.

d. When separating 2 electrical connectors, depress the retaining clip and pull on the electrical connector housings and *not* the wires.

NOTE
Electrical connectors can be serviced by disconnecting them and cleaning with aerosol electrical contact cleaner. Multiple pin connectors should be packed with a dielectric compound (available at most automotive and motorcycle supply stores).

e. After locating a defective circuit, check the electrical connectors to make sure they are clean and properly connected. Make sure there are no bent metal pins on the male side of the connector (**Figure 120**). Check all wires going into an electrical connector housing to make sure each wire is properly positioned and that the wire end is not loose (**Figure 121**).

(116) DIRECTIONAL SIGNAL SWITCH CONNECTIONS

	W/G	BK/Y	W/R	BL/W	G	O	GY
L			●	●	●	●	
N	●	●	●				
R			●	●		●	●

(117) OIL PRESSURE SWITCH CONNECTIONS

	SW Terminal	🜲
When engine is stopped	●	●
When engine is running		

(119) NEUTRAL SWITCH CONNECTIONS

	LG	🜲
When transmission is in neutral	●	●
When transmission is not in neutral		

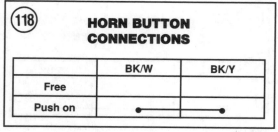

(118) HORN BUTTON CONNECTIONS

	BK/W	BK/Y
Free		
Push on	●	●

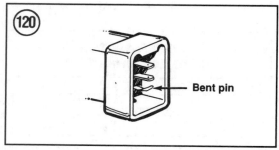

(120)

Bent pin

f. To attach the electrical connectors properly, push them together until they click and are locked into place (**Figure 122**).

g. When replacing handlebar switch assemblies, make sure the wiring is routed correctly so that it is not crimped when the handlebar is turned from side to side. Also secure the wiring to the handlebar with the plastic tie wraps.

Ignition Switch
Removal/Installation

1. Disconnect the battery negative (–) lead as described in this chapter.

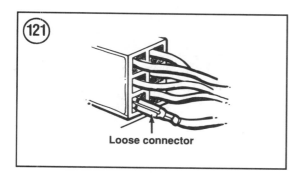

Loose connector

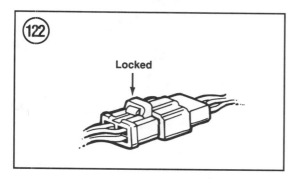

Locked

2. Remove the meter assembly (A, **Figure 123**) as described in this chapter.

3. Follow the wiring harness from the ignition switch to the wiring harness.

4. Disconnect the ignition switch 6-pin electrical connector containing 5 wires (1 yellow, 1 black, 1 red, 1 white/black and 1 orange/green). Also disconnect the 2 individual wire connectors (1 brown/white and 1 white).

5. From the under side of the upper fork bridge, remove the Allen bolts and lockwashers securing the ignition switch to the upper fork bridge.

6. Remove the switch assembly (B, **Figure 123**) from the upper fork bridge.

7. Install the new ignition switch and tighten the bolts securely.

8. Reconnect the 6-pin electrical connector and the 2 individual connectors. Make sure the electrical connectors are free of corrosion and are tight.

9. Connect the battery negative (–) lead as described in this chapter.

10. Install the meter assembly.

Right-hand Combination Switch and
Front Brake Light Switch
(On U.K. models the Headlight Switch)
Removal/Installation

The right-hand combination switch assembly contains both the engine start, engine stop switch and on U.K. models the headlight switch. If any portion of the switch is faulty, the entire switch assembly must be replaced.

1. Remove the seat as described under *Seat Removal/Installation* in Chapter Thirteen.

2. Disconnect the battery negative (–) lead as described in this chapter.

3. Remove the fuel tank as described under *Fuel Tank Removal/Installation* in Chapter Seven.

4. Remove the tie wraps securing the switch wiring harness to the handlebar.

NOTE
The location of the electrical connectors, and the color of the wiring, vary with the different years and with the country in which the bike was originally sold. Therefore the exact location of the connector(s) is not shown in this procedure.

5. Follow the right-hand switch electrical wiring harness on the handlebar to the frame area.

6. Locate and disconnect the electrical connector(s).

7. Disconnect the electrical connector (**Figure 124**) from the front brake light switch. The brake light switch wires are part of the right-hand switch electrical wiring harness.

8. Remove the electrical wire harness from any clips on the frame and carefully pull the harness out from the frame.

9. Remove the screws securing the right-hand combination switch together and remove the switch assembly (**Figure 125**).

10. Install a new switch and tighten the screws securely. Do not over-tighten the screws or the plastic switch housing may crack.

11. Reconnect the electrical connector(s)

12. Make sure the electrical connector(s) are free of corrosion and are tight. Install the tie wrap to hold the electrical wires to the front of the frame. The wires must be retained in this manner to allow room for the fuel tank.

13. Connect the battery negative (–) lead as described in this chapter.

14. Install the fuel tank as described in Chapter Seven.

15. Install the seat as described in Chapter Thirteen.

**Left-hand Combination Switch and
Starter Interlock Switch
(Headlight Dimmer Switch, Directional Signal
Switch, Horn Switch, Hazard Switch [U.S. and
Canadian] and on U.K. Models
the Passing Switch)
Removal/Installation**

The left-hand combination switch assembly contains the headlight dimmer switch, directional signal switch, horn switch, hazard and on U.K. models the Passing Switch. If any portion of the switch is faulty, the entire switch assembly must be replaced.

1. Remove the seat as described under *Seat Removal/Installation* in Chapter Thirteen.

2. Disconnect the battery negative (–) lead as described in this chapter.

3. Remove the fuel tank as described under *Fuel Tank Removal/Installation* in Chapter Seven.

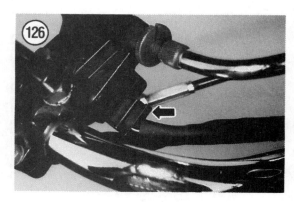
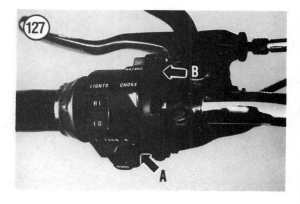

NOTE
The location of the electrical connectors, and the color of the wiring, vary with the different years and with the country in which the bike was originally sold. Therefore, the exact location of the connector(s) is not shown in this procedure.

4. Follow the left-hand switch electrical wiring harness on the handlebar to the frame area.

5. Locate and disconnect the electrical connector(s).

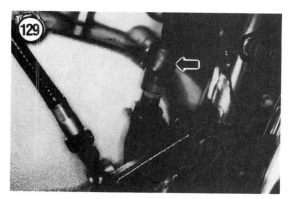

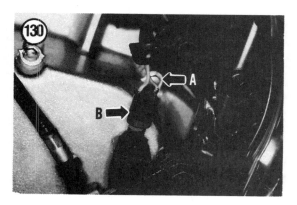

6. Disconnect the electrical connector (**Figure 126**) from the starter interlock switch. The starter interlock switch wires are part of the left-hand switch electrical wiring harness.

7. Remove the electrical wire harness from any clips on the frame and carefully pull the harness away from the frame.

8. Remove the screws attaching halves of the left-hand combination switch together, then remove the switch assembly (A, **Figure 127**).

9. Disconnect the choke lever (B, **Figure 127**) and cable from the left-hand switch assembly.

10. Install a new switch and tighten the screws securely. Do not over-tighten the screws or the plastic switch housing may crack.

11. Attach the electrical connector(s).

12. Make sure the electrical connector(s) are free of corrosion and are tight. Install the tie wrap to hold the electrical wires to the frame.

13. Connect the battery negative (–) lead as described in this chapter.

14. Install the fuel tank as described in Chapter Seven.

15. Install the seat as described in Chapter Thirteen.

Front Brake Light Switch Removal/Installation

1. Disconnect the electrical connectors (A, **Figure 128**) from the front brake light switch.

2. Remove the screw (B, **Figure 128**) securing the brake light switch (C, **Figure 128**) to the master cylinder and remove the switch.

3. Install the new switch and tighten the screws securely.

4. Make sure the electrical connectors are free of corrosion and are tight.

Rear Brake Light Switch Removal/Installation

1. Remove the seat and frame right-hand side cover as described in Chapter Thirteen.

2. Disconnect the return spring from the switch located behind the right-hand footpeg bracket.

3. Slide the rubber boot (**Figure 129**) up and off the electrical connectors on top of the switch assembly.

4. Disconnect the electrical connectors (A, **Figure 130**) from the top of the switch.

5. Remove the switch (B, **Figure 130**) from the frame mounting bracket on the frame.

6. Install by reversing these removal steps while noting the following:
   a. Make sure the electrical connectors are free of corrosion and are tight.
   b. Adjust the switch as described in this chapter.

Rear Brake Light Switch Adjustment

1. Turn the ignition switch to the ON position.

2. Depress the brake pedal. The brake light should come on just as the brake begins to work.

3. To make the brake light come on earlier, hold the brake light switch body (A, **Figure 131**) and turn the adjusting nut *clockwise* as viewed from the top. Turn the adjusting nut (B, **Figure 131**) *counterclockwise* to delay the light from coming on.

> *NOTE*
> *Some riders prefer the brake light to come on a little early. This way, they can tap the pedal without braking to warn drivers who are following too closely.*

Neutral Switch
Removal/Installation

The neutral switch (**Figure 132**) is located on the lower right-hand rear surface of the crankcase below the engine mounting lower through bolt boss.

1. Place the bike securely on the centerstand on level ground.

2. Drain the engine oil as described under *Engine Oil and Filter Change* in Chapter Three.

3. Working under the right-hand side of the engine crankcase, disconnect the electrical connector from the neutral switch (**Figure 133**).

> *NOTE*
> *Step 4 is shown with the engine removed from the frame for clarity. It is not necessary to remove the engine from the frame for this procedure.*

4. Unscrew the neutral switch (**Figure 132**) and washer from the right-hand crankcase.

5. Apply a non-hardening gasket sealer to the neutral switch threads prior to installation.

6. Install the neutral switch (**Figure 132**) and washer. Tighten the switch to the torque specification listed in **Table 1**.

7. Attach the electrical connector and make sure it is free of corrosion and is tight.

8. Refill the engine with the specified type and quantity engine oil as described in Chapter Three.

Sidestand Check Switch
Removal/Installation

1. Place the bike on the centerstand.

2. Follow the sidestand check switch electrical wiring harness up the left-hand side of the frame down tube.

3. Locate and disconnect the 2-pin electrical connector containing 2 wires (1 brown and 1 orange/white).

4. Disconnect the electrical connector from the main wiring harness.

5. Unhook the tie wraps securing the wiring harness to the frame.

6. Remove the screws securing the switch (**Figure 134**) to the frame and remove the switch.

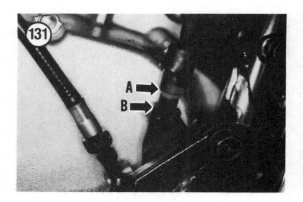

7. Install by reversing these removal steps while noting the following:

    a. Make sure the electrical connector is free of corrosion and is tight.

    b. Secure the electrical harness to the frame with tie wraps.

Oil Pressure Switch
Removal/Installation

1. Drain the engine oil as described under *Engine Oil and Oil Filter Change* in Chapter Three.

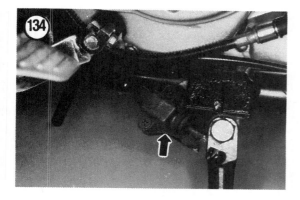

2. Remove the screw and disconnect the oil pressure sending switch wire (A, **Figure 135**).

3. Secure the external oil line fitting (B, **Figure 135**) with an open-end wrench and unscrew the oil pressure switch (C, **Figure 135**) from the fitting.

4. Apply a light coat of silicone sealer to the switch threads prior to installation.

5. Secure the external oil line fitting (B, **Figure 135**) with an open-end wrench and screw the oil pressure switch (C, **Figure 135**) into the fitting. Tighten the switch to the torque specification listed in **Table 2**.

6. Connect the oil pressure switch wire and tighten the screw securely.

7. Refill the engine with the specified type and quantity engine oil as described in Chapter Three.

ELECTRICAL COMPONENTS

    This section contains information on electrical components other than switches. Some of the test procedures covered in this section instruct taking a meter reading within the electrical connector attached to a specific part. Under these conditions make sure that the meter test lead has penetrated into the connector and is touching the bare metal wire *not* the insulation on the wire. If the test lead does not touch the bare metal wire the readings will be false and may lead to the unnecessary purchase of an expensive electrical part that cannot be returned for a refund. Most dealers and parts houses will not accept any returns on electrical parts.

    If you are having trouble with some of these components, performing some quick preliminary checks may save you a lot of time.

    a. Disconnect each electrical connector and check that there are no bent metal pins on the male side of the electrical connector. A bent pin will not connect to its mating receptacle in the female end of the connector causing an open circuit.

    b. Check each female end of the connector. Make sure that the metal connector on the end of each wire is pushed in all the way into the plastic connector. If not, carefully push them in with a narrow-bladed screwdriver.

    c. Check all electrical wires where they enter the individual metal connector in both the male and female plastic connector.

    d. After all is checked out, push the connectors together and make sure they are fully engaged and locked together.

8

Battery Case
Removal/Installation

1. Remove the battery as described under *Battery* in Chapter Three.

2. Remove the rear ignition coil as described in this chapter.

3. Disconnect the electrical connector(s) from the following components:

   a. I.C. ignitor unit (**Figure 136**).

   b. Directional signal control unit (**Figure 137**).

   c. Junction box/fuse panel (**Figure 138**).

   d. Voltage regulator/rectifier (**Figure 139**).

4. On the right-hand side of the battery case, remove the following:

   a. Remove the screws securing the reserve lighting switch (**Figure 140**).

   b. Remove the starter relay (A, **Figure 141**) as described in this chapter.

NOTE
The engine ground strap may be located on either side of the frame, depending on model and year.

5. Remove the bolts (B, **Figure 141**) securing the battery box to the frame on each side. Move the engine ground strap (C, **Figure 141**) out of the way.

6. Move the battery box to the right and tip it on its right-hand side to expose the bottom of the box.

7. Remove the bolts securing the voltage regulator/rectifier to the bottom of the box and remove it.

8. Turn the battery box back down to its normal position.

9. Slide the battery box out of the right-hand side of the frame and remove it.

10. If the battery case is corroded by electrolyte spillage, thoroughly clean with baking soda and water and rinse thoroughly. Then clean with solvent and dry completely. Repaint any areas of bare metal.

11. Install by reversing these removal steps while noting the following:

   a. Make sure all electrical connectors are free of corrosion and are tight.

   b. Be sure to attach the engine ground strap (C, **Figure 141**) to either the right- or left-hand side of the battery case.

   c. Tighten the battery case mounting bolts securely.

Meter Assembly (Speedometer, Tachometer and Indicator Lights) Removal/Installation

Refer to **Figure 142** for meter assembly components and **Figure 143** for the electrical schematic of the meter assembly.

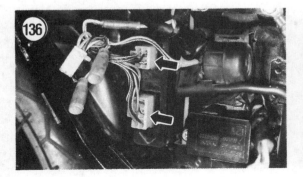

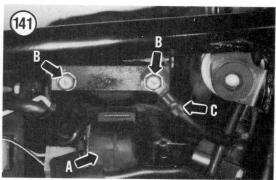

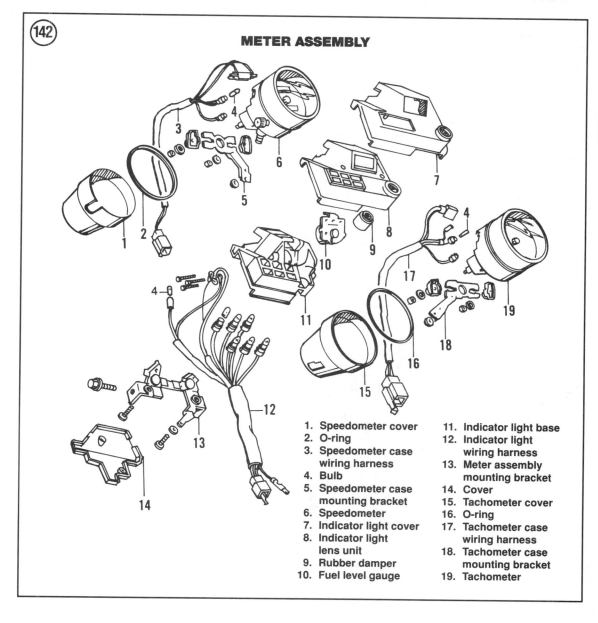

METER ASSEMBLY

1. Speedometer cover
2. O-ring
3. Speedometer case wiring harness
4. Bulb
5. Speedometer case mounting bracket
6. Speedometer
7. Indicator light cover
8. Indicator light lens unit
9. Rubber damper
10. Fuel level gauge
11. Indicator light base
12. Indicator light wiring harness
13. Meter assembly mounting bracket
14. Cover
15. Tachometer cover
16. O-ring
17. Tachometer case wiring harness
18. Tachometer case mounting bracket
19. Tachometer

8

1. Remove the headlight lens (A, **Figure 144**) assembly as described in this chapter.

2. Unscrew the speedometer drive cable (B, **Figure 144**) from the speedometer assembly.

3. Within the headlight case, disconnect the following electrical connectors (**Figure 145**):

   a. 9-pin electrical connector.
   b. 6-pin electrical connector.
   c. 4-pin electrical connector.
   d. Light green/red individual electrical connector.
   e. Red individual electrical connector (models so equipped).

4. Withdraw the electrical wiring harness multi-pin connectors and the individual connector(s) from the opening in the base of the headlight case. Make sure all electrical connectors going to the meter assembly are disconnected prior to removing the meter assembly.

5. Remove the flange bolt (C, **Figure 144**) on each side securing the meter assembly to the upper fork bridge.

NOTE
The ignition switch will not come off with the meter assembly, it will stay attached to the upper fork bridge.

6. Carefully pull the meter assembly straight up and off the upper fork bridge and the ignition switch.

7. Remove the meter assembly and wiring harnesses from the steering head area.

8. Install by reversing these removal steps while noting the following:

   a. Make sure the electrical connectors are free of corrosion and are tight.
   b. Tighten the meter assembly mounting bolts securely.

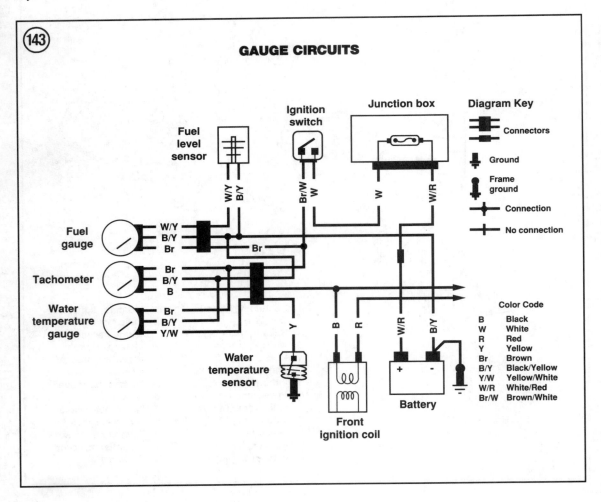

Tachometer Testing

Refer to **Figure 146** for this procedure.

The tachometer works directly with the ignition system. If the tachometer is malfunctioning, first make sure the ignition system is operating correctly.

1. Remove the headlight lens assembly as described in this chapter.

2. Within the headlight case, disconnect the 6-pin electrical connector going to the tachometer.

3. Install a *bare* jumper wire between the BROWN wire terminals in both the male and female connectors.

4. Connect another jumper wire to the BLACK terminal in the female side of the connector.

5. Turn the ignition switch to the ON position.

CAUTION
*In the following step, only touch the BLACK wire to the brown jumper wire, then **release it immediately**. A good ta-*

chometer will be damaged if electrical contact is made for any length of time.

6. Touch, then release, the BLACK terminal jumper wire to the bare jumper wire between the BROWN terminals. When contact is made, the tachometer needle should move slightly or "flick."

7. If the tachometer needle does not move or "flick", it is faulty and must be replaced.

8. Disconnect both jumper wires from the electrical connectors.

9. Within the headlight case, connect the 6-pin electrical connector going to the tachometer. Make sure the electrical connector is free of corrosion and is tight.

10. Install the headlight lens assembly as described in this chapter.

Fuel Gauge Testing

1. Remove the seat as described in Chapter Thirteen.

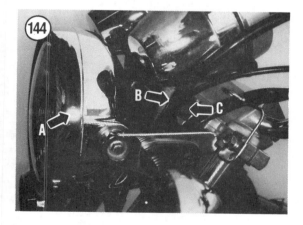

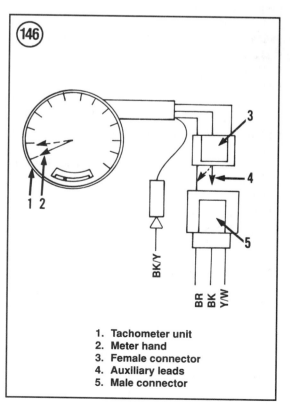

1. Tachometer unit
2. Meter hand
3. Female connector
4. Auxiliary leads
5. Male connector

2. Disconnect the fuel level sensor 2-pin electrical connector (**Figure 147**) (1 white/yellow and 1 black/yellow) at the end of the fuel tank.

3. Turn the ignition switch to the ON position.

4. The fuel level gauge should read "E."

CAUTION
*In the following step, only touch the jumper wire to the terminals in the electrical connector until the fuel gauge needle swings to the "F" mark, then **release it immediately**. A good fuel gauge will be damaged if electrical contact is made for any length of time.*

NOTE
In Step 5 connect the jumper wire to the harness side of the electrical connector—not the fuel tank side.

5. Touch, then release, the jumper wire between the 2 terminals in the fuel level sensor 2-pin electrical connector (**Figure 148**). With the jumper wire connected, the fuel level gauge should read "F." Disconnect the jumper wire immediately.

6. With the jumper wire disconnected, the fuel level gauge should read "E."

7. If the fuel level gauge readings are *correct* as indicated in Step 5 and Step 6, the fuel level gauge is okay.

8. If the readings in Step 7 and Step 8 are okay, the fuel level sensor in the fuel tank is faulty or the electrical wiring between the fuel tank sensor and the 2-pin electrical connector are faulty. Inspect the wiring and/or replace the fuel level sensor in the fuel tank.

9. If the fuel level gauge readings are *incorrect* in Step 5 and Step 6, the fuel gauge is faulty and must be replaced.

10. Install the frame left-hand side cover.

11. Install the seat.

Temperature Gauge Testing

1. Remove the fuel tank as described under *Fuel Tank Removal/Installation* in Chapter Seven.

2. Remove the steering head right-hand cover.

3. Disconnect the yellow electrical connector (**Figure 149**) from the thermostat housing.

4. Turn the ignition switch to the ON position.

5. The temperature gauge should read "C."

6. Attach a short jumper wire to the yellow wire electrical connector.

CAUTION
*In the following step, only touch the jumper wire to ground until the temperature gauge needle swings to the "H" mark, then **release it immediately**. A good temperature gauge will be damaged if electrical contact is made for any length of time.*

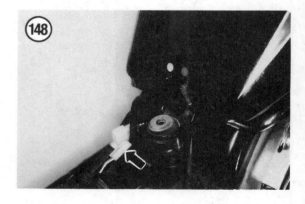

7. Touch, then release, the jumper wire to a good ground like the thermostat housing. With the jumper wire connected, the temperature gauge should read "H." Disconnect the jumper wire immediately.

8. With the jumper wire disconnected, the temperature gauge should read "C."

9. If the temperature gauge readings are *correct* as indicated in Step 7 and Step 8, the temperature gauge is okay, but the coolant temperature sensor may be faulty. Inspect the coolant temperature sensor as described in this chapter.

10. If the temperature gauge readings are *incorrect* in Step 7 and Step 8, the temperature gauge is faulty or the electrical wiring between the temperature gauge and the yellow electrical connector is faulty. Inspect the wiring and/or check the coolant temperature sensor as described in this chapter.

11. Disconnect the jumper wire and connect the yellow electrical connector (**Figure 149**) onto the thermostat housing.

12. Install the frame left-hand side cover.

13. Install the fuel tank as described in Chapter Seven.

Cooling Fan Thermo Switch Removal/Testing/Installation

The cooling fan thermo switch controls the radiator fan according to engine coolant temperature. When the coolant temperature gauge needle is in the HOT range, the cooling fan should operate. This cooling fan thermo switch is attached to the lower left-hand side of the radiator.

Figure 150 is a schematic of the cooling fan thermo switch circuit.

NOTE
If the cooling fan is not operating correctly, make sure that the cooling fan fuse has not blown prior to starting this test. Also clean off any rust or corrosion from the electrical terminals on the thermo switch at the radiator.

8

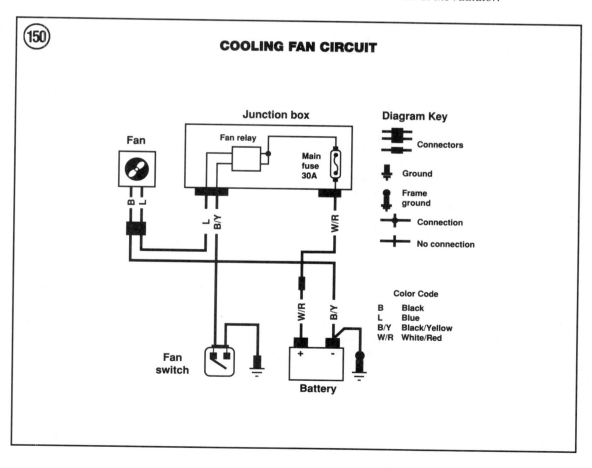

COOLING FAN CIRCUIT

1. Disconnect the electrical connector (A, **Figure 151**) from the cooling fan thermo switch.

2. Place a jumper wire between the cooling fan thermo switch yellow electrical connector and a good ground.

4. Turn the ignition switch ON, the cooling fan should start running.

5. If the cooling fan does not run, either the cooling fan or the electrical wiring to the cooling fan is faulty.

6. If the fan now runs, the cooling fan thermo switch may be defective; test the cooling fan thermo switch as follows.

7. Drain the coolant from the radiator as described under *Coolant Change* in Chapter Three.

8. Unscrew the cooling fan thermo switch (B, **Figure 151**) from the radiator.

> *WARNING*
> *Wear safety glasses or goggles and gloves during this test. Protect yourself accordingly as the coolant is heated to a high temperature.*

9. Place the cooling fan thermo switch in a small pan of 50/50 mixture of distilled water and anti-freeze. The cooling fan thermo switch must be positioned so that all of its threads are submerged in the coolant.

10. Place a shop thermometer in the pan (use a thermometer that is rated higher than the test temperature).

11. Use an ohmmeter and check the resistance between the terminal on the switch and ground (side of switch) as shown in **Figure 152**. At room temperature there should be no continuity (infinite resistance).

12. Do not let the switch or the thermometer touch the pan as it will give a false readings.

13. Heat the coolant slowly until the temperature reaches 94-100° C (201-212° F). Watch the ohmmeter needle while the coolant is heating. The needle should move from infinity to 0.5 ohms. Maintain this temperature for at least 3 minutes before taking the final reading. A sudden change in temperature will cause a different ohmmeter reading. After this 3 minute interval is completed, check the ohmmeter; there should be continuity (0.5 ohms).

14. Turn the heat off and keep the ohmmeter test leads attached. When the coolant reaches 91° C (196° F), check the ohmmeter; there should be no continuity (infinite resistance).

15. If the cooling fan thermo switch fails either of these tests, the switch must be replaced.

16. If the cooling fan thermo switch tests okay, allow it to cool down and remove it from the small pan.

17. Apply a light coat of silicone based sealant to the threads of the cooling fan thermo switch and install the switch in the radiator.

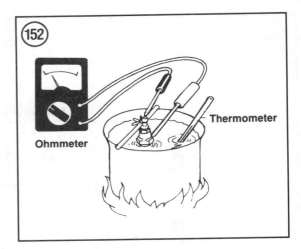

18. Tighten the cooling fan thermo switch to the torque specification listed in **Table 1**.

19. Refill the cooling system with the recommended type and quantity of coolant. Refer to Chapter Three.

20. Attach the electrical wires to the cooling fan thermo switch. Make sure the connections are tight and free from oil and corrosion.

Coolant Temperature Sensor
Removal/Testing/Installation

The coolant temperature sensor controls the temperature gauge on the instrument cluster. This sensor is attached to the thermostat housing.

1. Remove the fuel tank as described under *Fuel Tank Removal/Installation* in Chapter Seven.

2. Partially drain the cooling system as described under *Coolant Change* in Chapter Three. Drain just enough coolant to lower the coolant level in the radiator to below the radiator upper hose. This will lessen the loss of coolant onto the front cylinder head when the sensor is removed.

3. Disconnect the electrical connector (A, **Figure 153**) from the end of the coolant temperature sensor.

4. Unscrew the coolant temperature sensor (B, **Figure 153**) from the thermostat housing.

> *WARNING*
> *Wear safety glasses or goggles and gloves during this test. Protect yourself accordingly as the coolant is heated to a very high temperature and can result in severe burns if not handled properly.*

5. Place the coolant temperature sensor in a small pan of 50:50 mixture of distilled water and antifreeze. The coolant temperature sensor must be po-

sitioned so that all of its threads are submerged in the coolant.

6. Place a shop thermometer in the pan (use a thermometer that is rated higher than the test temperature).

7. Use an ohmmeter and check the resistance between the terminal on the switch and ground (side of switch) as shown in **Figure 152**. At room temperature there should be no continuity (infinite resistance).

8. Do not let the switch or the thermometer touch the pan as it will give a false reading.

9. Heat the coolant slowly until the temperature reaches 80° C (176° F). At this temperature there should be 42-62 ohms of resistance.

10. Continue to heat the coolant until the temperature reaches 100° C (212° F). At this temperature the resistance should reduce to 22-33 ohms.

11. Turn off the heat source.

12. If the coolant temperature sensor fails either of these tests, the sensor must be replaced.

13. Allow it to cool down and remove it from the small pan.

14. Apply a light coat of silicone based sealant to the threads of the coolant temperature sensor and install the sensor in the thermostat housing and tighten securely (B, **Figure 153**).

15. Refill the cooling system with the recommended type and quantity of coolant. Refer to Chapter Three.

16. Attach the electrical connector (A, **Figure 153**) to the coolant temperature sensor. Make sure the connection is tight and free from oil and corrosion.

17. Refill the cooling system as described in Chapter Three.

18. Install the fuel tank as described in Chapter Seven.

Horn Testing

1. Disconnect horn wires from harness.

2. Connect a 12 volt battery to the horn.

3. If the horn is good, it will sound. If not, replace it.

Horn
Removal/Installation

1. Disconnect the electrical connectors (**Figure 154**) from each horn.

2. Remove the front fork cover (**Figure 155**).

3. Remove the bolts (A, **Figure 156**) securing the horn assembly (B, **Figure 156**) and front brake 3-way joint to the lower fork bridge. Remove the horn assembly and reinstall the bolts to hold the brake 3-way joint in place.

4. Install by reversing these removal steps. Make sure the electrical connectors are free of corrosion and are tight.

JUNCTION BOX AND FUSE PANEL

The junction box and fuse panel assembly is located under the frame left-hand side cover. The junction box circuit for U.S. and Canadian models is shown in **Figure 157** and the circuit for U.K. models is shown in **Figure 158**.

Whenever the fuse blows, find out the reason for the failure before replacing the fuse. Usually, the trouble is a short circuit in the wiring. This may be

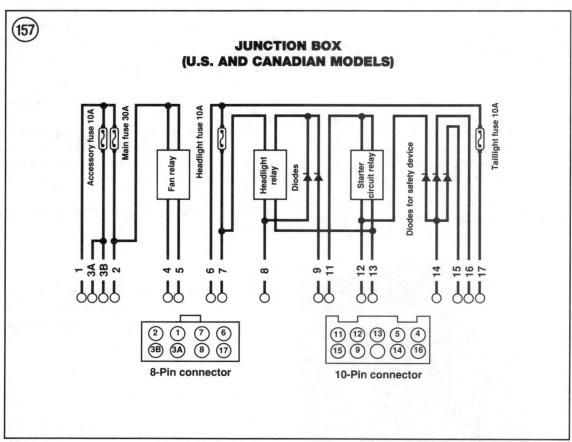

JUNCTION BOX (U.S. AND CANADIAN MODELS)

8-Pin connector

10-Pin connector

caused by worn-through insulation or a disconnected wire shorted to ground.

CAUTION
Never substitute metal foil or wire for a
fuse. Never use a higher amperage fuse
than specified. An overload could result
in a fire and complete loss of the bike.

CAUTION
When replacing a fuse, make sure the
ignition switch is in the OFF position.

This will lessen the chance of a short
circuit.

Fuse Replacement

1. Remove the frame left-hand side cover.

2. Unhook the lower end of the fuse panel cover
(**Figure 159**), lift it up and remove the cover.

3. Remove the fuse (**Figure 160**) with your fingers
or needlenose pliers and inspect it. If the fuse is

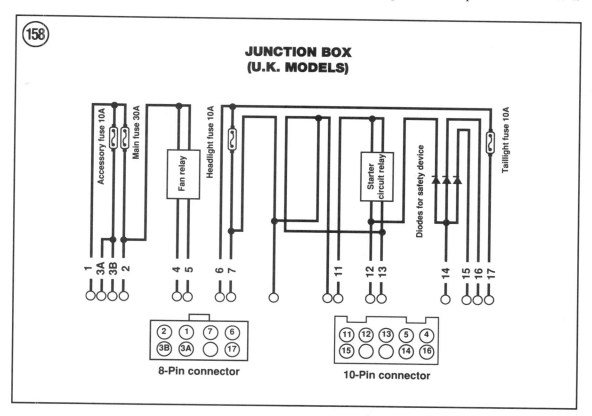

8

blown, there will be a break in the element (**Figure 161**). The 2 lower fuses (A, **Figure 162**) are spare fuses.

4. The fuse location and description label (B, **Figure 162**) is attached to the backside of the fuse panel cover.

NOTE
After using spare fuse, install a new spare fuse as soon as possible to avoid being stranded.

5. Install the new fuse and push it all the way down until it seats completely, then install the cover. Push the lower end of the cover on until it locks in place.
6. Install the frame left-hand side cover.

Junction Box and Fuse Panel Assembly Removal/Installation

1. Remove the frame left-hand side cover.
2. Disconnect both multi-pin electrical connectors (**Figure 163**) from the side of the junction box and fuse panel assembly.
3. Remove the bolt securing the upper retainer bracket (A, **Figure 164**) and remove the bracket.
4. Remove the junction box and fuse panel assembly (B, **Figure 164**) and the rubber isolator (C, **Figure 164**) from the left-hand side of the battery case.
5. Install the rubber isolator behind the junction box and fuse panel assembly and install onto the side of the battery case.
6. Install the upper retainer bracket and tighten the bracket bolt securely.
7. Make sure both multi-pin electrical connectors are free of corrosion and are tight.
8. Install the frame left-hand side cover.

WIRING DIAGRAMS

Wiring diagrams for all models are located at the end of this book.

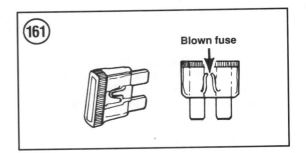
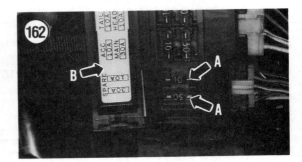

Table 1 ELECTRICAL SYSTEM TIGHTENING TORQUES

Item	N•m	ft.-lb.
Alternator rotor bolt	125	92
Alternator stator assembly mounting bolts	12	9
Starter clutch retainer 6 mm Allen bolts	34	25
Oil pressure switch	12	9
Cooling fan thermo switch	7.8	5.7
Neutral switch	15	11

Table 2 IGNITION TROUBLESHOOTING

Symptoms	Probable cause
Weak spark	Poor connections in circuit (clean and retighten all connections) High voltage leak (replace defective wire) Defective ignition coil (replace coil)
No spark	Broken wire (replace wire) Defective ignition coil (replace coil) Defective signal generator (replace signal generator assembly) Defective ignitor unit (replace ignitor unit) Faulty engine stop switch (replace switch)

Table 3 ELECTRICAL SYSTEM SPECIFICATIONS

Regulator/rectifier	Transistorized, non-adjustable
Regulated voltage	14-15 V at 5,000 rpm
Battery Capacity	12V/16 amp hour
Starter motor Brush length limit	8.5 mm (0.33 in.)
Commutator diameter limit	27 mm (1.063 in.)
Ignition pickup coil resistance	355-535 ohms
Ignition coil resistance Primary resistance	1.8-2.2 ohms
Secondary resistance	19,000-29,000 ohms
Spark plug cap resistance	3.75-6.25 ohms
Alternator stator coil resistance	0.34-0.52 ohms
Cooling fan thermo switch resistance 94-100° C (201-212° F)	from infinity to 0.5 ohms
91° C (196° F) and lower	from 0.5 ohm to infinity

Table 4 REPLACEMENT BULBS

Item	U.S. and Canadian Models Voltage/wattage
Headlight (high/low beam)	12V 60/55W
Taillight/brake light	12V 8/27W
Directional signal Front (plus running position)	12V 23/8W
Rear	12V 23W
	(continued)

Table 4 REPLACEMENT BULBS (continued)

U.S. and Canadian Models (continued)	
Item	Voltage/wattage
License plate light	12V 8W
Indicator lights	12V 3.4W
Instrument illumination lights	12V 3W

Other than U.S. and Canadian Models	
Item	Voltage/wattage
Headlight (high/low beam)	12V 60/55W
City light	12V 4W
Taillight/brake light	
South Africa	12V 8/27W
All other models	12V 5/21W
Directional signal (front and rear)	
Australia and South Africa	12V 23W
All other models	12V 21W
License plate light	
Australia and South Africa	12V 8W
All other models	12V 5W
Indicator lights	12V 3.4W
Instrument illumination lights	12V 3W

Table 5 COOLANT TEMPERATURE SENSOR READINGS

Temperature	Resistance (ohms)
80° C (176° F)	42-62
100° C (212° F)	22-33

CHAPTER NINE

LIQUID COOLING SYSTEM

9

The pressurized liquid cooling system consists of a radiator, water pump, thermostat, coolant reserve tank and an electric cooling fan.

The system uses a radiator fill cap with a designed relief pressure of 75-105 kPa (10.7-14.9 psi).

The water pump requires no routine maintenance and replacement parts are available if any parts are found defective.

CAUTION
*Drain and flush the cooling system at least every 2 years. Refer to **Coolant***

*Change in Chapter Three. Refill with a mixture of ethylene glycol antifreeze (formulated for aluminum engines) and distilled or purified water. Do not reuse the old coolant as it deteriorates with use. **Do not** operate the cooling system with only purified water (even in climates where antifreeze protection is not required). This is important because the engine is all aluminum; it will not rust but it will oxidize internally and have to be replaced. Refer to **Coolant Change** in Chapter Three.*

This chapter describes the repair and replacement of the cooling system components. **Table 1** at the end of this chapter lists all of the cooling system specifications. For routine maintenance and pressure testing of the system, refer to Chapter Three.

The cooling system must be cool prior to removing any component of the system.

WARNING
*Do **not** remove the radiator fill cap (**Figure 1**) when the engine is HOT. The coolant is very hot and is under pressure. Severe scalding could result if the*

escaping coolant comes in contact with your skin. Allow the cooling system to cool down prior to loosening the cap and then loosen the cap slowly to the first detent to allow any built-up pressure to escape safely.

HOSES AND HOSE CLAMPS

The small diameter coolant hoses are very stiff and are sometimes difficult to install onto the metal

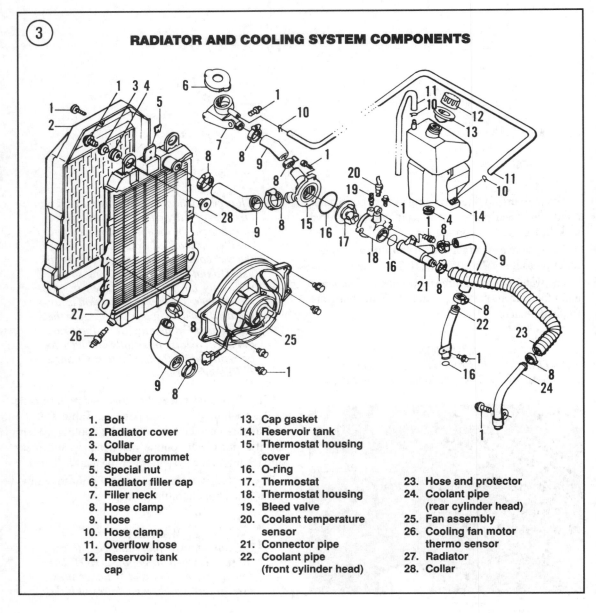

RADIATOR AND COOLING SYSTEM COMPONENTS

1. Bolt
2. Radiator cover
3. Collar
4. Rubber grommet
5. Special nut
6. Radiator filler cap
7. Filler neck
8. Hose clamp
9. Hose
10. Hose clamp
11. Overflow hose
12. Reservoir tank cap
13. Cap gasket
14. Reservoir tank
15. Thermostat housing cover
16. O-ring
17. Thermostat
18. Thermostat housing
19. Bleed valve
20. Coolant temperature sensor
21. Connector pipe
22. Coolant pipe (front cylinder head)
23. Hose and protector
24. Coolant pipe (rear cylinder head)
25. Fan assembly
26. Cooling fan motor thermo sensor
27. Radiator
28. Collar

fittings of the various cooling system parts. Prior to installing the hoses, apply a small amount of Armor All or rubber lube to the inside surface of these hoses and they will slide on much easier.

Different types of hose clamps are used on the various hoses. The majority of the hose clamps used are the clamping screw type that are released and tightened with a screwdriver. On some of the smaller hoses, the clamping band type are used and on this type the ends must be pinched open with a pair of gas pliers. The different types of clamps are used at specific locations due to space limitations around a specific part. Be sure to reinstall the correct type of clamp at the correct location.

COOLING SYSTEM CHECK

Two checks should be made before disassembly if a cooling system fault is suspected.

1. Run the engine until it reaches operating temperature. While the engine is running, a pressure surge should be felt when the coolant outlet hoses at the top of the cylinder heads (**Figure 2**) are squeezed.

2. If a substantial coolant loss is noted, one of the head gaskets may be blown. In extreme cases, suffi-

cient coolant will leak into a cylinder(s) when the bike is left standing for several hours so that the engine cannot be turned over with the starter. White smoke (steam) might also be observed at the muffler(s) when the engine is running. Coolant may also find its way into the oil supply. Check the dipstick; if it looks like green chocolate malt (milky or foamy) there is coolant in the oil system. If so, correct the cooling system immediately.

CAUTION
After the cooling system is corrected, drain and thoroughly flush the engine oil system to eliminate all coolant residue from the internal portions of the engine. Refill with fresh engine oil; refer to Chapter Three. Recheck the condition of the oil and drain and refill if necessary.

PRESSURE CHECK

If the cooling system requires repeated refilling, there is probably a leak somewhere in the system. Perform the *Cooling System Inspection* described in Chapter Three.

RADIATOR

Removal/Installation

Refer to **Figure 3** for this procedure.

WARNING
The cooling fan is connected directly to the battery. The radiator fan may run even with the ignition switch in the OFF position, therefore the battery negative lead must be disconnected prior to starting this procedure.

1. Disconnect the battery negative lead as described under *Battery* in Chapter Three.

2. Drain the cooling system as described under *Coolant Change* in Chapter Three.

3. On the left-hand side, disconnect the cooling fan motor electrical connector (**Figure 4**) containing 2 wires (one blue, one black).

4. On the lower left-hand side of the radiator, disconnect the electrical connector (**Figure 5**) from the fan motor thermo switch.

5. Remove the bolts securing the radiator cover (**Figure 6**) and remove the cover.

6. Loosen the clamping screw on the upper hose clamp (**Figure 7**). Move the clamp back onto the hose and off of the neck of the fitting on the radiator. Leave the hose attached to the thermostat housing cover.

7. Loosen the clamping screw on the lower hose clamp (A, **Figure 8**). Move the clamp back onto the hose and off of the neck of the fitting on the radiator. Leave the hose attached to the fitting on the crankcase.

8. Remove the upper 2 bolts (**Figure 9**) and the lower 2 bolts (B, **Figure 8**) that secures the radiator at the top and bottom on each side.

9. Carefully pull the radiator and cooling fan assembly (C, **Figure 8**) slightly forward and down. Remove the radiator and cooling fan assembly from the frame.

10. Install by reversing these removal steps while noting the following:

  a. Replace both radiator hoses if either is starting to deteriorate or is otherwise damaged.

  b. Make sure the fan motor and fan motor switch electrical connections are free of corrosion and are tight.

  c. Thoroughly clean off any road dirt, oil and/or rust from the frame area prior to attaching the fan motor ground wire to the frame. Tighten the bolt securely (**Figure 10**).

  d. Make sure the collar is in place on each of the radiator mounts.

  e. Refill the cooling system with the recommended type and quantity of coolant as described in Chapter Three.

Inspection

1. If not already removed, remove the screws securing the radiator cover and remove the cover from the front of the radiator.

2. If compressed air is available, use short spurts of air directed to the *backside* of the radiator and blow out dirt and bugs.

3. Flush off the exterior of the radiator with a garden hose on low pressure. Spray both the front and the back to remove all road dirt and bugs. Carefully use a whisk broom or stiff paint brush to remove any stubborn dirt.

> *CAUTION*
> *Do not press too hard or the cooling fins and tubes may be damaged causing a leak. Do not use a wire brush.*

4. Carefully straighten out any bent cooling fins with a broad tipped screwdriver or putty knife.

5. Check for cracks or leakage (usually a moss-green colored residue) at the filler neck, the inlet and outlet hose fittings and the upper and lower tank seams.

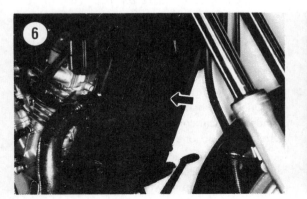

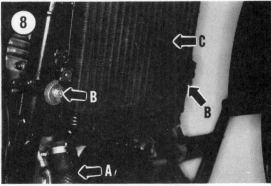

6. Inspect the upper and lower mounting brackets. Check for cracks or fractures and repair if necessary.

7. If the condition of the radiator is doubtful, have it checked as described under *Pressure Check* in Chapter Three. The radiator can be pressure checked while removed or installed on the bike.

8. To prevent oxidation to the radiator, touch up any area where the black paint is worn off. Use a good quality spray paint and apply several *light* coats of paint. Do not apply heavy coats as this will cut down on the cooling efficiency of the radiator.

9. If necessary, unscrew the cooling fan motor thermo switch from the radiator. Apply a silicone

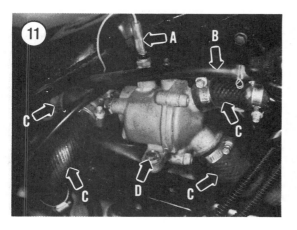

based sealant to the threads of the switch and install the switch in the radiator and tighten securely.

COOLING FAN AND SHROUD

Removal/Installation

Refer to **Figure 3** for this procedure.

The cooling fan and shroud are replaced as an assembly. They cannot be purchased separately

1. Remove the radiator as described in this chapter.

> *NOTE*
> *Note the location of the cooling fan ground cable located under one of the shroud mounting bolts. The cable must be reinstalled in the exact same location during installation.*

2. Remove the bolts securing the cooling fan motor and shroud assembly to the backside of the radiator.

3. Remove the assembly from the radiator.

4. Install by reversing these removal steps while noting the following:

    a. Attach the cooling fan ground wire to the correct location under the upper left-hand bolt. Make sure the contact area is free of oil and rust. Clean off if necessary.

    b. Apply blue Loctite (No. 242) to the threads on the fan shroud mounting bolts. Install the bolts and tighten securely.

    c. Refill the cooling system with the recommended type and quantity of coolant as described in Chapter Three.

THERMOSTAT AND HOUSING

Thermostat Housing
Removal/Installation

The thermostat is located on the right-hand side of the engine above the front cylinder head.

1. Drain the cooling system as described under *Coolant Change* in Chapter Three.

2. Remove the fuel tank as described under *Fuel Tank Removal/Installation* in Chapter Seven.

3. Remove the steering head right-hand cover as described in Chapter Thirteen.

4. Disconnect the electrical connector (A, **Figure 11**) from the coolant temperature sensor.

5. Disconnect the reservoir hose (B, **Figure 11**) from the filler neck and move it out of the way.

6. Loosen the clamping screws of the hose clamps on the hoses (C, **Figure 11**) attached to the thermostat housing and connector pipe. Move the clamp back onto each hose and off of the neck of the fitting on the thermostat housing and the connector pipe.

7. Remove the bolt (D, **Figure 11**) securing the thermostat housing to the frame and remove the assembly.

8. To remove the thermostat from the housing, perform the following:

   a. Remove the bolts securing the thermostat cover and remove the cover and O-ring seal.

   b. Remove the thermostat from the housing.

   c. If necessary, test the thermostat as described in this chapter.

   d. If reusing the same thermostat, make sure the return spring is operating correctly and has not sagged. Replace the thermostat if necessary.

9. Position the thermostat with the air bleeder hole facing up and install the thermostat into the thermostat housing. Push it in until it seats completely.

10. Inspect the O-ring seal for hardness or deterioration, replace if necessary. Install the O-ring seal.

11. Install the thermostat cover and bolts. Tighten the bolts securely in 2-3 stages in a crisscross pattern.

12. Install the thermostat housing onto the frame mounting area.

13. Install the bolt (A, **Figure 12**) securing the thermostat housing to the frame and tighten securely.

14. Move all 4 hoses (B, **Figure 12**) back onto the fittings on the thermostat housing and connector pipe.

15. Move the clamps back onto each hose and tighten the clamping screw on each of the 4 hose clamps.

16. Connect the reservoir hose (C, **Figure 12**) onto the filler neck.

17. Connect the electrical connector (D, **Figure 12**) onto the coolant temperature sensor.

18. Install the steering head right-hand cover.

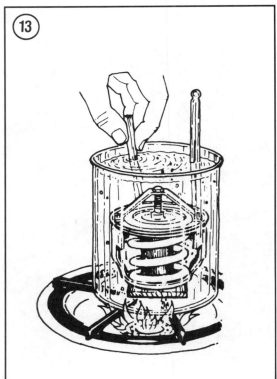

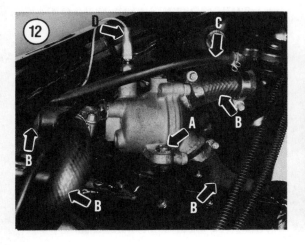

19. Install the fuel tank as described in Chapter Seven.

20. Refill the cooling system with the recommended type and quantity of coolant as described in Chapter Three.

21. Start the engine and check for coolant leaks.

Thermostat Testing

Test the thermostat to ensure proper operation. The thermostat should be replaced if it remains open at normal room temperature or stays closed after the specified temperature has been reached during the test procedure.

1. Place the thermostat on a small piece of wood in a pan of water (**Figure 13**).

2. Place a thermometer in the pan of water (use a cooking or candy thermometer that is rated higher than the test temperature).

3. Gradually heat the water and continue to gently stir the water until it reaches 80-84° C (176-183° F).

At this temperature the thermostat valve should start to open.

4. Continue to heat the water until the temperature reaches 95° C (203° F) and beyond. At this temperature, the thermostat valve should have opened at least 8.0 mm (0.31 in.).

NOTE
Valve operation is sometimes sluggish; it usually takes 3-5 minutes for the valve to operate properly.

5. If the valve fails to open in Step 3 or to the dimension listed in Step 4, the thermostat should be replaced (it cannot be serviced). Be sure to replace it with one of the same temperature rating.

WATER PUMP

The water pump is not a separate unit that can be removed as an assembly. It is an integral part of the right-hand crankcase half and the right-hand crankcase cover. The only parts that can be serviced are the impeller, the impeller drive shaft and the mechanical seal.

Impeller
Removal/Inspection/Installation

1. Remove the right-hand crankcase cover as described under *Right-hand Crankcase Cover Removal/Installation* in Chapter Four.

2. Remove the nut (**Figure 14**) securing the water pump impeller and remove the impeller (**Figure 15**).

3. Remove the O-ring seal (**Figure 16**) from the shaft and discard it. A new O-ring seal must be installed every time the impeller is removed.

4. Inspect the impeller for corrosion and/or damage. Check the blades for cracks. Replace the impeller if necessary.

5. Install by reversing these removal steps, while noting the following:

    a. Install a new O-ring seal on the shaft and apply a light coat of clean engine oil to it.

    b. Install the impeller and tighten the nut securely.

Mechanical Seal
Removal/Installation

1. Remove the impeller as described in this chapter.

2. Use a flat-bladed screwdriver and pry the flange (**Figure 17**) loose from the crankcase.

> *CAUTION*
> *Do not damage the inner surface of the crankcase receptacle or the water pump shaft while removing the mechanical seal.*

3. Use needlenose pliers and carefully pull the mechanical seal out of the receptacle in the crankcase. Discard the old seal.
4. Thoroughly clean out the receptacle in the crankcase of all old seal residue.

> *NOTE*
> *The body of the new mechanical seal has an adhesive coating. Do **not** apply any type of liquid gasket sealer to the seal receptacle in the crankcase or the exterior of the seal.*

5. Place the new mechanical seal (A, **Figure 18**) into the receptacle in the crankcase (**Figure 19**).
6. Use a 28 mm socket and socket extension (B, **Figure 18**) and press the seal into the receptacle until it is seated.
7. Remove the socket and extension.
8. Clean the sliding surface of the new seal with solvent and thoroughly dry with a lint-free cloth.
9. Apply a light coat of straight coolant (anti-freeze) to the sliding surfaces of the mechanical seal for initial lubrication.
10. Apply a light coat of straight coolant (anti-freeze) to the rubber seal and sealing seat on the backside of the impeller (**Figure 20**).

HOSES

Hoses deteriorate with age and should be replaced periodically or whenever they show signs of cracking or leakage. To be safe, replace the hoses every 4 years. The spray of hot coolant from a cracked hose can injure the rider and passenger. Loss of coolant can also cause the engine to overheat and result in extensive damage.

Whenever any component of the cooling system is removed, inspect the hose(s) and determine if replacement is necessary.

This procedure represents a typical hose replacement procedure for all flexible hoses in the cooling system. The replacement of the metal coolant pipes

from the cylinder heads and crankcase are covered in Chapter Four.

Flexible Hose Replacement

1. Drain the cooling system as described under *Coolant Change* in Chapter Three.

> *NOTE*
> *The sections of hose attached to the thermostat housing are very short and*

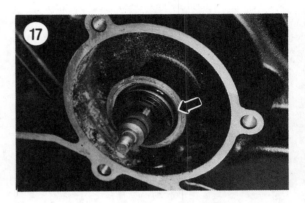

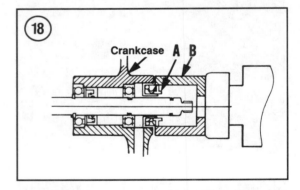

also very stiff. The working area around these hoses is very limited, therefore it is suggested that the thermostat housing be removed from the frame and then the hoses replaced.

2. Loosen the clamping screw (A, **Figure 21**) on the hose clamp.

3. Move the clamp back onto the hose and off the neck of the fitting where the hose was attached.

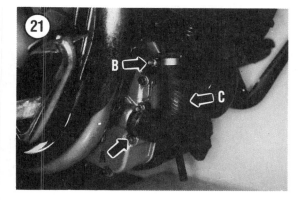

4. Repeat Step 2 and Step 3 for the hose clamp at the other end of the hose (B, **Figure 21**).

5. Carefully twist the hose (C, **Figure 21**) to release it from each fitting. If the hose has been installed for some time, it may be difficult to break loose. If so, carefully cut the hose parallel to the fitting with a knife. Carefully pry the hose from the fitting with a broad-tipped screwdriver.

6. Inspect the fitting for cracks or other damage. Replace or repair the fitting if necessary. If the fitting is okay, clean off any old hose and/or sealant residue that may have been used. Clean off all rust or oxidation with fine sandpaper and wipe clean with a cloth dipped in solvent. Dry with a lint-free cloth.

7. Inspect the hose clamps and replace if necessary. The hose clamps are as important as the hoses. If they do not hold the hose tightly in place, the coolant will leak.

8. Prior to installing the hoses, apply a small amount of Armor All or rubber lube to the inside surface of these hoses and they will slide on much easier.

9. Push the hose (C, **Figure 21**) completely onto each fitting.

10. Place the hose clamp as near the end of the hose as possible in order to clear the raised rib on the fitting. Make sure the clamp is not on the raised rib as it will result in a coolant leak.

11. Tighten the hose clamps (A and B, **Figure 21**) securely, but not so tight that the clamps may cut into the hose.

12. Install all components removed.

13. Refill the cooling system with the recommended type and quantity of coolant. Refer to *Coolant Change* in Chapter Three.

14. Start the engine and check for leaks.

9

Table 1 COOLING SYSTEM SPECIFICATIONS	
Coolant capacity	1.8 liters (1.9 U.S. qt./1.6 Imp. qt.)
Radiator cap relief pressure	93-123 kPa (14-18 psi)
Thermostat	
Begins to open	80-84° C (176-183° F)
Valve lift	Minimum of 8 mm (0.31 in.)
	@ 95° C (203° F)

CHAPTER TEN

FRONT SUSPENSION AND STEERING

This chapter describes the repair and maintenance for the front wheel, front forks and steering components.

Front suspension torque specifications are covered in **Table 1**. **Tables 1-4** are at the end of this chapter.

NOTE
Where differences occur relating to the United Kingdom (U.K.) models they are identified. If there is no (U.K.) designation relating to a procedure, photo or illustration, it is identical to the United States (U.S.) models.

FRONT WHEEL

Removal

CAUTION
Care must be taken when removing, handling and installing a wheel with a disc brake rotor on each side. The rotor is relatively thin in order to dissipate heat and to minimize unsprung weight. The rotors are designed to withstand tremendous rotational loads but can be damaged when subjected to side impact

*loads. If the rotor is knocked out of true by a side impact, a pulsation will be felt in the front brake lever when braking. The rotor is too thin to be trued and must be replaced with a new one. Protect the rotor when transporting a wheel to a dealer or tire specialist for tire service. Do **not** place a wheel in a car trunk or pickup bed without protecting the rotor from side impact.*

1. Place the bike on the sidestand.

2. Remove the front axle nut (**Figure 1**) from the left-hand side.

3. Loosen the front axle pinch bolt nut (**Figure 2**).

4. Remove one of the brake calipers (either one) as described under *Front Brake Caliper Removal/Installation* in Chapter Twelve. The other caliper can be left in place.

5. Place the bike on the centerstand.

6. Place a small jack, with a piece of wood to protect the crankcase, under the crankcase. Apply a small amount of jack pressure to support the bike securely with the front wheel off the ground.

7. Unscrew and remove the speedometer cable (**Figure 3**) from the speedometer gear box.

8. Withdraw the front axle from the right-hand side.

9. Pull the wheel down and forward to remove it from the front fork and the remaining brake caliper.

> *NOTE*
> *Insert a piece of vinyl tubing or wood in both calipers in place of the brake discs. That way if the brake lever is inadvertently squeezed, the piston will not be forced out of the cylinders. If this happens, the calipers may have to be disassembled to reseat the piston and the system will have to be bled. Also, by using the vinyl tubing or wood, it will not be necessary to bleed the brake when installing the wheel.*

> *CAUTION*
> *Do not set the wheel down on the disc surface as it may get scratched or warped. Set the sidewalls on 2 wood blocks (**Figure 4**).*

10. Remove the right-hand spacer (**Figure 5**) from the hub.

11. Remove the speedometer gear box (**Figure 6**) from the other side of the hub.

12. Inspect the wheel as described in this chapter.

10

Installation

1. Make sure the axle bearing surfaces of the fork sliders and axle are free from burrs and nicks.

2. Align the tangs of the speedometer drive gear (A, **Figure 7**) with the notches (B, **Figure 7**) in the front hub and install the speedometer gearbox (**Figure 6**). Make sure the gear box seats completely. If the speedometer components do not mesh properly, the hub components of the wheel will be too wide for installation.

3. Install the right-hand spacer (**Figure 5**) onto the hub.

4. Position the wheel into place. Insert the brake disc into the caliper being careful not to damage the brake pads.

5. Apply a light coat of grease to the front axle. Insert the front axle through the fork leg, speedometer gear box and the wheel hub.

6. Make sure the spacer (**Figure 8**) is still in place on the right-hand side of the wheel.

7. Position the speedometer housing so the raised tab on the fork leg indexes into the notch in the speedometer housing (**Figure 9**). This procedure locates the speedometer housing and prevents it from rotating when the wheel turns.

8. Install the front axle, then install the front axle nut, but do not tighten it.

9. Rotate the wheel slowly and install the speedometer cable into the speedometer housing (**Figure 3**). Position the speedometer housing and cable so that the cable does not have a sharp bend in it.

10. Place a long drift in the hole in the right-hand end of the front axle to prevent it from turning. Tighten the front axle nut (**Figure 10**) to the torque specification listed in **Table 1**. Remove the drift from the front axle.

11. Remove the jack and wood block from under the crankcase. Leave the bike on the centerstand.

12. Install the removed brake caliper as described in Chapter Twelve.

13. With the front brake applied, push down hard on the handlebars and pump the forks several times to seat the front axle.

14. Tighten the front axle pinch bolt and nut (**Figure 2**) to the torque specification listed in **Table 1**.

15. After the wheel is completely installed, rotate it several times to make sure that it rotates freely. Apply the front brake as many times as necessary to

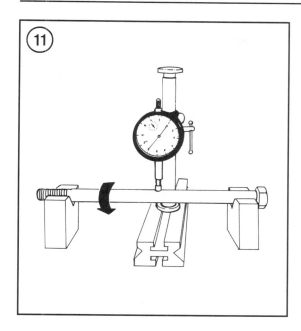

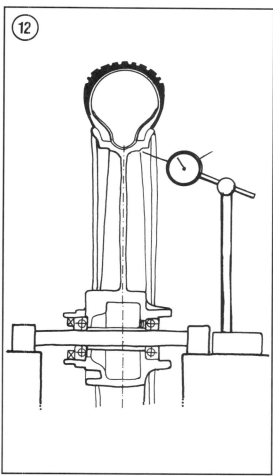

make sure all brake pads are against both brake discs correctly.

Inspection

1. Remove any corrosion on the front axle with a piece of fine emery cloth. Clean it with solvent, then wipe the axle clean with a lint-free cloth.

2. Check axle runout. Place the axle on V-blocks and place the tip of a dial indicator in the middle of the axle (**Figure 11**). Rotate the axle and check runout. If the runout exceeds the specification listed in **Table 1**, replace the axle; do not attempt to straighten it.

3. Check rim runout as follows:
   a. Remove the tire from the rim as described in this chapter.
   b. Measure the radial (up and down) runout of the wheel rim with a dial indicator as shown in **Figure 12**. If runout exceeds the wear limit specification listed in **Table 1**, check the wheel bearings.
   c. Measure the axial (side to side) runout of the wheel rim with a dial indicator as shown in **Figure 12**. If runout exceeds the wear limit specification listed in **Table 1**, check the wheel bearings.
   d. Check the wheel bearings as described under *Front Hub* in this chapter. If the rear wheel bearings are okay, the cast wheel is faulty and must be replaced. Cast wheels cannot be serviced.
   e. Replace the front wheel bearings as described under *Front Hub* in this chapter.

4. Inspect the wheel rim (**Figure 13**) for dents, bending or cracks. Check the rim and rim sealing surface for scratches deeper than 0.5 mm (0.01 in.).

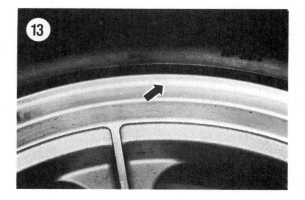

10

If any of these conditions are present, the wheel is unsafe for use and should be replaced.

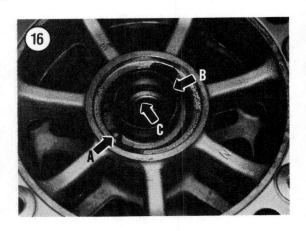

Speedometer Gear Box
Inspection and Lubrication

1. Remove the front wheel as described in this chapter.

2. Inspect the speedometer drive gear housing (**Figure 14**) for wear or damage. Replace the assembly if necessary.

3. Inspect the oil seal (**Figure 15**) for leakage.

4. Inspect the tangs of the speedometer drive gear for wear or damage.

5. If necessary, remove the oil seal with a hook and remove the drive gear. Replace if necessary.

6. Clean out all old grease from the gear housing and gear. Apply a good coat of high-temperature grease and install the drive gear into the housing. Install a new grease seal.

7. Inspect the drive ring (B, **Figure 7**) in the front hub for wear or damage. If necessary, remove the drive ring as follows:

    a. Remove the circlip (A, **Figure 16**) and remove the drive ring (B, **Figure 16**) from the hub.

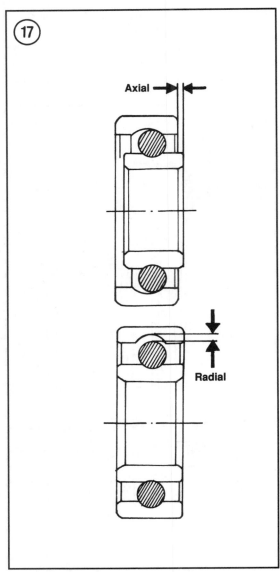

b. Align the drive ring tabs with the grooves in the front hub and install the drive gear. Push it down until it stops.

c. Position the circlip with the sharp side facing out and install the circlip. Make sure the circlip is correctly seated in the hub groove.

d. Apply a good coat of high-temperature grease to the drive gear.

FRONT HUB

Inspection

Inspect each wheel bearing prior to removing it from the wheel hub.

CAUTION
Do not remove the wheel bearings for inspection because they will be damaged during the removal process. Remove wheel bearings only if they are to be replaced.

CAUTION
*Do not set the wheel down on the disc surface as it may get scratched or warped. Set the sidewalls on 2 wood blocks (**Figure 4**).*

1. Perform Steps 1-4 of *Disassembly* in this chapter.

2. Turn the inner race of each bearing by hand. Make sure bearings turn smoothly.

3. Inspect the play of the inner race (C, **Figure 16**) of each wheel bearing. Check for excessive axial play and radial play (**Figure 17**). Replace the bearing if it has an excessive amount of free play.

4. Replace the bearings if necessary; always replace as a complete set. When replacing the bearings, be sure to take your old bearings along to ensure a perfect matchup.

NOTE
Fully sealed bearings are available from many bearing specialty shops. Fully sealed bearings provide better protection from dirt and moisture that may get into the hub.

Disassembly

Refer to **Figure 18** for this procedure.

10

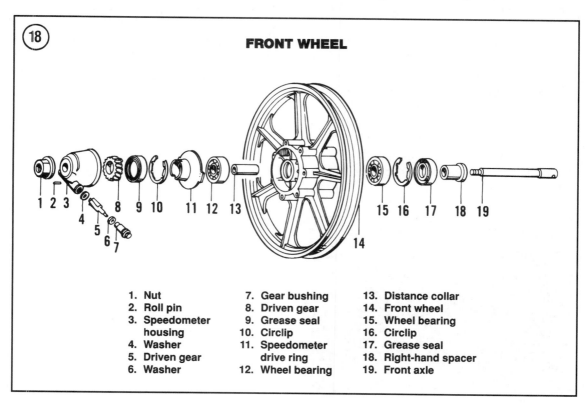

(18) **FRONT WHEEL**

1. Nut	7. Gear bushing	13. Distance collar
2. Roll pin	8. Driven gear	14. Front wheel
3. Speedometer housing	9. Grease seal	15. Wheel bearing
4. Washer	10. Circlip	16. Circlip
5. Driven gear	11. Speedometer drive ring	17. Grease seal
6. Washer	12. Wheel bearing	18. Right-hand spacer
		19. Front axle

1. Remove the front wheel as described in this chapter.

> *CAUTION*
> *Do not set the wheel down on the disc surface as it may get scratched or warped. Set the sidewalls on 2 wood blocks (**Figure 4**).*

2. Remove the right-hand spacer (**Figure 5**) from the hub.

3. Remove the speedometer gear box (**Figure 6**) from the other side of the hub.

4. If necessary, remove the bolts securing the brake disc (**Figure 19**) and remove the disc.

5. Before proceeding further, inspect the wheel bearings as described in this chapter. If they must be replaced, proceed as follows.

6. On the right-hand side of the hub; perform the following:
   a. Remove the grease seal (**Figure 20**).
   b. Remove the circlip securing the bearing.

7. On the left-hand side of the hub; perform the following:
   a. Remove the circlip (A, **Figure 16**).
   b. Remove the drive ring (B, **Figure 16**) from the hub.

8. To remove the right- and left-hand bearings and distance collar, insert a soft aluminum or brass drift into one side of the hub (**Figure 21**).

9. Push the distance collar over to one side and place the drift on the inner race of the lower bearing.

10. Tap the bearing out of the hub with a hammer, working around the perimeter of the inner race.

11. Repeat for the bearing on the other side.

12. Clean the inside and the outside of the hub with solvent. Dry with compressed air.

Assembly

1. On non-sealed bearings, pack the bearings with a good-quality bearing grease. Work the grease in between the balls thoroughly; turn the bearing by hand a couple of times to make sure the grease is distributed evenly inside the bearing.

2. Blow any dirt or foreign matter from the hub prior to installing the bearings.

> *CAUTION*
> *Install non-sealed bearings with the single sealed side facing outward. Tap the bearings squarely into place and tap on the outer race only. Do not tap on the inner race or the bearing might be damaged. Be sure that the bearings are completely seated.*

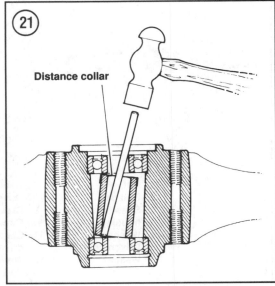

Distance collar

3. Tap the right-hand bearing squarely into place and tap on the outer race only. Use a socket (**Figure 22**) that matches the outer race diameter. Do not tap on the inner race or the bearing might be damaged. Be sure that the bearing is completely seated.

4. Turn the wheel over (right-hand side up) on the workbench and install the distance collar.

5. Use the same tool set-up and drive in the left-hand bearing.

6. If the brake disc was removed, perform the following:

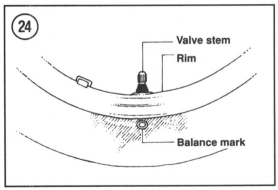

Valve stem
Rim
Balance mark

a. Apply red Loctite (No. 271) to the brake disc bolts prior to installation.

b. Install the brake disc (**Figure 19**) and bolts. Tighten to the torque specifications listed in **Table 1**.

7. Install the right-hand spacer (**Figure 2**) into the hub.

8. Align the tangs of the speedometer drive gear (A, **Figure 7**) with the notches in the front hub (B, **Figure 7**) and install the speedometer gearbox. Make sure the gear box seats completely (**Figure 6**). If the speedometer components do not mesh properly, the hub components of the wheel will be too wide for installation.

9. Install the front wheel as described in this chapter.

WHEELS

Wheel Balance

An unbalanced wheel is unsafe. Depending on the degree of unbalance and the speed of the motorcycle, the rider may experience anything from a mild vibration to a violent shimmy which may even result in loss of control.

The weights are attached to the wheel rim (**Figure 23**). Weight kits are available from motorcycle dealers. These kits contain test weights and strips of adhesive-backed weights that can be cut to the desired length and weight and attached directly to the rim or clamp-on type shown in **Figure 23**. Kawasaki offers clamp-on weights of 10, 20 and 30 grams each.

Before you attempt to balance the wheel, check to be sure that the wheel bearings are in good condition and properly lubricated. The wheel must rotate freely. Also check that the tire balance mark (paint dot on the tire) is aligned with the valve stem (**Figure 24**). If not, break the tire loose from the rim and align it correctly prior to trying to balance the wheel. Refer to *Tire Changing* in this chapter.

NOTE
When balancing the wheels, do so with the brake discs attached. These components rotate with the wheel and it will affect the balance.

1. Remove the wheel as described in this chapter or Chapter Eleven.

2. Mount the wheel on a fixture such as the one shown in **Figure 25** so it can rotate freely.

3. Give the wheel a spin and let it coast to a stop. Mark the tire at the lowest point (6 o'clock).

4. Spin the wheel several more times. If the wheel keeps coming to rest at the same point, it is out of balance.

5. Tape a test weight to the upper, or light, (12 o'clock) side of the wheel.

6. Rotate the wheel 1/4 turn (3 o'clock), let go of the wheel and observe the following:

   a. If the wheel does not rotate—stays at the 3 o'clock position. The correct balance weight was installed. The wheel is balanced.

   b. If the wheel rotates and the weighted portion goes *up*. Replace the weight with the next heavier size.

   c. If the wheel rotates and the weighted portion goes *down*. Replace the weight with the next lighter size.

   d. Repeat this step until the wheel remains at rest after being rotated 1/4 turn. Rotate the wheel another 1/4 turn, and another 1/4 turn, and another turn to see if the wheel is correctly balanced.

7. Remove the test weight and install the correct size weight.

> *CAUTION*
> *Do not attach more than 60 grams of balance weight to the wheel. If the balance weight required exceeds this amount, take the wheel to a Kawasaki dealer for inspection and balancing.*

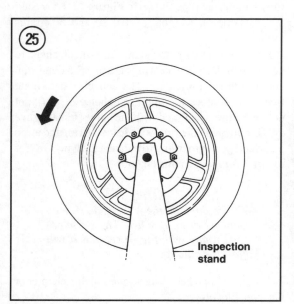

Figure 25. Inspection stand

TIRES

Tire Safety

After installing new tires on the bike, break them in correctly. Remember that a new tire has relatively poor adhesion to the road surface until it is broken in properly. Don't subject a new tire to any high speed riding for at least the first 60 miles (100 km).

Even after the tires are broken in properly, always warm them up prior to the first ride of the day. This will lessen the possibility of loss of control of the bike. If you have purchased a tire brand other than those originally installed by the factory, maintain the correct tire inflation pressure recommended by *that tire manufacturer* and not those listed in **Table 2** in

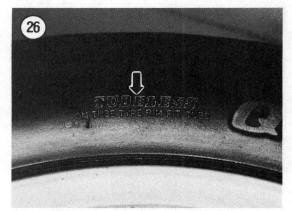

this chapter. **Table 2** is for original equipment tires only.

Tubeless Tires

> *WARNING*
> *Do not install an inner tube inside a tubeless tire. The tube will cause an abnormal heat buildup in the tire.*

Tubeless tires have the word "TUBELESS" (**Figure 26**) molded into the tire sidewall and the rims have "SUITABLE FOR TUBELESS TIRES," "TUBELESS TIRE," (**Figure 27**) or equivalent cast into them.

When a tubeless tire has gone flat, it should be removed from the rim to inspect the inside of the tire and to apply a combination plug/patch from the inside. Don't rely on a plug or cord repair applied from outside the tire. They might be okay on a car, but they're too dangerous on a motorcycle.

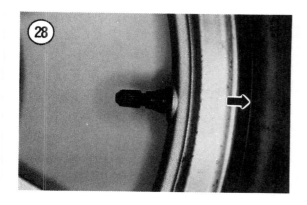

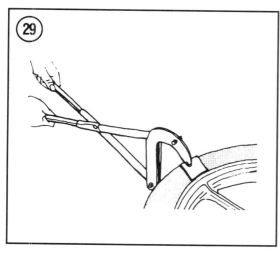

After repairing a tubeless tire, don't exceed 50 mph (80 kph) for the first 24 hours. The patch could work loose from tire flexing and heat.

TIRE CHANGING

The wheels can easily be damaged during tire removal. Special care must be taken with tire irons when changing a tire to avoid scratches and gouges to the outer rim surface. Insert scraps of leather between the tire iron and the rim to protect the rim from damage. The stock cast wheels are designed for use with tubeless tires.

When removing a tubeless tire, take care not to damage the tire beads, inner liner of the tire or the wheel rim flange. Use tire levers or flat handled tire irons with rounded ends.

Removal

1. If you are going to reinstall the existing tire, mark the valve stem location on the tire (**Figure 28**) so the tire can be installed in the same position for easier balancing.
2. Remove the valve stem core to deflate the tire.

> *NOTE*
> *Removal of a tubeless tire from its rim can be very difficult because of the exceptionally tight bead/rim seal. Breaking the bead seal may require the use of a special tool (**Figure 29**). If you are unable to break the seal loose, take the wheel to a motorcycle dealer and have them break it loose.*

> *CAUTION*
> *The inner rim and tire bead are sealing surfaces for the tubeless tire. Do not scratch the inside of the rim or damage the tire bead as this will result in an air leak.*

3. Press the entire bead on both sides of the tire into the center of the rim. Make sure the tire is broken loose around the entire perimeter of the wheel.
4. Lubricate the beads with soapy water.

> *CAUTION*
> *Use rim protectors (**Figure 30**) or insert scraps of leather between the tire irons*

and the rim to protect the rim from damage.

5. Insert the tire iron under the bead next to the valve (**Figure 31**). Force the bead on the opposite side of the tire into the center of the rim and pry the bead over the rim with the tire iron.

6. Insert a second tire iron next to the first to hold the bead over the rim. Then work around the tire with the first tire iron, prying the bead over the rim (**Figure 32**).

7. Stand the tire on end or turn it over. Insert the tire iron between the second bead and the side of the rim that the first bead was pried over (**Figure 33**). Force the bead on the opposite side from the tire iron into the center of the rim. Pry the second bead off the rim, working around as with the first. Remove the tire from the rim.

8. Inspect the rim as described in this chapter.

Tire and Rim Inspection

1. Wipe off the inner surfaces of the wheel rim. Clean off any rubber residue or any oxidation.

2. If a can of pressurized tire sealant was used for a temporary fix of a flat, thoroughly clean off all sealant residue from the rim surfaces. Any remaining residue will present a problem when reinstalling the tire and achieving a good seal of the tire bead against the rim.

3. Inspect the rim inner flange. Smooth any scratches on the rim-to-tire sealing surface with emery cloth. If a scratch is deeper than 0.5 mm (0.020 in.), the wheel should be replaced.

> *WARNING*
> *Carefully consider whether a tire should be patched or replaced. If there is any doubt about the quality of the existing tire, **replace it with a new one**. Don't take a chance on a tire failure at any speed.*

4. If a tire is going to be patched, thoroughly inspect the tire.

5. If any one of the following are observed, do not repair the tire; *replace it with a new one*:

  a. A puncture or split whose total length or diameter exceeds 6 mm (0.24 in.).

  b. A scratch or split on the side wall.

  c. Any type of ply separation.

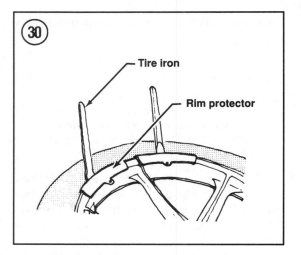

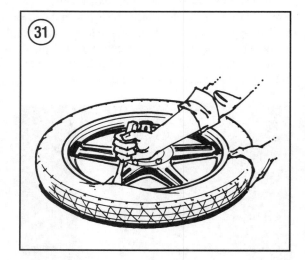

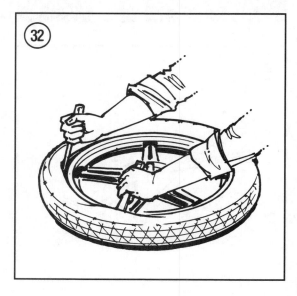

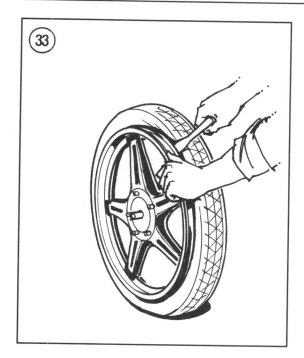

d. Tread separation or excessive abnormal wear pattern.

e. Tread depth of less than 1.6 mm (0.06 in.) in the front tire or less than 2.0 mm (0.08 in.) in the rear tire for original equipment tires. Aftermarket tires tread depth minimum may vary.

f. Scratches on either sealing bead.

g. The cord is cut in any place.

h. Flat spots in the tread from skidding.

i. Any abnormality in the inner liner.

6. Do not rely on a plug or cord patch applied from outside the tire. Use a combination plug/patch (**Figure 34**) applied from inside the tire. Apply the plug/patch, following the instructions supplied with the patch kit.

7. Inspect the valve stem seal. Because rubber deteriorates with age, it is advisable to replace the valve stem when replacing the tire.

8. Inspect the valve stem hole in the rim. Remove any dirt or corrosion from the hole and wipe dry with a clean cloth.

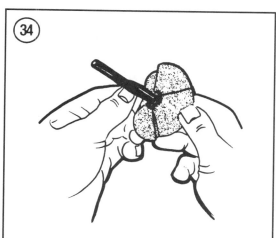

Installation

1. A new tire may have balancing rubbers inside. These are not patches and should not be disturbed or removed.

NOTE
Step 2 relates to metal valve stems only.

2. Install a new valve stem as follows:

a. Insert the new valve stem into the rim.

b. Install the nut and tighten with your fingers only. Do not use pliers and overtighten the nut as it may distort the rubber sealing grommet that could result in an air leak.

c. Hold onto the nut and install and tighten the locknut securely.

d. Inspect the valve stem core rubber seal for hardness or deterioration. Replace the valve stem core if necessary.

3. If the tire was completely removed, lubricate both beads of the tire with soapy water. If only one side was removed, lubricate the exposed rim bead.

4. When installing the tire onto the rim make sure the correct tire, either front or rear is installed onto the correct wheel and also that the direction arrow (**Figure 35**) faces the direction of wheel rotation.

5. If remounting the old tire, align the mark made in Step 1, *Removal* with the valve stem. If a new tire

10

is being installed, align the colored spot near the bead (indicating a lighter point on the tire) with the valve stem.

6. If the tire was completely removed from the rim, place the backside of the tire into the center of the rim (**Figure 36**). The lower bead should go into the center of the rim and the upper bead outside. Work around the tire in both directions (**Figure 37**). Use a tire iron for the last few inches of bead (**Figure 38**).

7. Press the upper bead into the rim opposite the valve stem. Pry the bead into the rim on both sides of the initial point with a tire iron, working around the rim to the valve (**Figure 39**).

8. Check the bead on both sides of the tire for an even fit around the rim.

9. Bounce the wheel several times, rotating it each time. This will force the tire beads against the rim flanges. After the tire beads are in contact with the rim evenly, inflate the tire to seat the beads.

10. Place an inflatable band around the circumference of the tire. Slowly inflate the band until the tire beads are pressed against the rim. Inflate the tire enough to seat it, deflate the band and remove it.

> **WARNING**
> *In the next step, inflate the tire to approximately 10-15% over the recommended inflation pressure. Do not exceed this pressure as the tire could burst causing severe injury. Never stand directly over a tire while inflating it.*

11. After inflating the tire, check to see that the beads are fully seated and that the tire rim lines (**Figure 40**) are the same distance from the rim all the way around the tire. If the beads won't seat, deflate the tire and re-lubricate the rim and beads with soapy water.

12. Re-inflate the tire to the required pressure listed in **Table 2**. Install the valve stem cap (**Figure 41**). Always make sure to install the cap as the cap prevents small pebbles and dirt from collecting in the valve stem; this could allow air leakage or result in incorrect tire pressure readings.

13. Balance the wheel as described in this chapter.

> **WARNING**
> *If you have repaired a tire, do not ride the bike any faster than 30 mph (50 km/h) for the first 24 hours. It takes at least 24 hours for a patch to cure. Also*

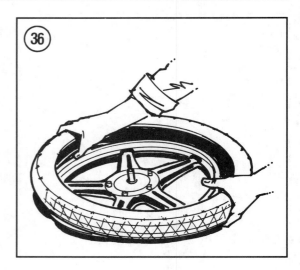

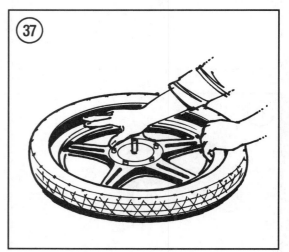

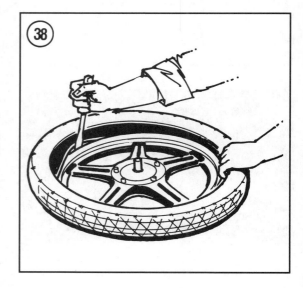

never ride the bike faster than 80 mph (130 km/h) with a repaired tire.

TIRE REPAIRS

Patching a tube or tubeless tire on the road is very difficult. A can of pressurized tire sealant may inflate the tire and seal the hole, although this is only a temporary fix. On tubeless tires, the beads must be against the rim for this method to work. Another temporary solution is to carry a spare inner tube that could be installed and inflated. Either temporary solution may enable you to get to a service station where the tire can be correctly repaired.

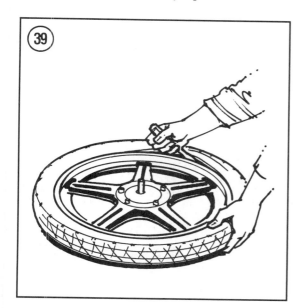

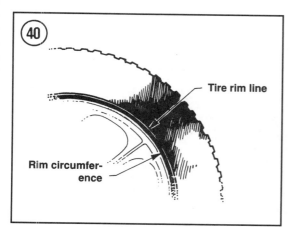

Kawasaki (and the tire industry) recommends that the tubeless tire be patched from the inside. Use a combination plug/patch applied from the inside the tire (**Figure 34**). Do not patch the tire with an external type plug. If you find an external patch on the tire, it is recommended that it be patch-reinforced from the inside. Due to the variations of material supplied with different tubeless tire repair kits, follow the instructions and recommendations supplied with the repair kit.

HANDLEBAR

Handlebar Assembly Removal/Installation

> *NOTE*
> *If it is not necessary to remove the components from each end of the handlebar for service, perform the following steps. If component removal is necessary, refer to the* **Disassembly/Assembly** *in the next procedure.*

1. Remove the fuel tank as described under *Fuel tank Removal/Installation* in Chapter Seven.
2. Disconnect the brake light switch electrical connector (**Figure 42**) from the brake lever.

10

3. Disconnect the starter interlock switch electrical connector (**Figure 43**) from the clutch lever.

> *CAUTION*
> *Cover the surrounding area with a heavy cloth or plastic tarp to protect it from accidental spilling of clutch and brake fluid. Wash any spilled clutch or brake fluid from any painted or plated surface immediately, as it will destroy the finish. Use soapy water and rinse thoroughly.*

4. Remove the trim caps (**Figure 44**) from the Allen bolts.

5. Remove the Allen bolts (**Figure 45**) securing the handlebar upper holders.

6. Remove the upper holders and the handlebar assembly.

7. Move the handlebar assembly back and rest it on the frame.

8. Secure the handlebar assembly so the brake master cylinder reservoir remains in the upright position. This is to minimize loss of hydraulic fluid and to keep air from entering into the brake system. It is not necessary to remove the hydraulic line.

9. Install by reversing these removal steps while noting the following:

    a. Tighten the Allen bolts to the torque specification listed in **Table 1**. Tighten the front bolts first then the rear so there is no gap at the front and an even gap at the rear between the handlebar upper and lower holders (**Figure 46**).

    b. Check the throttle operation. If necessary, adjust the throttle operation as described in Chapter Three.

> *WARNING*
> *After installation is completed, make sure the brake lever does not come in contact with the throttle grip assembly when it is pulled on fully. If it does, the brake fluid may be low in the reservoir; refill if necessary. Refer to **Front Disc Brakes** in Chapter Twelve.*

Handlebar and Component Removal/Installation

> *NOTE*
> *If it is necessary to remove the components from the handlebar for service,*

perform the following steps. If component removal is not necessary, refer to the preceding procedure.

Right-hand side of handlebar

1. Remove the fuel tank as described under *Fuel tank Removal/Installation* in Chapter Seven.

2. Disconnect the brake light switch electrical connector (**Figure 42**) from the brake switch.

3. Unscrew and remove the rear view mirror (A, **Figure 47**) from the master cylinder.

4. Remove the screws securing the right-hand handlebar switch assembly (B, **Figure 47**) together.

5. Partially remove the upper half and disconnect the throttle cables from the throttle assembly. Carefully lay the throttle cable over the fender or back over the frame. Be careful that the cable does not get crimped or damaged.

6. Remove the lower half of the right-hand switch assembly from the handlebar and lay it over the fender or back over the frame.

7. Remove the throttle grip assembly (C, **Figure 47**).

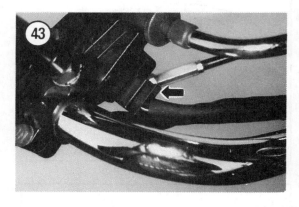

CAUTION
Cover the surrounding area with a heavy cloth or plastic tarp to protect it from accidental spilling of brake fluid. Wash any spilled brake fluid off any painted or plated surface immediately, as it will destroy the finish. Use soapy water and rinse thoroughly.

8. Remove the clamping bolts and clamp securing the front brake master cylinder (D, **Figure 47**) to the handlebar.

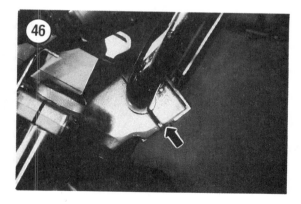

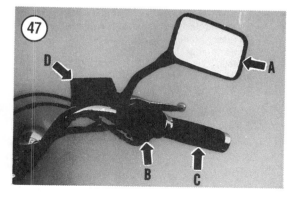

9. Remove the front brake master cylinder from the handlebar. Tie the front brake master cylinder to the frame and keep the reservoir in the upright position. This is to minimize loss of brake fluid and to keep air from entering into the brake system. It is not necessary to remove the hydraulic brake line.

10. Remove the components from the left-hand side of the handlebar as described in this chapter.

11. To remove the handlebar from the fork bridge, perform the following:
   a. Remove the trim caps (**Figure 44**) from the Allen bolts.
   b. Remove the Allen bolts (**Figure 45**) securing the handlebar upper holders.
   c. Remove the upper holders and the handlebar assembly.
   d. Move the handlebar assembly back and rest it on the frame.

12. Install by reversing these removal steps while noting the following:
   a. Apply a light coat of multipurpose grease to the throttle grip area on the handlebar prior to installing the throttle grip assembly.
   b. Tighten the front brake master cylinder clamping upper bolt first and then the lower bolt. Tighten the clamping bolts securely.

WARNING
After installation is completed, make sure the brake lever does not come in contact with the throttle grip assembly when it is pulled on fully. If it does, the brake fluid may be low in the reservoir. Refill if necessary. Refer to ***Front Disc Brakes*** *in Chapter Eleven.*

   c. Adjust the throttle operation as described in Chapter Three.
   d. Tighten the handlebar mounting Allen bolts to the torque specification listed in **Table 1**. Tighten the front bolts first then the rear so there is a slight gap at the rear between the handlebar upper and lower holders (**Figure 46**).

Left-hand side of handlebar

1. Remove the fuel tank as described under *Fuel Tank Removal/Installation* in Chapter Seven.

2. Disconnect the starter interlock switch electrical connector (**Figure 43**) from the clutch lever.

3. Unscrew the rear view mirror (A, **Figure 48**) from the clutch lever assembly.

4. Remove the screws securing the left-hand handlebar switch assembly (B, **Figure 48**) together and remove the upper half of the switch.

5. Disconnect the choke cable from the choke lever (C, **Figure 48**) on the switch assembly.

6. Remove the lower half of the switch from the handlebar and lay it over the fender or back over the frame.

7. Slide the hand grip assembly (D, **Figure 48**) off the end of the handlebar.

8. Loosen the pinch bolt securing the clutch lever assembly (E, **Figure 48**) to the handlebar. Slide the assembly off the end of the handlebar.

9. Remove the components from the left-hand side of the handlebar as described in this chapter.

10. To remove the handlebar from the fork bridge, perform the following:

   a. Remove the trim caps (**Figure 44**) from the Allen bolts.

   b. Remove the Allen bolts (**Figure 45**) securing the handlebar upper holders.

   c. Remove the upper holders and the handlebar assembly.

   d. Move the handlebar assembly back and rest it on the frame.

11. Install by reversing these removal steps while noting the following:

   a. Tighten the bolts to the torque specification listed in **Table 1** or if not listed, tighten securely.

   b. Adjust the choke operation as described in Chapter Three.

   c. Tighten the handlebar mounting Allen bolts to the torque specification listed in **Table 1**.

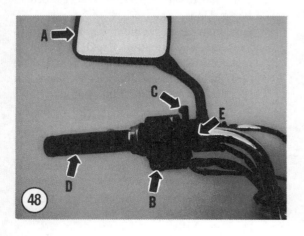

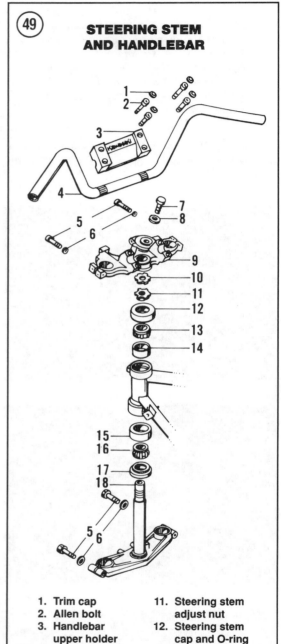

STEERING STEM AND HANDLEBAR

1. Trim cap
2. Allen bolt
3. Handlebar upper holder
4. Handlebar
5. Bolts
6. Washers
7. Steering stem bolt
8. Washer
9. Upper fork bridge
10. Locknut
11. Steering stem adjust nut
12. Steering stem cap and O-ring
13. Upper roller bearing
14. Upper roller bearing race
15. Lower roller bearing race
16. Lower roller bearing
17. Oil seal
18. Steering stem

Tighten the front bolts first then the rear so there is a slight gap at the rear between the handlebar upper and lower holders (**Figure 46**).

STEERING HEAD AND STEM

Disassembly

Refer to **Figure 49** for this procedure.

1. Remove the front wheel as described in this chapter.

2. Remove the handlebar assembly (A, **Figure 50**) as described in this chapter.

3. Remove the headlight case as described under *Headlight Case Removal/Installation* in Chapter Eight.

4. Disconnect the speedometer cable from the meter assembly (B, **Figure 50**).

5. Disconnect the electrical connector from the horns, headlight, meter and indicator light assembly.

6. Remove the steering stem head bolt and washer.

7. Loosen the upper fork bridge bolts.

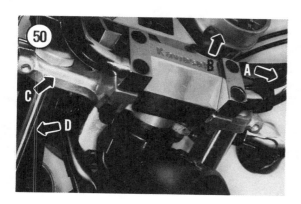

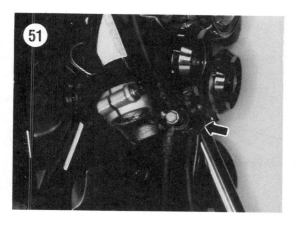

NOTE
The headlight mounting brackets and the meter/indicator light assembly can remain attached to the upper fork bridge and be removed as an assembly.

8. Remove the upper fork bridge assembly (C, **Figure 50**).

9. Remove the front forks (D, **Figure 50**) as described in this chapter.

10. Remove the screws securing the fork cover and remove the cover.

11. Remove the front brake 3-way joint (**Figure 51**) from the steering stem as described under *Front Brake 3-way Joint Removal/Installation* in Chapter Twelve.

12. Loosen the locknut and the steering stem adjust nut with a spanner wrench or use the easily improvised tool shown in **Figure 52**.

13. Hold onto the lower end of the steering stem assembly and remove the following:

   a. The steering stem locknut and adjust nut.

   b. The steering stem cap and the O-ring seal on models so equipped.

14. Lower the steering stem assembly down and out of the steering head. Don't worry about catching any loose steel balls as the steering stem is equipped with assembled roller bearings.

15. Remove the upper roller bearing from the top of the steering head section of the frame.

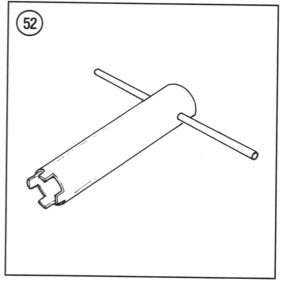

Inspection

1. Clean the outer bearing races in the steering head and the roller bearings with solvent.

2. Check the welds around the steering head for cracks and fractures. If any are found, have them checked by a Kawasaki dealer or a competent frame shop.

3. Check the bearing rollers for pitting, scratches or discoloration indicating wear or corrosion. Replace the upper and lower roller bearings as a set if either bearing is faulty.

4. Check the outer races for pitting, galling and corrosion. If any of these conditions exist, replace the races as described in this chapter.

5. Check the steering stem for cracks, damage or wear. If damaged in any way, replace the steering stem.

Steering Stem Assembly

Refer to **Figure 49** for this procedure.

1. Make sure the steering head outer races are properly seated.

2. Apply an even complete coat of wheel bearing grease to the steering head outer races (**Figure 53**) and to both bearings.

3. Install the upper roller bearing into the steering head.

4. Install the steering stem into the head tube and hold it firmly in place.

5. Install the steering stem cap and the O-ring seal, on models so equipped.

6. Position the lower steering stem locknut with the smaller diameter facing down and install it.

NOTE
The following step is best performed using the Kawasaki special tool (Stem Nut Wrench, part No. 57001-1100).

7. Seat the bearings as follows:

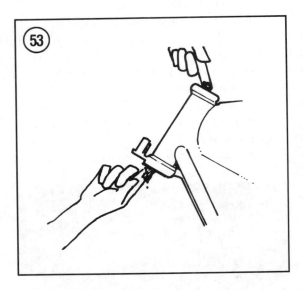

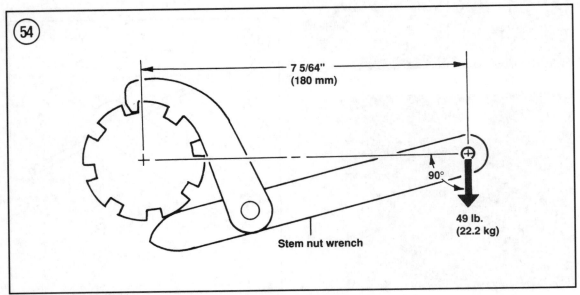

7 5/64"
(180 mm)

90°

49 lb.
(22.2 kg)

Stem nut wrench

a. Tighten the steering stem nut to 39 N•m (29 ft.-lb.). If using the Kawasaki steering stem wrench with the same dimensions shown in **Figure 54**, apply a 49 lb. (22.2 kg) force to the end of the wrench to obtain the desired 39 N•m (29 ft.-lb.) torque on the steering stem nut.

NOTE
If the stem nut wrench is not available, tighten the steering stem nut by feel using a large pair of adjustable pliers. Tighten the nut until tight, then turn the steering stem back and forth to seat the bearings. Loosen the nut 1/16 to 1/8 turn, then retighten it until the steering stem turns smoothly with no trace of play.

b. When the steering stem adjust nut is tightened properly, the steering stem should turn smoothly with no play.

c. Loosen the steering stem adjust nut 1/16 to 1/8 of a turn until it turns lightly.

d. Turn the adjust nut lightly *clockwise*, as viewed from the top, until it just starts to be hard to turn. Do not overtighten or the steering will be too tight.

e. Turn the steering stem by hand to make sure it turns freely and does not bind. Repeat if necessary.

8. Install the steering stem locknut. Secure the steering stem adjust nut in its present location and tighten the locknut securely.

9. Install the front brake 3-way joint (**Figure 51**) onto the steering stem as described in Chapter Twelve.

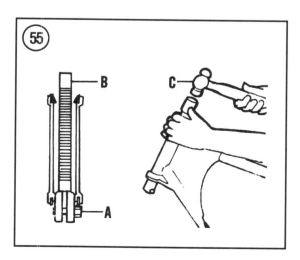

10. Install the fork cover and tighten the screws securely.

11. Install the front forks (D, **Figure 50**) as described in this chapter.

12. Install the upper fork bridge assembly (C, **Figure 50**).

13. Tighten the upper fork bridge bolts to the torque specification listed in **Table 1**.

14. Install the steering stem head bolt and washer, then tighten to the torque specification listed in **Table 1**.

15. Connect the electrical connector onto the horns, headlight, meter and indicator light assembly.

16. Connect the speedometer cable onto the meter assembly (B, **Figure 50**).

17. Install the headlight case as described in Chapter Eight.

18. Install the handlebar assembly (A, **Figure 50**) as described in this chapter.

19. Install the front wheel as described in this chapter.

STEERING HEAD BEARING RACES

The headset and steering stem bearing races are pressed into the headset portion of the frame. The races are easily bent so they should not be removed unless they require replacement.

Headset Bearing Race Removal/Installation

1. Remove the steering stem as described in this chapter.

2A. A special Kawasaki tool (Stem Bearing Remover part No. 57001-1107) can be used to remove the headset bearing race as follows:

a. Install the outer race remover (A, **Figure 55**) into one of the outer races.

b. Insert an aluminum rod or a drift against the top of the outer race remover (B, **Figure 55**).

c. Tap on the end of the rod or drift with a hammer (C, **Figure 55**) and drive the bearing outer race out of the steering head. Remove the special tool from the outer race.

d. Repeat for the bearing outer race at the other end of the headset.

2B. If the special tools are not used, perform the following:

10

a. Insert a hardwood stick or soft punch into the head tube and carefully tap the outer race out from the inside (**Figure 56**).

b. After it is started, work around the outer race so that neither the race nor the head tube is damaged.

c. Repeat for the bearing outer race on the other end of the headset.

3. Thoroughly clean the bearing receptacles in the headset with solvent and thoroughly dry with compressed air.

4. Inspect the receptacles for damage or burrs that may make installation of the new bearing races difficult. Carefully remove any burrs prior to installing new bearing races.

5. Apply a light coat of multi-purpose grease to the headset receptacles and to the outer surface of the new bearing races. This will make installation easier.

6A. A special Kawasaki tool set-up (Driver Press Shaft part No. 57001-1075, Driver 57001-1106 and Driver 57001-1076) can be used to install the headset bearing race as follows:

a. Position the outer races into the headset and just start them into position lightly with a soft-faced

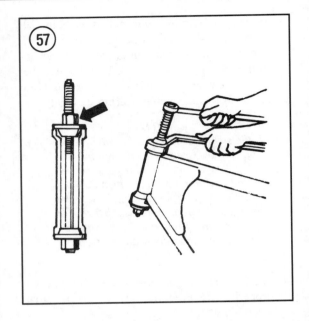

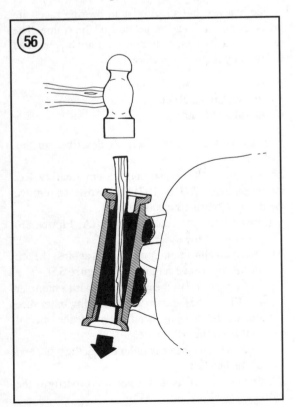

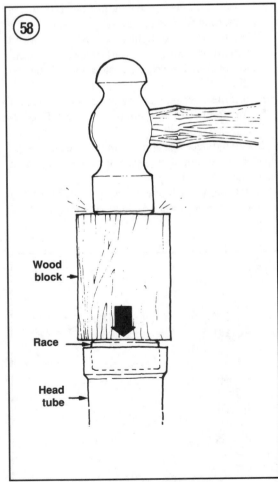

Wood block

Race

Head tube

mallet. Just tap them in enough to hold them in place until the special tools can be installed.

  b. Install the bearing Drivers into both of the outer races.

  c. Tighten the nut (**Figure 57**) on the bearing Driver Press Shaft and pull the outer races into place in the headset. Tighten the nut until both bearing outer races are completely seated in the head set and are flush with the steering head surface.

  d. Remove the special tool.

6B. If the special tools are not used, perform the following:

  a. Position one of the outer races into the headset and just start it into position lightly with a

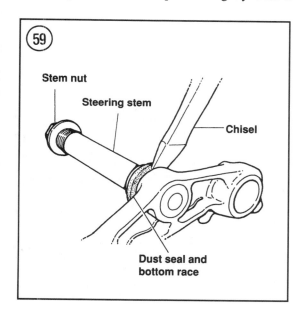

Stem nut

Steering stem

Chisel

Dust seal and bottom race

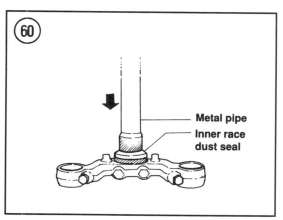

Metal pipe

Inner race dust seal

soft-faced mallet. Just tap it in enough to hold it in place.

  b. Tap the outer race in slowly with a block of wood, a suitable size socket or piece of pipe (**Figure 58**). Make sure that the race is squarely seated in the headset race bore before tapping it into place. Tap the race in until it is flush with the steering head surface.

  c. Repeat for the other outer race.

Steering Stem Lower Bearing Removal/Installation

1. Install the steering stem adjust nut and locknut onto the steering stem to protect the threads during this procedure.

2. Clamp the steering stem shaft in a vise with soft jaws.

3. Carefully drive the bearing and oil seal up from the base of the steering stem with a chisel and hammer (**Figure 59**) working around in a circle so that the bearing will not bind on the stem.

4. Remove the steering stem from the vise.

5. Remove the steering stem locknut and adjust nut.

6. Remove the bearing and oil seal from the steering stem shaft and discard both parts.

7. Clean all old grease from the steering stem bearing area.

8. Inspect the bearing location of the steering stem for damage or burrs that may make installation of the new bearing races difficult. Carefully remove any burrs before installing new bearing races.

9. Apply a light coat of multi-purpose grease to the steering stem and to the inner surface of the new bearing. This will make installation easier.

10. Install the oil seal and the lower bearing on the steering stem. Slide the bearing down onto the top of the shoulder at the base of the steering stem.

11. Align the bearing with the machined surface of the steering stem and slide an appropriate size piece of pipe down against the *inner* bearing race (**Figure 60**).

12. Use a hammer and carefully tap the lower bearing into place. Tap it into place until it bottoms out.

13. Remove the piece of pipe.

14. Make sure it is seated squarely and is all the way down.

10

FRONT FORKS

Front Fork Service

Before suspecting major trouble, drain the front fork oil and refill with the proper type and quantity fork oil; refer to *Front Fork Oil Change* in Chapter Three. If you still have trouble, such as poor damping, a tendency to bottom or top out or leakage around the rubber seals, follow the service procedures in this section.

To simplify fork service and to prevent the mixing of parts, the legs should be removed, serviced and installed individually.

Removal/Installation

1. Place the bike on the centerstand on a level surface.

2. Remove the cap (**Figure 61**) from the top of both fork tubes.

> *WARNING*
> *Always bleed off all air pressure; failure to do so may cause personal injury when partially disassembling the fork for changing the oil.*

> *NOTE*
> *Release air pressure gradually. If released too fast, fork oil will spurt out with the air. Protect your eyes and clothing accordingly.*

3. On models so equipped, depress the valve stem and bleed off *all* air pressure. Repeat for the other fork assembly.

> *NOTE*
> *Insert a piece of vinyl tubing or wood in the caliper in place of the brake disc. That way if the brake lever is inadvertently squeezed, the pistons will not be forced out of the cylinders. If this does happen, the caliper may have to be disassembled to reseat the piston and the system will have to be bled. By using the wood, bleeding the brake is not necessary when installing the wheel.*

4. Remove the brake caliper as follows:

  a. Loosen, then remove the bolts (A, **Figure 62**) securing the brake caliper assembly to the front fork.

  b. Remove the caliper assembly (B, **Figure 62**) from the brake disc.

5. Remove the front wheel (C, **Figure 62**) as described in this chapter.

6. Remove the screws securing the front fender to the front forks.

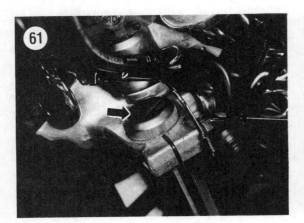

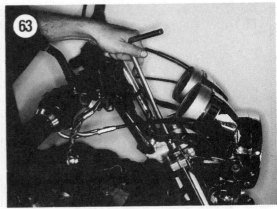

NOTE
The Allen bolt at the base of the slider has been secured with a thread locking agent and is often very difficult to remove because the damper rod will turn inside the slider. It sometimes can be removed with an air impact driver. If you are unable to remove it, take the fork tubes to a dealer and have the bolts removed.

7. If the fork assembly is going to be disassembled, perform the following:

    a. Use an Allen wrench to loosen (just break it loose) the Allen bolt at the base of the slider. If the bolt is loosened too much, fork oil may start to drain out of the slider.

    b. Use a suitable size socket and T-handle extension (**Figure 63**) to depress the top cap while removing the retaining ring (**Figure 64**). Discard the old retaining ring as a new one must be installed every time the ring is removed.

c. Remove the top cap and spring spacer.

8. Loosen the upper and lower fork bridge bolts (**Figure 65**).

9. Twist the fork tube slightly and withdraw it from the upper and lower fork bridges.

10. Install by reversing these removal steps while noting the following:

    a. Install the fork tube and push it up until it is flush with the top surface of the upper fork bridge (**Figure 66**).

    b. Install the front axle into both fork sliders to assure correct alignment between both fork assemblies.

    c. Tighten the upper and lower fork bridge bolts to the torque specifications listed in **Table 1**.

    d. Remove the front axle from both fork sliders.

    e. On models so equipped, add air pressure to the fork assemblies if so desired. Refer to **Table 4** for recommended air pressure.

Disassembly

Refer to **Figure 67** during the disassembly and assembly procedures.

1. On models so equipped, make sure all air pressure is released from the fork assembly prior to disassembly. Depress the valve stem and bleed off *all* air pressure.

NOTE
The top cap and spring spacer were removed during fork assembly removal.

2. Carefully withdraw the fork spring and spring seat from the fork tube.

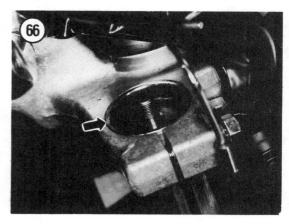

10

3. Turn the fork assembly upside down and drain the fork oil into a suitable container. Pump the fork several times by hand to expel most of the remaining oil. Dispose of the fork oil properly.

NOTE
*If you recycle your engine oil, do **not** add the fork oil to the engine oil because the recycler probably will not accept the oil.*

4. Remove the Allen bolt and gasket from the slider. If the Allen bolt was not loosened during the removal procedure, use special Kawasaki tools and perform the following:
   a. Install the adapter (part No. 57001-1057) onto the extension bar and handle (part No. 57001-183).
   b. Insert this special tool setup into the fork tube and index it into the hex receptacle in the top of the damper rod to hold the damper rod in place.
   c. Using an Allen wrench, loosen then remove the Allen bolt and washer from the base of the slider.

4. Remove the dust seal from the slider.

5. Remove the stopper ring from the top of the slider.

NOTE
On this type of fork, force is needed to remove the fork tube from the slider.

6. Install the fork tube in a vise with soft jaws.

7. There is an interference fit between the bushing in the fork slider and the bushing on the fork tube. In order to remove the fork tube from the slider, pull hard on the fork tube using quick in-and-out strokes (**Figure 68**). Doing so will withdraw the bushing, washer and the oil seal from the slider.

NOTE
It may be necessary to heat slightly the area on the slider around the oil seal prior to removal. Use a rag soaked in hot water; do not apply a flame directly to the fork slider.

8. Withdraw the fork tube from the slider.

NOTE
Do not remove the fork tube bushing unless it is going to be replaced. Inspect it as described in this chapter.

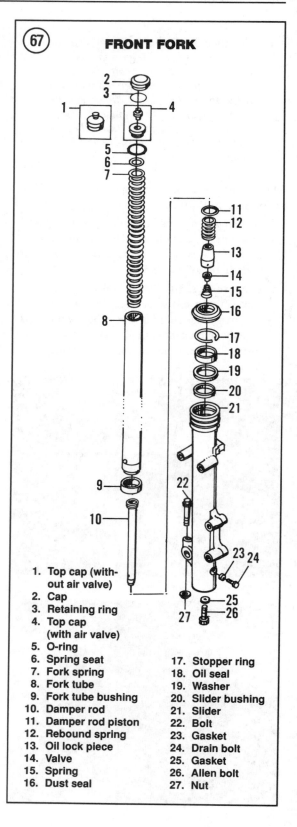

(67) **FRONT FORK**

1. Top cap (without air valve)
2. Cap
3. Retaining ring
4. Top cap (with air valve)
5. O-ring
6. Spring seat
7. Fork spring
8. Fork tube
9. Fork tube bushing
10. Damper rod
11. Damper rod piston
12. Rebound spring
13. Oil lock piece
14. Valve
15. Spring
16. Dust seal
17. Stopper ring
18. Oil seal
19. Washer
20. Slider bushing
21. Slider
22. Bolt
23. Gasket
24. Drain bolt
25. Gasket
26. Allen bolt
27. Nut

9. Remove the oil lock piece, spring and valve from the damper rod.

10. Remove the damper rod and rebound spring from the slider.

11. Inspect the components as described in this chapter.

Inspection

1. If still installed, remove the drain screw and sealing washer (**Figure 69**).

2. Thoroughly clean all parts in solvent and dry them. Check the fork tube for signs of wear or scratches.

3. Check the damper rod for straightness. **Figure 70** shows one method. The damper rod should be replaced if the runout is 0.2 mm (0.008 in.) or greater.

4. Make sure the oil holes (**Figure 71**) in the damper rod are clear. Clean out if necessary.

5. Inspect the damper rod (**Figure 72**) and its piston ring (**Figure 73**) for wear or damage. Replace as necessary.

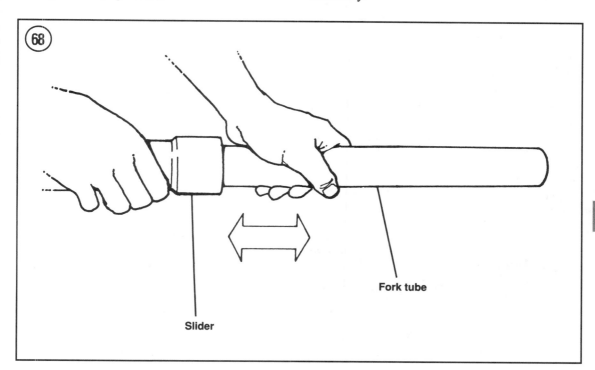

Slider

Fork tube

10

6. Check the fork tube for straightness. If bent or severely scratched, it should be replaced.

7. Check the slider for dents or exterior damage that may cause the upper fork tube to hang up during riding. Replace if necessary.

8. Inspect the brake caliper mounting bosses (**Figure 74**) and the front axle pinch bolt area (**Figure 75**) on the slider for crack or damage. If damaged, replace the slider.

9. Inspect the bushings on the slider (**Figure 76**) and fork tube (**Figure 77**) bushings. If either is scratched or scored they must be replaced. If the Teflon coating is worn off so that the copper base material is showing on approximately 3/4 of the total surface, the bushing must be replaced.

10. Inspect the fork cap retaining ring groove (**Figure 78**) in the fork tube for wear or damage. The groove cannot be "rounded off" at the upper portion since that would allow the retaining ring to slip out when riding. If necessary, replace the fork tube.

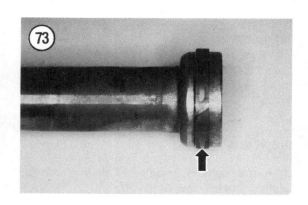

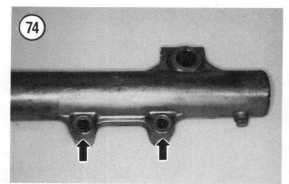

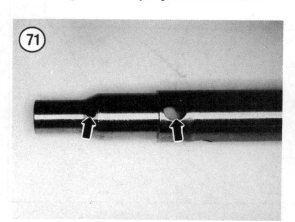

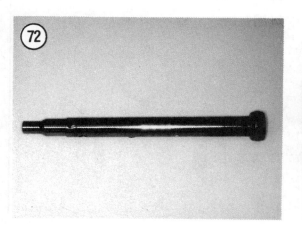

11. Inspect the fork top cap for wear or damage. Check the O-ring seal for hardness or deterioration, replace if necessary.

12. Inspect the oil seal seating area (**Figure 79**) in the slider for damage or burrs. Clean up if necessary.

13. Inspect the gasket on the Allen bolt (**Figure 80**), replace if damaged.

NOTE
Kawasaki does not provide any dimensions for either a new spring or for a

service limit dimension for the un-compressed length of the fork spring. If you suspect the spring has sagged, take the spring to a Kawasaki dealer and compare the length to a new spring. Replace if necessary.

14. Inspect the fork spring for wear or damage, replace if necessary.

15. Any parts that are worn or damaged should be replaced. Simply cleaning and reinstalling unserviceable components will not improve performance of the front suspension.

Assembly

1. Coat the sliding portions of all parts with fresh SAE 10W-20 fork oil prior to installation.

2. Install the rebound spring onto the damper rod (**Figure 81**) and insert this assembly into the fork

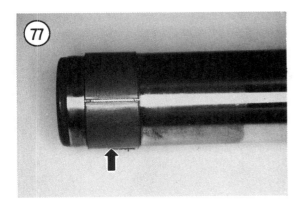

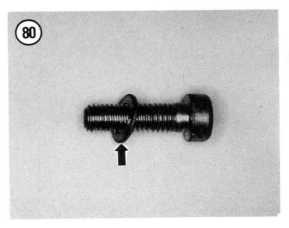

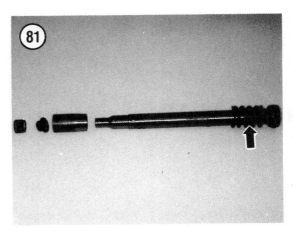

10

tube (**Figure 82**). Push the damper rod in until it exits the bottom of the fork tube (**Figure 83**).

3. Temporarily install the fork spring (**Figure 84**), spring seat (A, **Figure 85**) and spacer (B, **Figure 85**) to hold the damper rod in place. Push the spacer in until it bottoms out (**Figure 86**).

4. Apply a strip of duct tape (**Figure 87**) over the end of the fork tube to temporarily hold the fork spring, seat and spacer in place.

5. Position the oil lock piece with the tapered end (A, **Figure 88**) going on first and install it onto the damper rod. Push it on until it stops (B, **Figure 88**).

6. Position the valve with the flange side going in first (**Figure 89**) and install the valve into the end of the oil lock piece.

7. Position the spring with the smaller diameter coils going in first (**Figure 90**) and apply a small amount of cold grease (**Figure 91**) to the smaller diameter coils.

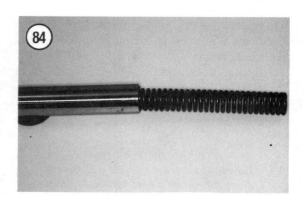

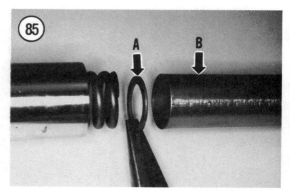

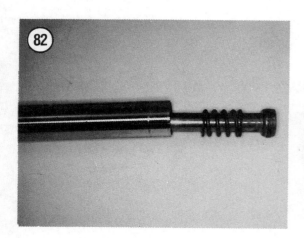

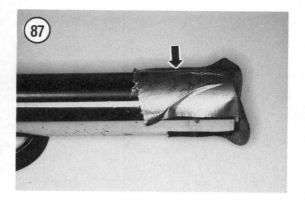

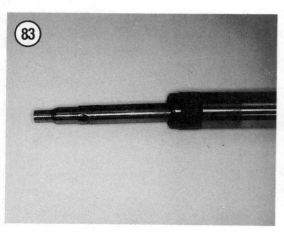

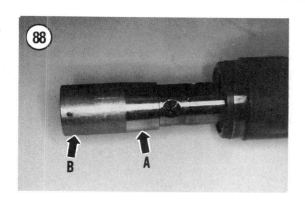

8. Install the spring into the end of the valve. Push the spring in until it stops and is held in place on the valve (**Figure 92**).

9. Install the upper fork assembly into the slider (**Figure 93**).

10. Make sure the gasket (**Figure 80**) is on the Allen bolt.

11. Apply blue Loctite (No. 242) to the threads of the Allen bolt prior to installation. Install it in the fork slider (**Figure 94**) and screw it into the base of

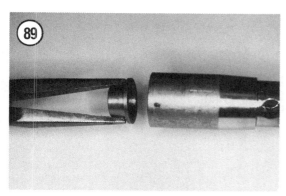

10

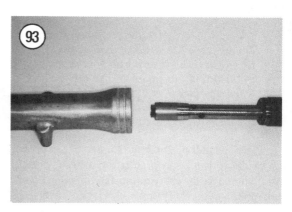

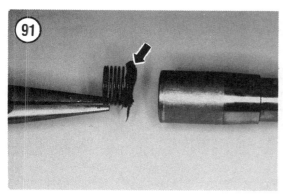

the damper rod. Tighten to the torque specification listed in **Table 1**.

12. Remove the strip of duct tape from the top of the fork tube.

13. Slide the fork slider bushing (A, **Figure 95**) and the washer (B, **Figure 95**) down the fork tube and rest it on top of the fork slider.

> *NOTE*
> *The following special tool is **very expensive**. If you work on a lot of different bikes, this special tool is a must for your tool box. It is adjustable and will work on almost all Japanese fork assemblies (including Japanese "Showa" forks installed on some late model Harley-Davidson motorcycles).*

14. Install the special tool (A, **Figure 96**) down onto the washer (B, **Figure 96**) and slider bushing (C, **Figure 96**).

15. Drive the slider bushing into the slider with the special tool. Drive the bushing in until it bottoms out in the slider.

16. Remove the special tool.

> *CAUTION*
> *Do not use a "reclosable" type of plastic bag as the closure portion of the bag is thick and can damage the oil seal when it passes over it. If using this type of bag, cut off the closure portion, then use the modified bag.*

17. Place a small plastic bag (**Figure 97**) over the top of the fork tube to protect the oil seal during installation over the sharp top surface opening of the fork tube.

18. Coat the new seal with fresh SAE 10W-20 fork oil.

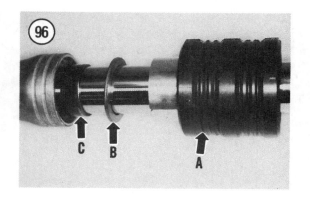

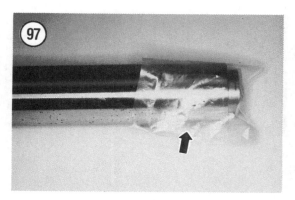

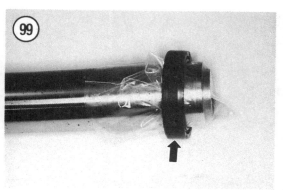

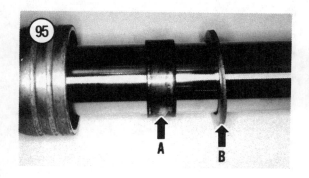

19. Position the seal with the open groove facing upward (**Figure 98**) and slide the oil seal (**Figure 99**) over the plastic bag and down the fork tube.

20. Remove the plastic bag.

21. Use the same special tool set-up used in Step 14 to drive in the oil seal (A, **Figure 100**).

22. Drive the oil seal into the slider with the special tool (B, **Figure 100**) until the groove in the slider can be seen above the top surface of the oil seal.

23. Remove the special tool.

24. Install the stopper ring and slide it down the fork tube.

25. Install the stopper ring and make sure it is completely seated in the groove in the fork slider (**Figure 101**).

26. Install the dust seal (**Figure 102**) into the slider. Press it in until it is completely seated.

27. Install the fork assembly into the frame, as described in this chapter, then fill it with fork oil.

NOTE
Kawasaki recommends that the fork oil level be measured, if possible, to ensure a more accurate filling.

NOTE
To measure the correct amount of fluid, use a plastic baby bottle or a mixing container. These bottles or containers have measurements in milliliters (ml) on the side.

28. Add the recommended amount of fork oil to the fork assembly (**Figure 103**). Refer to **Table 3** for the recommended viscosity and quantity.

29. Compress the fork assembly completely, hold it in this position, and measure the fork oil level.

30. Use an accurate ruler or oil level gauge (**Figure 104**), to achieve the correct oil level listed in **Table 3**.

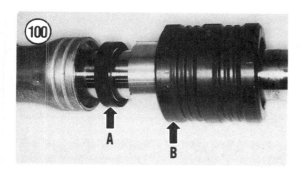

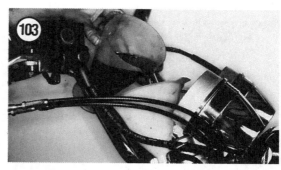

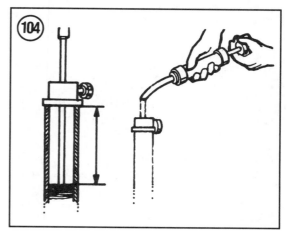

10

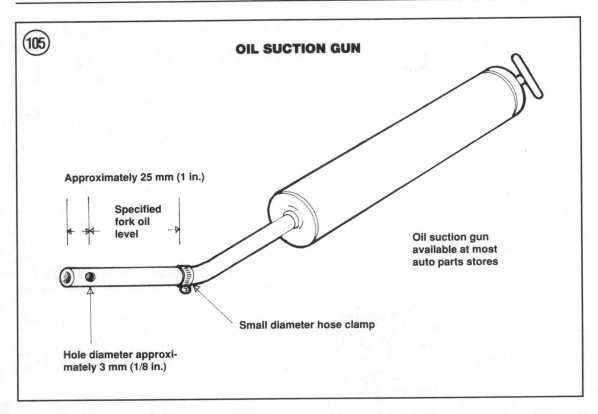

OIL SUCTION GUN

Approximately 25 mm (1 in.)

Specified
fork oil
level

Oil suction gun
available at most
auto parts stores

Small diameter hose clamp

Hole diameter approximately 3 mm (1/8 in.)

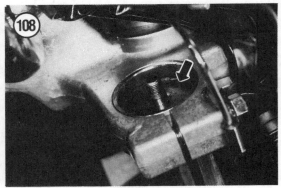

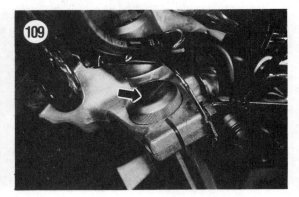

NOTE
*An oil level measuring device can be made as shown in **Figure 105**. Position the lower edge of the hose clamp the specified oil level distance up from the small diameter hole. Fill the fork with a few ml's more than the required amount of oil. Position the hose clamp on the top edge of the fork tube and draw out the excess oil. Oil is sucked out until the level reaches the small diameter hole. A precise oil level can be achieved with this simple device.*

31. Allow the oil to settle completely and recheck the oil level measurement. Adjust the oil level if necessary.

32. Extend the fork slider.

33. Repeat Steps 1-32 for the other fork assembly. Both fork assemblies must be installed to complete this procedure.

34. Install the front fender and the front wheel. Maintain jack pressure under the engine.

35. Install the fork spring with the smaller diameter coils going in first.

36. Install the spring seat, spacer and top cap (**Figure 106**).

WARNING
Make sure the retaining ring is seated correctly in the fork tube groove. If the ring works loose while riding, the fork assembly will compress and could result in an accident.

37. Use a suitable size socket and extension; depress the top cap and spring. Install a *new* retaining ring (**Figure 107**) and make sure the retaining ring is seated correctly in the fork tube groove (**Figure 108**).

38. Remove the jack from under the engine.

39. On models so equipped, add air pressure to the fork assemblies if so desired. Refer to **Table 4** for recommended air pressure.

40. Install the cap (**Figure 109**) onto the top of both fork tubes.

10

Table 1 FRONT SUSPENSION TIGHTENING TORQUES

Item	N•m	ft.-lb.
Front axle nut	59	43
Front axle pinch bolt and nut	13	9.5
Brake disc bolts	23	16.5
Handlebar upper holder Allen bolts	24	17.5
Steering stem bolt	39	29
Fork cap bolt air valve	7.8	5.7
Fork drain bolt	7.8	5.7
Fork bridge bolts		
Upper	20	14.5
Lower	25	18
Fork slider Allen bolt	20	14.5

Table 2 TIRE SIZE AND INFLATION PRESSURE (COLD)*

	Tire size			
Front	100/90-19H tubeless			
Rear	150/90-15 74H, 150/90 B15 M/C 74H or 150/90-15 M/C 74H tubeless			

	Tire Pressure			
	Front		Rear	
Load	psi	kPa	psi	kPa
Up to 215 lbs. (97.5 kg) U.S., Canada, Australia, South Africa models	28	200	28	200
215 to 406 lbs. (97 to 184 kg) All other models	28	200	32	225
215 to 397 lbs. (97 to 180 kg)	28	200	32	225

* Tire inflation pressure for factory equipped tires. Aftermarket tires may require different inflation pressure; refer to manufacturer's specifications.

Table 3 FORK OIL CAPACITY AND DIMENSIONS

Fork oil
  Viscosity — SAE 10W-20 fork oil
  Capacity per leg
    Oil change only — 310-320 ml (10.48-10.82 U.S. oz. 8.73-9.0 Imp. oz.)
    After disassembly
      U.S and Canadian models — 359-364 ml (12.04-12.31 U.S. oz. 10.11-10.25 Imp. oz.)
      All other models — 370-375 ml (12.51-12.68 U.S. oz. 10.42-10.56 Imp. oz.)
  Oil level each leg
    U.S. and Canadian models — 220-240 mm (8.66-9.45 in.)
    All other models — 205-225 mm (8.07-8.86 in.)

Table 4 FRONT SUSPENSION SPECIFICATIONS

Item	Wear limit
Front axle runout	0.2 mm (0.01 in.)
Front wheel rim runout	
Radial	0.8 mm (0.031 in.)
Axial	0.5 mm (0.019 in.)
Front fork spring free length limit	NA*
Front fork air pressure	
Standard	atmospheric pressure
Usable range	0-49 kPa (0-7.1 psi)

* Kawasaki does not provide any standard length or service limit dimensions for the fork spring.

CHAPTER ELEVEN

REAR SUSPENSION AND FINAL DRIVE

This chapter includes repair and replacement procedures for the rear wheel and rear suspension components. Refer to Chapter Ten for procedures relating to tire changing and wheel balancing.

Refer to **Table 1** for rear suspension torque specifications. **Table 1** and **Table 2** are located at the end of this chapter.

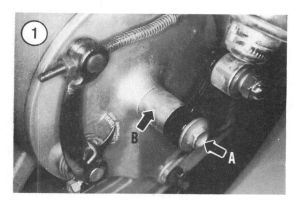

REAR WHEEL

Removal/Installation

1. Place the bike on the side stand on level ground.

2. Remove the right-hand muffler as described under *Right-hand Exhaust Pipe and Muffler Removal/Installation* in Chapter Seven.

3. Hold the right-hand end of the axle (A, **Figure 1**) with a wrench to prevent the rear axle from rotating during the next step.

4. Remove the cotter pin and loosen the rear axle nut (**Figure 2**). Discard the cotter pin, never reuse a cotter pin as the ends could brake off and the cotter pin may fall out.

5. Remove the safety clip, then remove the bolt and nut (**Figure 3**) securing the torque link arm to the rear brake panel. Swing the torque link arm down and out of the way.

11

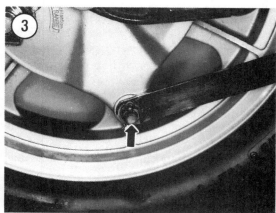

6. Completely unscrew the rear brake adjusting nut (**Figure 4**).

7. Depress the brake pedal and remove the brake rod from the pivot joint in the brake arm. Remove the pivot joint from the brake lever and install the pivot joint and the adjusting nut onto the brake rod to avoid misplacing them.

8. Place the bike on the centerstand on level ground with the rear wheel off the ground. If necessary, place a small jack, with a piece of wood to protect the crankcase, under the crankcase. Apply a small amount of jack pressure to support the bike securely with the rear wheel off the ground.

9. Remove the rear axle nut and washer (**Figure 2**).

10. Withdraw the axle (A, **Figure 1**). Don't lose the spacer (B, **Figure 1**) on the right-hand side between the brake panel and the swing arm.

11. Slide the wheel to the right to disengage it from the hub drive splines and remove the wheel.

12. Install the spacer, washer and nut back onto the rear axle (**Figure 5**) to avoid misplacing the small parts.

13. Inspect the wheel as described in this chapter.

Installation

1. Apply a light coat of grease (lithium based NLGI No. 2 grease with molybdenum disulfide) to the final driven flange spline (**Figure 6**) and to the rear wheel coupling (**Figure 7**).

2. Position the rear wheel so that the splines of the final driven flange and the final drive align. Slowly move the wheel back and forth and push the wheel to the left until it completely seats.

3. Position the spacer (B, **Figure 1**) on the right-hand side between the brake panel and the swing arm.

4. Install the rear axle (A, **Figure 1**) from the right-hand side and install the axle washer and nut (**Figure 2**). Tighten the nut only finger-tight at this time.

5. To install the brake torque link, perform the following:

   a. Swing the brake arm up and into position.

   b. Install the bolt, washer and nut. Tighten the bolt and nut to the torque specification listed in **Table 1**.

   c. Install the safety clip into the hole in the bolt (**Figure 3**).

6. To prevent a soft or "spongy feel" to the rear brake, rotate the rear wheel and apply the rear brake

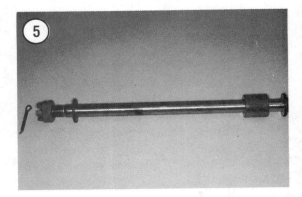
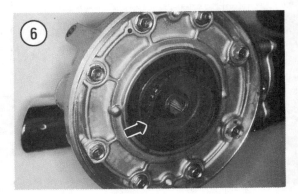

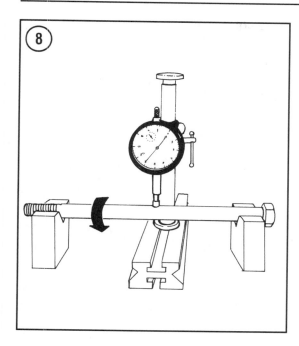

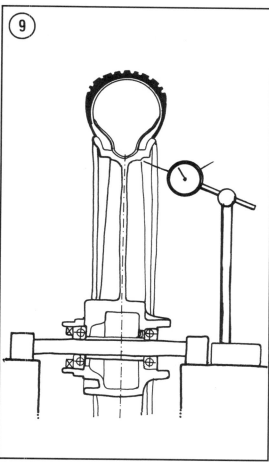

several times. This will center the brake panel within the brake drum, resulting in a solid feel to the rear brake.

7. Install a wrench on the axle to keep the axle from turning.

8. Tighten the rear axle nut to the torque specifications listed in **Table 1**.

9. Install a new cotter pin and bend the ends over completely.

10. Completely unscrew the rear brake adjusting nut from the brake rod.

11. Install the pivot joint into the brake lever.

12. Depress the brake pedal and insert the brake rod into the pivot joint in the brake arm. Install the adjust nut onto the brake rod and turn it in until brake action can be accomplished by depressing the brake pedal.

13. After the wheel is installed, completely rotate it and apply the brake several times to make sure it rotates freely and that the brake still works properly.

14. Adjust the rear brake free play as described in Chapter Three.

Inspection

1. Remove any corrosion on the rear axle with a piece of fine emery cloth. Clean off with solvent, then wipe the axle clean with a lint-free cloth.

2. Check axle runout. Place the axle on V-blocks and place the tip of a dial indicator in the middle of the axle (**Figure 8**). Rotate the axle and check runout. If the runout exceeds the specification listed in **Table 2**, replace the axle; do not attempt to straighten it.

3. Check rim runout as follows:

　　a. Remove the tire from the rim as described in this chapter.

　　b. Measure the radial (up and down) runout of the wheel rim with a dial indicator as shown in **Figure 9**. If runout exceeds the wear limit specification listed in **Table 1**, check the wheel bearings.

　　c. Measure the axial (side to side) runout of the wheel rim with a dial indicator as shown in **Figure 9**. If runout exceeds the wear limit specification listed in **Table 2**, check the wheel bearings.

　　d. Check the wheel bearings as described under *Rear Hub* in this chapter. If the rear wheel bearings are okay, the cast wheel is faulty and must be replaced. Cast wheels cannot be serviced.

e. Replace the rear wheel bearings as described under *Rear Hub* in this chapter.

4. Inspect the wheel rim (**Figure 10**) for dents, bending or cracks. Check the rim and rim sealing surface for scratches that are deeper than 0.5 mm (0.01 in.). If any of these conditions are present, replace the wheel as it is unsafe for use.

REAR HUB

Inspection

Inspect each wheel bearing prior to removing it from the wheel hub.

> *CAUTION*
> *Do not remove the wheel bearings for inspection as they will be damaged during removal. Remove wheel bearings only if they are to be replaced.*

1. Perform Step 1 and Step 2 of *Disassembly* in this chapter.

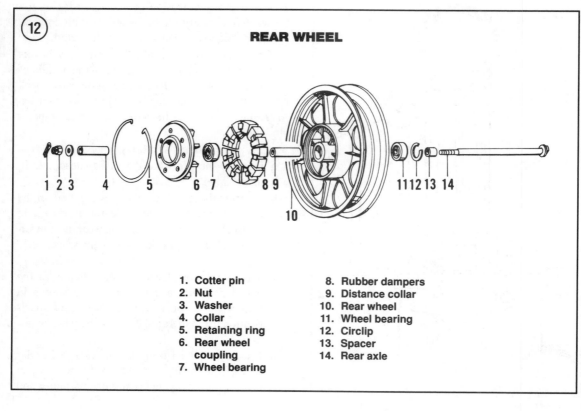

REAR WHEEL

1. Cotter pin
2. Nut
3. Washer
4. Collar
5. Retaining ring
6. Rear wheel coupling
7. Wheel bearing
8. Rubber dampers
9. Distance collar
10. Rear wheel
11. Wheel bearing
12. Circlip
13. Spacer
14. Rear axle

2. Turn each wheel bearing inner race (**Figure 11**) by hand. Make sure the bearings turn smoothly.

3. Replace the bearings if necessary; always replace as a complete set. When replacing the bearings, be sure to take your old bearings along to ensure a perfect matchup.

4. Inspect the splines of the rear wheel coupling (**Figure 7**). If any are damaged, the rear wheel coupling must be replaced.

Disassembly

Refer to **Figure 12** for this procedure.

1. Remove the rear wheel as described in this chapter.

2. Pull straight up and remove the brake panel assembly (**Figure 13**) from the hub.

3. Use a flat-bladed screwdriver and pry the retaining ring (**Figure 14**) securing the rear wheel coupling to the rear wheel. Remove the retaining ring.

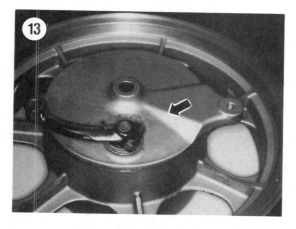

NOTE
If the hub is corroded around the rear wheel coupling, it may be necessary to use a 3 or 4 finger puller to remove the rear wheel coupling from the hub. If there is no corrosion, the rear wheel coupling can be removed from the hub without the use of a puller.

4A. If a puller is necessary for removal, perform the following:

  a. Install a socket or piece of metal (A, **Figure 15**) on the hub (B, **Figure 15**) surface adjacent to the wheel bearing. Do *not* set it on the wheel bearing as the bearing will be damaged.

  b. Insert the fingers of the puller in the holes in the coupling (C, **Figure 15**).

NOTE
If the coupling will not work free from the hub, spray WD-40 around the coupling perimeter and allow it to set for 10-15 minutes. If you are still unable to work the coupling loose, take the wheel to a dealer for removal.

CAUTION
Do not apply excessive force with the puller as the coupling holes may fracture from the pressure applied by the puller fingers.

  c. Slowly apply pressure on the puller to work the coupling loose.

  d. Withdraw the coupling from the wheel hub and remove the puller.

4B. Pull straight up and remove the rear wheel coupling from the hub.

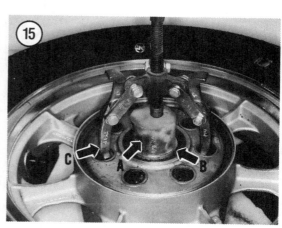

5. Remove the rubber cushion assembly (**Figure 16**) from the rear hub.

6. Before proceeding further, inspect the wheel bearings as described in this chapter. If they must be replaced, proceed as follows.

7. To remove the right-hand bearing, remove the circlip (A, **Figure 17**) securing the bearing.

8. To remove the right- and left-hand bearings (B, **Figure 17**) and distance collar, insert a soft aluminum or brass drift into one side of the hub.

9. Push the distance collar over to one side and place the drift on the inner race of the lower bearing.

10. Tap the bearing out of the hub with a hammer, working around the perimeter of the inner race. Remove the distance collar.

11. Repeat Steps 8-10 for the other bearing.

12. Clean the inside and the outside of the hub with solvent. Dry with compressed air.

13. Inspect the raised ribs (**Figure 18**) for the rubber dampers for wear or fractures. If damage is severe or any of the ribs are missing, replace the rear wheel.

14. Clean the inside and the outside of the rear wheel coupling with solvent. Dry with compressed air.

15. Inspect each rubber cushion assembly (**Figure 19**) for wear or deterioration. Replace if necessary.

16. Inspect the rear wheel coupling as follows:

   a. Inspect the inner splines (**Figure 20**) for wear or missing teeth.

   b. Inspect the raised bosses (A, **Figure 21**) for cracks or damage.

   c. Inspect the entire flange (B, **Figure 21**) for cracks or warping.

   d. Replace the rear wheel coupling if any of these areas are damaged.

Assembly

The rear hub bearings are packed with grease and sealed at time of manufacture. This type of bearing cannot be packed with new grease.

1. Blow any dirt or foreign matter out of the hub prior to installing the bearings.

> *CAUTION*
> *Position the bearings with the marked side facing outward.*

2. Tap the right-hand bearing squarely into place and tap on the outer race only. Use a socket that matches the outer race diameter. Do not tap on the inner race or the bearing might be damaged. Be sure that the bearing is completely seated in the hub.

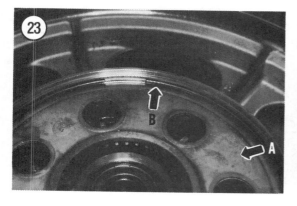

3. Install the circlip and make sure it is correctly seated in the hub groove (**Figure 22**).

4. Turn the wheel over (left-hand side up) on the workbench and install the distance collar.

5. Use the same tool set-up and drive in the left-hand bearing. Drive the bearing in until there is a minimal amount of clearance between the distance collar and the inner race. Kawasaki does not specify the amount of clearance, but the important thing is that the inner races of both bearings are not binding against the distance collar.

6. Install the rubber damper assembly (**Figure 16**) and make sure it is properly seated in the hub.

7. Apply a light coat of grease (lithium based NLGI No. 2 grease with molybdenum disulfide) to the splines and the outer perimeter of the rear wheel coupling (**Figure 20**).

8. Install the rear wheel coupling (A, **Figure 23**) straight down into the rear hub. Push it down until it is completely seated in the rear hub.

9. Inspect the rear wheel coupling retaining ring for wear, distortion or damage. Replace if necessary.

10. Install the retaining ring (B, **Figure 23**) securing the rear wheel coupling to the rear wheel. Make sure the ring is correctly seated in the rear hub groove.

11. Install the brake panel assembly (**Figure 13**) into the hub.

12. Install the rear wheel as described in this chapter.

11

FINAL DRIVE UNIT

Removal

1. Remove the rear wheel as described in this chapter.

2. Remove the left-hand muffler (A, **Figure 24**) as described under *Left-hand Exhaust Pipe and Muffler Removal/Installation* in Chapter Seven.

3. Drain the final drive unit oil as described in Chapter Three.

4. Remove the left-hand shock absorber upper and lower mounting nuts, lockwashers and washers and remove the left-hand shock absorber (B, **Figure 24**).

NOTE
In **Figure 25** *only 3 of the 4 nuts are shown. Be sure to remove all 4 nuts.*

5. Remove the nuts (**Figure 25**) securing the final drive unit to the swing arm.

6. Pull the final drive unit straight back until it is disengaged from the splines on the drive shaft. The coil spring (**Figure 26**) will usually stay with the final drive shaft. Either place a piece of duct tape over the end of the drive shaft to hold the spring in place, or remove the spring from the end of the drive shaft so it won't be misplaced.

7. The drive shaft will stay within the swing arm.

Inspection

Disassembly and assembly of the final drive unit requires a considerable number of special Kawasaki tools. The price of all of these tools could be more than the cost of most repairs or seal replacement on the unit by a Kawasaki dealer.

1. Check that the bearing case flange bolts (A, **Figure 27**) are in place and are tight.

2. Inspect the splines on the final driven ring gear (**Figure 28**). If they are damaged or worn, the ring gear must be replaced.

NOTE
*If these splines are damaged, also inspect the splines (**Figure 29**) on the rear*

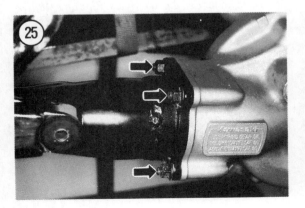

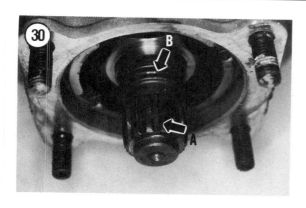

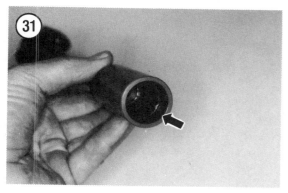

wheel coupling; it may also be damaged and require replacement.

3. Inspect the pinion joint input splines (A, **Figure 30**) of the final drive unit for wear or damage.

NOTE
*If these splines are damaged, also inspect the splines (**Figure 31**) on the drive shaft; it may also be damaged and require replacement.*

4. Check the threads on the mounting studs (**Figure 32**) and shock absorber stud (**Figure 33**) for wear or thread damage. If necessary, clean the threads with an appropriate size metric die.

5. Check that gear oil has not been leaking from either the ring gear side (B, **Figure 27**) or pinion joint side (**Figure 34**) of the unit. If there are traces of oil leakage, take the unit to a dealer for oil seal replacement.

6. Inspect the O-ring seal (B, **Figure 30**) on the pinion joint input splines for deterioration or damage. Replace if necessary.

7. Make sure the small Allen bolt (**Figure 35**) is in place and is tight.

11

Installation

1. During final drive unit removal, the drive shaft may have moved back slightly and away from the splines on the front bevel gear unit. Perform the following to make sure the drive shaft is still engaged properly:

   a. At the front bevel gear unit, pull the rubber boot back to gain access to the front of the drive shaft.

   b. If necessary, slowly rotate the drive shaft at the rear and properly align the splines of the drive shaft with the front bevel gear unit. Push the drive shaft all the way forward until it seats completely as shown in **Figure 36**.

2. If removed, install the spring (**Figure 26**) into the end of the drive shaft fitting. If the spring remained in place, remove the piece of duct tape used during removal.

3. Apply a light coat of molybdenum disulfide grease (NGLI No. 2) to the splines at the rear end of the drive shaft joint.

4. If removed, install the collar (**Figure 37**) into the final drive unit. Push it in until it is completely seated (**Figure 38**).

5. Install the final drive unit onto the swing arm and drive shaft.

6. Slowly push the final drive unit forward and mesh it with the drive shaft. It may be necessary to slightly rotate the final driven spline back and forth to align the splines of the drive shaft and the final drive unit.

7. Push the final drive unit all the way forward until it is seated correctly (**Figure 39**).

8. Install the final drive unit's mounting nuts (**Figure 25**) only finger-tight at this time. Do not tighten the nuts until the rear wheel and rear axle are in place.

9. Move the rubber boot back into position at the front of the swing arm. Make sure it is correctly installed to keep out dirt and water.

10. Install the rear wheel as described in this chapter.

11. Tighten the final drive unit nuts to the specifications listed in **Table 1**.

12. Install the shock absorber and the upper and lower washers and nuts. Tighten to the torque specifications listed in **Table 1**.

13. Refill the final drive unit with the correct amount and type of gear oil. Refer to Chapter Three.

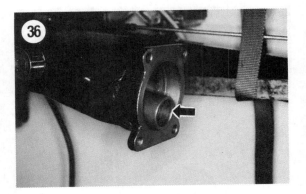

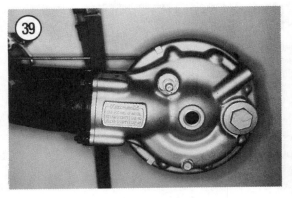

DRIVE SHAFT

Removal/Installation

NOTE
The drive shaft can be removed two different ways. Either remove the swing arm or the front bevel gear case. This procedure is shown with the swing arm removed.

1A. Remove the swing arm as described in this chapter.

1B. Remove the front bevel gear unit as described under *Front Bevel Gear Unit Removal/Installation* in Chapter Four.

CAUTION
The small coil spring fitted between the final drive gear splines and the universal joint splines will usually stay on the drive shaft spline. This coil spring must

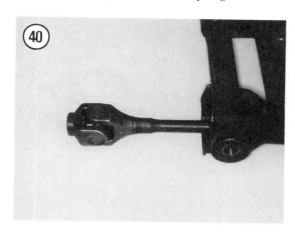

be in place when the drive shaft is reinstalled.

2. Carefully pull the drive shaft out through the front opening of the swing arm (**Figure 40**) and remove it.

3. Thoroughly clean out the grease from the inner surface of the drive shaft sliding joint (**Figure 41**).

4. Inspect the drive shaft as described in this chapter.

5. Re-lubricate the inner surfaces of the sliding joint with 17 ml of high-temperature grease.

6. Apply high-temperature grease to the front splines of the drive shaft universal joint and the output splines of the front bevel gear unit.

CAUTION
Do not forget to reinstall the small coil spring between the drive shaft and the final drive unit.

7. If the small coil spring separated from the final drive unit, reinstall it into the end of the drive shaft sliding joint (**Figure 42**).

8. Install the drive shaft into the front of the swing arm (**Figure 40**).

9A. Install the swing arm as described in this chapter.

9B. If the front bevel gear unit was removed, perform the following:

    a. Slowly push the drive shaft toward the rear and mesh it with the final drive unit splines. It may be necessary to rotate the drive shaft back and forth slightly to align the splines of the drive shaft and the final drive unit.

    b. Push the drive shaft all the way toward the rear until it is seated correctly.

11

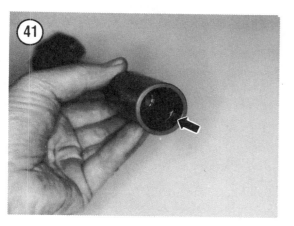

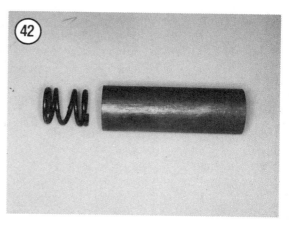

c. Install the front bevel gear unit as described in Chapter Four.

Inspection

1. Inspect the drive shaft (**Figure 43**) for damage and fatigue. Kawasaki does not provide and service specifications for the drive shaft. Replace the drive shaft if necessary.

2. Clean the universal joint in solvent and thoroughly dry with compressed air.

3. Inspect the universal joint pivot points for play (**Figure 44**). Rotate the joint in both directions. If there is noticeable side play, the universal joint must be replaced.

4. Inspect the front splines (**Figure 45**) on the universal joint end of drive shaft and the rear splines (**Figure 41**). If they are damaged or worn, the drive shaft must be replaced. If these splines are damaged, also inspect the splines on the front bevel gear unit and the final drive unit; they may also need to be replaced.

5. Apply a light coat of molybdenum disulfide grease (NGLI No. 2) to the splines on each end.

SWING ARM

In time, the roller bearings will wear and will have to be replaced. The condition of the bearings can greatly affect handling performance and if worn parts are not replaced they can produce erratic and dangerous handling. Common symptoms are wheel hop, pulling to one side during acceleration and pulling to the other side during braking.

Refer to **Figure 46** for this procedure.

Removal

1. Remove the rear wheel as described in this chapter.

2. Remove the final drive unit (A, **Figure 47**) and drive shaft as described in this chapter.

3. Remove the upper and lower mounting nuts and washers securing the right-hand shock absorber (B, **Figure 47**). Remove the shock absorber.

4. Remove the pivot point trim cap (**Figure 48**) from each side.

5. Grasp the rear end of the swing arm and try to move it from side to side in a horizontal arc. There should be no noticeable side play. If play is evident and the pivot bolt nut is tightened correctly, the bearings should be replaced.

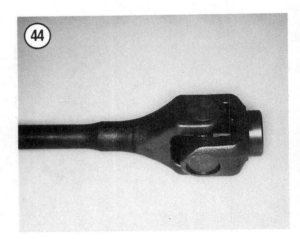

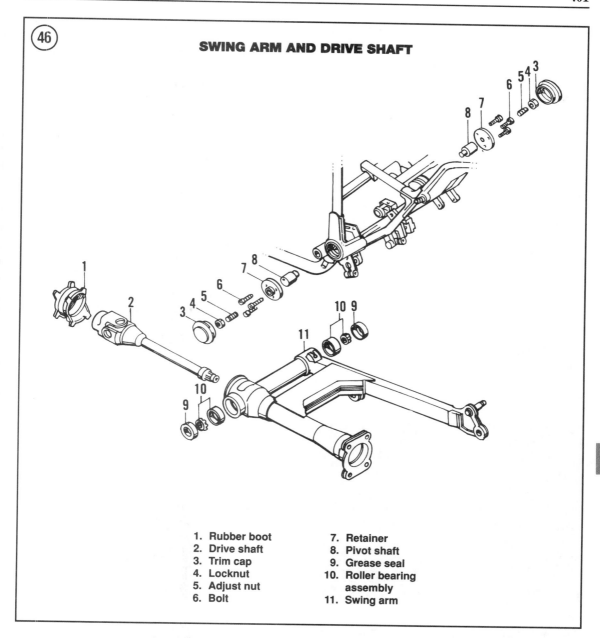

SWING ARM AND DRIVE SHAFT

1. Rubber boot
2. Drive shaft
3. Trim cap
4. Locknut
5. Adjust nut
6. Bolt
7. Retainer
8. Pivot shaft
9. Grease seal
10. Roller bearing assembly
11. Swing arm

11

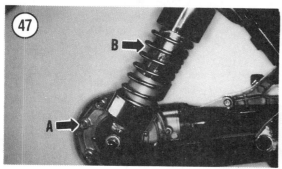

6. Loosen the pivot shaft adjust bolt 17 mm locknut (A, **Figure 49**) and back out the 6 mm Allen adjust bolt (B, **Figure 49**). It is not necessary to remove these items, just loosen them.

7. Remove the bolts (C, **Figure 49**) securing the pivot shaft retainer (D, **Figure 49**) and remove the retainer. Repeat for the other side of the swing arm.

8. Screw a 5 mm bolt (A, **Figure 50**) into the pivot shaft (B, **Figure 50**).

9. Pull the pivot shaft partially out of the swing arm needle bearing. Leave this pivot shaft in place until the pivot shaft on the other side is loosened.

10. Screw a 5 mm bolt into the other pivot shaft.

11. Pull this pivot shaft completely out of the swing arm needle bearing.

12. Place a box under the swing arm or hold onto the swing arm and remove the pivot shaft loosened in Step 8.

13. Carefully pull the rubber boot from the front bevel gear unit, but leave it on the swing arm.

14. Pull back on the swing arm, free it from the frame pivot area, then remove it from the frame.

15. Withdraw the drive shaft and remove the rubber boot from the swing arm.

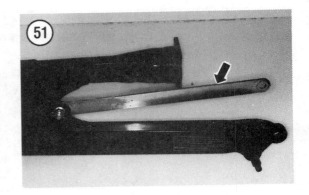

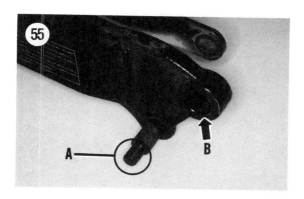

16. Inspect the swing arm and bearings as described in this chapter.

Inspection

1. If necessary, remove the rear brake panel torque link (**Figure 51**).

2. Check the welded sections on the swing arm for cracks or fractures. Refer to **Figure 52** and **Figure 53**.

3. Inspect the final drive unit mounting bolt holes (**Figure 54**) in the swing arm. If the holes are elongated or worn, replace the swing arm.

4. Inspect the right-hand shock absorber lower mounting threaded stud (A, **Figure 55**) on the swing arm. If the threads are damaged, clean them with an appropriate size metric die.

5. Inspect the rear axle mounting boss for wear or damage (B, **Figure 55**).

6. Turn the bearing inner race (**Figure 56**) of each pivot bearing by hand. Make sure the bearings turn smoothly.

7. Replace the bearings if necessary; always replace as a complete set. When replacing the bearings, be sure to take your old bearings along to ensure a perfect matchup.

8. Inspect the pivot shafts (**Figure 57**) for wear or damage, replace if necessary.

9. Inspect the pivot shaft adjust bolt locknut (A, **Figure 58**) and pivot shaft adjust bolt (B, **Figure 58**) in the retainer for wear or damage. Both must rotate freely on each other, replace as a set if either is faulty.

10. Inspect the mounting holes (**Figure 59**) in the retainer. If any of the holes are elongated, replace the retainer.

11

11. Inspect the pivot shaft receptacle (**Figure 60**) on both sides of the frame for rust or corrosion. Clean out if necessary, then apply molybdenum disulfide grease to the surface.

12. Inspect the rubber boot for cracks, damage or deterioration, replace if necessary.

Installation

1. Apply molybdenum disulfide grease to the bearings, the grease seals, the pivot shafts and to the frame pivot shaft receptacle.

2. Apply molybdenum disulfide grease to the splines on the front bevel gear unit (**Figure 61**).

3. Install the drive shaft into the swing arm (**Figure 62**) and install the rubber boot (**Figure 63**).

4. Position the swing arm into the mounting area of the frame. Align the holes in the swing arm with the holes in the frame (**Figure 64**).

5. The universal joint at the front of the drive shaft will usually pivot down during swing arm installation and will not align with the splines on the front bevel gear. Insert a long screwdriver (**Figure 65**), or metal rod, into the swing arm and move the front portion of the universal joint up to align with the front bevel gear unit splines. If necessary, rotate the drive shaft slightly until alignment is correct, then push the drive shaft all the way on until it bottoms.

6. Install the 5 mm bolt into the pivot shaft (**Figure 66**).

7. Install one of the pivot shafts (B, **Figure 50**) through the frame and into the swing arm bearing. Push the pivot shaft all the way in.

8. Install the other pivot shaft through the frame and into the swing arm bearing. Push the pivot shaft all the way in.

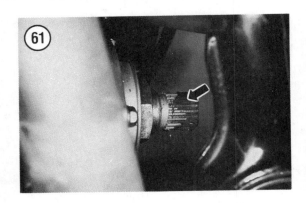

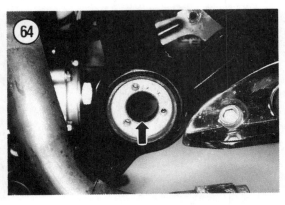

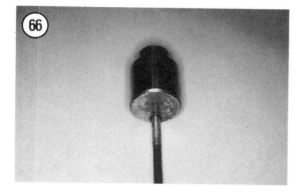

9. Back out both pivot shaft adjust bolts until they are flush with the inner surface of their retainer (**Figure 67**). This is necessary for clearance adjustment later in this procedure.

10. Install the pivot shaft retainer (D, **Figure 49**) on each side. Tighten the retainer mounting bolts securely (C, **Figure 49**).

11. Pull the rubber boot up into position on the front bevel gear unit (**Figure 68**). The boot must be installed correctly to keep dirt and moisture from the universal joint.

12. Refer to **Figure 69** and adjust the swing arm-to-frame clearance as follows:

NOTE
*A handy tool to use in the next step is a valve adjustment shim (**Figure 70**).*

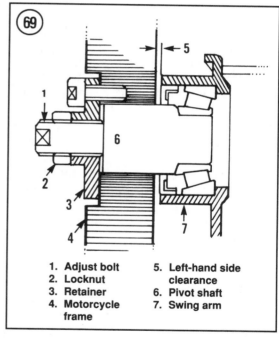

1. Adjust bolt
2. Locknut
3. Retainer
4. Motorcycle frame
5. Left-hand side clearance
6. Pivot shaft
7. Swing arm

These shims are not used on the Vulcan engine but they are available in various thickness from most motorcycle dealers.

a. Use needlenose pliers (**Figure 71**) and insert a 2.5 mm (0.10 in.) shim or spacer between the frame gusset and the left-hand pivot point of the swing arm (**Figure 72**).

b. Use a 6 mm Allen wrench (**Figure 73**) and screw in the right-hand retainer adjust bolt until the left-hand side of the swing arm moves up against the shim. Do not overtighten as you must be able to remove the shim.

c. Hold onto the 6 mm adjust bolt with the Allen wrench (A, **Figure 74**) so it will not rotate, then tighten the 17 mm locknut (B, **Figure 74**) on the right-hand retainer adjust bolt to the torque specification listed in **Table 1**.

d. Remove the shim from the left-hand side.

e. Screw in the left-hand retainer adjust bolt until it stops against the pivot shaft then stop.

f. Hold onto the 6 mm adjust bolt with an Allen wrench so it will not rotate, then tighten the 17 mm locknut on the left-hand retainer adjust bolt to the torque specification listed in **Table 1**.

13. Move the swing arm up and down several times to make sure all components are properly seated.

14. Install the pivot point trim cap (**Figure 75**) onto each side. Make sure they are seated completely.

15. Install the final drive unit, drive shaft and shock absorber as described in this chapter.

16. Install the rear wheel as described in this chapter.

Bearing Replacement

The roller bearing outer races are installed in each side of the swing arm pivot points. Whenever a bearing outer race is removed from the frame it must be discarded. Never reinstall a bearing outer race that has been removed.

The bearing must be removed with special tools that are available from a Kawasaki dealer. The special tools are as follows.

a. Bearing remover: part No. 57001-1058.

b. Adapter: part No. 57001-1061.

c. Bearing driver set: part No. 57001-1129.

1. Remove the swing arm as described in this chapter.

2. Remove the grease seal (A, **Figure 76**) from each side of the swing arm.

3. Remove the roller bearing (B, **Figure 76**) from each side of the swing arm.

CAUTION
Do not try to remove the bearing outer races without the use of these special tools as the bearing mounting receptacle in the swing arm may be damaged. If damaged, the new roller bearings will

not be properly aligned and the swing arm will not pivot correctly.

4. Insert the bearing outer race adapter into the swing arm and attach it to the backside of the bearing race. Attach the remover (similar to a body shop slide hammer) to the bearing remover.

5. Use the slide hammer and withdraw the bearing outer race slowly from the swing arm receptacle.

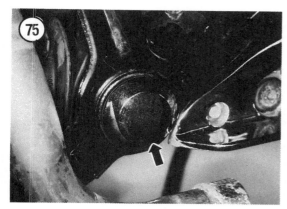

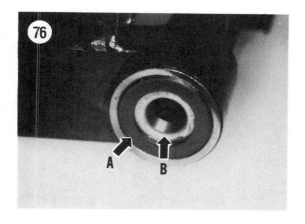

Remove the special tools and discard the bearing outer race.

6. Repeat Step 4 and Step 5 for the other bearing outer race. Discard this needle bearing also.

7. Thoroughly clean out the inside of the swing arm pivot area with solvent and dry with compressed air.

8. Apply a light coat of molybdenum disulfide grease to all parts before installation.

CAUTION
Never reinstall a bearing outer race that has been removed. During removal it becomes slightly damaged and is no longer true to alignment and will create an unsafe riding condition.

NOTE
Either the right- or left-hand bearing outer race can be installed first.

9. Place the bearing outer race over the bearing receptacle in the swing arm.

10. Place the suitable size bearing driver (from bearing driver set: part No. 57001-1129) into the race and press or drive the bearing outer race into place slowly and squarely. Remove the bearing driver.

11. Apply a light coat of molybdenum disulfide grease to the bearing surface of the inner race.

12. Thoroughly pack the new roller bearing with molybdenum disulfide grease. Work the grease into all of the rollers and their cavities. Rotate the bearing within the inner race several times to make sure the bearing is completely packed with grease.

13. Apply molybdenum disulfide grease to the new grease seal and install the grease seal. Press the grease seal in until it stops.

14. Repeat Steps 9-13 for the bearing on the other side of the swing arm.

15. Install the swing arm as described in this chapter.

11

SHOCK ABSORBERS

The shock absorbers are spring controlled and hydraulically dampened. The shocks can be adjusted by changing the air pressure and damping force to suit various riding and load requirements.

The shocks are sealed and cannot be disassembled or rebuilt. Service is limited to refilling the internal oil supply in each damping unit.

Refer to **Figure 77** for these procedures.

Removal/Installation

Removal and installation of the rear shocks is easier if done separately. The remaining unit will support the rear of the bike and maintain the correct relationship between the top and bottom shock mounts.

1. Place the bike on the centerstand on level ground.

NOTE
Seat removal is only a precaution to avoid damage to the seat should a tool slip while removing the upper nut.

2. Remove the seat as described in Chapter Thirteen.

3. Remove the air valve cap (**Figure 78**) and depress the valve stem core (**Figure 79**) to bleed off all air pressure. Reinstall the cap to avoid misplacing it.

4. Adjust both shocks to their softest rebound setting, completely *counterclockwise*.

NOTE
This procedure is shown with the rear wheel removed for clarity. It is not nec-

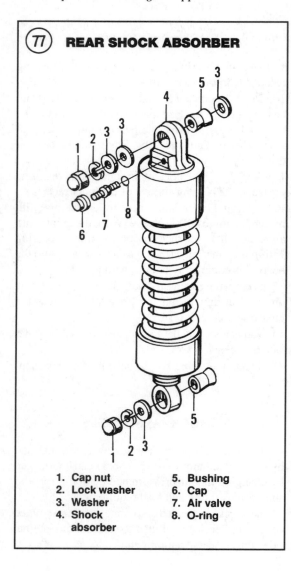

REAR SHOCK ABSORBER

1. Cap nut
2. Lock washer
3. Washer
4. Shock absorber
5. Bushing
6. Cap
7. Air valve
8. O-ring

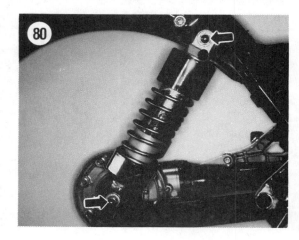

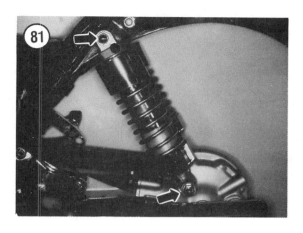

essary to remove the wheel for this procedure.

5. On the right-hand side, remove the upper and lower nuts, lockwashers and washers (**Figure 80**) securing the shock absorber to the frame and to the swing arm.

6. On the left-hand side, remove the upper and lower nuts and washers (**Figure 81**) securing the shock absorber to the frame and to the final drive unit.

7. Pull the unit straight off the upper and lower mounts to remove it.

8. Install by reversing these removal steps. Tighten the upper and lower mounting nuts to the torque specification listed in **Table 1**.

Preliminary Inspection

1. Check the damper unit (A, **Figure 82**) for leakage.

> *NOTE*
> *The damper unit cannot be rebuilt; it*
> *must be replaced as a unit.*

2. Inspect the rubber bushings in the upper (**Figure 83**) and lower (**Figure 84**) joints for wear or deterioration. Replace if necessary.

3. Inspect the spring (B. **Figure 82**) for wear, damage or sagging. If damaged, replace the shock absorber as the spring cannot be replaced.

4. Remove the cap (**Figure 85**) and inspect the air valve assembly for damage. Make sure it is tight. Replace if damaged.

11

Damping Oil Refilling

1. Remove the shock absorber from the bike as described in this chapter.

2. Remove the cap (**Figure 85**) and completely unscrew the air valve assembly and O-ring seal.

3. Insert a small funnel into the air valve opening in the shock and hold the shock vertical.

4. Use SAE 5W oil and fill the shock absorber to the top of the damper unit (A, **Figure 86**). Remove the funnel.

5. Drain the oil from the damper unit into a graduated beaker (B, **Figure 86**).

6. Observe the amount of oil in the beaker. Stop draining the oil when the oil in the beaker is equal to the **air volume** (not oil volume) in the damper unit (C, **Figure 86**). Refer to **Table 2** for **air volume** capacity.

7. The shock absorber damper unit should have the specified amount of air and oil (D, **Figure 86**).

8. Inspect the O-ring seal on the air valve assembly and replace if necessary.

9. Install the air valve assembly and new O-ring seal. Tighten the air valve assembly securely.

10. Install the shock absorber onto the bike as described in this chapter.

Damping Adjustment

The damping can be adjusted to any of 4 settings. The softest setting is No. 1 and the stiffest setting is No. 4. The standard factory setting is No. 2 and the setting should be adjusted to personal preference to accommodate rider weight and riding conditions.

> *WARNING*
> *Both shock absorbers must be adjusted to the same setting. If they are set to different settings, it will result in an unsafe riding conditions that could lead to an accident.*

Rotate the damping adjuster (A, **Figure 87**) to the desired position from No. 1 (softest) to No. 4 (hardest). Align the number with the index mark on the upper mount.

Air Pressure Adjustment

The air pressure can be adjusted from atmospheric pressure to the maximum pressure listed in **Table 2**.

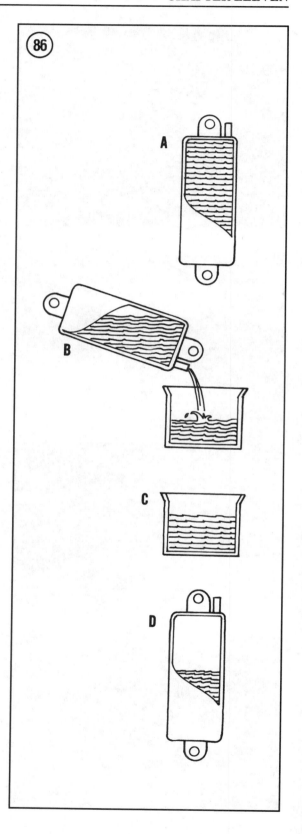

Atmospheric pressure is suggested for an average rider weight (150 lbs [68 kg]) with no passenger and no accessories or luggage. If the rider is heavier, carries a passenger and/or added accessories or luggage the air pressure should be increased to accommodate this additional weight.

The standard factory pressure is atmospheric pressure and the pressure should be adjusted to personal preference to accommodate rider weight and riding conditions.

NOTE
The air pressure in the shock must be checked when the shock is cold (room temperature), prior to the first ride of the day and with the bike setting in a cool place (not in the hot sun).

1. Place the bike on the centerstand, on level ground and with the rear wheel off the ground.
2. Remove the air valve cap (B, **Figure 87**).

NOTE
Do not use a tire gauge as there will be an air loss when the gauge is attached and removed from the valve stem.

3. Check the air pressure with a small capacity air pressure gauge designed for use on air pressurized shock absorbers and front forks.

NOTE
The air pressure in both shock absorbers should be as close as possible to provide safe handling.

4. To lower air pressure, push in on the valve stem core and release the desired amount of air.

CAUTION
*Add air pressure gradually to **avoid exceeding** the maximum air pressure of 500 kPa (71 psi). Exceeding this air pressure will damage internal seals and cause an oil leak.*

5. To increase air pressure, use a hand held air pump and add the desired air pressure.
6. After the desired air pressure is obtained, install the air valve cap and tighten securely.

11

Table 1 REAR SUSPENSION TIGHTENING TORQUES

Item	N·m	ft.-lb.
Rear axle nut	110	80
Brake torque rod bolt and nut	29	22
Shock absorber mounting nuts		
Upper and lower	35	26
Swing arm		
Retainer adjust bolt locknut	13	9.6
Final drive unit		
Mounting nuts	24	17.5
Bearing case flange bolts	34	25

Table 2 REAR SUSPENSION SPECIFICATIONS

Item	Wear limit
Rear wheel rim runout	
Radial	0.8 mm (0.031 in.)
Axial	0.5 mm (0.019 in.)
Shock absorber damping oil	
Viscosity	SAE 5W motor oil
Capacity per unit	
U.S. and Canada	136.5-141.5 ml
	(4.61-4.78 U.S. oz., 3.84-3.98 Imp. oz.)
U.K.	139.5-144.5 ml
	(4.72-4.89 U.S. oz., 3.93-4.07 Imp. oz.)
Air chamber capacity	
U.S. and Canada	91 ml (3.07 U.S. oz., 2.58 Imp. oz.)
U.K.	88 ml (2.97 U.S. oz., 2.50 Imp. oz.)
Shock absorber air pressure	
Standard	atmospheric pressure
Usable range	0-294 kPa (0-43 psi)
Maximum	500 kPa (71 psi)

CHAPTER TWELVE

BRAKES

The brake system on all models consists of a dual disc on the front wheel and a drum brake on the rear. This chapter describes repair and replacement procedures for all brake components.

Table 1 contains the brake system torque specifications and **Table 2** contains brake system specifications. **Table 1** and **Table 2** are located at the end of this chapter.

FRONT DISC BRAKES

The front disc brakes are actuated by hydraulic fluid and are controlled by a hand lever that is attached to the front master cylinder. As the brake pads wear, the brake fluid level drops in the reservoir and automatically adjusts for wear.

When working on hydraulic brake systems, it is necessary that the work area and all tools be absolutely clean. Any tiny particles of foreign matter and grit in the caliper assembly or the master cylinder can damage the components. Also, sharp tools must not be used inside the caliper or on the piston. If there is any doubt about your ability to correctly and safely carry out major service on the brake components, take the job to a Kawasaki dealer or brake specialist.

> *NOTE*
> *If you recycle your old engine oil, **never** add used brake fluid to the old engine oil. Recyclers may not accept the oil if other fluids (fork oil, brake fluid or any other type of petroleum based fluids) have been combined with it.*

Consider the following when servicing the disc brake system.

1. Disc brake components rarely require disassembly, so do not disassemble them unless necessary.

> *WARNING*
> *Do not intermix silicone based (DOT 5) brake fluid as it can cause brake component damage leading to brake system failure.*

12

2. Use only DOT 3 or DOT 4 brake fluid from a sealed container.

3. Do not allow disc brake fluid to contact any plastic, painted or plated surfaces or surface damage will occur.

4. Always keep the master cylinder reservoir and spare cans of brake fluid closed to prevent dust or moisture from entering. If moisture enters the brake fluid it would result in brake fluid contamination and brake problems.

5. Use only DOT 3 or DOT 4 disc brake fluid to wash parts. Never clean any internal brake components with solvent or any other petroleum base cleaners.

6. Whenever *any* component has been removed from the brake system the system is considered "opened" and must be bled to remove air bubbles. Also, if the brake feels "spongy," this usually means there are air bubbles in the system and it must be bled. For safe brake operation, refer to *Bleeding the System* in this chapter.

CAUTION
Do not use solvents of any kind on the brake systems' internal components.

Solvents will cause the seals to swell and distort. When disassembling and cleaning brake components (except brake pads) use new DOT 3 or DOT 4 brake fluid.

WARNING
*When working on the brake system, do **not** inhale brake dust. It may contain asbestos, which can cause lung injury and cancer. Wear a face mask that meets OSHA requirements for trapping asbes-*

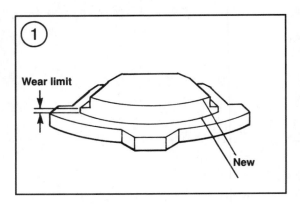

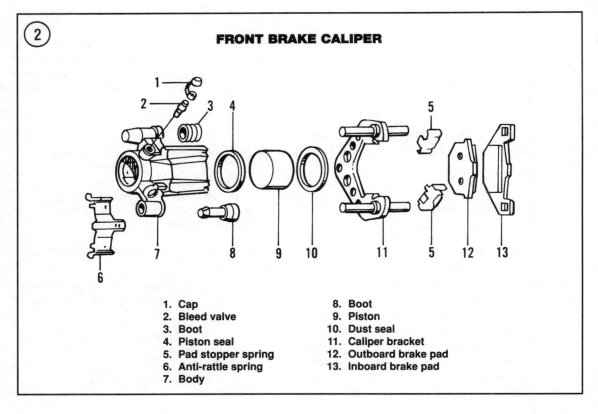

FRONT BRAKE CALIPER

1. Cap
2. Bleed valve
3. Boot
4. Piston seal
5. Pad stopper spring
6. Anti-rattle spring
7. Body
8. Boot
9. Piston
10. Dust seal
11. Caliper bracket
12. Outboard brake pad
13. Inboard brake pad

tos particles, and wash your hands and forearms thoroughly after completing the work.

FRONT BRAKE PAD REPLACEMENT

There is no recommended mileage interval for changing the friction pads in the disc brakes. Pad wear depends greatly on riding habits and conditions. The pads should be checked for wear every 6 months and replaced when the wear indicator (**Figure 1**) reaches the edge of the brake disc. To maintain an even brake pressure on the disc always replace both pads in both calipers at the same time.

Disconnecting the hydraulic brake hose from the brake caliper is not necessary for brake pad replacement. Disconnect the hose only if the caliper assembly is going to be removed and serviced.

CAUTION
Check the pads more frequently when the wear line approaches the disc. On some pads the wear line is very close to the metal backing plate. If pad wear happens to be uneven for some reason,

the backing plate may come in contact with the disc and cause damage.

Front Brake Pad Replacement

Refer to **Figure 2** for this procedure.
1. Place the bike on the centerstand on level ground.
2. Remove the caliper mounting bolts (**Figure 3**) and remove the caliper from the disc.
3. Remove both brake pads from the caliper assembly.
4. Check the brake pad friction surface (**Figure 4**) for oil contamination or fraying. Check the pad plates for cracks or other damage. If the brake pads appear okay, measure the friction thickness with a vernier caliper (**Figure 5**). Replace the pads as a set if the friction thickness is worn to the wear limit listed in **Table 2** or less.

WARNING
The brake pads must be replaced as a set. When servicing the front brakes, both the left- and right-hand brake caliper pads must be replaced at the same time to maintain brake effectiveness.

5. Clean the pad recess and the end of the piston with a soft brush. Do not use solvent, a wire brush or any hard tool which would damage the cylinders or pistons.
6. Carefully remove any rust or corrosion from the disc.
7. Lightly coat the end of the piston and the backs of the new pads *not* the friction material with disc brake lubricant.

NOTE
When purchasing new pads, check with your dealer to make sure the friction compound of the new pad is compatible

12

with the disc material. Remove any roughness from the backs of the new pads with a fine-cut file; blow them clean with compressed air.

NOTE
*There are 2 different types of master cylinders used among the different models. The master cylinder shown in **Figure 6** is used on 1985-1990 models. Service procedures for 1991 and later models is identical except that the top cover is round instead of rectangular.*

8. When new pads are installed in the caliper, the master cylinder brake fluid level will rise as the caliper piston is repositioned. Perform the following:

    a. Clean the top of the master cylinder of all dirt and foreign matter.

    b. Remove the screws (A, **Figure 6**) securing the cover (B, **Figure 6**). Remove the cover and the diaphragm from the master cylinder.

    c. Slowly push the caliper piston into the caliper. Constantly check the reservoir to make sure brake fluid does not overflow. Remove brake fluid, if necessary, before it overflows.

    d. The piston should move freely. If it doesn't and there is evidence of it sticking in the cylinder, the caliper should be removed and serviced as described in this chapter.

9. Push the caliper piston in all the way to allow room for the new pads.

10. Make sure the anti-rattle spring (A, **Figure 7**) is still in place in the caliper.

11. Install the outboard pad into the caliper. Push it all the way down until it stops (B, **Figure 7**).

12. Push the posts on the caliper carrier (**Figure 8**) onto the piston portion of the caliper to allow room for installation of the inboard pad.

13. Install the inboard pad (A, **Figure 9**) into the caliper and align the holes in the pad with the caliper carrier posts (B, **Figure 9**).

14. Push the pad all the way down until it stops (A, **Figure 10**), release the caliper carrier and make sure the posts engage the holes in the inboard pad (B, **Figure 10**).

15. Hold the brake pads in position and install the caliper onto the brake disc, being careful not to damage the leading edge of the new pads on the disc.

16. Install the caliper mounting bolts (**Figure 3**) and tighten to the torque specification listed in **Table 2**.

17. Repeat Steps 2-7 and Steps 10-16 for the brake pads in the other caliper assembly.

18. Tie the back of the bike down or have an assistant sit on the pillion seat to raise the front wheel off the ground.

19. Spin the front wheel and activate the front brake lever as many times as it takes to refill the cylinders in the caliper and correctly locate the brake pads.

WARNING
Use brake fluid clearly marked DOT 3 or DOT 4 from a sealed container. Other types may vaporize and cause brake failure. Always use the same brand name, because some brands are not compatible. Do not intermix silicone based (DOT 5) brake fluid as it can cause brake component damage leading to brake system failure.

20. Refill the master cylinder reservoir, if necessary, to maintain the correct fluid level as seen through the viewing port (**Figure 11**) on the side. Install the diaphragm (**Figure 12**) and cover (**Figure 13**). Tighten the screws securely.

WARNING
Do not ride the motorcycle until you are sure the brakes are operating correctly with full hydraulic advantage. If necessary, bleed the brake as described under ***Bleeding the System*** *in this chapter.*

21. Bed the pads in gradually for the first 10 days of riding by using only light pressure as much as possible. Immediate hard application will glaze the new friction pads and greatly reduce the effectiveness of the brake.

FRONT BRAKE CALIPER

Removal

Refer to **Figure 2** for this procedure.

It is not necessary to remove the front wheel in order to remove the caliper assembly.

CAUTION
Do not spill any brake fluid on the front fork or front wheel. Wash off any spilled brake fluid immediately, as it will destroy the finish. Use soapy water and rinse completely.

12

1. Clean the top of the master cylinder of all dirt and foreign matter.

NOTE
There are 2 different types of master cylinders that have been used. The master cylinder shown in Figure 6 is used on 1985-1990 models. Service procedures for 1991 and later models are identical except that the top cover and body are round instead of rectangular.

2. Loosen the screws (A, **Figure 6**) securing the master cylinder cover (B, **Figure 6**). Slightly loosen the cover and the diaphragm. This will allow air to enter the reservoir and allow the brake fluid to drain out more quickly in the next step.

NOTE
By performing Step 3, compressed air may not be necessary for piston removal during caliper disassembly.

3. If the caliper assembly is going to be disassembled for service, perform the following:
   a. Remove the brake pads as described in this chapter.
   b. Slowly apply the brake lever to push the piston part way out of the caliper assembly for ease of removal during caliper service.
4. Place a small drain under the caliper to catch the expelled brake fluid.
5. Loosen the union bolt (A, **Figure 14**) securing the brake hose to the caliper assembly.
6. Remove the union bolt, brake hose (B, **Figure 14**) and sealing washer from the brake hose adaptor nut, then let the brake fluid drain from the brake hose into the container. Dispose of this brake fluid— never reuse brake fluid.
7. If Step 3 was not performed, loosen, then remove the bolts (**Figure 3**) securing the brake caliper assembly to the front fork.
8. Remove the caliper assembly from the brake disc.
9. Place the loose end of the brake hose in a reclosable plastic bag to prevent brake fluid from dribbling out.

Installation

1. If removed, install the brake pads into the caliper as described in this chapter.

2. Carefully install the caliper assembly onto the disc being careful not to damage the leading edge of the brake pads.
3. Install the bolts (**Figure 3**) securing the brake caliper assembly to the front fork and tighten to the torque specifications listed in **Table 1**.
4. Install the brake hose (A, **Figure 15**), with a *new* sealing washer on each side of the fitting, onto the caliper.
5. Install the union bolt through the sealing washers (B, **Figure 15**) and fitting. Correctly position the brake hose onto the caliper and tighten the union bolt securely.
6. Remove the master cylinder top cover and diaphragm.

WARNING
Use brake fluid clearly marked DOT 3 or DOT 4 from a sealed container. Other types may vaporize and cause brake failure. Always use the same brand name, because some brands are

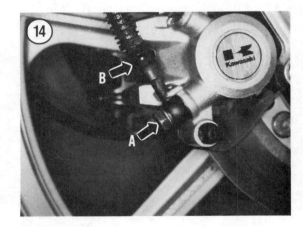

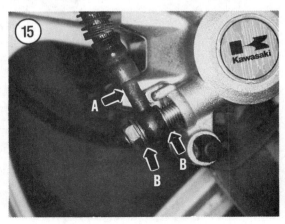

not compatible. Do not intermix silicone-based (DOT 5) brake fluid as it can cause brake component damage leading to brake system failure.

7. Tie the back of the bike down or have an assistant sit on the seat to raise the front wheel off the ground.

8. Refill the master cylinder reservoir. Install the diaphragm and cover. Do not tighten the screws at this time.

9. Bleed the brake as described under *Bleeding the System* in this chapter.

WARNING
Do not ride the motorcycle until you are sure that the brakes are operating properly.

Front Caliper Rebuilding

Refer to **Figure 2** for this procedure.

1. Remove the caliper and brake pads as described in this chapter.

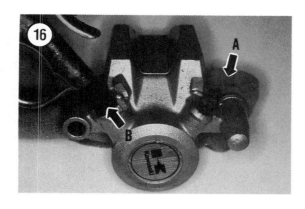

2. Separate the caliper bracket from the caliper body.

NOTE
If the piston was partially forced out of the caliper body during removal, Steps 3-5 may not be necessary. If the piston or caliper bore is corroded or very dirty, additional compressed air may be necessary to remove the piston completely.

3. Place a shop cloth (A, **Figure 16**) or piece of soft wood over the end of the piston.

4. Perform this step over and close to a workbench top. Hold the caliper body with the piston facing away from you.

WARNING
*In the next step, the piston may shoot out of the caliper body like a bullet. Keep your fingers out of the way. Wear shop gloves and apply air pressure gradually. Do **not** use high pressure air or place the air hose nozzle directly against the hydraulic line fitting inlet in the caliper body. Hold the air nozzle away from the inlet allowing some of the air to escape.*

5. Apply the air pressure in short spurts to the hydraulic fluid passageway or brake hose inlet (B, **Figure 16**) and force the piston out. Use a service station air hose if you don't have an air compressor.

CAUTION
In the following step, do not use a sharp tool to remove the dust and piston seals from the caliper cylinders. Do not damage the cylinder surface.

6. Use a piece of plastic or wood and carefully push the piston and dust seals (**Figure 17**) in toward the caliper cylinder and out of their grooves.

7. Inspect the caliper as described in this chapter.

NOTE
Never reuse the old dust seals or piston seals. Very minor damage or age deterioration can make the seals useless.

8. Coat the new dust seals and piston seals with fresh DOT 3 or DOT 4 brake fluid.

9. Carefully install the new piston seal (**Figure 18**) and then the dust seal (**Figure 19**) in the grooves in the caliper cylinder. Make sure the seals are properly seated in their respective grooves (**Figure 17**).

10. Coat the piston, seals and caliper cylinder with fresh DOT 3 or DOT 4 brake fluid. This will make piston installation easier.

11. Position the piston with the machined side (**Figure 20**) going in first and install the piston into the caliper cylinder (**Figure 21**). Push the piston in until it bottoms.

12. Make sure the rubber boots (A, **Figure 22**) are installed on the caliper bracket.

13. Apply a thin coat of silicone grease to the caliper bracket posts (B, **Figure 22**).

14. Install the caliper bracket (A, **Figure 23**) onto the caliper body (B, **Figure 23**). Push the bracket on until it bottoms.

15. If removed, install the anti-rattle spring (**Figure 24**) in the caliper.

16. Install the brake pads and caliper as described in this chapter.

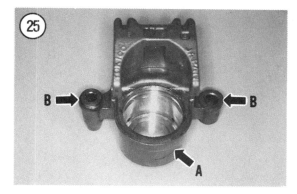

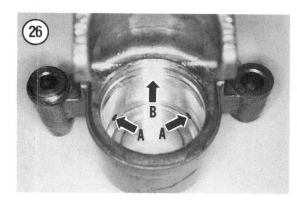

Front Caliper Inspection

1. Inspect the piston and dust seal grooves in the caliper body for damage. If damaged or corroded, replace the caliper assembly.

2. Inspect the caliper body (A, **Figure 25**) for cracks or damage. Check mounting bolt holes (B, **Figure 25**). If worn or damaged, replace the caliper assembly.

3. Inspect the hydraulic fluid passageways (A, **Figure 26**) in the base of the piston bore. Make sure it is clean and open. Apply compressed air to the opening and make sure it is clear. Clean out if necessary with fresh brake fluid.

NOTE
Kawasaki does not provide new or service limit dimensions for the piston O.D. or the cylinder I.D.

4. Inspect the cylinder wall (B, **Figure 26**) and the piston (**Figure 27**) for scratches, scoring or other damage. If either is rusty or corroded, replace either the piston or the caliper assembly.

5. Remove the bleed screw (**Figure 28**).

6. Inspect the threaded holes in the body for the bleed screw (A, **Figure 29**) and for the hydraulic line

12

(B, **Figure 29**) for wear or damage. Clean out with an appropriate size metric tap and flush with solvent.

7. Inspect the bleed screw. Make sure the hole (**Figure 30**) is clean and open. Apply compressed air to the opening and make sure it is clear. Clean out if necessary with fresh brake fluid.

8. Inspect the anti-rattle spring (**Figure 31**) for wear or damage, replace if necessary.

9. If serviceable, clean the caliper body and piston with fresh hydraulic brake fluid, isopropyl alcohol or ethyl alcohol and rinse with fresh hydraulic brake fluid.

10. Inspect the caliper bracket (**Figure 32**) for fractures or damage, replace if necessary.

11. Inspect the caliper bracket posts (**Figure 33**) for burrs, wear or damage. Clean off any burrs or replace the bracket if necessary.

12. Make sure the pad stopper springs (**Figure 34**) are in good condition and stay in place on the caliper bracket. If they are loose, replace the springs.

13. Inspect the rubber boots (**Figure 35**) for wear, deterioration or tears, replace as a pair if either is damaged.

FRONT MASTER CYLINDER

Removal/Installation

> *NOTE*
> *There are 2 different types of master cylinders that have been used among the different models. The master cylinder shown in this procedure is used on 1985-1990 models. Service procedures for 1991 and later models are identical*

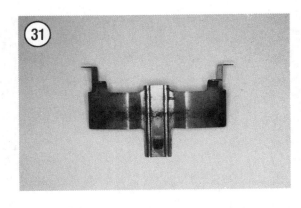

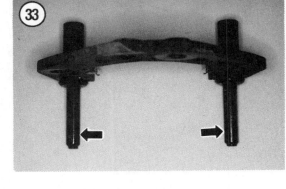
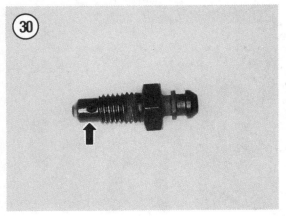

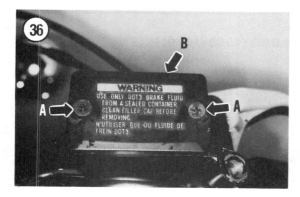

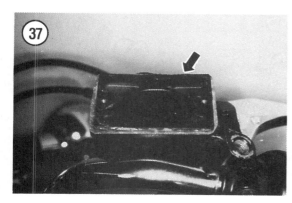

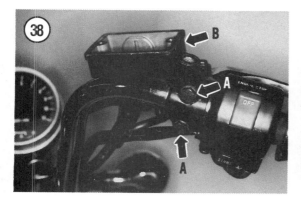

except that the top cover and body are round instead of rectangular.

CAUTION
Cover the surrounding areas with a heavy cloth or plastic tarp to protect them from accidental brake fluid spills. Wash brake fluid from any painted or plated surfaces or plastic parts immediately, as it will destroy the finish. Use soapy water and rinse completely.

1. Clean the top of the master cylinder of all dirt and foreign matter.

2. Unscrew the rear view mirror from the master cylinder.

3. Remove the screws (A, **Figure 36**) securing the cover (B, **Figure 36**). Remove the cover and the diaphragm (**Figure 37**).

WARNING
*If a cooking baster is used for this purpose, do **not** reuse it for cooking purposes due to brake fluid residue within it.*

4. If you have a shop syringe or a cooking baster, draw all of the brake fluid out of the master cylinder reservoir.

5. Loosen the master cylinder clamping bolts (A, **Figure 38**).

6. Disconnect the brake light switch electrical connector (A, **Figure 39**) from the brake switch.

7. Slide the rubber boot (B, **Figure 39**) off the union bolt.

8. Place a shop cloth under the union bolt to catch any spilled brake fluid that will leak out.

9. Unscrew the union bolt (C, **Figure 39**) securing the brake hose to the master cylinder. Don't lose the sealing washer from each side of the hose fitting. Tie the loose end of the hose up to the handlebar and cover the end to prevent the entry of moisture and

12

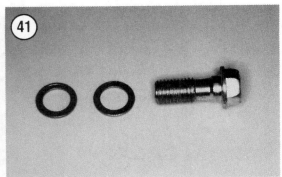

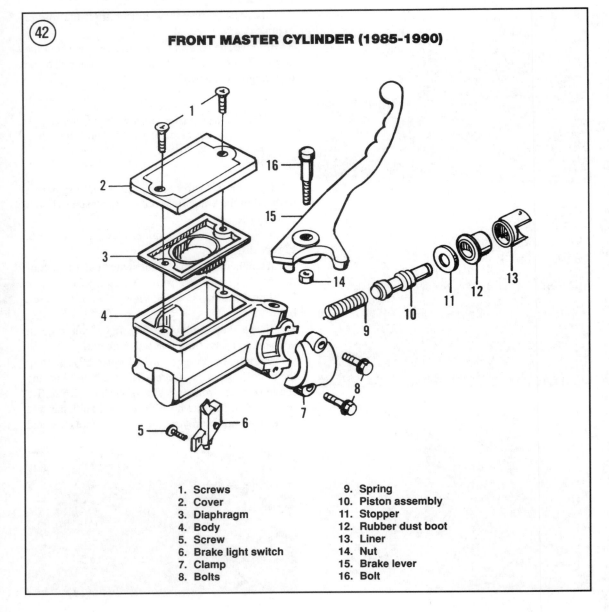

FRONT MASTER CYLINDER (1985-1990)

1. Screws	9. Spring
2. Cover	10. Piston assembly
3. Diaphragm	11. Stopper
4. Body	12. Rubber dust boot
5. Screw	13. Liner
6. Brake light switch	14. Nut
7. Clamp	15. Brake lever
8. Bolts	16. Bolt

foreign matter. Cover the loose end with a re-closable plastic bag (**Figure 40**).

10. Remove the clamping bolts and clamp that secures the master cylinder to the handlebar, then remove the master cylinder (B, **Figure 38**) from the handlebar.

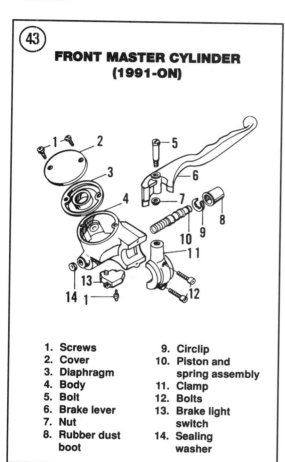

FRONT MASTER CYLINDER (1991-ON)

1. Screws
2. Cover
3. Diaphragm
4. Body
5. Bolt
6. Brake lever
7. Nut
8. Rubber dust boot
9. Circlip
10. Piston and spring assembly
11. Clamp
12. Bolts
13. Brake light switch
14. Sealing washer

11. Install by reversing these removal steps while noting the following:

a. Position the clamp with the small projection facing toward the throttle grip.

b. Install the master cylinder, clamp and bolts. Tighten the upper bolt first, then the lower bolt. Tighten the bolts securely.

c. Place a sealing washer on each side of the brake hose fitting (**Figure 41**) and install the union bolt.

d. Tighten the union bolt to the torque specification listed in **Table 1**.

e. Bleed the front brakes as described under *Bleeding the System* in this chapter.

Disassembly

Refer to the following illustrations for this procedure:

a. **Figure 42**: 1985-1990 models.
b. **Figure 43**: 1991-on models.

NOTE
There are 2 different types of master cylinders that have been used. The master cylinder shown in this procedure is used on 1985-1990 models. Service procedures for 1991 and later models are identical except that the top cover and body are round instead of rectangular.

1. Remove the master cylinder as described in this chapter.

2. If still in place, remove the top cover (**Figure 44**) and diaphragm (**Figure 45**) from the master cylinder.

12

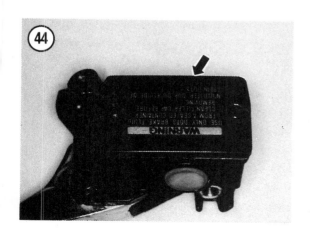

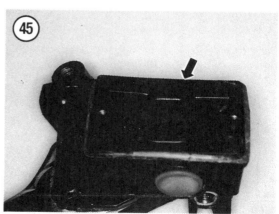

3. Remove the bolt and nut securing the hand lever and remove the lever (**Figure 46**).

4A. On 1985-1990 models, perform the following:

  a. Use a thin-bladed screwdriver to release the liner tabs from the holes in the master cylinder body, then remove the liner (**Figure 47**).

  b. Remove the rubber dust boot (**Figure 48**) from the area where the hand lever actuates the piston assembly.

  c. Remove the stopper (**Figure 49**) from the end of the piston assembly.

4B. On 1991-on models, perform the following:

  a. Remove the rubber dust boot from the area where the hand lever actuates the piston assembly.

  b. Use circlip pliers, remove the internal circlip from the body.

5. Remove the piston assembly and the spring (**Figure 50**).

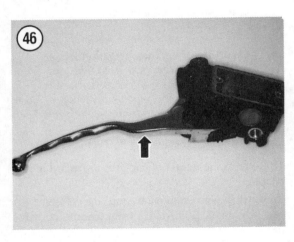

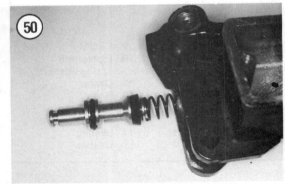

6. If necessary, remove the screw securing the brake light switch to the master cylinder and remove the switch assembly (**Figure 51**).

Inspection

NOTE
Kawasaki does not provide new or service limit dimensions for the body cylinder bore I.D. or the piston assembly O.D.

1. Clean all parts in fresh hydraulic brake fluid, isopropyl alcohol or ethyl alcohol.

2. Inspect the body cylinder bore (**Figure 52**) surface for signs of wear and damage. If less than perfect, replace the master cylinder assembly. The body cannot be replaced separately.

3. Make sure the passage (**Figure 53**) in the bottom of the master cylinder body is clear. Clean out if necessary.

4. Inspect the threads for the union bolt (**Figure 54**) in the body. If worn or damaged, clean out with a suitable size metric thread tap or replace the master cylinder assembly.

5. Check the hand lever pivot lugs (**Figure 55**) on the master cylinder body for cracks or elongation. If damaged, replace the master cylinder assembly.

6. Inspect the piston contact surfaces (A, **Figure 56**) for signs of wear and damage. If less than perfect, replace the piston assembly.

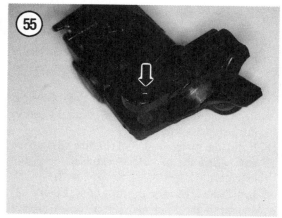

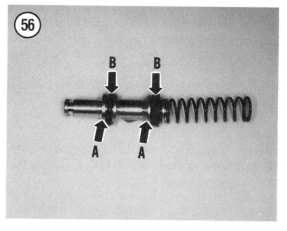

12

7. Check the end of the piston (**Figure 57**) for wear caused by the hand lever. If worn, replace the piston assembly.

8. Inspect the piston cups (B, **Figure 56**) for any signs of wear or damage. Cups are not available separately and must be replaced as an assembly.

9. Inspect the pivot hole (**Figure 58**) in the hand lever. If worn or elongated, the lever must be replaced.

10. Inspect the top cover and the diaphragm (**Figure 59**) for wear or deterioration, replace if necessary.

Assembly

1. Soak the piston assembly and new cups in fresh brake fluid for at least 15 minutes to make them pliable. Coat the inside of the cylinder bore with fresh brake fluid prior to the assembly of parts.

> *CAUTION*
> *When installing the piston assembly, do not allow the cups to turn inside out as they will be damaged and allow brake fluid leakage within the cylinder bore.*

2. Position the spring with the tapered end facing toward the primary cup and install it onto the piston (**Figure 60**).

3A. On 1985-1990 models, perform the following:
   a. Install the stopper (**Figure 49**) onto the end of the piston assembly.
   b. Install the rubber dust boot (**Figure 48**) into the area where the hand lever actuates the piston assembly.
   c. Install the liner onto the dust boot (**Figure 61**) and push the liner and piston down until it bottoms in the master cylinder body (**Figure 62**). Make sure the piston is locked in place.

3B. On 1991-on models, perform the following:
   a. Using circlip pliers, install the circlip into the body. Make sure it seats correctly in the groove in the body.
   b. Install the rubber dust boot over the end of the piston and make sure it seats correctly.

4. Install the hand lever (**Figure 46**), the bolt and nut. Tighten nut securely.

5. If removed, install the brake light switch (**Figure 51**) and screw to the master cylinder. Tighten the screw securely.

6. Install the master cylinder as described in this chapter.

FRONT BRAKE HOSE REPLACEMENT

Kawasaki recommends replacing the brake hose every four years or when it shows signs of cracking or damage.

Removal/Installation

Refer to **Figure 63** for this procedure.

> *CAUTION*
> *Cover the surrounding area with a heavy cloth or plastic tarp to protect*

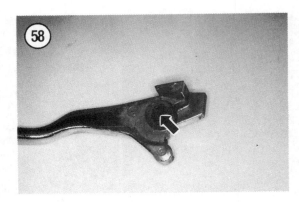

them from accidental brake fluid spills. Wash brake fluid from any painted or plated surfaces or plastic parts immediately, as it will destroy the finish. Use soapy water and rinse completely.

1. Remove the caps from the bleed screws (**Figure 64**) of both front calipers.

2. Attach a piece of hose to each bleed screw (**Figure 65**) and place the loose end in a container.

3. Open both bleed screws and operate the master cylinder lever to pump the brake fluid from the master cylinder, the brake hoses and the caliper assemblies. Operate the lever until the system is clear of brake fluid.

4. Clean all dirt and foreign matter from the top of the master cylinder.

5. Remove the screws securing the cover (**Figure 66**). Remove the cover and the diaphragm (**Figure 67**).

> *WARNING*
> *If a cooking baster is used for this purpose, do **not** reuse it for cooking purposes due to brake fluid residue within it.*

6. If you have a shop syringe or a cooking baster, draw any residual brake fluid from the master cylinder reservoir.

7. Slide the rubber boot (A, **Figure 68**) off the union bolt.

8. Unscrew the union bolt (B, **Figure 68**) securing the upper brake hose to the master cylinder. Don't lose the sealing washer on each side of the hose fitting.

9. Remove the union bolt and sealing washers (A, **Figure 69**) securing the lower hose to each of the brake calipers.

10. Remove each brake hose (B, **Figure 69**) and allow residual brake fluid to drain into the container used in Step 2. Dispose of this brake fluid—never reuse brake fluid.

11. Unhook both lower brake hoses from the guide on the front fender.

12. Remove the screws securing the front fork cover (**Figure 70**) and remove the cover.

13. Remove the union bolt and sealing washers (A, **Figure 71**) that secure the upper hose (A, **Figure 72**) and the lower left-hand hose (B, **Figure 72**) to the 3-way connector.

14. Remove the upper brake hose (A, **Figure 72**).

15. Remove the lower left-hand hose (B, **Figure 71**).

16. Remove the union bolt and sealing washers that secure the lower right-hand hose (C, **Figure 71**) to the 3-way connector.

17. Remove the lower right-hand hose (D, **Figure 71**).

18. If necessary, remove the bolts securing the 3-way joint (E, **Figure 71**) to the lower fork bridge, then remove the 3-way joint.

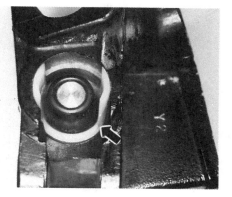

12

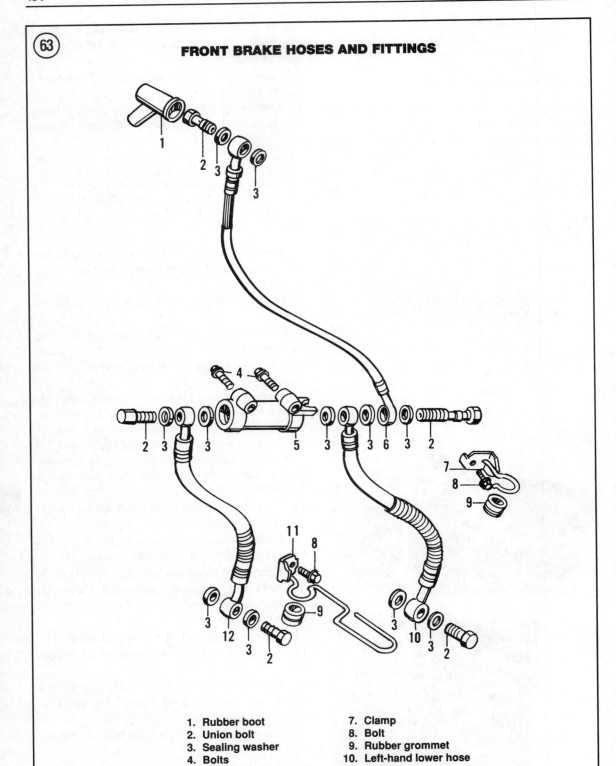

FRONT BRAKE HOSES AND FITTINGS

1. Rubber boot
2. Union bolt
3. Sealing washer
4. Bolts
5. 3-way connector
6. Upper hose
7. Clamp
8. Bolt
9. Rubber grommet
10. Left-hand lower hose
11. Clamp
12. Right-hand lower hose

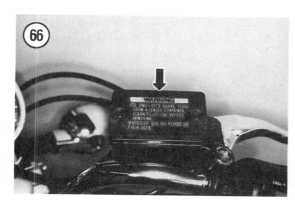

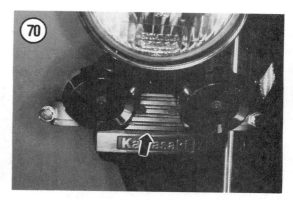

12

19. Refer to **Figure 63** and install new hoses, sealing washers and union bolts in the reverse order of removal while noting the following:

    a. Be sure to install new sealing washers (**Figure 73**) in their correct positions on each side of the brake hose fittings.

    b. Tighten the union bolts to the torque specifications listed in **Table 1**.

    c. Bleed the brake as described under *Bleeding the System* in this chapter.

FRONT BRAKE DISC

Removal/Installation

1. Remove the front wheel as described in Chapter Ten.

> *NOTE*
> *Place a piece of wood or vinyl tube in the caliper in place of the disc. This way, if the brake lever is inadvertently squeezed, the pistons will not be forced out of the cylinders. If this does happen, the caliper might have to be disassembled to reseat the pistons and the system will have to be bled. By using the wood or vinyl tube, bleeding the system is not necessary when installing the wheel.*

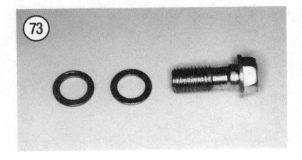

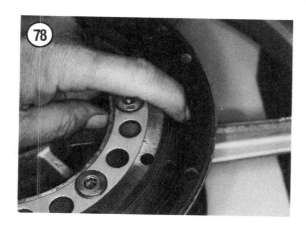

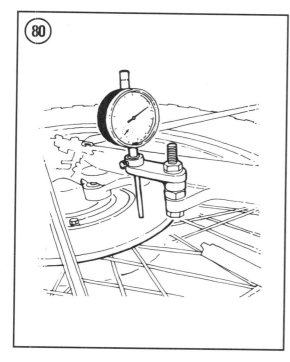

12

> *CAUTION*
> *Do not set the wheel down on the disc surface, as it may get scratched or warped. Set the wheel on 2 blocks of wood (**Figure 74**).*

2. Remove the speedometer housing (**Figure 75**) from the left-hand side.

3. Turn the wheel over and remove the spacer (**Figure 76**) from the right-hand side.

4. Remove the bolts securing the brake disc (**Figure 77**) to the hub and remove the disc.

5. Repeat Step 4 for the other brake disc if necessary.

6. Install by reversing these removal steps while noting the following:

    a. Apply blue Loctite (No. 271) to the disc mounting bolts prior to installation.

    b. Tighten the disc mounting bolts to the torque specifications listed in **Table 1**.

Inspection

It is not necessary to remove the disc from the wheel to inspect it. Small marks on the disc are not important, but radial scratches deep enough to snag a finger nail (**Figure 78**) reduce braking effectiveness and increase brake pad wear. If these grooves are found, the disc should be replaced.

1. Measure the thickness of the disc at several locations around the disc with a micrometer (**Figure 79**). The disc must be replaced if the thickness in any area is less than that specified in **Table 2**.

2. Make sure the disc bolts are tight prior to running this check. Check the disc runout with a dial indicator as shown in **Figure 80**. Rotate the wheel slowly and watch the dial indicator. If the runout exceeds that listed in **Table 1** the disc(s) must be replaced.

3. Clean the disc (**Figure 81**) of any rust or corrosion and wipe clean with lacquer thinner. Never use

an oil-based solvent that may leave an oil residue on the disc.

BLEEDING THE SYSTEM

This procedure is not necessary unless the brakes feel spongy, there has been a leak in the system, a component has been replaced or the brake fluid has been replaced.

NOTE
Start with the right-hand caliper first as it is the farthest away from the master cylinder.

1. Remove the dust cap from the bleed valve (**Figure 82**) on the right-hand caliper assembly.
2. Connect a piece of clear tubing to the bleed valve of the right-hand caliper assembly.

CAUTION
Cover the wheel with a heavy cloth or plastic tarp to protect it from the accidental spilling of brake fluid. Wash any brake fluid from any plastic, painted or plated surface immediately; as it will destroy the finish. Use soapy water and rinse completely.

3. Clean the top cover or cap of the master cylinder of all dirt and foreign matter.

NOTE
There are 2 different types of master cylinders that are used among the different models. The master cylinder shown in this procedure is used on 1985-1990 models. Service procedures for 1991 and later models are identical except that the top cover and body are round instead of rectangular.

4. Remove the screws (A, **Figure 83**) securing the cover (B, **Figure 83**). Remove the cover and the diaphragm (**Figure 84**).
5. Fill the reservoir almost to the top lip; insert the diaphragm and the cover, or cap, loosely. Leave the cover, or cap, in place during this procedure to prevent the entry of dirt.
6. Place the other end of the tube into a clean container.
7. Fill the container with enough fresh brake fluid to keep the end submerged.

WARNING
Use brake fluid from a sealed container marked DOT 3 or DOT 4 only (specified for disc brakes). Other types may vaporize and cause brake failure. Do not intermix different brands or types because some may not be compatible. Do not intermix a silicone based (DOT 5) brake fluid as it can cause brake component damage leading to brake system failure.

NOTE
During this procedure, it is very important to check the fluid level in the brake master cylinder reservoir often. If the reservoir runs dry, you'll introduce more air in the system which will require starting over.

8. If the master cylinder was drained, it must be bled first as follows:
   a. Slide the rubber boot (A, **Figure 85**) off the union bolt.
   b. Place a shop rag under the master cylinder as some brake fluid will leak out during this procedure.

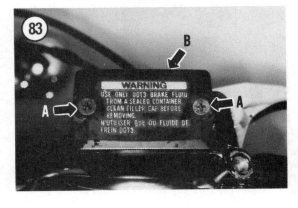

c. Remove the union bolt (B, **Figure 85**) and hose from the master cylinder.

d. Slowly apply the brake lever several times while holding your thumb over the opening in the master cylinder and perform the following:

e. With the lever applied, slightly release your thumb pressure. Some of the brake fluid and air bubbles will escape.

f. Apply thumb pressure and pump lever once more.

g. Repeat this procedure until you can feel resistance at the lever.

9. Quickly reinstall the hose, sealing washers and the union bolt. Refill the master cylinder with brake fluid.

10. Tighten the union bolt, pump the lever again and perform the following at the master cylinder:

a. Loosen the union bolt (B, **Figure 85**) 1/4 turn. Some brake fluid and air bubbles will escape.

b. Tighten the union bolt and repeat this procedure until no air bubbles escape.

11. Tighten the union bolt to the torque specification listed in **Table 1**.

12. Slowly apply the brake lever several times as follows:

a. Pull the lever in and hold it in the applied position.

b. Open the bleed valve on the right-hand caliper about one-half turn. Allow the lever to travel to its limit.

c. When this limit is reached, tighten the bleed valve.

13. As the fluid enters the system, the level will drop in the reservoir. Maintain the level to just about the top of the reservoir to prevent air from being drawn into the system.

14. Continue to pump the lever and fill the reservoir until the fluid emerging from the hose is completely free of bubbles.

NOTE
Do not allow the reservoir to empty during the bleeding operation or more air will enter the system. If this occurs, the entire procedure must be repeated.

NOTE
If you are having trouble getting all of the bubbles out of the system, refer to **Reverse Flow Bleeding** *at the end of this section.*

15. Hold the lever in, tighten the bleed valve, remove the bleed tube and install the bleed valve dust cap.

16. If necessary, add fluid to correct the level in the reservoir.

17. Repeat Step 1 and Step 2, Steps 5-8 and Steps 13-17 for the left-hand brake caliper.

18. Install the diaphragm (**Figure 84**) and the cover (B, **Figure 83**) onto the front master cylinder. Tighten the screws (A, **Figure 83**) securely.

19. Test the feel of the brake lever. It should be firm and should offer the same resistance each time it's operated. If it feels spongy, it is likely that there is still air in the system and it must be bled again. When all air has been bled from the system and the fluid level is correct in the reservoir, double-check for leaks and tighten all fittings and connections.

WARNING
Before riding the bike, make certain that the brakes are operating correctly. Spin the front wheel and apply the lever sev-

12

eral times. The wheel must come to a complete stop each time.

20. Test ride the bike slowly at first to make sure that the brakes are operating properly.

Reverse Flow Bleeding

This bleeding procedure can be used if you are having a difficult time freeing the system of all bubbles.

Using this procedure, the brake fluid will be forced into the system in a reverse direction. The fluid will enter the caliper, flow through the brake hose and into the master cylinder reservoir. If the system is already filled with brake fluid, the existing fluid will be flushed out of the top of the master cylinder by the new brake fluid being forced into the caliper. Siphon fluid from the reservoir, then hold a shop cloth under the master cylinder reservoir to catch any additional fluid that will be forced out.

A special reverse flow tool called the EZE Bleeder is available or a home made tool can be fabricated for this procedure.

To make this home made tool, perform the following:

> *NOTE*
> *The brake fluid container must be plastic—not metal. Use vinyl tubing of the correct inner diameter to ensure a tight fit on the caliper bleed valve.*

a. Purchase a 12 oz. (345 ml) *plastic* bottle of DOT 3 or DOT 4 brake fluid.

b. Remove the cap, drill an appropriate size hole and adapt a vinyl hose fitting onto the cap.

c. Attach a section of vinyl hose to the hose fitting on the cap and secure it with a hose clamp. This joint must be a tight fit as the plastic brake fluid bottle will be squeezed to force the brake fluid out past this fitting and through the hose.

d. Remove the moisture seal from the plastic bottle of brake fluid and screw the cap and hose assembly onto the bottle.

1. Remove the dust cap from the bleed valve (**Figure 82**) on the right-hand caliper assembly.

2. Clean the top cover of the master cylinder of all dirt and foreign matter.

3. Remove the screws (A, **Figure 83**) securing the cover (B, **Figure 83**). Remove the cover and the diaphragm (**Figure 84**).

4. Attach the vinyl hose to the bleed valve on the right-hand caliper. Make sure the hose is tight on the bleed valve.

5. Open the bleed valve and squeeze the plastic bottle forcing this brake fluid into the system.

> *NOTE*
> *If necessary, siphon brake fluid from the reservoir to avoid overflow of fluid.*

6. Observe the brake fluid entering the master cylinder reservoir. Continue to apply pressure from the

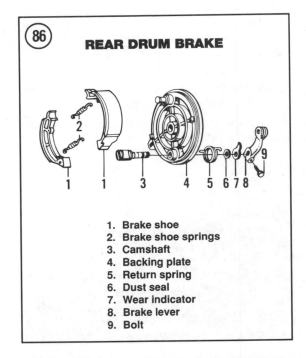

86

REAR DRUM BRAKE

1. Brake shoe
2. Brake shoe springs
3. Camshaft
4. Backing plate
5. Return spring
6. Dust seal
7. Wear indicator
8. Brake lever
9. Bolt

87

tool, or bottle, until the fluid entering the reservoir is free of all air bubbles.

7. Close the bleed valve and disconnect the bleeder or hose from the right-hand caliper bleed valve.

8. Install the dust cap on the caliper bleed valve.

9. Repeat Steps 1-8 for the left-hand caliper assembly.

10. At this time the system should be free of bubbles. Apply the brake lever and check for proper brake operation. If the system still feels spongy, perform the typical bleeding procedure described at the beginning of this section.

11. Install the diaphragm (**Figure 84**) and the cover (B, **Figure 83**) on the front master cylinder. Tighten the screws (A, **Figure 83**) securely.

REAR DRUM BRAKE

Pushing down on the brake foot pedal pulls the cable/rod assembly which moves the brake arm that

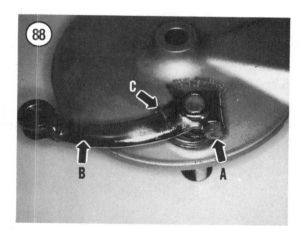

in turn rotates the camshaft. The rotating camshaft forces the brake shoes out into contact with the brake drum.

Pedal free play must be maintained to minimize brake drag and premature brake wear and maximize braking effectiveness. Refer to Chapter Three for complete rear drum brake adjustment procedures.

Disassembly

Refer to **Figure 86** for this procedure.

> *WARNING*
> *When working on the brake system, do **not** inhale brake dust. It may contain asbestos, which can cause lung injury and cancer. Wear a face mask that meets OSHA requirements for trapping asbestos particles, and wash your hands and forearms thoroughly after completing the work.*

1. Remove the rear wheel as described in Chapter Eleven.

2. Pull the brake assembly (**Figure 87**) straight up and out of the brake drum.

3. Carefully pull up on both brake shoes in a V-formation and remove the brake shoes and return springs as an assembly.

4. Disconnect the return springs from the brake shoes.

> *NOTE*
> *Before removing the brake camshaft, mark the end of the camshaft in relation to the split on the brake lever. This reference will be used during installation.*

5. If necessary, remove the bolt (A, **Figure 88**) securing the brake lever (B, **Figure 88**) and remove the brake lever, wear indicator and return spring. Withdraw the camshaft from the backing plate and remove the dust seal from the backing plate.

Inspection

1. Thoroughly clean and dry all parts except the brake linings.

2. Check the contact surface of the drum for scoring (**Figure 89**). If there are grooves deep enough to snag your fingernail, the drum should be reground.

3. Measure the inside diameter of the brake drum (**Figure 90**). If the measurement is greater than the service limit listed in **Table 2**, the rear wheel must be replaced.

4. If the drum can be machined oversize (turned) and still stay within the maximum service limit diameter, the linings will have to be replaced and the new ones arced to conform to the new drum contour.

5. Measure the brake lining thickness with a vernier caliper (**Figure 91**). They should be replaced if the lining portion is worn to the service limit dimension or less. Refer to specifications listed in **Table 2**.

6. Inspect the linings (**Figure 92**) for imbedded foreign material. Dirt can be removed with a stiff wire brush. Check for any traces of oil or grease; if they are contaminated they must be replaced.

7. Inspect the brake shoe assemblies (**Figure 93**) for wear, cracks or other damage. Replace as a set if necessary.

8. Inspect the cam lobe and pivot pins (A, **Figure 94**) for wear or corrosion. Minor roughness can be removed with a fine emery cloth.

9. Inspect the backing plate (B, **Figure 94**) for wear, cracks or other damage. Replace if necessary.

10. Inspect the rear axle bushing (C, **Figure 94**) in the backing plate for wear, scoring or other damage. Replace the backing plate if necessary, the bushing cannot be replaced.

11. Inspect the brake shoe return springs (**Figure 95**) for wear. If they are stretched, they will not fully retract the brake shoes. Replace as necessary.

Assembly

1. If removed, grease the camshaft with a light coat of molybdenum disulfide grease. Install the cam into the backing plate from the backside with the triangular mark facing toward the center of the brake panel.

2. Install a new dust seal and wear indicator onto the camshaft from the outside of the backing plate.

3. Install the spring and the camshaft.

4. Align the brake lever split with the mark made on the end of the camshaft and install the brake lever (B, **Figure 88**).

5. Index the spring onto the brake arm (C, **Figure 88**) as shown.

6. Install and securely tighten the bolt (A, **Figure 88**) securing the brake lever.

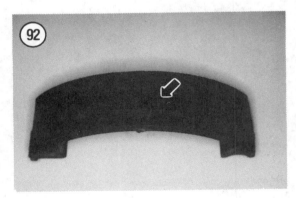

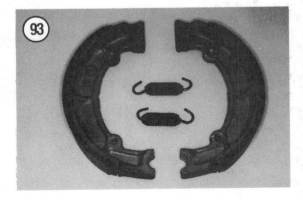

7. Grease the camshaft and pivot post (A, **Figure 94**) with a light coat of molybdenum disulfide grease; avoid getting any grease on the brake backing plate where the brake linings may come in contact with it.

8. Assemble the return springs onto the brake shoes.

9. Hold the brake shoes in a "V" formation with the return springs attached and snap them into place on the brake backing plate. Make sure they are firmly seated on it (**Figure 96**).

10. Install the brake panel assembly into the brake drum.

11. Install the rear wheel as described in Chapter Eleven.

12. Adjust the rear brake as described in Chapter Three.

REAR BRAKE PEDAL AND CABLE/ROD ASSEMBLY

Removal/Installation

Refer to **Figure 97** for this procedure.

1. Place the bike on the centerstand on level ground.

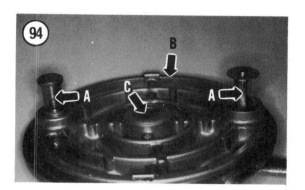
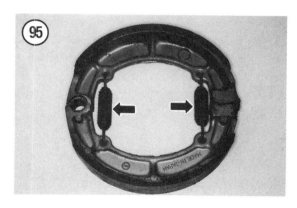

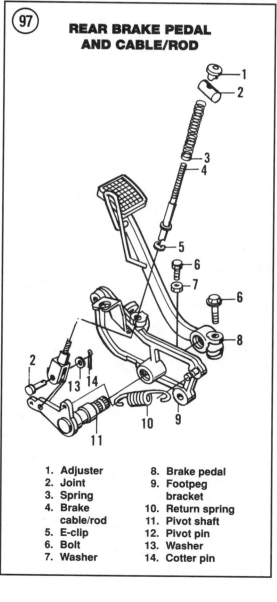

REAR BRAKE PEDAL AND CABLE/ROD

1. Adjuster
2. Joint
3. Spring
4. Brake cable/rod
5. E-clip
6. Bolt
7. Washer
8. Brake pedal
9. Footpeg bracket
10. Return spring
11. Pivot shaft
12. Pivot pin
13. Washer
14. Cotter pin

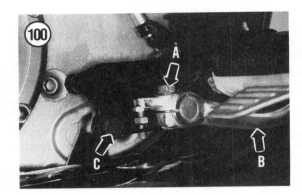

NOTE
The rear brake control cable/rod assembly is a combination of a cable where it attaches to the rear brake pedal and then changes into a brake rod where it attaches to the rear brake lever at the rear brake panel and lever. This is a single assembly joined at the center of the assembly and if any portion of the assembly is faulty, the entire cable/rod assembly must be replaced.

2. Completely unscrew the rear brake adjusting nut (A, **Figure 98**).

3. Depress the brake pedal and remove the brake rod (B, **Figure 98**) from the pivot joint in the brake lever. Remove the pivot joint from the brake lever and install the pivot joint and the adjusting nut onto the brake rod to avoid misplacing them.

4. Loosen the locknut (A, **Figure 99**) on the pedal height adjust bolt and completely back off the adjust bolt (B, **Figure 99**) from the brake pedal.

5. Remove the brake pedal clamping bolt (A, **Figure 100**) and remove the brake pedal (B, **Figure 100**) from the pivot shaft.

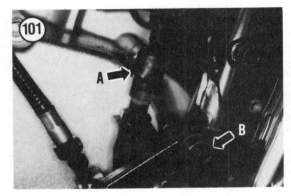

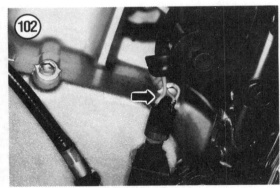

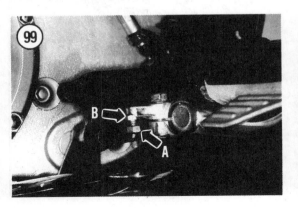

6. Slide the rubber boot (A, **Figure 101**) up and off the brake light switch.

7. Disconnect the rear brake light switch electrical connectors (**Figure 102**).

8. Remove the footpeg bracket upper (B, **Figure 101**) and lower (C, **Figure 100**) mounting bolts and move the assembly off the frame.

9. Unhook the cable/rod from the mounting bracket on the frame (**Figure 103**).

10. Carefully withdraw the cable/rod assembly out from behind the coolant reservoir tank and out of the clamp (**Figure 104**) on the crankcase.

11. Install by reversing these removal steps while noting the following:

    a. Apply a light coat of grease to all pivot areas prior to installing any parts.

    b. Always install new cotter pins—never reuse a cotter pin as the ends may break off and the cotter pin could fall out disabling the brake system.

    c. Securely tighten the bolts securing the footpeg assembly to the frame.

    d. Align the index mark on the brake lever with the pivot shaft and tighten the bolt to the torque specification listed in **Table 1**.

    e. Adjust the rear brake as described in Chapter Three.

12

Table 1 BRAKE SYSTEM TIGHTENING TORQUES

Item	N•m	ft.-lb.
Union bolt	25	18
Front caliper		
Bleed valve	7.8	5.8
Mounting bolts	32	24
Brake disc bolts	23	16.5
Rear drum brake arm bolt	19	13.5
Rear brake pedal bolt	25	18

Table 2 BRAKE SYSTEM SPECIFICATIONS

Item	Specifications	Wear limit
Front brake disc		
Thickness	4.8-5.1 mm (0.189-0.200 in.)	4.5 mm (0.18 in.)
Disc runout	less than 0.2 mm (0.008 in.)	0.3 mm (0.012 in.)
Front brake pad thickness	4.85 mm (0.191 in.)	1.0 mm (0.039 in.)
Rear brake		
Drum I.D.	180.00-180.16 mm (7.086-7.093 in.)	180.7 mm (7.11 in.)

CHAPTER THIRTEEN

FRAME

This chapter contains removal and installation procedures for all body panels and frame components.

SEAT

Removal/Installation

1. Insert the ignition key in the document holder door, open and remove the door.

2. Remove the bolts (**Figure 1**) securing the seat to the grab rail.

3. Pull up on the rear of the seat (**Figure 2**) and move the seat toward the rear to disengage it from the front retaining bracket on the frame. Remove the seat.

4. To install, insert the seat's front tab under the retaining bracket on the frame. Push the seat forward and make sure the tab is located correctly under the bracket.

5. Push the front of the seat down and align the front mounting bolt holes with the mounting bracket on the grab rail.

6. Install the bolts (**Figure 1**) and tighten securely.

7. Install the document holder door, push it closed and lock it.

> *WARNING*
> *After the seat is installed, pull up on it*
> *firmly to make sure it is securely locked*

in place. If the seat is not correctly locked in place, it may slide to one side or the other when riding the bike. This could lead to a loss of control and a possible accident.

FRAME SIDE COVERS

Removal/Installation

1. Remove the bolt (A, **Figure 3**) securing the frame side cover to the frame rail at the bottom.
2. Carefully pull the front and rear sections of the frame side cover off the mounting posts at locations shown in B, **Figure 3** and remove the cover.

3. To install, make sure the rubber cushions are in place in the mounting brackets on the frame.
4. Push the frame side covers onto the rubber cushions and make sure they are secured in place.

5. Install the bolt and tighten securely.

FRAME HEAD SIDE COVERS

Removal/Installation

1. Remove the fuel tank as described in Chapter Seven.
2. On the right-hand side, remove the screws (A **Figure 4**) securing the frame head side cover and pull the cover (B, **Figure 4**) straight off the frame and remove it.
3. On the left-hand side, remove the screws (A **Figure 5**) securing the frame head side cover and pull the cover (B, **Figure 5**) straight off the frame and remove it.
4. Install by reversing these removal steps.

FOOTPEGS

Front Footpeg
Removal/Installation

> *NOTE*
> *The right-hand footpeg is attached to the rear brake lever bracket assembly. If the entire footpeg bracket must be re-*

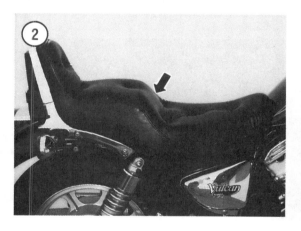

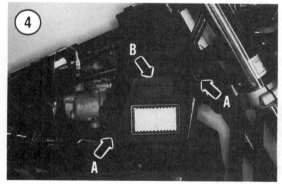

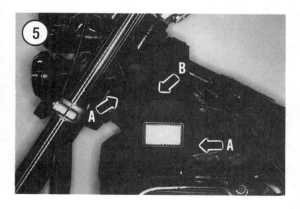

13

*moved, refer to **Rear Brake Pedal and Rod/Cable Assembly Removal/Installation** in Chapter Twelve.*

1. To remove the right-hand footpeg, perform the following:

    a. Remove the E-clip from the end of the pivot pin.

    b. Withdraw the pivot pin and remove the footpeg (**Figure 6**) and spring from the bracket.

2. To remove the left-hand footpeg and bracket, perform the following:

    a. Remove the bolts (A, **Figure 7**) securing the bracket assembly (B, **Figure 7**) to the frame and remove the assembly.

    b. Remove the E-clip from the end of the pivot pin.

    c. Withdraw the pivot pin and remove the footpeg and spring from the bracket.

3. Install by reversing these removal steps while noting the following:

    a. Apply a light coat of multi-purpose grease to the pivot pin prior to installation.

    b. Make sure the spring is positioned correctly to hold the footpeg in the *down* position.

    c. Make sure the E-clip is positioned correctly in the pivot shaft.

    d. Tighten the mounting bolts securely.

Rear Footpeg and Bracket
Removal/Installation

1. To remove the right-hand footpeg and bracket, remove the bolts (A, **Figure 8**) securing the bracket assembly (B, **Figure 8**) to the frame and remove the assembly.

2. To remove the left-hand footpeg and bracket, remove the bolts (A, **Figure 9**) securing the bracket assembly (B, **Figure 9**) to the frame and remove the assembly.

3. To remove the footpeg from the bracket, perform the following:

    a. Remove the E-clip from the end of the pivot pin.

    b. Withdraw the pivot pin and remove the footpeg and spring from the bracket.

4. Install by reversing these removal steps while noting the following:

    a. Apply a light coat of multi-purpose grease to the pivot pin prior to installation.

    b. Make sure the spring is positioned correctly to hold the footpeg in the *up* position.

    c. Make sure the E-clip is positioned correctly in the pivot shaft.

    d. Tighten the mounting bolts securely.

SIDESTAND

Removal/Installation

1. Place the bike on the centerstand on level ground to support the bike securely.

2. Place the sidestand in the up position.

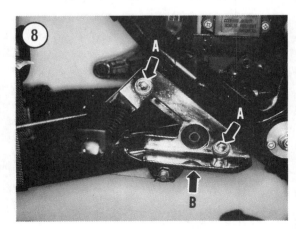

3. Use vise-grip pliers and disconnect the return springs (A, **Figure 10**) from the pin on the sidestand.

4. Remove the nut (B, **Figure 10**) from the bolt securing the sidestand to the frame mounting boss.

5. Withdraw the bolt and remove the sidestand (C, **Figure 10**) from the frame.

6. Install by reversing these removal steps while noting the following:

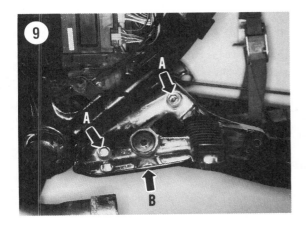

a. Apply a light coat of multipurpose grease to the pivot point on the frame, sidestand and pivot bolt prior to installation.

b. Tighten the bolt and nut securely.

CENTERSTAND

Removal/Installation

1. Place wood block(s) under the engine to support the bike securely.

2. Place a small jack, with a piece of wood to protect the crankcase, under the crankcase. Apply a small amount of jack pressure to support the bike securely with the front wheel off the ground.

3. Place the centerstand in the down position.

4. Loosen the nuts (A, **Figure 11**) on the clamping bolts securing the centerstand pivot shaft to the frame mounting bosses.

5. Remove the cotter pin (B, **Figure 11**) from the right-hand end of the pivot shaft. Discard the cotter pin.

6. Place the centerstand in the up position.

7. Use vise-grip pliers and disconnect the return spring (C, **Figure 11**) from the pin (D, **Figure 11**) on the centerstand and lower the centerstand.

8. Hold onto the centerstand and remove the pivot shaft (E, **Figure 11**) from the centerstand and the frame mounting bosses.

9. Remove the centerstand (F, **Figure 11**) from the frame.

10. Install by reversing these removal steps while noting the following:

13

a. Apply a light coat of multipurpose grease to the pivot points on the frame, centerstand assembly and pivot shaft prior to installation.

b. Install a new cotter pin and bend the ends over completely.

c. Tighten the bolts and nuts securely.

FRONT FENDER

Removal/Installation

1. Remove the front wheel as described under *Front Wheel Removal/Installation* in Chapter Ten.

NOTE
Prior to removal, mark the front under-side of the fender with a piece of tape with a "F" mark on it. This identifica-

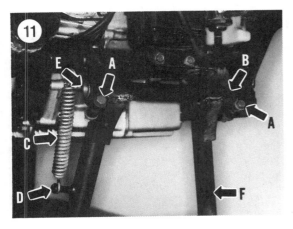

*tion is necessary for use during instal-
lation.*

2. Remove the flange bolts (**Figure 12**) securing
the front fender to both fork sliders and remove the
front fender (**Figure 13**).

3. Install by reversing these removal steps while
noting the following:

   a. The front fender is *almost symmetrical*, but the
     front portion is slightly longer and must be
     installed in the correct orientation or it will
     touch the front wheel.

   b. Position the front fender with the longer portion
     toward the front of the bike. Refer to the mark
     made during removal.

   c. Tighten the flange bolts securely. Do not over-
     tighten as the plastic fender may fracture in the
     mounting hole area.

REAR FENDER

Removal/Installation

1. Remove the seat as described in this chapter.

2. Disconnect the taillight/brake light 3-pin connector and license plate light 2 individual electrical
connectors (**Figure 14**) (1 red wire and 1 black/yel-
low wire) on top of the rear fender.

3. Remove the front top bolts (**Figure 15**) and the
rear side bolts (A, **Figure 16**) securing the rear
fender to the frame. The taillight/brake light and the
license plate light assemblies will come off with the
rear fender.

4. Carefully move the rear fender (B, **Figure 16**)
toward the rear, then remove it from the frame.

5. Install by reversing these removal steps while
noting the following:

   a. Tighten the flange bolts securely. Do not over-
     tighten as the plastic fender may fracture in the
     mounting hole area.

   b. Make sure the electrical connectors are free of
     corrosion and are tight.

REAR HAND GRIP

Removal/Installation

1. Remove the seat as described in this chapter.

2. Remove the bolts securing the tool box to the rear
hand grip and remove the tool box (A, **Figure 17**).

3. Disconnect the electrical connectors from the
rear turn signals. The turn signal assemblies can
remain attached to the side rails of the rear hand grip
assembly.

4. Remove the bolts (B, **Figure 17**) securing the
side rails to the frame.

5. Carefully remove the rear hand grip assembly (C,
Figure 17) from the frame and rear fender.

6. Install by reversing these removal steps while
noting the following:

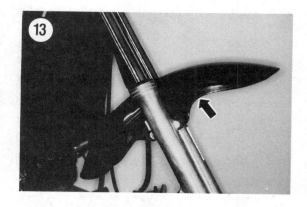

a. Tighten the bolts securely. Do not overtighten as the plastic fender may fracture in the mounting hole area.

b. Make sure the electrical connectors are free of corrosion and are tight.

FRAME

The frame does not require routine maintenance. However, it should be inspected immediately after any accident or spill.

Component Removal/Installation

1. Remove the seat, frame side covers, frame head side covers, and fuel tank.
2. Remove the engine as described in Chapter Four.
3. Remove the front wheel, steering stem and front forks as described in Chapter Ten.
4. Remove the speedometer and headlight case as described in Chapter Eight.
5. Remove the rear wheel, shock absorbers and swing arm as described in Chapter Eleven.

6. Remove the front and rear fenders as described in this chapter.
7. Remove the radiator as described in Chapter Nine.
8. Remove the battery as described in Chapter Three and the battery case as described in Chapter Eight.
9. Remove the wiring harness.
10. Remove the steering head races from the steering head tube as described in Chapter Ten.
11. Inspect the frame for bends, cracks or other damage, especially around welded joints and areas that are rusted.
12. Assemble by reversing these removal steps.

Stripping and Painting

Remove all components from the frame. Thoroughly strip off all old paint. The best way is to have it sandblasted down to bare metal. If this is not possible, you can use a liquid paint remover and steel wool and a fine, hard wire brush.

> *CAUTION*
> *The fenders and frame head side covers are molded plastic and the color is an integral part of the component. If you wish to change the color of these parts, consult an automotive paint supplier for the proper procedure. Do not use any type of paint remover on these components as it will damage the surface.*

When the frame is down to bare metal, have it inspected for hairline and internal cracks. Magnaflux is the most common and complete process.

Make sure that the paint primer that you use is compatible with the type of paint you are going to

13

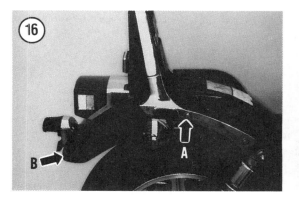

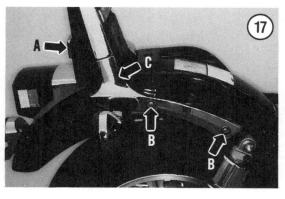

use for the finish color. Spray on one or two coats of primer as smoothly as possible. Let it dry thoroughly and use a fine grade of wet sandpaper (400-600 grit) to remove any flaws. Carefully wipe the surface clean and then spray a couple of coats of the final color. Use either lacquer or enamel base paint and follow the manufacturer's instructions.

A shop specializing in painting will probably do the best job. However, you can do a surprisingly good job with a good grade of spray paint. Spend a few extra dollars and get a good grade of paint as it will make a difference in how good it looks and how long it will stand up. It's a good idea to shake the can and make sure the ball inside the can is loose when you purchase the can of paint. Shake the can as long as is stated on the can. Then immerse the can **upright** in a pot or bucket of **warm** water (not hot—not over 120° F).

WARNING
*Higher temperatures could cause the can to burst. Do **not** place the can in direct contact with any flame or heat source.*

Leave the can in the water for several minutes. When thoroughly warmed, shake the can again and spray the frame. Be sure to get into all the crevices where there may be rust problems. Several light mist coats are better than one heavy coat. Spray painting is best done in temperatures of 70-80° F (21-26° C); any temperature above or below this will cause problems.

After the final coat has dried completely, at least 48 hours, any over spray or orange peel may be removed with a *light* application of Dupont rubbing compound (red color) and finished with Dupont polishing compound (white color). Be careful not to rub too hard or you will go through the finish.

Finish off with a couple coats of good wax prior to reassembling all the components.

It's a good idea to keep the frame touched up with fresh paint if any minor rust spots or scratches appear.

INDEX

14

14

WIRING DIAGRAMS

VN700-A1, VN750-A1, A2, A3, A4 1985-1988
(U.S. AND CANADA)

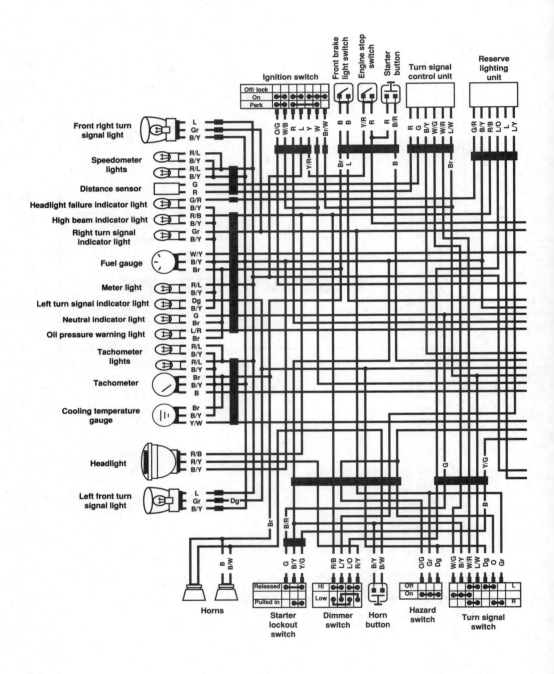

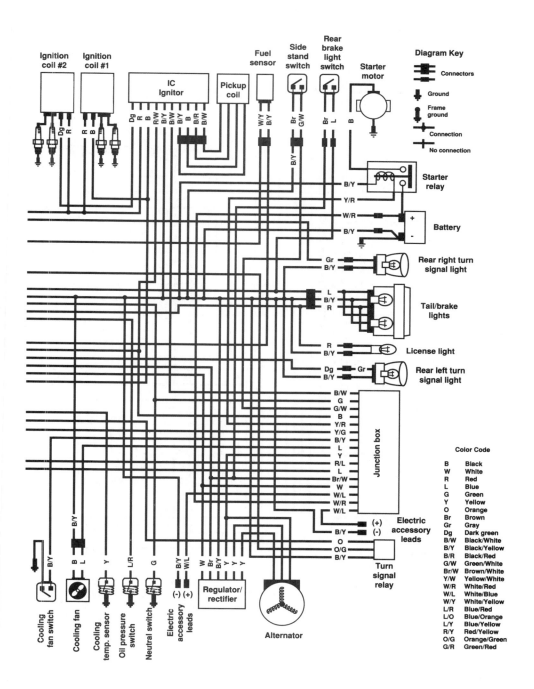

Ignition coil #2
Ignition coil #1
IC Ignitor
Pickup coil
Fuel sensor
Side stand switch
Rear brake light switch
Starter motor

Diagram Key

Connectors
Ground
Frame ground
Connection
No connection

Starter relay
Battery
Rear right turn signal light
Tail/brake lights
License light
Rear left turn signal light
Junction box
Electric accessory leads
Turn signal relay

Cooling fan switch
Cooling fan
Cooling temp. sensor
Oil pressure switch
Neutral switch
Electric accessory leads
Regulator/ rectifier
Alternator

Color Code

B	Black
W	White
R	Red
L	Blue
G	Green
Y	Yellow
O	Orange
Br	Brown
Gr	Gray
Dg	Dark green
B/W	Black/White
B/Y	Black/Yellow
B/R	Black/Red
G/W	Green/White
Br/W	Brown/White
Y/W	Yellow/White
W/R	White/Red
W/L	White/Blue
W/Y	White/Yellow
L/R	Blue/Red
L/O	Blue/Orange
L/Y	Blue/Yellow
R/Y	Red/Yellow
O/G	Orange/Green
G/R	Green/Red

15

VN750-A2, A3, A4 1986-1988
(OTHER THAN U.S. AND CANADA)

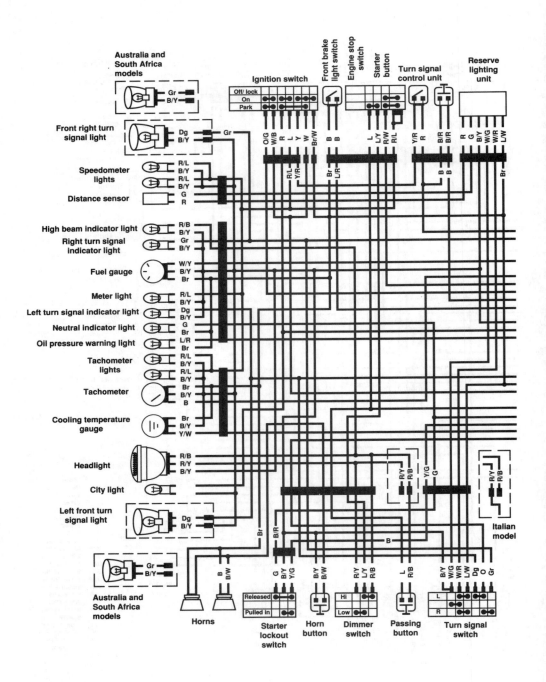

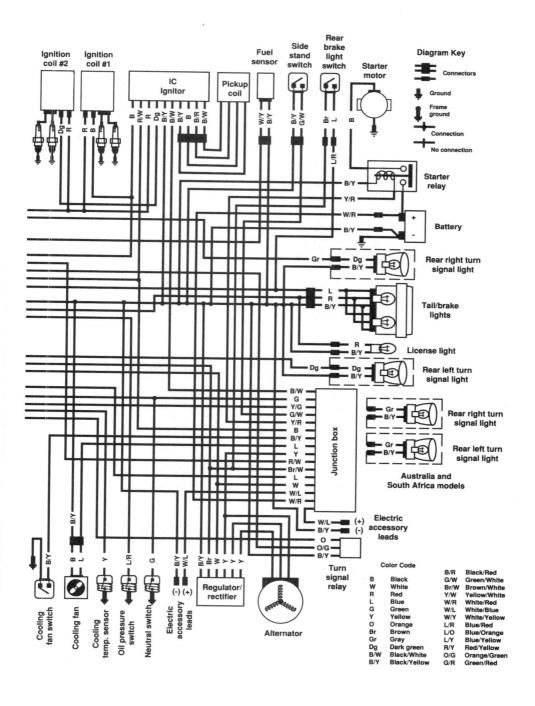

VN750-A5, A6, A7, A8, A9, A10, A11, A12, A13, A14, A15, A16, A17 1989-2001 (U.S. AND CANADA)

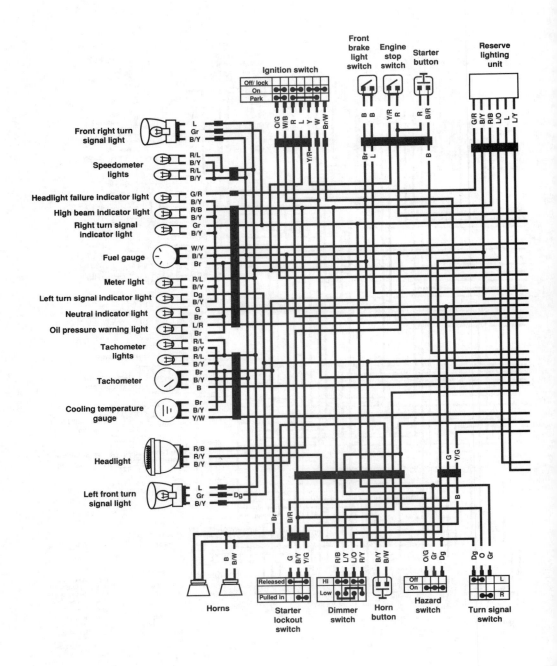

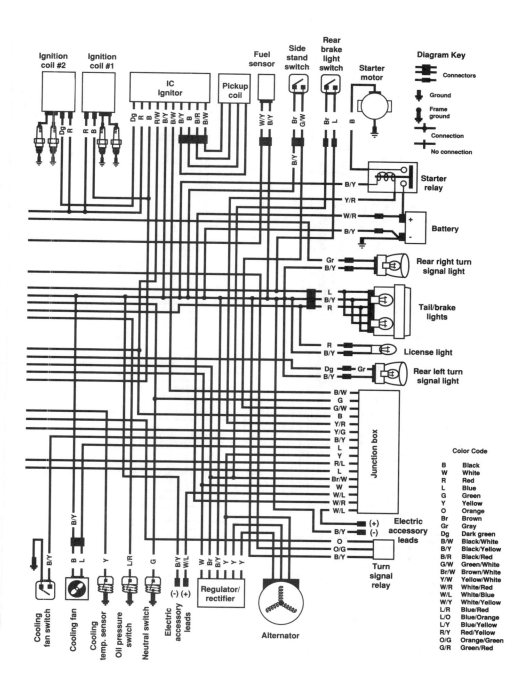

15

VN750-A5, A6, A7, A8, A9, A10, A11, A12, A13, A14, A15, A16, A17 1989-2001 (OTHER THAN U.S. AND CANADA)

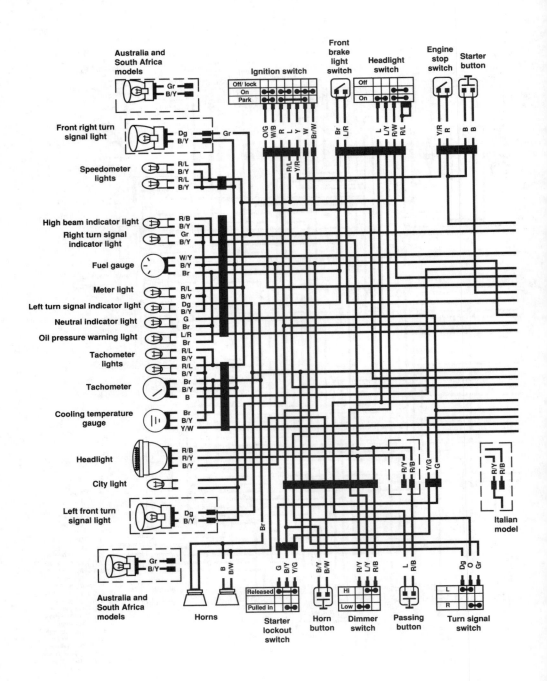

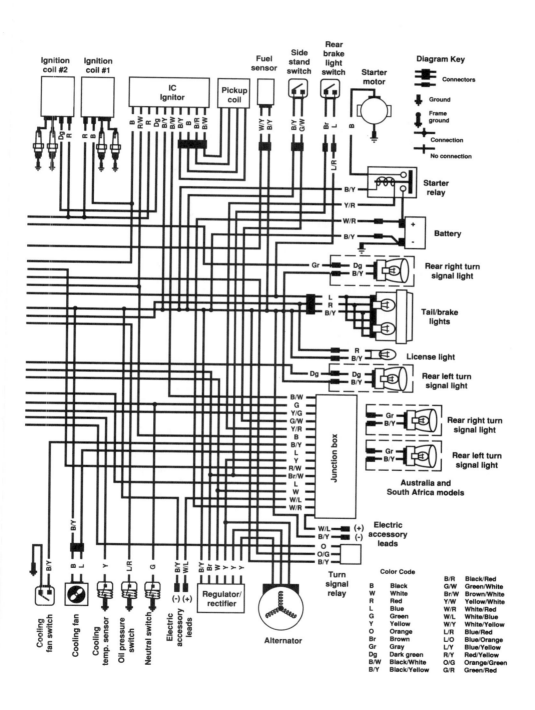

15

NOTES

NOTES

Bought Bike On
2-20-03 mi: 6354

MAINTENANCE LOG

Service Performed **Mileage Reading**

Oil change (example)	2,836	5,782	8,601		
3-21-04 Finial Drive: GL5 mi: 8855 OIL: 10W40 CASTROL					
6-22-04 NEW TIRES mi: 11918					